Tacit Alliance

Edinburgh Studies in Anglo-American Relations

Series Editors: Steve Marsh and Alan P. Dobson

Published and forthcoming titles

Post-War Planning on the Periphery: Anglo-American Economic Diplomacy in South America, 1939–1945
Thomas C. Mills

The Arsenal of Democracy: Aircraft Supply and the Anglo-American Alliance, 1938–1942
Gavin J. Bailey

Reagan and Thatcher's Special Relationship: Latin America and Anglo-American Relations
Sally-Ann Treharne

Jimmy Carter and the Anglo-American 'Special Relationship'
Thomas K. Robb

The Politics of Diplomacy: U.S. Presidents and the Northern Ireland Conflict, 1967–1998
James Cooper

A Not-So-Special Relationship: The US, the UK and German Reunification, 1945–1990
Luca Ratti

The Pilgrims Society and Public Diplomacy, 1895–1945
Stephen Bowman

Tacit Alliance: Franklin Roosevelt and the Anglo-American 'Special Relationship' before Churchill, 1937–1939
Tony McCulloch

euppublishing.com/series/esar

Tacit Alliance

Franklin Roosevelt and the Anglo-American 'Special Relationship' before Churchill, 1937–1939

Tony McCulloch

EDINBURGH
University Press

Edinburgh University Press is one of the leading university presses in the UK. We publish academic books and journals in our selected subject areas across the humanities and social sciences, combining cutting-edge scholarship with high editorial and production values to produce academic works of lasting importance. For more information visit our website: edinburghuniversitypress.com

© Tony McCulloch, 2022

Edinburgh University Press Ltd
The Tun – Holyrood Road, 12(2f) Jackson's Entry, Edinburgh EH8 8PJ

Typeset in 11/14 Sabon by
IDSUK (DataConnection) Ltd

A CIP record for this book is available from the British Library

ISBN 978 0 7486 5638 7 (hardback)
ISBN 978 0 7486 5639 4 (webready PDF)
ISBN 978 0 7486 5641 7 (epub)

The right of Tony McCulloch to be identified as the author of this work has been asserted in accordance with the Copyright, Designs and Patents Act 1988, and the Copyright and Related Rights Regulations 2003 (SI No. 2498).

Contents

Preface and Acknowledgements vi

Part 1 Roosevelt I and II, 1933–1937

1. Introduction: A 'Tacit Alliance'? 3
2. Roosevelt I, March 1933–January 1937 22
3. Roosevelt II, January–May 1937 40

Part 2 Parallel Action, 1937–1938

4. Roosevelt and Chamberlain, May–September 1937 63
5. Quarantine Speech, October–December 1937 83
6. Roosevelt Initiatives, January–February 1938 107

Part 3 Appeasement, 1938

7. *Anschluss*, March–May 1938 129
8. Munich Crisis, May–September 1938 148
9. 'Unspoken Alliance', October–December 1938 169

Part 4 Peace Front, 1939

10. 'Methods Short of War', January–April 1939 191
11. 'A Special Character', May–June 1939 211
12. Polish Crisis, July–September 1939 229

Part 5 Tacit Alliance, 1939

13. 'Winston Is Back', September–October 1939 251
14. Allies' Arsenal, October–November 1939 266
15. Conclusions: 'Tacit Alliance' Revisited 281

Bibliography and Primary Sources 300
Index 322

Preface and Acknowledgements

In his book *Alliance Politics*, the eminent political scientist Richard Neustadt, referring (p. 65) to the highs and lows in Anglo-American relations during the early Cold War, wrote that:

> In an alliance such as this the membrane between sovereign states is paper-thin and porous. Transatlantic reticence is of a piece with reticence at home. For any word to friends across the ocean may come back to other ears at home. As well, a word to friends at home may skip across the water. The relationship is reciprocal. Either way the motive is the same; prudence counsels reticence.

Anglo-American relations during the late 1930s were similarly characterised by an aura of sensitivity and a deep-seated reticence on the part of policy makers in both Washington and London, who were reluctant to discuss their countries' relationship in any detail in case their words aroused domestic criticism, especially from American isolationists – for whom any sign of close Anglo-American cooperation on political matters was anathema. A case in point occurred in February 1938 when Senator William Borah, picking up on some ambiguous wording by the British Foreign Secretary, Anthony Eden, in a Commons speech, accused the Roosevelt Administration of forming a 'tacit alliance' with Britain.

Taking Borah's remark as its starting point, this work analyses the place of Anglo-American relations in Roosevelt's foreign policy from the start of his second term in January 1937 through to the outbreak of war in Europe and the repeal of the arms embargo clause of the US Neutrality Act in November 1939. The book's central argument is that, despite the mutual doubts afflicting the governments, and public opinion, on both sides of the Atlantic during these years, there was nevertheless considerable progress – thanks largely to Franklin Roosevelt – in establishing an ideological and strategic understanding between the two democracies that laid the foundation for the 'special relationship' so desired by Winston Churchill during and after the Second World War.

A work such as this obviously requires research in a wide variety of archives, both in person and on-line. These archives have been identified in the primary sources and bibliography section at the end of the book and, without exception, they conjure up very pleasant memories of working in libraries, universities and other locations in the United States, Canada and Britain while gathering the material for this volume. I happily acknowledge my debt to the owners, past and present, of these collections and to the staff who have so diligently organised and catalogued them and made access to them possible. I am especially grateful to the Revd Dr Ann Shukman, a granddaughter of Walter Runciman, for hosting me so well at her home, Elshieshields Tower, in Scotland, while I researched his private papers. I am now working on a biography of Runciman.

My thanks also go to the many friends and colleagues who have taken an interest in my work over the years, both while I was Head of History and American Studies at Canterbury Christ Church University and more recently as Senior Fellow in North American Studies at the UCL Institute of the Americas. I am fortunate to be working in a first-class department at University College London, where I began my interest in US history and politics as a student many years ago. Special thanks are due to all of my colleagues there, particularly Maxine Molyneux and Iwan Morgan. Special thanks are also due to Alan Dobson and Steve Marsh, friends and colleagues for many years in the Transatlantic Studies Association, and patient editors of the 'Edinburgh Studies in Anglo-American Relations'. Edinburgh University Press have also been very supportive publishers and I am also grateful to Palgrave-Macmillan, and again to Alan Dobson, for permission to quote from my articles published in the *Journal of Transatlantic Studies*. Finally, thanks are due to Jane McKenna for her interest in the book during its final stages and for compiling the index. Above all, I must thank my family – especially Heather, Jack and Holly – for their unfailing support during the entirety of this project. The book is dedicated to them.

Part I

Roosevelt I and II, 1933–1937

1 Introduction: A 'Tacit Alliance'?

On 1 February 1938, William Borah, the veteran isolationist from Idaho, stood up in the Senate and, in the words of the *New York Times*, accused the Roosevelt Administration of 'risking war by letting the world believe that the United States was in a "tacit alliance" with Great Britain'. Borah was referring to a statement by Anthony Eden in the Commons on 21 December, in which, according to the Senator, he implied 'a secret understanding between Great Britain and the United States'. The Foreign Secretary's comments needed clarification, argued Borah, as he had said that 'Britain and the United States had an understanding and were in consultation. When asked what that relationship was', Borah continued, 'Eden replied he could not reveal it.' Borah felt that this statement was disturbing 'because there has gone to the world an understanding that the United States and Great Britain have a working relationship of such a nature that it must be secret'.[1]

Borah's outburst came in the wake of the fierce debate in the United States and abroad that ensued when Franklin Roosevelt said in his Chicago speech on 5 October 1937 that the peace-loving countries of the world should 'quarantine the aggressors'. The President's announcement on 28 January 1938 that the United States now required a much larger defence budget, including a 20 per cent increase in the size of the Navy, to cope with the dangers inherent in the international situation, together with reports of a meeting between US and British naval officials, confirmed the suspicions of isolationists that Roosevelt's 'Quarantine' speech was the harbinger of a more interventionist policy. Borah now accused the Roosevelt Administration of having an understanding with the British whereby both powers would enlarge their navies so as to counteract the expansionist policy of Japan. Senator Hiram Johnson, another well-known isolationist, took a similar view and demanded a public statement confirming that the President had not abandoned the traditional American policy of avoiding entangling alliances with the nations of Europe.[2]

Both Borah and Johnson had been amongst the so-called 'Irreconcilables' opposed to US entry to the League of Nations in 1919–20, and ever since they had been suspicious of any sign of American political cooperation with European powers, especially Britain. Nor were the two Senators thinking only of naval relations and Japan. It is clear from their private papers, as well as their speeches, that they felt that the Roosevelt Administration was cooperating too readily with the British Government over a range of issues relating to Europe, as well as the Far East. Other signs of a close Anglo-American relationship that suggested an 'informal alliance' were felt to include the Tripartite Currency Agreement of September 1936 with France and the periodic speculation that a deal might be in the offing to settle the British war debt that was suspended in 1934 following Johnson's War Debt Act. The visit to Washington of Walter Runciman, the British Trade Secretary, in January 1937 also caused concern. A trade agreement had been concluded with Canada in November 1935 and there were suspicions that one with Britain would have more than economic significance. The increasingly friendly relations with Canada, which was the senior Dominion in the British Empire, and the continuing efforts of the Roosevelt Administration to gain more discretion in interpreting the Neutrality laws were also noted. Above all, the President's 'Quarantine speech', in October 1937, and the revelation of secret naval talks in London in January 1938, aroused deep suspicions among the isolationists.[3]

Borah and Johnson would have been even more alarmed had they been aware of Roosevelt's initiative in January 1938, when the President sent a secret message to the British Government suggesting that he call a conference to discuss the international tensions at that time. In fact, this initiative was rebuffed by Neville Chamberlain – much to the chagrin of the Foreign Secretary, Anthony Eden – and the President agreed to postpone it. Eden's subsequent resignation in mid-February 1938 highlighted the fact that there were divisions in London at this time, as well as in Washington, as to the best strategy to adopt towards the growing threat from Germany, Italy and Japan and the role of the USA in that strategy. Chamberlain's preferred policy was one of direct negotiations with the dictator powers to gain their cooperation in bringing about a peaceful readjustment of the international status quo. This approach was not popular in the United States, especially after the Munich agreement, and it did not sit well with Roosevelt and his Administration. But nor did the policy of American isolationism favoured by Borah and Johnson.[4]

The main aim of the current work is to examine Borah's view that a 'tacit alliance' existed between the United States and Britain at this time for the purpose of deterring the dictator states of Germany, Italy and Japan – a purpose that, in his opinion, brought with it the prospect of American involvement in another world war. For the historian, such a claim raises several key questions about the nature of Anglo-American relations on the eve of the Second World War. Firstly, was Borah justified in his suspicions of FDR's foreign policy, and especially the fear that FDR was working towards a closer relationship with Britain than the Administration was admitting in public? Secondly, how did FDR's foreign policy square with the policy of appeasement being pursued by the Chamberlain Government and with the views of the Labour and Liberal Opposition, and Conservative critics such as Churchill? Thirdly, how important was the role played by Canada in Anglo-American relations in the late 1930s, and especially by William Lyon Mackenzie King, the Canadian Prime Minister in this period? Fourthly, what was the attitude in Berlin at this time towards Anglo-American relations and the existence or otherwise of an understanding between London and Washington? The answers to these questions will help to answer a fifth and final question – was there a 'tacit alliance' between the United States and Britain in the late 1930s that acted as a precursor to the 'special relationship' identified by Churchill in his post-war Fulton speech?[5]

Definitions

Before proceeding further, it is necessary to establish clear definitions – as far as possible, given the controversy surrounding them – of the key terms used in the debates of the 1930s. The contemporary meaning of these terms is the one favoured by the current writer rather than any later variants suggested by historians or political scientists. Five terms in particular were much used in the 1930s, ranging from total non-intervention in international conflicts to a readiness to intervene 'when and where necessary' – pacificism, isolationism, appeasement, internationalism and interventionism. There was some overlap between them, and especially between pacifism and isolationism, and between internationalism and interventionism. FDR regarded himself as an internationalist who wanted to cooperate with Britain and France to contain Nazi Germany. He rejected the idea of isolationism but was also opposed to outright interventionism – in the sense of sending US troops abroad – until 1941. At the same time, he was reluctant to support the kind of appeasement policy favoured by Chamberlain prior to the outbreak of war.[6]

Pacifism

Although the pacifists of the 1930s do not receive much attention today, they were an important factor in both the United States and Britain until at least 1939. For example, the 'Keep America Out of War Congress' (KAOWC) was officially founded at a rally held in New York in March 1938. As Doenecke has written:

> The main sponsor was the Socialist Party, and the chairman was the veteran pacifist reformer Oswald Garrison Villard. For most of its life, the KAOWC was a coalition composed of the Socialist Party and six militant peace organisations: the Peace Section of the American Friends Service Committee; the Fellowship of Reconciliation; the World Peace Commission of the Methodist Church; the American Section of the Women's International League for Peace and Freedom; the National Council for the Prevention of War; and the War Resisters League.

Like many other pacifist and isolationist organisations, it was dissolved when the US joined the war following Pearl Harbor. Pacificism was also a significant force in the Labour Party for much of the 1930s and it handicapped the party's attitude towards rearmament until at least 1937. The best-known pacifist in Britain was George Lansbury, the erstwhile Labour Party leader, who Ernest Bevin famously criticised for 'hawking his conscience from one conference to another'.[7]

Isolationism

It has been suggested by some historians that 'isolationism' is a misleading term because the United States has never been completely isolated from the affairs of other countries, especially since the war with Spain in 1898. It is also true that 'isolationists', including Borah and Johnson, often disagreed on specific issues.

Other terms such as 'non-intervention' and 'unilateralism' have been put forward as representing the real views of the isolationists. However, 'isolationism' was a ubiquitous term in the 1930s and therefore cannot simply be ignored. It also had a reasonably clear meaning at that time, which was the view that the US should hold to the advice of the Founding Fathers to avoid involvement in the political affairs of Europe, especially Britain, and to shun 'entangling alliances'. These familiar warnings of George Washington and Thomas Jefferson were frequently quoted by Borah, Johnson and other isolationists throughout the 1930s. Less often quoted by the isolationists was the rider added by Washington about 'temporary alliances for extraordinary emergencies'. Whatever their disagreements over specific issues, most isolationists shared a deep suspicion of Britain and, to a lesser extent, France. Historians have sometimes referred to 'the myth of American isolationism' – but it was no myth as far as Franklin Roosevelt was concerned.[8]

Internationalism

The term 'internationalism' has also been criticised because of its very broad and variable meaning. But, like isolationism, it was one of the key terms used in the 1930s and therefore it must be defined as clearly as possible rather than disregarded. In the 1930s most 'internationalists' argued that, even in their own day, Washington and Jefferson had been unable to avoid the US becoming involved in European events, and that the growth of American economic and strategic interests since then had made it impossible for the US to ignore political rivalries in the wider world. However, the degree of involvement that the US should undertake was a continual matter of debate. Critics of such a policy in the 1930s tended to use the terms 'internationalist' and 'interventionist' interchangeably – or, to describe 'interventionists' as 'extreme internationalist'. The definitional goal posts also moved as public support for aid to the Allies increased between 1939 and 1941. Many of the self-identified internationalists of the 1930s were supporters of Woodrow Wilson – Democrats like Cordell Hull, Norman Davis and FDR himself – who maintained their faith in the value of international cooperation and wished to cooperate with the League of Nations and its leading members, especially Britain, as far as was politically possible. What this meant in practice, given the strength of isolationism, especially in Congress, was a policy of parallel rather than joint action, in both Europe and the Far East.[9]

Appeasement

As had often been pointed out, 'appeasement' was the accepted term in the early 1930s for a desire to achieve international peace and stability, especially in Europe, by redressing legitimate grievances amongst dissatisfied nations. In this sense, most public figures were in favour of 'appeasement', which was partly a response to the view that the Paris peace settlement was flawed and needed to be amended. Similarly, 'economic appeasement' was seen by many, not least Cordell Hull, Roosevelt's Secretary of State, as essential if international peace and stability were to be achieved. This notion of general or international appeasement was rather different from the direct or bilateral appeasement policy towards Hitler and Mussolini that became such a prominent feature of British and French foreign policies during the late 1930s, culminating in the Munich agreement of September 1938. It was this trend towards direct concessions to the dictator states, especially Germany, under the threat of force rather than a greater focus on rearmament and deterrence that gave appeasement the unenviable reputation that it still has today.[10]

Interventionism

In his attitude towards Europe, Woodrow Wilson moved from internationalism during the early years of the First World War, when attempts were made, notably by his special envoy, Colonel Edward House, to broker an agreement between the Allies and the Central Powers to end the war, to interventionism in April 1917. The US then became a belligerent, joined the Allies as an 'Associated Power', and sent an expeditionary force to the battlefields of Europe. Military intervention had already been urged by Theodore Roosevelt, and admirers of TR – such as Henry Stimson and Frank Knox – were to be among the leading interventionists in the late 1930s. The line between internationalism – that is, cooperation with like-minded nations that might include financial and economic aid – and interventionism was a flexible and rather subjective one. If this line was occasionally straddled by Wilson between 1914 and 1917, it was deliberately obscured by FDR after January 1939, when he announced in his State of the Union address that there were 'many methods short of war, but stronger and more effective than mere words' that the US could employ against 'aggressor governments'. However, interventionism, in the sense of sending an expeditionary force to

Europe, had very few advocates prior to 1941 and FDR was not one of them.[11]

The question of whether there was, in fact, a 'tacit alliance' between the United States and Britain prior to the outbreak of the Second World War is one that is situated at the junction of four historical debates that together have generated a very large body of writing and scholarship. Firstly, there is the US isolationism debate regarding the nature of FDR's foreign policy in the 1930s, and the extent to which it was constrained by the strength of American isolationism at that time. Secondly, the British appeasement debate has examined Neville Chamberlain's foreign policy, its causes and consequences, and whether there were any alternatives to appeasement. Thirdly, the North Atlantic Triangle debate has explored the role of Canada, especially while Mackenzie King was Prime Minister, in acting as a bridge between the US and Britain. Fourthly, there is the debate about what might be termed 'the view from Berlin'. What was the attitude of the German Foreign Ministry and of the Nazi regime to British and US foreign policies in the 1930s and the possibility of American intervention in another European conflict? Each of these debates has influenced historians writing about Anglo-American relations in the late 1930s.[12]

American isolationism

As regards US foreign policy, Borah's notion of a 'tacit alliance' between the US and UK in February 1938 represented an early manifestation of the 'isolationist' school of thought that was critical of Roosevelt's diplomacy. Borah's views were echoed by 'isolationist' historians such as Charles Beard, who argued that Roosevelt had acted and spoken in public like an 'isolationist' during his first term but reversed this policy and took the United States into war in 1941. Many of the early isolationists were progressives like Senator Burton K Wheeler who argued that involvement in European affairs had mainly benefitted financiers and big business, especially arms manufacturers, etc. New Left historians echoed these views and interpreted US intervention as being largely driven by economic imperialism. This interpretation of US foreign policy was championed by William Appleman Williams in *The Tragedy of American Diplomacy*, while Lloyd Gardner's *Economic Aspects of New Deal Diplomacy* deprecated the traditional emphasis by historians on isolationism, interventionism and internationalism and argued that more attention should be paid to American economic diplomacy. More specifically, he stressed the role of FDR's Secretary of State, Cordell Hull, whose trade agreements programme aimed to promote a free trade or 'Open Door' policy, especially with Britain.[13]

More recently, the main line of attack on FDR's foreign policy has come from what might be termed the 'interventionist' school of historians. Arguing the opposite of the isolationists, these historians have criticised the Roosevelt Administration for not doing more to stand up to Germany, Italy and Japan rather than for doing too much. They have taken the view that FDR effectively pandered to isolationism by not taking a stronger stand against them, and in favour of the democracies, until 1939. There were not many contemporaries who took this view although erstwhile TR supporters such as Henry Stimson and Frank Knox were often frustrated with FDR's cautious policy during the 1930s. Robert Divine, a leading member of this school of thought, portrayed Roosevelt as a genuine 'isolationist' in the early years of his Presidency who, after 1939, became an 'internationalist'. Divine and other 'interventionist' historians pointed to Roosevelt' Bombshell message to the London Economic Conference in 1933 and his signing of the Neutrality Acts as evidence of FDR's isolationism during his first term, and to US policy during the Spanish Civil War and the Munich crisis as indications of his isolationism during his second term.[14]

Finally, there is what might be termed the 'internationalist' school that has broadly supported the record of US foreign policy in the late 1930s. This school argues that the Roosevelt Administration did as much as it could within the limits of US isolationism, especially in educating American public opinion. This was the view of the State Department as set out in *Peace and War: United States Foreign Policy, 1931–1941*, published in 1943. This view gained strong support from Basil Rauch who argued that New Deal foreign policy, rather like the domestic New Deal, while not being perfect, managed to achieve as much as was possible at the time, given the circumstances of the time. He argued that Roosevelt had always been an 'internationalist' and had tried to educate American public opinion towards a more realistic foreign policy while striving to keep the United States out of war until the Japanese attack on Pearl Harbor. William Langer and Everett Gleason, although more critical of FDR, were still essentially sympathetic is their early study. Similarly, Robert Dallek's major work is critical of Roosevelt for pandering to the isolationists in Congress but defends him from his most outspoken critics. More enthusiastic recent defences of FDR's foreign policy include the work by Dominic Tierney on the Spanish Civil War and the broader analysis of Roosevelt's foreign policy by David Schmitz.[15]

British appeasement

Turning next to British foreign policy, the appeasement debate has been central to writing on the Chamberlain Government's foreign policy ever since the collapse of France and the desperate Dunkirk evacuation in May–June 1940. The polemical *Guilty Men*, written under the pseudonym 'Cato' – taken from the name of the principled Roman Senator who opposed the ambitions of Julius Caesar – denounced fifteen key figures who were deemed especially culpable for the situation in which Britain found itself. These were headed by the three prime ministers who held office up to 1940 – MacDonald, Baldwin and, above all, Chamberlain. The list also included Lord Halifax, Sir John Simon and Sir Samuel Hoare – key figures in the National Governments of the 1930s. *Guilty Men* was followed by many other works on British foreign policy in the lead-up to the Second World War, including the multi-volume opus of Sir Winston Churchill, knighted in 1953 for his service to the nation. Although by no means as polemical as *Guilty Men*, Churchill's writings left little doubt as to where the failings lay for Britain's perilous position in 1940. Nor did A. J. P. Taylor, who, while pointing out that Chamberlain's appeasement policy was popular at the time, also argued that Hitler was essentially an opportunist and that Chamberlain had led him to believe that Great Britain and France would not fight for Poland, just as they had not fought for Czechoslovakia.[16]

Such views were met by a sustained defence of British appeasement policy on the grounds that it was the only viable option at the time, given the threats confronting British power in Europe and the Far East, the attitude of the Dominions and the lack of Allies apart from France. Chamberlain's defenders also pointed out that he had a dual policy of rearmament as well as appeasement, and that the extra year gained by the Munich agreement at least gave Britain more time to rearm and enable a united response by Britain and the Dominions, given the lengths to which Chamberlain had gone to achieve peace. Such views were championed, amongst others, by Donald Cameron Watt, who identified what he saw as 'the rise of a revisionist school' in the 1960s. Since then, a wide-ranging debate over British appeasement has continued unabated between 'revisionist' historians and 'counter-revisionists' who adhere to a more nuanced version of the original orthodoxy that judged Chamberlain and other key figures in the National Government as guilty of serious misjudgements in their handling of Hitler and Nazi Germany, a debate well reviewed in Sidney Aster's essay. Recent contributors continue to disagree. Stedman's work on 'the alternatives to appeasement', while not uncritical of Chamberlain, concludes by defending Chamberlain very much along revisionist lines, whereas two other recent works by Tim Bouverie and Adrian Phillips essentially support the Churchillian critique of appeasement and underline Chamberlain's shortcomings.[17]

Canada and the North Atlantic Triangle

In terms of Canada's role, the Canadian historian C. P. Stacey once referred to 'the peculiar relationship of Franklin D. Roosevelt to Canada'. Pointing out that 'Mr Roosevelt is perhaps the first American President of whom it could be said that he was genuinely popular in Canada,' he raised the question of how is one to explain Roosevelt's evident special interest in Canada? He was certainly not obsessed with the country, but he seems to have had a more genuine interest in relations with Canada than any other President has ever had' – especially in the case of defence. Stacey had no answer to this question himself, beyond saying that the enigmatic FDR was often difficult to fathom. While stating that too much influence on US foreign policy should not be attributed to the Canadian Prime Minister, Mackenzie King, he argued that 'possibly as good an explanation as any is the one he himself gave during his visit to Quebec City in 1936: "since the age of two I have spent the majority of my summers in the Province of New Brunswick"'.[18]

In fact, FDR's attitude towards Canada needs to be seen within the context of the 'North Atlantic Triangle' – a term coined by John Bartlet Brebner in 1945. Brebner argued that a significant triangular relationship had emerged between the US, Britain and Canada – politically and economically – during the late nineteenth century. This development was underlined by Canada's strong contribution to victory during the First World War, her status at the Paris Peace Conference and her membership of the League of Nations. The uneasy relations of the 1920s between the US, Britain and Canada were followed by 'the perplexing triangular interplay during the prelude to war' but cooperation was much closer between 1939 and 1945, including a 'triangular economic integration for war'. This broad canvas has been filled by several later historians and political scientists, and while opinions vary on the usefulness of the term, there is no doubt that Mackenzie King saw Canada as a bridge between the USA and Britain, and that the Canadian role in the years 1937–39 therefore needs to be addressed in order to examine fully the notion of an Anglo-American 'tacit alliance'.[19]

Nazi Germany and the view from Berlin

Finally, the perspective of the enemies of an Anglo-American alliance, tacit or otherwise, needs to be borne in mind, as well as the perspective of an important ally such as Canada. Given that much of the driving force behind closer Anglo-American relations in the late 1930s was provided by fear of Nazi Germany in Washington and London, and that the US President's words and deeds suggested that, as in the Great War, US neutrality was unlikely to prove permanent if war broke out in Europe, were these warnings heeded in Berlin? What was the attitude of the German Embassy in Washington towards the signs of a closer relationship between Washington and London in Roosevelt's second term as President, compared with his first? To what extent did the Embassy warn the German Foreign Ministry about the growing closeness between Britain and the United States, and how far were any such warnings heeded by the German Foreign Ministry and by the Nazi hierarchy, especially the Foreign Minister, von Ribbentrop, and by Hitler himself?[20]

Early authorities, such as Gerhard Weinberg and Saul Friedlander, argued that Hitler had a low regard for the United States as a military threat in 1939, especially as he was convinced that Britain and France would not fight over Poland. However, when the Allies declared war and refused his peace offer, Hitler took more notice of the United States and was keen to keep it out of the war. This view has been elaborated upon by later writers such as Ian Kershaw but not changed in its essentials. Klaus Fischer, for example, has provided a very detailed and nuanced picture of Hitler's image of America, including his disdain for the bureaucrats in the German Foreign Ministry. Even Ribbentrop, his Foreign Minister, although hardly a bureaucrat, lost influence after 1939 as Hitler turned more to his military advisers for support. Nor did he have a very high opinion of the diplomats at the German Embassy in Washington, with the exception of the Military Attaché, General Friedrich von Bötticher, whose views he was more ready to read and take notice of. However, the reports of the Washington Embassy provide important evidence as to how well Berlin was informed about FDR's foreign policy and Anglo-American relations.[21]

Anglo-American relations, 1937–39

Most of the recent historiography on Anglo-American relations in the late 1930s has tended to stress the policy differences between the Roosevelt Administration and the Chamberlain Government, with individual historians empathising more with one side or the other. Relations between Britain and the United States were certainly troubled for much of the 1930s. One early historian, Harry Allen, even referred to the 'almost total lack of Anglo-American history in these years' – presumably meaning political cooperation, as he was well aware of the economic and naval issues involving the two governments. Herbert Nicholas, on the other hand, argued that there was continuous diplomatic activity between Washington and London, which contributed to the close relations between the two after war had broken out. David Adams, however, saw Roosevelt as an internationalist whose 'attempted policy of parallel action was doomed to failure because, quite apart from the problem of internal American dissent, the powers with whom he hoped to become aligned were themselves following a policy of appeasement'.[22]

A. J. P. Taylor's work, while critical of British policy, also maintained that the Roosevelt Administration made no worthwhile contribution towards dealing with the European crisis. 'The vote of November 1932 was a victory for "isolationism",' he claimed, arguing that Roosevelt's election in 1932 was soon followed by the end of American cooperation in disarmament and reparations. Referring to the Neutrality Acts, he continued, with more force than accuracy: 'President Roosevelt accepted these measures without any sign of disagreement. Their effect was reinforced by the intensely nationalistic economics of the New Deal.' Roosevelt could provide only oral exhortation during the European crisis but what Britain and France required was material strength. 'None was forthcoming from the United States.' Lack of American support contributed towards the British and French retreat at the Munich conference, he argued. 'Roosevelt, entangled in troubles over domestic policy, had no mind to add to his difficulties by provoking controversy over foreign affairs. Europe could go its own way without America.'[23]

Taylor's reputation was not based on his knowledge of American history. But his opinion on American appeasement received strong support from influential American historians such as Robert Divine, who saw Roosevelt as a genuine 'isolationist' in the early years of his presidency. Divine argued that, by the time of the Munich conference in 1938, 'American isolation had become the handmaiden of European appeasement.' Similarly, Arnold Offner, who traced American policy towards Germany from 1933 to 1938, wrote: 'A.J.P. Taylor is correct: Americans, whatever misgivings they might have had at the time, only later condemned the British and French for doing what they would have done in their place'. Following Taylor's thesis that Hitler was essentially an opportunist who was frequently fearful of foreign response and prepared to alter his immediate policy, and arguing that 'Roosevelt perpetually inclined towards appeasement,' Offner added: 'Bolder American policy might not only have encouraged others to greater daring and resistance, but could have changed, in a way highly advantageous to the democracies, the critical political circumstances in which German, and European, policy developed.'[24]

The first detailed treatment of Anglo-American relations in the 1930s based on newly released British documents in the UK National Archives, and still a significant contribution to the field, was by Ritchie Ovendale. Like much of the new scholarship of the 1970s, it was undertaken following the 1967 Public Records Act in the UK, which reduced the fifty-year rule for the release of British government records to thirty years. Ovendale's book focused more on Chamberlain and British policy, including the influence of Canada and the other Dominions, rather than on Roosevelt and US policy, and found more cooperation between London and Washington than some earlier – and later – works. Ovendale gave Chamberlain much of the credit for this.

> It was largely Chamberlain's policy of appeasement which ensured that when war came in 1939 the commonwealth was united. Britain, too, had behind it a sympathetic United States, and Roosevelt's assurance that the industrial resources of his country would be at Britain's disposal. This was a considerable achievement.

Callum MacDonald, on the other hand, stressed the tensions between FDR and Chamberlain, arguing that American policy-makers believed that the Prime Minister was 'the agent of selfish City interests'. Differences in policy towards Europe and Far East 'explain the considerable degree of mistrust which marked the attitude of the Roosevelt Administration towards the Chamberlain government', MacDonald wrote.[25]

Not long after the publication of the works by Ovendale and MacDonald, another very significant book appeared, by David Reynolds, on the 'creation of the Anglo-American alliance'. Reynolds's book, which he has supplemented with a number of other important writings, traced the development of Anglo-American relations from Chamberlain's appointment as Prime Minister in 1937 to American entry into the Second World War. The book's subtitle, 'A study in competitive cooperation', was also revealing. Reynolds's main focus was British foreign policy and, adopting a broadly revisionist stance, he was generally sympathetic to Chamberlain and the problems he faced that led the British Government to pursue a policy of appeasement. One of these problems was a tradition of American unreliability, dating back to Woodrow Wilson's failure to secure American membership of the League of Nations, that had given rise to what Reynolds characterised as 'doubts, hopes and fears' in London about the reliability of US foreign policy in the 1930s. Reynolds argued that FDR's efforts to reassure Chamberlain about US support for Britain and France were undermined by the strength of US isolationism, especially prior to the Munich crisis in September 1938, and the President's own lack of a clear policy until the crisis of May/June 1940 made this an urgent necessity.[26]

Reynolds's work, with its emphasis on the problems affecting Anglo-American relations in the late 1930s, has been followed by a number of important books that have tended to adopt a similar interpretation. Donald Cameron Watt, a leading advocate of the revisionist view of Chamberlain, was more critical of Roosevelt's policy, prior to 1939 at least. William Rock's very detailed treatment of Anglo-American relations during Chamberlain's premiership again focused mainly on the British perspective. While critical of both Chamberlain and Roosevelt, he agreed that the 'doubts, hopes, fears' of the British Government in its attitude towards the US were an important factor in hampering their cooperation. Brian McKercher, examining the Anglo-American relationship in the context of the 'transition of power' from Britain to the US in the period 1930–45, has also been very critical of Roosevelt's foreign policy as being generally unhelpful to Britain and thereby contributing indirectly to the appeasement of the dictator states. Robert Self, a biographer of Chamberlain, has excoriated FDR and US policy towards war debts. More recently, Stedman's discussion of 'alternatives to appeasement' has largely supported Chamberlain's foreign policy while downplaying the value of the United States as an ally.[27]

This is not to say that Roosevelt has been without his recent defenders amongst historians of Anglo-American relations in the 1930s. Edward Bennett has written: 'If a judgement must be made concerning where the Anglo-American relationship broke down in the 1930s there is blame a plenty, but the main culprit must be judged to be Neville Chamberlain.' According to Bennett, Chamberlain was the 'miscreant' who refused to work more closely with FDR and frustrated the President's attempts to bring pressure to bear on the aggressor nations. Greg Kennedy, while critical of Chamberlain, has maintained that Anglo-American relations became much closer during the 1930s and that the situation in the Far East was more important than Europe in facilitating this improvement. 'The basis of the "special relationship" of the Grand Alliance had been formed in the Far East by the events between 1933 and 1939,' he wrote. Simon Rofe has also blamed the British Prime Minister for the limitations on Anglo-American cooperation in the late 1930s. 'Chamberlain exhibited a lack of understanding of the complexity of American opinion and how it informed US foreign policy. In turn this meant that cooperation between President and Prime Minister was minimal.'[28]

The 'special relationship'

Following this brief review of the historiography of Anglo-American relations in the late 1930s, a final point must be made about the legacy of the 'special relationship' label used by Winston Churchill in his Fulton speech in March 1946 to describe Anglo-American relations during the Second World War. This description has resulted in what might be termed the 'glass half-full or half-empty' syndrome: that is, the tendency to measure the closeness of the Anglo-American relationship against impossibly high standards. No one was more aware than Churchill that the wartime relationship was far from harmonious, even though it was ultimately victorious, in conjunction with the rest of the United Nations, including Canada and the Soviet Union. There were frequent disagreements between the two sides over military, economic, financial and political issues – for example, the 'Imperial Preference' system of the British Empire and the timing and location of 'the Second Front' to help relieve some of the pressure on the Soviet Union after 1941. Historians of the war are obviously aware of the constant in-fighting that took place amongst the Allies, as can be seen in the titles of many of their works. And yet there was a high degree of cooperation, albeit on the implicit understanding that, once the immediate crisis was over, less urgent issues, such as trade relations and the future of the British colonial empire, would come to the fore. This needs to be borne in mind when evaluating the closeness or otherwise of the Anglo-American relationship in the late 1930.[29]

Notes

1. *NYT*, 2 February 1938.
2. Congressional debates, Borah and Johnson, 1 February 1938. See also FO/371/21491, A965/1/45, Lindsay to Halifax, 2 February 1938.
3. For US isolationism see Adler, *Isolationist Impulse*; Cole, *Roosevelt and Isolationists*; Jonas, *Isolationism in America*; Wapshott, *The Sphinx*; Maddox, *William E Borah*; McKenna, *Borah*; Lower, *Hiram W Johnson*; Cole, *Senator Gerald P Nye*.
4. For Roosevelt's initiative see Dallek, *FDR*, pp. 155–7; Bennett, 'Roosevelt Peace Plan'.

5. For Churchill's speech on the special relationship see 'The Sinews of Peace', 5 March 1946, available at <https://winstonchurchill.org/resources/speeches/1946-1963-elder-statesman/the-sinews-of-peace/>.
6. For a recent discussion of these terms see the special issue of the *Journal of Transatlantic Studies* edited by Simon Rofe, 'Isolationism and Internationalism in Transatlantic Affairs', especially Rofe, Introduction, pp. 1–6; and Johnstone, 'Isolationism and Internationalism in American Foreign Relations', pp. 7–20.
7. For KAOWC see Doenecke, 'Non-Interventionism of the Left', especially pp. 222–3; for Lansbury see Shepherd, *George Lansbury*.
8. For a critique of the term 'isolationism' see Johnstone, 'Isolationism and Internationalism'; for another view see McCulloch, 'American Isolationism in the 1930s'; see also Johnson, 'Myth of American Isolationism'; Washington's Farewell Address, 1796, and Jefferson's First Inaugural Address, 1801, can be accessed via American Presidency Project, available at <https://www.presidency.ucsb.edu/>.
9. Johnstone, 'Isolationism and Internationalism'; McCulloch, 'American Isolationism in the 1930s'; Schmitz, *Triumph of Internationalism*.
10. For a critique of British appeasement see Shen, *Age of Appeasement*; for a defence see Stedman, *Alternatives to Appeasement*; for the idea of American appeasement see Offner, *American Appeasement*.
11. Franklin Roosevelt, State of the Union address, 4 January 1939, available at <https://www.presidency.ucsb.edu/documents/annual-message-congress>.
12. See Baylis, *Enduring Alliance*, pp. 1–17 for a brief historiography and methodology of the Anglo-American relationship; also Reynolds, 'Rethinking Anglo-American Relations'.
13. Beard, *President Roosevelt*; see also Tansill, *Back Door to War*; Williams, *Tragedy of American Diplomacy*; Gardner, *Economic Aspects*.
14. Divine, *Reluctant Belligerent*; Doenecke and Wilz, *From Isolation to War*; Doenecke and Stoler, *Debating Franklin D Roosevelt's Foreign Policies*; Marks, *Wind Over Sand*; Graebner, *Roosevelt and the Search for a European Policy, 1937–1939*.
15. State Department, *Peace and War*; Rauch, *Roosevelt*; Langer and Gleason, *Challenge to Isolation*; Dallek, *FDR*; Tierney, *Spanish Civil War*; Schmitz, *Triumph of Internationalism*; Schmitz, *The Sailor*.
16. Cato, *Guilty Men*; Churchill, *Gathering Storm*; Taylor, *Origins of Second World War*.
17. Watt, 'Revisionist School'; see also *Personalities and Policies*; *Succeeding John Bull*; *How War Came*; Aster, 'Appeasement'; Stedman, *Alternatives to Appeasement*; Bouverie, *Appeasing Hitler*; Phillips, *Fighting Churchill, Appeasing Hitler*.

18. Stacey, *Canada and the Age of Conflict*, II, p. 230 for quotes; *NYT*, 1 August 1936, quoted in Stacey, p. 231; see also Eayrs, *In Defence of Canada*, II; Perras, *FDR and Origins of Canadian–American Security Alliance*.
19. Brebner, *North Atlantic Triangle, 1945*; Kottman, *North Atlantic Triangle*; McKercher and Aronson, *North Atlantic Triangle in a Changing World*; Haglund, 'Brebner's North Atlantic Triangle at Sixty'; McCulloch, 'North Atlantic Triangle: A Canadian Myth?'.
20. Dallek, *FDR*, pp. 192, 207; MacDonald, 'German Moderates'.
21. Friedlander, *Prelude to Downfall*; Weinberg, 'Hitler's Image of the United States'; Kershaw, *Fateful Choices*; Fischer, *Hitler and America*.
22. Allen, *Great Britain and United States*, p. 29; Nicholas, *Britain and USA*, p. 29; see also Nicholas, *United States and Britain*; Adams, *America in Twentieth Century*, pp. 76–9. See also Adams, *FDR, New Deal and Europe*; Adams, 'The Concept of Parallel Action'; Adams, *Before the Special Relationship*.
23. Taylor, *Origins of Second World War*, p. 95, pp. 165–6, p. 237.
24. Divine, *Reluctant Belligerent*, p. 55; see also Divine, *Illusion of Neutrality*; Offner, *American Appeasement*, pp. 279–80; Offner, *Origins of Second World War*, p. 127.
25. Ovendale, '*Appeasement*', p. 320; see also his chapter 'Canada, Britain, the United States' in Eldridge, *Kith and Kin*; MacDonald, *The United States, Britain and Appeasement*, Introduction, pp. ix–xi; see also articles by Harrison at this time, e.g. 'A Presidential "Demarche"'; 'The Runciman Visit to Washington'.
26. Reynolds, *Creation*, pp. 7–36 for section on 'Doubts, Hopes and Fears'; pp. 7–23 for Chamberlain's attitude towards the US; pp. 26–7 for view that the Roosevelt Administration did not have a coherent foreign policy until 1940; p. 95 for summary of his view of period 1937–40; see also Reynolds, *Munich to Pearl Harbor*; for other writings by Reynolds consult the Bibliography.
27. Watt, *Succeeding John Bull*; Rock, *Chamberlain and Roosevelt*; McKercher, *Transition of Power*; Self, *Britain, America and the War Debt Controversy;* Stedman, *Alternatives to Appeasement*, pp. 140–5 for the role of the United States.
28. Bennett, *Separated by a Common Language*, p. 231; Kennedy, *Anglo-American Strategic Relations*, p. 267; see also Kennedy, 'Neville Chamberlain and Strategic Relations with the United States'; Rofe, *Welles Mission*, p. 44.
29. For an excellent recent overview of the Anglo-American relationship see Dobson, 'The Evolving Study of Anglo-American Relations'. Some of the disagreements between the British and US Governments during the war can be seen, for example, in Thorne, *Allies of*

a Kind; for British criticisms of France as an ally see Dockrill, *British Establishment Perspectives on France, 1936–40*. For the 'glass half-full' versus the 'glass half-empty' viewpoint see Allen, 'A Special Relationship', a review essay of Watt's critical appraisal of Anglo-American relations in *Succeeding John Bull*. For a very critical view of the 'special relationship' see Self, *Britain, America and the War Debt Controversy*. For a balanced view see Burk, 'Is There an Anglo-American Alliance?'.

2 Roosevelt I, March 1933–January 1937

In the lead-up to FDR's landslide re-election in November 1936, the British Foreign Office began to receive reports that the President intended to take a more active role in foreign affairs in his second term and that he was toying with the idea of calling an international conference to discuss the growing threats to peace. These reports came from a variety of sources, including the British Embassy in Washington and the Canadian Prime Minister, Mackenzie King, via the Dominions Secretary, Malcolm MacDonald. They were supplemented after the election by a telegram from Sir Eric Phipps, the British Ambassador in Berlin, who said that his American counterpart, William Dodd, had told him that Roosevelt was all in favour of 'keeping the present Germany lean' and had in mind the summoning of a world peace conference in the following spring. 'If the "gangster" powers of Germany, Italy and Japan declined to attend or to give satisfactory undertakings at the conference, then the "peace-loving" states should come into close agreement amongst themselves to contain them.'[1]

Dodd's conversation with Phipps attracted a great deal of attention in the Foreign Office, especially the American Department. Perhaps its most dramatic effect was upon the attitude of Sir Robert Vansittart, the Permanent Under Secretary at the Foreign Office. While cool towards the idea of an American peace conference, he was gratified by Roosevelt's reported attitude towards economic relations with Germany, which mirrored his own mantra of 'no advantages to Germany without corresponding advantages to peace'. Since 1933, Vansittart had been in favour of 'keeping Germany lean' until Hitler's intentions were clearer. 'I frankly regard this telegram as the confirmation of the views that I have expressed for the last four years,' he wrote. 'There are signs that something <u>might</u> be made out of Mr Franklin Roosevelt II who may not be the same man as Mr F. Roosevelt I.' Similarly, Anthony Eden, the Foreign Secretary, felt that the telegram from Phipps was highly significant. 'It is of the utmost importance that we should lose no opportunity of cooperating with Roosevelt II in every sphere,' he said.[2]

FDR's conference idea

The main purpose of this chapter is to review FDR's foreign policy during his first term as President – Roosevelt I – in order to explain his desire to become more involved in international, and especially European, affairs in his second term – as Roosevelt II. One aspect of FDR's thinking was clearly the conference idea that reached the British Foreign Office towards the end of 1936. In fact, FDR had shared his idea with Arthur Krock, the Pulitzer Prize-winning *New York Times* columnist, who reported in August 1936 that he had met FDR at the President's home in Hyde Park, New York State, and the President had outlined his 'great design', as Krock called it, for a small meeting of the key heads of state -representing Britain, France, Germany, Italy, Japan, China and the Soviet Union – to forestall the worsening international situation, especially in Europe, and to prevent a second world war. FDR did not confirm or deny the story when it was published, and similar reports circulated in Washington prior to the election. A modified version of the idea was proposed secretly to the British Government in January 1938 and it was this proposal that Chamberlain turned down, contributing to Eden's resignation in the following month.[3]

As regards the British attitude to any kind of international conference, the overriding concern – as Vansittart's comments showed – was the potential threat posed by Nazi Germany and, to a lesser extent, by Fascist Italy and Imperial Japan. Hope remained that it would be possible to reach a modus vivendi with Hitler through a policy of negotiation and appeasement but at the same time a degree of rearmament was clearly advisable and was steadily increased between 1934 and 1937, although not as rapidly as events demanded. As regards relations with the US, Eden saw distinct possibilities in the summoning of a conference by the American President. 'Maybe it will not succeed, but if the attempt were made, & failure the fault of the dictator powers, the process of education of world opinion (& particularly U.S. opinion) should be salutary,' he wrote. Sir Ronald Lindsay, the British Ambassador in Washington, was accordingly informed that, while the Foreign Office would not encourage Roosevelt to call a conference, it was also vital not to discourage him and to try to arrange for confidential discussions and preparation with London beforehand.[4]

One of the sources of the information reaching London about FDR's conference idea was Malcolm MacDonald, the Dominions Secretary, and son of Ramsay MacDonald, the former Prime Minister. MacDonald had met Mackenzie King, the Canadian Prime Minister, in Geneva on 20 September 1936 and the two men discussed the international situation in some depth. Mackenzie King saw Canada as an 'interpreter' and 'mediator' between Great Britain and the US, and was anxious to facilitate closer relations between them. Returning to power in the Canadian general election of October 1935, he travelled to Washington to meet FDR and other US officials and quickly finalised a trade agreement with the US. FDR paid a return visit to Canada in July 1936 and met not only Mackenzie King but also John Buchan, Lord Tweedsmuir, the Governor General. Mackenzie King told MacDonald that at a meeting between him, Tweedsmuir and Roosevelt, the latter had 'thrown out the idea of calling a conference of heads of States, including King Edward, Herr Hitler, the President of the French Republic, and others', if he was re-elected.[5]

Roosevelt bombshell

As the comments by Vansittart and Eden suggest, the British Foreign Office felt that FDR had not been especially helpful during his first term, despite the fact that his election in November 1932 had been welcomed in London in preference to the return to power of Herbert Hoover. As a member of Woodrow Wilson's wartime Administration, more had been expected of him than of the discredited Hoover. Indeed, his Inaugural Address on 4 March was well received by the British Embassy and the American Department of the Foreign Office. Lindsay characterised it as 'a courageous speech', full of leadership, inspiring in both its language and its delivery. He also felt that Roosevelt had chosen internationalists for key positions in his Cabinet. His Secretary of State was Cordell Hull, an internationalist who was especially interested in the liberalisation of trade. As Secretary of the Treasury Roosevelt chose William Woodin, another internationalist who, however, resigned because of ill health and was replaced in January 1934 by FDR's good friend and Hyde Park neighbour Henry Morgenthau Junior, the son of Woodrow Wilson's ambassador to Turkey. FDR's Ambassador-at-Large was Norman Davis, a convinced Wilsonian and a close friend of Cordell Hull.[6]

However, following initial optimism, the British Government had been disappointed by Roosevelt's failure to persuade Congress to offer a more generous settlement on war debts than Britain had obtained in the 1923 agreement negotiated in Washington by Stanley Baldwin. The British were also unhappy at FDR's decision to take the dollar off the gold standard in April 1933 while Prime Minister Ramsay MacDonald was crossing the Atlantic to meet him, and then dismayed by his attitude towards the issue of currency stabilisation at the World Economic Conference in London, culminating in the infamous 'bombshell message' from FDR to the conference, rejecting any form of stabilisation. In October 1933 Sir Frederick Leith-Ross, a British Treasury official, visited Washington for talks on the war debt issue. But the main effect of the Leith-Ross visit was to annoy Roosevelt, in view of the British assumption that the onus was on him to come up with a solution. A bill that forbade loans to foreign countries in default on their war debts was introduced by Hiram Johnson in January 1934 and was signed by the President in April 1934. As a result, the British Government, which had been making token payments, promptly ended them.[7]

Inevitably, these financial and economic issues affected wider Anglo-American relations. The policies of London and Washington towards Japan's ambitions in the Far East were still strained following the Manchurian incident in 1931, when Japan had invaded China and established the puppet state of 'Manchukuo' under Japanese control. Henry Stimson, Hoover's Secretary of State, had said that the US would refuse to recognise Japanese sovereignty over Manchuria but felt let down by the less than enthusiastic attitude of Sir John Simon, the British Foreign Secretary. In February 1933 Japan announced its withdrawal from the League of Nations. The Tangku truce in May 1933 ended hostilities for the time being but Japan's designs on China remained. This was demonstrated by the so-called Amau statement, issued by the Japanese Foreign Ministry on 17 April 1934, which stated that Japan would oppose any foreign intervention that threatened her position in China. Further Japanese threats against China led to the Ho-Umezu agreement in June 1935, which ceded virtual control of Hebei province from China to Japan. This further truce held until the Marco Polo Bridge incident, which marked the start of the Sino-Japanese War in July 1937.[8]

Neville Chamberlain, the Chancellor of the Exchequer, was especially incensed by Roosevelt's actions, which he saw as demonstrating the inherent unreliability of the United States in international affairs – an unreliability that dated back to the Senate's rejection in 1920 of the League of Nations, championed by President Woodrow Wilson. Chamberlain argued that Britain should reduce its defence costs by coming to terms with Japan over naval parity in the Far East, regardless of the attitude of the United States, and he put this view forward in the British Cabinet in the second half of 1934. Even Sir John Simon, British Foreign Secretary at that time, who had had his differences with the United States over the Japanese invasion of Manchuria in 1931, balked at this idea but it was only the Japanese decision to denounce the Washington naval treaty in December 1934 that laid Chamberlain's idea to rest – for the time being at least. In March 1936 the London naval agreement was signed between Britain and the US, in the absence of Japan, and Anglo-American relations in the Far East were significantly improved. Indeed, a leading historian in this field has argued that 'a new era in Anglo-American relations had been forged in the fires of the naval disarmament process'. A formal alliance against Japan was not possible but London and Washington 'now knew that informal consultation and cooperation, along parallel but not joint lines, was a useful strategic reality'.[9]

Advent of Hitler

Meanwhile, the situation in Europe was steadily deteriorating. Hitler had become the German Chancellor in January 1933 and, following the Reichstag Fire in February, the Nazi Party had issued emergency decrees and taken full control of the government. Nazi propaganda, masterminded by Joseph Goebbels, had attacked both the Versailles peace treaty of 1919 and 'the Jewish conspiracy' for supposedly undermining Germany's domestic strength and her place in Europe. In October 1933 Hitler announced that Germany was leaving the Geneva Disarmament Conference and the League of Nations. Germany had been secretly rearming since the 1920s and this had greatly increased under Nazi rule. In March 1935 Berlin confirmed that Germany had developed its own Air Force. Military conscription was introduced and it was announced that the armed forces would be increased to a peace-time strength of 550,000 men – actions that violated not only the Versailles treaty but also Germany's separate peace treaty with the United States. In public, the State Department issued a disapproving statement that pointed out the importance of maintaining treaties. In private, FDR told William Phillips, the Under Secretary of State, that he did not want the United States to become involved in the European situation at that time but the possibility of some intervention in the future was at the back of his mind. An alarmed Phillips noted in his diary that 'the President, for once, was completely off the straight road'.[10]

Alongside continuing attempts to negotiate with Nazi Germany over rearmament, Britain had herself started to rearm after the low point of 1932–33, when defence expenditure reached what a distinguished historian described as the 'nadir' of £102.7 million. The 'ten-year rule' (that war was not to be expected in the next ten years) was abandoned in 1932, and in November 1933 the Defence Requirements Sub-Committee was established to identify the main deficiencies in British defences. The Committee was handicapped by differences of opinion between the armed services and the tight limit on expenditure imposed by Chamberlain and the Treasury. However, some progress was made in 1934, especially in British air power, and this was extended following the White Paper, *Statement Relating to Defence*, issued in March 1935, when the Government announced 'a further expansion of the air force which would bring its strength in first-line planes at home to 1500 by 1937, treble the existing home strength and double that which would have been reached by 1937 against the programme of 1934'.[11]

Neutrality laws

In June 1935 a change of government in Britain – welcomed by Roosevelt and other Administration officials – opened the way for better relations between London and Washington. Not only was the tired and disillusioned MacDonald succeeded as Prime

Minister by the more palatable Stanley Baldwin, but also Sir John Simon gave way as Foreign Secretary to Sir Samuel Hoare, and Anthony Eden entered the Cabinet as Minister for League Affairs. However, the new Government signed the Anglo-German naval agreement in June – which upset France and Italy – and soon faced a major crisis in Europe when it became clear that Mussolini was intent on invading the kingdom of Ethiopia (known then as Abyssinia) as part of his ambition to create an Italian empire and to avenge an infamous defeat at the hands of the Ethiopians back in 1896. The deteriorating situation in Europe was the immediate background to the introduction of new US Neutrality laws that were to hamper Roosevelt's foreign policy and complicate Anglo-American relations for the rest of the 1930s.[12]

Isolationists such as Borah and Johnson wanted strict and impartial Neutrality legislation that would 'embargo arms, bar loans and limit trade to all belligerents', and this approach was increasingly supported by peace organisations such as the National Council for the Prevention of War. FDR, on the other hand, and advocates of international cooperation and collective security, wanted as much discretion as possible to be able to discriminate between the 'aggressor' and 'victim', as was the policy of the League of Nations. Roosevelt tried to block new Neutrality legislation but the pressure of public opinion on Congress grew as the situation in Europe worsened. FDR eventually agreed to a compromise that introduced a mandatory embargo on the export of 'arms, ammunition and the implements of war' during wartime but gave the President discretion in deciding when the embargo should go into effect and in defining 'implements of war'. He hoped that the Neutrality Bill he signed on 31 August would be temporary, but it was renewed in February 1936, including the arms embargo, with an additional ban on loans or credits to belligerents.[13]

The governments of Britain and France had looked to Italy as an ally against Hitler's Germany and leaders of the three powers had met together at Stresa in April 1935 to confer over the implications of German rearmament. Mussolini assumed that London and Paris would oppose but not resist the Italian invasion of Ethiopia in October but the British Cabinet reluctantly decided to support whatever sanctions against Italy the other League members could agree upon. On 1 October the Labour Party conference in Brighton also voted overwhelmingly in favour of sanctions against Italy. However, during November, the Baldwin Government became increasingly alarmed at the prospect of economic sanctions against Italy, especially on oil, that might lead to a war that was likely to be to the benefit of Germany. Britain and France were also keen to revive the so-called Stresa Front and it was in these circumstances that Sir Samuel Hoare met Pierre Laval, the French Foreign Minister, in Paris on 7 and 8 December and agreed to a 'compromise' plan, whereby Ethiopia would make large territorial concessions to Italy in return for peace. When news of the so-called 'Hoare–Laval pact' became public on 9 December there was an outcry against it and Hoare was forced to resign.[14]

Roosevelt's annual address to Congress on 3 January 1936 was more concerned with foreign affairs than any of his earlier messages. Since the summer of 1933, he said, the policies of several powers had become increasingly aggressive so that the world now faced the prospect of general war. He made it quite clear which powers he had in mind. 'The evidence before us clearly proves that autocracy in world affairs endangers peace and that such threats do not spring from the nations devoted to the democratic ideal,' he said. Lindsay described this address as 'a slashing indictment of the policies followed by the Italian, German and Japanese Governments'. The speech confirmed the view, he wrote, 'that, while a technical neutrality will be rigidly observed, there can be no question of an effort to inculcate intellectual neutrality such as was made by President Wilson in the beginning of the Great War'.[15]

Lindsay felt that, despite the Neutrality law of August 1935, Roosevelt might still be able to discriminate in Britain's favour if she found herself at war – for example, with Italy. But this possibility had not been increased by 'the Paris episode'. Indeed, the British Ambassador was clearly appalled by the conduct of his own Government and he warned London about the very bad impression that the Hoare–Laval pact had made in the United States. 'They filled the friends of Great Britain with dismay and they provided equal exultation to her critics,' he wrote. The uproar in Britain and Hoare's subsequent resignation had repaired some of the damage, he continued, 'but it would be too much to suggest that the episode itself is now forgotten, for it is not the way of politicians or of editors to forget the *lache* of a great country'. The last part of Lindsay's despatch was omitted from the copy that was sent to the Dominions but the Hoare–Laval episode was clearly an absolute public relations disaster for the Government and a reminder that

British public opinion, like public opinion in the United States, required careful handling.[16]

In March 1936 German troops occupied the demilitarised zone of the Rhineland, thus violating another part of the Versailles treaty. While the British Government refused to take military action against Germany, the episode did encourage further steps towards rearmament, including the establishment of a new post of Minister of Co-ordination of Defence in March 1936. Such a post had been advocated by Winston Churchill alongside his dire warnings of the threat posed by a resurgent Germany, but the position was given to Sir Thomas Inskip, a 'safe pair of hands', and he held it until January 1939. At the same time as Inskip's appointment, the British Government also began a rearmament programme that included the modernisation of the Army and the addition of four new battalions. The Navy was to receive two new battleships and an aircraft carrier, while existing battleships were to be modernised, and the number of cruisers substantially increased. The first-line strength of the Air Force for home defence was to rise to 1,750 planes, rather than the 1,500 originally planned, and twelve more squadrons were to be allocated to Imperial defence.[17]

Alarm bells were also ringing in Washington. FDR told Sir Arthur Willert, a former British diplomat and journalist, and a friend from the First World War, who was visiting him at the White House, that Britain and France needed to stand up to the dictators. While Hull and the State Department wanted to improve economic relations with Germany, if Berlin adopted a more liberal trade policy, Henry Morgenthau, the Secretary of the Treasury, favoured a more robust approach, especially after the Rhineland episode. Morgenthau was keen to act against the currency practices that subsidised German exports to the US and elsewhere, and with the President's approval and the support of the US Attorney General he decided to announce the imposition of countervailing duties on German goods at a press conference in June 1936. After protesting about these duties, the German Government eventually backed down and modified its practices, so that in August 1936 the American Treasury announced that the duties would be withdrawn. The episode was an indication of the outlook and influence of the Secretary of the Treasury that were to be a prominent feature of Anglo-American relations during FDR's second term. 'Contrary to the fears of the State Department and the bluster of the German press', Morgenthau later wrote, 'the Treasury policy worked. . . . It was the first check to Germany's career of economic conquest.'[18]

Spanish Civil War

By May 1936 Ethiopia had been overrun by Italian forces and Haile Selassie had left Addis Ababa for exile in England. The limited economic sanctions imposed by the League were removed on 15 July 1936. Just two days later, a military revolt in Morocco marked the onset of the Spanish Civil War. Events in Spain were of great concern to both London and Washington because of their international ramifications. In the months following the outbreak of the Spanish Civil War in July 1936 the governments of Italy and Germany intervened quite openly on the side of the Nationalist rebels, led by General Franco, while the Soviet Union provided equally open military support for the Republican Government, and the French Government was divided over the best course of action to take. The conflict was seen by many – not least by liberals and socialists in the United States – as a struggle between democracy and fascism but the complexity of the issues involved belied simple definition. A Non-intervention Committee was set up in London, which all of the major European powers joined, but foreign intervention continued unabated and cemented what became known as the Rome–Berlin Axis, following a show of solidarity between Mussolini and Hitler in October 1936.[19]

C. P. Stacey argued that Franklin Roosevelt had 'a more genuine interest in relations with Canada than any other President has ever had'. FDR certainly paid a great deal of attention to relations with Canada during his presidency and assiduously courted Mackenzie King, the Liberal Prime Minister during this period. Roosevelt viewed Mackenzie King, as the Canadian viewed himself, as a bridge between the governments of the United States and Britain. Canada was especially important as a trading partner and during the 1930s became increasingly significant in terms of both continental and Imperial defence. Mackenzie King was out of office in 1932 at the time of the Ottawa agreements that were central to the system of Imperial Preference, developed within the Empire as a response to the Great Depression and high US tariffs. He was therefore quite happy to see the agreements modified, and trade barriers in general reduced, as long as this was not done at the expense of Canada. Returning to power in the Canadian general election of October1935, he travelled to Washington to meet FDR and other US officials and the two leaders quickly finalised a trade agreement in November 1935.[20]

FDR paid a brief return visit to Canada on 31 July 1936, at the invitation of the Governor General, Lord Tweedsmuir – the former John Buchan, the novelist. Roosevelt spent most of this visit in Quebec City, where he was greeted with great pomp and ceremony and a twenty-one-gun salute. In an article entitled 'Roosevelt visit links 3 nations', the point was made that the official visit – the first by an American President to Canada – was as significant for the Anglo-American relationship as it was for Canada–US relations, especially at a time of rising tensions in Europe. George V had died in January 1936, and while in Quebec Roosevelt extended an invitation to the new King, Edward VIII, to visit Washington, as well as welcoming Mackenzie King to return to the US capital at any time. He also made a brief speech, delivered partly in English and partly in French, stressing the friendship between the US and Canada and, of course, their undefended border. According to Mackenzie King, it was during this trip that the President had 'thrown out the idea of calling a conference of heads of States, including King Edward, Herr Hitler, the President of the French Republic, and others', if he was re-elected. This information was subsequently shared with Malcolm MacDonald, the Dominions Secretary and son of Ramsay MacDonald, when he met Mackenzie King in Geneva on 20 September 1936.[21]

Roosevelt said very little about foreign affairs during the 1936 election campaign, beyond his speech at Chautauqua, New York, on 14 August, when he stated that the Administration's basic policy was to keep America out of war. 'We are not isolationists except in so far as we seek to isolate ourselves completely from war,' he maintained. But, he warned, while war existed, there was always a danger of involvement. The Neutrality laws were some defence, but the real need was to prevent war in the first place. This was a consistent theme of Roosevelt's foreign policy from 1936 onwards – the need to prevent war rather than trying to cope with it once it had broken out, as Woodrow Wilson had been forced to do. The implication was that the US should cooperate with like-minded powers – that is, the democracies of Britain and France – to prevent war. In this regard he mentioned Cordell Hull's trade agreements programme and highlighted the 'good neighbour' policy of the Administration, especially within the Western hemisphere, and above all towards Canada.[22]

Tripartite Currency Agreement

Hitler's obvious determination to destroy the Versailles peace settlement, together with the growing militarisation of Nazi Germany, placed enormous pressure on France at a time when there were also rising internal tensions between left and right. As a result, the French currency came under increasing strain and made devaluation more and more likely. This was a matter of great concern to London and Washington for political as well as financial and economic reasons, as a weak France would encourage further moves by Germany. The announcement of German conscription and rearmament in March 1935 and the reoccupation of the Rhineland in March 1936 added to the pressure on the franc, as did the outbreak of the Spanish Civil War. Roosevelt was sympathetic towards the Popular Front Government of Léon Blum, formed in June 1936, and he allowed Morgenthau to open the negotiations with Neville Chamberlain and the French Finance Minister, Vincent Auriol, aided by Emmanuel Monick, the French financial attaché in London, that eventually led to the Tripartite Currency Agreement of September 1936. This consisted of separate statements by the French, British and US Treasuries agreeing a managed devaluation of the French franc while sterling and the dollar remained at their existing level.[23]

The Tripartite Currency Agreement, or 'Tripartite Pact' as Morgenthau liked to call it, did not put an end to French financial and political weakness, but it was of great importance in improving Anglo-American financial relations. The dissension of the London Economic Conference and the 'Roosevelt bombshell' had at least been forgiven, if not forgotten. The two Treasuries were now on better terms than they had been since at least 1933 and they agreed to keep in touch by means of informal meetings in London or Washington in the future. The currency agreement was an obvious contribution to currency stability, but it also had wider implications, both economic and political. It removed a major obstacle to Hull's trade agreements programme, and it was also an indication that, in the wake of the Johnson Act, war debts had been discounted by the financial markets as a major factor influencing currency levels. Not least, the currency agreement was also a demonstration of cooperation between the democracies. This became all the more significant when Germany and Japan announced the

Anti-Comintern Pact, signed in Berlin on 25 November 1936. Although ostensibly aimed at the Soviet Union, it was a warning to the democracies that there was growing cooperation between Rome, Berlin and Tokyo.[24]

Not the least remarkable feature of the Tripartite Currency Agreement was the fact that it was negotiated and announced during the Presidential election campaign of 1936. To a large extent, this campaign was dominated by the personality and performance of the President, but FDR also stressed the theme of defending democracy at home and abroad by recognising the need for reform within the United States and contributing to the maintenance of peace abroad. The Republican candidate, Governor Alf Landon of Kansas, attacked Hull's trade agreements programme for lowering tariffs against foreign goods, and also accused FDR of torpedoing the London Economic Conference in July 1933. The currency agreement with Britain and France therefore came at exactly the right time for Roosevelt and the Democrats. Hull also gave an effective defence of his trade agreements programme by arguing that it contributed to both American economic recovery and world peace. Frank Knox, the owner of the *Chicago News* and the Republican Vice-Presidential candidate, attacked the New Deal for what he regarded as its dictatorial tendencies. But he was also an internationalist who became a significant ally for Roosevelt's foreign policy during FDR's second term.[25]

FDR's victory was welcomed in Britain and France. From London, Robert Bingham, the US Ambassador, informed Roosevelt that Baldwin and Eden had told him that they were now ready to make a more definite statement welcoming a more liberal trade policy. From Paris, William Bullitt told the President that the Government had taken heart from his victory and that Blum was especially pleased. In a speech at the Guildhall on 9 November Baldwin declared that relations with America were excellent and that the Government looked forward to a further period of friendly cooperation with the Roosevelt Administration in all matters of common concern. It was particularly gratifying to note, continued Baldwin, that both governments were pledged to fight obstacles to international trade. 'A further bond of sympathy between the two countries has been the similarity of their outlook in the political field and a keen desire to help within the measure of their respective situations the cause of world peace.' Clearly, there was encouragement in London and Paris for the foreign policy of Roosevelt II to move well beyond that of Roosevelt I.[26]

Buenos Aires conference

After his re-election Roosevelt embarked on a trip to Latin America for the 'Special Conference for the Maintenance of Peace' that took place in Buenos Aires in December 1936. The conference, which had been suggested by FDR in response to the worsening international situation, agreed to consult if the peace of the Americas appeared to be threatened. It also adopted a protocol that confirmed the US acceptance of non-intervention in Latin America implied by the Good Neighbour policy. When FDR addressed the inaugural session on 1 December, he referred to the assembled representatives as a 'family' of nations and drew a contrast between the happy state of the Americas, where 'every nation of this hemisphere is at peace with its neighbours', and the rapid rearmament and growing threat of war in the rest of the world. 'Beyond the ocean we see continents rent asunder by old hatreds and new fanaticisms,' he said. But he expressed confidence that 'the Republics of the New World' could help 'the Old World' to avert the impending catastrophe. 'Democracy is still the hope of the world,' he declared. If it continued to succeed in the Americas, it could succeed elsewhere. Hull followed up Roosevelt's address to the conference with a speech of his own on 5 December, in which he put forward 'Eight Pillars of Peace', each of which appeared very bland but carried an implied criticism of Nazi Germany, Italy and Japan.[27]

The theme of defending and promoting democracy at home and abroad that Roosevelt employed during his re-election campaign and enlarged upon in his Buenos Aires speech was also central to his State of the Union message at the end of his first term. The threat to democracy, in the US and elsewhere, posed by the rise of Nazism and Fascism had been addressed in his 1936 State of Union message and he returned to this theme in his annual message in January 1937. In fact, there were no fewer than twenty-two references to 'democracy' or 'democratic' in his 1937 address – more than in any other State of the Union address in American history. Referring back to the reform movement of the Progressive Era associated with Theodore Roosevelt and Woodrow Wilson, during which he had come of age as a politician, FDR said that 'The World War, for all of its tragedy, encouraged these demands, and stimulated action to fulfil these new desires.' But where democracy had been replaced by oligarchy 'militarism has leapt forward, while in those Nations which have retained democracy, militarism has waned'.[28]

He then referred to his recent trip to Latin America for the Inter-American Conference held in Buenos Aires. 'The very cordial receptions with which I was greeted were in tribute to democracy,' he said. 'To me the outstanding observation of that visit was that the masses of the peoples of all the Americas are convinced that the democratic form of government can be made to succeed and do not wish to substitute for it any other form of government.' FDR regarded this as proof that the ordinary people of Latin America believed that 'democracies are best able to cope with the changing problems of modern civilization within themselves, and that democracies are best able to maintain peace among themselves'. He also said that the Inter-American Conference, operating on the 'fundamental principles of democracy', had done much to 'assure peace in this Hemisphere'. Furthermore,

> in a very real sense, the Conference in Buenos Aires sent forth a message on behalf of all the democracies of the world to those Nations which live otherwise. Because such other Governments are perhaps more spectacular, it was high time for democracy to assert itself.

This was a message that the President was to repeat many times during his second term – the democracies needed to stand up for their beliefs against Nazi Germany and the other dictator states before it was too late.[29]

The view from Berlin

The growing criticism of the Nazi regime by Roosevelt and members of his Administration was fully recognised by the German Foreign Ministry in Berlin. Rudolph Leitner, the Head of the American Political Division, wrote that 'the fundamental antithesis between the two ideologies seems to be unbridgeable, all the more since our exertions to enlighten the public have so far foundered on the hostile attitude of the media which mould public opinion (the press, radio, film and theatre) which are mostly dominated by Jewish capital'. According to Leitner, the speeches of Roosevelt and Hull reflected the general hostility in the United States towards Nazi Germany. Canada's attitude towards Germany was also unfriendly, he added, although this had not prevented a trade agreement being signed in Ottawa in October 1936. Hostility between Washington and Berlin, however, was clearly affecting trade relations between the two countries. In contrast, relations between the US, Britain and France were seen to have grown closer and the Tripartite Currency Agreement was regarded as 'proof of the beginnings of general political cooperation between the democracies, united by an ideology which they share'.[30]

The situation at the end of 1936 was summed up from the German perspective by Thomsen, the Chargé d'Affaires in Washington. 'A feeling of deep resentment against us has been steadily growing in recent weeks,' he said. Fresh evidence of this, he pointed out, was contained in Roosevelt's speech to the Pan-American Congress at Buenos Aires. 'While he did not once mention Germany by name in this speech, yet in substance and form it was really aimed at us,' said Thomsen. 'It is now generally held in America that our foreign exchange and economic policies will lead to a serious economic convulsion until, in Roosevelt's words, they collapse "like a house of cards".' It was clear from the President's speech that Berlin 'should count less and less on the United States taking a passive and detached attitude towards the events in Europe, at least with regard to their economic and ideological aspects'. The available evidence, he argued, 'with reference to events in the field of foreign currency, speaks of an economic ring being formed against us'.[31]

Early in 1937 Hans Luther, the German Ambassador, sent a despatch to the Foreign Ministry suggesting that Roosevelt's second term 'might be the beginning of a series of surprises which the energetic and enterprising President is preparing to extend to the sphere of foreign affairs'. There had been rumours for some time that he 'intended to invite the heads of the European Great Powers to a conference at Washington in order to discuss jointly and in friendly fashion the political and ideological issues that divided them, with a view to bringing about a general tranquilization'. Luther himself did not think that the President was likely to take any immediate steps, especially in view of the failure of the talks held in Washington prior to the London Economic Conference in 1933. But the Ambassador was in no doubt where the President's priorities lay. 'In practical terms, the foreign policy of the United States is at present – in contrast to the usual American concentration upon the Far East, next to Latin America – entirely focused upon Europe,' he reported. 'The starting point of all thinking on foreign affairs in this country is now the question of the part the United States should play in a future European conflict.'[32]

Notes

1. FO/371/20476, W11944/79/98, note by Malcolm MacDonald of conversation with Mackenzie King, 20 September 1936; FO/371/19827, A8860/103/45, Phipps to Simon, 6 November 1936.
2. Ibid., minutes by Sir R. Vansittart, 9 and 11 November 1936; and by Anthony Eden, 12 November 1936.
3. Dallek, *FDR*, pp. 129–131; Krock, *In The Nation*, pp. 62–6; Krock, *Memoirs*, pp. 175–6; *NYT*, 26 and 27 August 1936.
4. FO/371/19827, A8860/103/45, minute by Eden, 12 November 1936; Vansittart to Lindsay, 17 November 1936; comment by Eden on minute by Craigie, 13 November 1936.
5. FO 371, 20476, W11944/79/98, note by Malcolm MacDonald of conversation with Mackenzie King, 20 September 1936; Mackenzie King Diary, 20 September 1936.
6. FO/371/16599, A2141/17/45, Lindsay to Simon, 9 March 1933; A1778/17/45, Lindsay to Craigie, 24 February 1933, for an appreciation of the Roosevelt Cabinet; see also Freidel, *Roosevelt: Launching the New Deal*, pp. 137–60.
7. Dallek, *FDR*, pp. 23–58; McKercher, *Transition of Power*, pp. 157–85; Self, *Britain, America and the War Debt Controversy*, pp. 178–95; Watt, *Succeeding John Bull*, pp. 65–8.
8. Dallek, *FDR*, pp. 87–90; McKercher, *Transition of Power*, pp. 94–202; Shen, *Age of Appeasement*, pp. 1–35.
9. Kennedy, *Anglo-American Strategic Relations*, pp. 121–210, especially pp. 202–3.
10. Dallek, *FDR*, pp. 101–6; Phillips Diary, Box 6, 22 and 23 March 1935.
11. Mowat, *Britain Between the Wars*, pp. 475–9, 538–42; HMSO, White Paper, 'Statement Relating to Defence', Cmd 4827 (1935); see also Neilson, 'Defence Requirements Sub-Committee', pp. 651–84.
12. Dallek, *FDR*, pp. 106–21; Harris, *US and Italo-Ethiopian Crisis*.
13. Dallek, *FDR*, pp. 117–21; Divine, *Illusion of Neutrality*, pp. 122–61.
14. CAB/23, 50, (1935), item 2, 2 December 1935; Templewood, *Nine Troubled Years*, pp. 176–92.
15. Dallek, *FDR*, pp. 116–17; for FDR Annual Message see <https://www.presidency.ucsb.edu/documents/annual-message-congress-2>; FO/371/19826, A482/103/45, Lindsay to Eden, 16 January 1936.
16. Ibid., Lindsay to Eden, 16 January 1936; see also McCulloch, 'FDR as Founding Father', pp. 229–33.
17. Shen, *Age of Appeasement*, pp. 99–135; Mowat, *Britain Between the Wars*, pp. 563–72; HMSO, White Paper, 'Statement Relating to Defence', Cmd 5107 (1936).
18. FO/371/19828, A3150/170/45, Willert to Craigie, 9 April 1936; Harrison, 'Presidential Demarche', pp. 249–50; Blum, *Morgenthau Diaries I, 1928–1938*, pp. 149–59.

19. See Preston, *Spanish Civil War*; Thomas, *Spanish Civil War*; Tierney, *FDR and Spanish Civil War*; Traina, *American Diplomacy and Spanish Civil War*; Wiskemann, *Rome–Berlin Axis*; Steiner, *Triumph of the Dark*, pp. 181–251.
20. Stacey, *Canada and the Age of Conflict*, 2, p. 230; McCulloch, 'Mackenzie King and the North Atlantic Triangle', pp. 5–8.
21. *NYT*, 1 August 1936; FO/371/20476, W11944/79/98, note by Malcolm MacDonald of conversation with Mackenzie King, 20 September 1936; Mackenzie King Diary, 20 September 1936.
22. Dallek, *FDR*, pp. 122–30; for Chautauqua speech, 14 August 1936, <https://www.presidency.ucsb.edu/documents/address-chautauqua-ny>.
23. Blum, *Morgenthau Diaries I*, pp. 159–73.
24. Steiner, *Triumph of the Dark*, pp. 262–4.
25. Kennedy, *Freedom from Fear*, pp. 457–66 for 1936 election campaign and Frank Knox; for British Embassy reports on election campaign see FO/371/19829, A8033/170/45, Mallet to Eden, 29 September 1936 and A8357/170/45, Mallet to Eden, 10 October 1936.
26. Roosevelt papers, President's Secretary's File (PSF), Box 52, Bingham to Roosevelt, 13 November 1936; ibid., Box 43, Bullitt to Roosevelt, 8 November 1936; *The Times*, 10 November 1936 for Baldwin speech.
27. *NYT*, 2 December 1936 for FDR speech to conference; Hull, *Memoirs I*, pp. 493–503; Dallek, *FDR*, pp. 132–4; see also Haglund, *Latin America*, pp. 35–50, for a critical view of US foreign policy at this time.
28. McCulloch, 'FDR and Democracy Promotion', pp. 69–76.
29. See <https://www.presidency.ucsb.edu/documents/annual-message-congress-1> for FDR's annual message to Congress, 6 January 1937.
30. DGFP/C/VI, doc 37, 'Memorandum by Rudolph Leitner (the Head of Political Division IX), Berlin, 17 November 1936; doc 52, Luther to GFM, 24 November 1936.
31. DGFP/C/VI, doc 72, Thomsen, Chargé d'Affaires to GFM, 2 December 1936.
32. DGFP/C/VI, doc 207, Luther to GFM, 15 February 1937.

3 Roosevelt II, January–May 1937

On Saturday evening, 23 January 1937, after an informal dinner, Walter Runciman and Franklin Roosevelt talked alone in the President's room in the White House. 'By road of reminiscence he reached the subject of peace, and he told me . . . his fears for Europe,' Runciman later wrote. Roosevelt explained the difficulties surrounding the Administration's new Neutrality Bill in Congress but was confident of securing wider powers under it. 'He regarded the effect on the German mind of his possessing these powers as an important new fact,' noted Runciman.

> While he did not wish to exaggerate his influence, he told me plainly . . . that he thought that collaboration between England and America would be pacifying, although he did not overlook the fact that a German air attack would probably aim at obtaining a decision in a fortnight or three weeks. . . . I told the President that in my view Germany would make war at her convenient moment provided America was not taking any steps to come in or exercise an effective neutrality.[1]

The visit of Walter Runciman, the President of the British Board of Trade, to Washington a few days after FDR's second Inaugural, confirmed that Roosevelt II was greatly concerned about the world situation, especially in Europe, and keen to become more involved in international affairs than Roosevelt I, and to support the democracies of Britain and France in dealing with Germany and the other dictator states. Invited by the President to visit him after his second Inaugural Address, Runciman spent four days in Washington, where he discussed in depth not only the prospects for an Anglo-American trade agreement but also the deteriorating international situation, in both Europe and the Far East, and FDR's hopes that the US Neutrality laws would be modified in favour of the democracies. Thus although the ostensible reason for Runciman's winter-time trip across the Atlantic was to discuss trade issues, the agenda was, in fact, much broader and not at all confined to purely economic matters. As a senior member of the British Cabinet, his visit also catered to FDR's penchant for informal diplomacy and his desire to 'connect' at a personal level with the British Government.[2]

One hundred days

The main purpose of this chapter is to analyse the transition from Roosevelt I to Roosevelt II by examining FDR's foreign policy in the first hundred days of his second term, from his Inaugural Address on 20 January 1937 to his signing of the revised Neutrality Act on 1 May. Runciman's visit, in many ways, pointed in the direction of the President's foreign policy during this period and, indeed, for most of his second term. However, it has received relatively little attention from historians of Anglo-American relations. FDR's personal invitation to Runciman in May 1936 to visit him in Washington can be seen as a follow-up to his State of the Union message in January 1936, which contained an outspoken attack on the leaders of the 'dictator states' of Germany, Italy and Japan, who, he believed, were threatening international peace and stability, and thereby risking the onset of a second world war. Runciman's visit to Washington was followed by a series of initiatives by members of the Administration – including Henry Morgenthau (Secretary of the Treasury), Cordell Hull (Secretary of State), Norman Davis (Ambassador-at-Large) and Robert Bingham (Ambassador to Britain) – to enlist British support for a move to head off an international crisis.[3]

As for British policy, Stanley Baldwin had indicated, after the abdication of Edward VIII in December 1936, that he would retire from the premiership once the new king, George VI, was crowned in May 1937. It was taken for granted within the Government that Baldwin would be succeeded by Neville Chamberlain, the Chancellor of the Exchequer. The potential threat from Germany continued to loom large but British rearmament was now under way, albeit at a less urgent rate than in Germany. There was still a strong hope in London that it would be possible to come to terms with Hitler to avoid the need for full-scale rearmament and the danger of a European war. Foreign Office officials like Vansittart, who doubted that Nazi Germany could be appeased, hoped that it might be possible to split Mussolini from Hitler and they were also keen to avoid provoking Japan so that British forces could focus on Europe. Thus while Eden, Vansittart and others welcomed FDR's cooperation, the value of US support was seen very much in terms of how well it chimed with British appeasement strategy.[4]

The Canadian Prime Minister, William Lyon Mackenzie King, who was in London for the Imperial Conference, was a firm supporter of British appeasement policy towards Germany. He was also someone whose support Roosevelt and Hull were keen to enlist in negotiations for a trade agreement with Britain because of Canada's central role in facilitating the Ottawa agreements of August 1932 between Britain and the Dominions. The Ottawa system, based on the principle of Imperial Preference, was a major target of Hull's free trade philosophy and he hoped that Mackenzie King would help to promote an Anglo-American trade agreement that might help to dismantle it. Mackenzie King had been out of office between 1930 and 1935 – his only break in a premiership that lasted from 1921 to 1948 – and the Ottawa conference had been hosted by his Conservative rival, and bitter enemy, Richard Bennett. Like Hull, Mackenzie King was a free trader, in principle at least, and it was he who had helped Hull to persuade Roosevelt to support the Canadian–American trade agreement of November 1935.[5]

Runciman visit

Walter Runciman had been the President of the Board of Trade and a member of the British Cabinet since 1931, under first MacDonald and then Baldwin. A visit to Washington had been suggested in January 1933, before FDR's inauguration as President, by Arthur Murray, a British friend from the First World War who was Assistant Military Attaché at the British Embassy in 1917–18 while Roosevelt was Assistant Secretary of the Navy. Runciman had been President of the Board of Trade in Asquith's wartime ministry before returning to this position as a National Liberal in Ramsay MacDonald's National Government in 1931. The suggestion was renewed by Murray during his visit to Hyde Park in May 1936 and this led to an invitation from Roosevelt to the British Cabinet minister, delivered in person by Murray in June. In view of the impending Presidential election in November 1936, the final details of the trip were not arranged until Christmas Day, when Roosevelt suggested the weekend after the inaugural celebrations as the best time for his British visitor to arrive at the White House, and this was agreed.[6]

Runciman arrived in Washington on 23 January and, accompanied by Lindsay, first called on Hull at the State Department. 'Mr Hull was pleasant and genial, and he soon gave us to understand that his mind was centred on his liberalised trade policy,' recorded Runciman. The British Minister referred to his own trade agreements since Ottawa as having broadened world trade. Hull, for his part, repeated the doctrines he had been preaching for several years. 'The peace of the world, he declared, could only be secured by obliterating the obstacles to international trade which at present gave rise to friction,' Runciman recalled, 'and in so far as these barriers affected the supply of raw materials he thought they endangered European peace.' Runciman then put his own views. 'While not sharing his exaggerations, I told him that I thought his aspirations were well founded, even if expressed in language that went further than what I would use myself.'[7]

After dinner on the 23rd, Runciman and Roosevelt talked together, and the President expressed pleasure at the Tripartite Currency Agreement, saying that it enabled the three governments to work more closely together. The President said that 'we could talk now freely on subjects which formerly they would have been reluctant to discuss with us', Runciman recorded. 'I asked the President if we could now count on easier cooperation to which he replied "Yes".' Roosevelt then turned to the subject of an Anglo-American trade agreement and he asked about Runciman's talk with Hull. 'So far as he, the President is concerned, he said that he thought we could make and keep a trade agreement.' In fact, Runciman found the President much less critical of British policy than Hull. According to Runciman, 'while describing Mr Hull's attitude and speaking warmly of his perseverance, he, the President, was more sympathetic towards our point of view and understood more clearly our difficulties than Mr Hull had done earlier in the day'.[8]

Runciman said to Roosevelt that he felt peace could be secured if it were known by the world that 'so far as Britain and America are concerned the table is cleared of troublesome questions'. He asked the President whether they could not clear up some troublesome points while he was in Washington. Using vague phraseology, FDR indicated his desire to deal with one or two awkward problems but he remarked, ominously as Runciman thought, that Bonnet, the new French Ambassador, had been 'ass enough', in the President's words, to say that he was coming to deal with the French war debt. Roosevelt said: 'He will not be able to do anything with that you may bet your boots.' As for the British war debt, one of the first questions Runciman had been asked by the press when he arrived in the US was whether he intended to discuss debts, to which he replied, 'God forbid.' Roosevelt said that he had observed this remark, with which he entirely concurred. 'Neither he nor I explained what we meant!' commented Runciman.[9]

On Sunday evening, 24 January, after talks with various Administration members during the day, Runciman had another long session with Roosevelt and Hull. Runciman observed that Roosevelt was less concerned about trade than Hull. 'Fiscal questions are not the chief interest of the President', he noted, 'and it is only in connection with their bearing on the maintenance of peace that he discussed these questions at all.' Roosevelt mentioned Germany's complaints about her lack of colonies and raw materials. Runciman told Roosevelt that the British Government was not averse to Germany buying and accumulating raw materials, provided that they were not for purposes of rearmament. Roosevelt said that he had no objection to the Germans buying anything that they could pay for, but the time might come when he would have to prohibit the export of arms to Germany. 'In other words,' concluded Runciman, 'he was not prepared to give any assistance to Germany either to add to her armaments, or to borrow more freely in the American market.' This confirmed the message given by Dodds to Phipps in November 1936 about FDR's desire to 'keep Germany lean' until she mended her ways.[10]

On the issue of the American Neutrality laws, Roosevelt said that he wanted discretionary power to prohibit the export of arms and war material but that he faced great opposition to this in Congress from senators like Gerald Nye. Runciman asked him if the Administration had considered the effect that a mandatory embargo on arms and other war supplies imposed by Congress would have on American foreign trade. 'I told him that the natural result would be to make countries like the U.K. turn away from the U.S.A. to other sources of supply, because we could not run the risk of finding ourselves choked off some day, perhaps in our time of greatest need,' recorded Runciman. 'As a simple business precaution we would deal now with countries which would be our suppliers in the future, and we would avoid countries which might cut off our supplies at the behest of the Senator Nyes of this world.' Britain could not be expected to abandon the security of the Ottawa agreements and risk upsetting the Dominions for the benefit of the United States if she was likely to find herself at war and dependent upon the Empire for supplies.[11]

'Before going to bed late on Sunday night I asked the President how I might describe his having brought me across the Atlantic in the middle of the winter,' Runciman cabled to London. 'He replied "in order to bring us closer together".' Runciman gave this assessment of the President to Baldwin, Chamberlain and Eden: 'He is very friendly towards us, shudders at the thought of a European war, will not and cannot commit America to action, but is so well disposed that he can be regarded as a firm opponent of any steps which might lead to hostilities.' Runciman also felt that if the trade negotiations resulted in an agreement 'the course would be clear for more complete collaboration'. He repeated this point to Baldwin later. 'If we are able to reach a trade agreement with the present Administration, there is no doubt that it will make much easier their cooperation with us in case of trouble in Europe.'[12]

'The risks of war in Europe are present in his mind, and he returns repeatedly to his statement that the dictators are the danger. The only safe guardians of peace are the Parliamentary countries,' continued Runciman. 'The Middle West, however, do not understand the dangers as he does, and if war broke out he would have to do a great deal of leading.' At present Roosevelt must go slowly and British observers should be careful in what they said about America's attitude. 'The closer we are to their public opinion and to their rulers the more certainly can we count on American support sooner or later,' Runciman wrote. On Tuesday, 26 January, he and his wife again saw the President, at a Diplomatic Corps event. 'After the entertainment he sent for me', recorded Runciman, 'and said a final Goodbye to us, adding "I hope you have thought it worthwhile", to which I replied that one did not cross the North Atlantic in the winter merely for a holiday.'[13]

The Runciman visit confirmed that Roosevelt was primarily concerned at this time about the European crisis, which had dominated his conversations with the British Minister. He also expressed his fears about Japanese aims and said that he favoured a more consistent policy between Britain and the United States in the Far East, possibly involving the 'neutralisation' of the Pacific. He was clearly anxious for Anglo-American cooperation and was hostile towards Germany. He believed that he had some influence on the situation in Europe, especially if the Neutrality laws were modified to allow him greater discretion to embargo arms and ammunition in the event of war. His strategy was to warn Hitler and Mussolini that, if they did not come to terms with Britain and France, they would also face the hostility of the United States if war in Europe ensued, as had occurred during the Great War. He was also very mindful of the growth of the German Air Force and he asked Runciman for information about the capability of the British Air Force, especially its estimated strength at the end of 1937 and 1938. The Air Ministry agreed to supply this information and it was sent to him via Lindsay in mid-February.[14]

While somewhat disappointed over his trade talks with Hull, Runciman regarded the visit as worthwhile and he now joined Eden in favour of an economic approach to American friendship. 'My impression is that for the next four years President Roosevelt's Government will be more than friendly, provided one or two points of friction are overcome,' Runciman wrote to Baldwin. 'The President is obviously anxious to maintain a degree of intimacy with the British Government . . . I hope that we shall lose no chance of collaborating with him promptly and candidly.' When Runciman returned to London he reported on his visit to his Cabinet colleagues. Neville Chamberlain dined with Runciman soon after his return and thought he should have pressed Roosevelt more on various issues, especially regarding cooperation in the Far East. 'But', he continued, echoing Runciman, 'he brought away a general impression that the President (which of course means the Govt as he is more of a dictator than Hitler) is very friendly, very afraid of war, very anxious to avoid it if it came, but likely, if we should become involved, to be in it with us in a few weeks'.[15]

Naturally, Runciman's visit did not go unnoticed in the United States. Apart from press coverage, a number of politicians and commentators referred to Runciman's brief sojourn and warned against any movement towards closer relations with Britain. For example, the radio commentator Boak Carter, well known for his critical view of Britain, told his audience that the British Government was sending emissaries to America in an attempt to 'hoodwink' the country into becoming involved in European affairs. For his part, Lindsay, while somewhat disappointed that more had not been achieved on the trade front, also regarded the visit as useful, and made a point of discussing it with his German colleague. 'I rather hope that Berlin is more concerned about the visit than any other capital,' he wrote to Craigie, in the Foreign Office. Indeed, Runciman's visit did not go unnoticed by the German Embassy in Washington and Luther sent a report on it to Berlin soon after. He took the view that it was mainly concerned with financial and economic issues – currency stability, war debts and trade – but he also saw it as part of a trend whereby Britain and France were moving closer to the United States in these areas, in contrast to the stand-off in German–American trade relations.[16]

Morgenthau initiative

During his visit to Washington the most important member of the Roosevelt Administration that Runciman met, apart from the President and Hull, was Henry Morgenthau Jr, the Secretary of the Treasury and a close confidant of FDR – unlike Hull. Morgenthau told the British Minister that, as a result of the currency agreement, he – like Roosevelt – felt that the two governments were now on a different and more intimate footing and that the American Treasury was now ready to exchange information on various subjects. Soon after, on 11 February 1937, he sent for Bewley, Financial Adviser at the British Embassy, and asked him to deliver a 'personal message' to Chamberlain as soon as possible. Believing that the approach of the State Department was 'timorous' and 'conventional', and that Hull 'was obsessed by his trade agreements programme', Morgenthau was determined to employ financial diplomacy, as far as possible, to fill the gap left by Hull's slow and cumbersome policy. He believed that the 1936 Tripartite Currency Agreement – or Pact – was an important breakthrough and he wanted to build on the momentum it had created and that had been referred to during the Runciman visit.[17]

On 9 February Morgenthau had lunch with the President. 'The world is just drifting rapidly towards war,' said Morgenthau. 'The European countries are gradually going bankrupt through preparing for war. You are the only person who can stop it.' FDR replied that Norman Davis had told him the same thing. But, acknowledging Morgenthau's argument that Hull's trade agreements programme would take time, he agreed to a secret approach to

Chamberlain. A few days later Morgenthau had a further discussion with the President, during which FDR said that if he called a conference, he would invite just half a dozen countries. He would tell the delegates that the problem was theirs and send them to some other building to work out a solution and come back with it. He would offer no advice about political issues, the President added, but he would try to get disarmament started at an accelerating pace over a five-year period. 'Any nation refusing to comply with the majority rule', he said, 'should then be hit by an economic boycott imposed by the others at the conference.' The implicit aim of such a conference was therefore to call out Germany and the aggressor states and to help Britain and France.[18]

On 11 February Morgenthau gave Bewley his message for Chamberlain 'from one finance minister to another'. But Chamberlain's response, largely drafted by the Foreign Office, was mostly confined to a plea to revise the Neutrality laws in Britain's favour. There was no mention of a conference or of any other concrete proposal. As Lindsay pointed out, 'while the burden of Morgenthau's words – and still more his thoughts – was how to prevent a war . . . the burden of the Chancellor's reply is to say how the United States can best help us if a war comes'. Not that Lindsay felt that there were any realistic steps that the US could take to prevent a war from coming.

> The only thing I can think of is that they should continue to make the greatest possible parade of their sympathies for the democratic ideology, and thereby bring it home to the Germans that an aggression on their part will greatly affect the US attitude. This perhaps might give pause to Berlin.

Indeed, this was the approach that FDR was pursuing, but it was constrained by scepticism in London as well as by the Neutrality laws and the strength of isolationism at home.[19]

Bingham and Eden

While Morgenthau was sending his secret message to Chamberlain, and Hull was making clear the importance of Britain to his trade agreements policy, Robert Bingham, the American Ambassador in London, was inviting Eden to dine alone with him on 20 March 1937 for an especially significant talk. This was another initiative that had been taken by the President. Bingham told Eden that Roosevelt's main concern was to avoid the fate of Woodrow

Wilson, whose programme of domestic reforms had been halted by American involvement in the Great War. Thus the President wanted to do all he could to prevent war breaking out in Europe and the British Government could therefore count upon his wholehearted collaboration in the preservation of peace. Bingham said that it was quite true the President was considering an initiative in the international field but that he was determined to act in close cooperation with the British Government.[20]

Bingham told Eden that Roosevelt 'was not only ready but eager to help, that he would be ready to take an initiative if and when we thought the moment was right, and that he would take none unless we were in accord as to its appropriateness'. Bingham added that he had been specifically instructed by Roosevelt to deliver this message personally to Eden. Both Bingham and Eden felt that the time for such an initiative had not yet come but both were equally anxious that a favourable opportunity should not be missed. Bingham urged that if the British Government, with its fuller information on the European situation, felt that the time had come to invite the President to take an initiative, it should not hesitate to do so. The American Government would likewise not hesitate to inform London if it thought the moment opportune.[21]

Trade agreement moves

At the beginning of March, the State Department followed up Runciman's visit to Washington by sending a 'refined' list of essential tariff reductions to the British Embassy. This consisted of the product groups in the American 'essentials' list of November 1936, with the omission of hog products, barley, oranges and glacé kid, and the addition of honey. Thus, the nine groups had been reduced to seven to help speed up negotiations for an Anglo-American trade agreement. Hull's determination to make progress with an Anglo-American trade agreement was shown in a cable sent to American representatives prior to a meeting of the League Raw Materials Committee in March 1937. 'We are ... very anxious to work at present in harmony with the British and French as far as possible,' it read.

> You are aware that our trade agreement conversations with the British are just now at a pivotal state. We should therefore move very cautiously during the entire meeting at Geneva ... Should you find yourself in sharp or definite disagreement with them would you mind consulting me before taking any action.[22]

In a significant despatch to London about the initiatives emanating from Washington, Lindsay wrote: 'Never in history have Anglo-American relations been so friendly and cordial as now, except during the eighteen months when the two countries were associated together in war.' Certainly, isolationism remained very strong in the United States, he said, and if war came in Europe, America would definitely be neutral. Nevertheless, there was a good deal that might be accomplished within the rather narrow limits laid down by the American attitude, 'for neutrality may be of many colours'. If war became imminent, the Neutrality laws were likely to be amended and the onus was on the British Government to ensure that the amendment was favourable. America might even enter the war, and if she did so, it would doubtless be on the British side. But if she came to such a decision, 'it will be postponed till the eleventh hour, when to the belligerents even a few minutes may be of inestimable value'.[23]

Lindsay continued: 'Some time may be saved if His Majesty's Government continue to practise a wise diplomacy.' To this end, London should refrain from any initiative on a major political issue as this would arouse the isolationists and embarrass the Roosevelt Administration. On the other hand, any American initiative should be welcomed. In this respect, unusually for the United States, an approach was possible along the path of economic cooperation, especially through the conclusion of a trade agreement. Despite difficulties with the Dominions over Imperial Preference, such an agreement was not only possible but vital, Lindsay suggested to Eden. 'I respectfully but forcibly submit to you, Sir, that an American hand is being proffered to us, and it is full of gifts.' Thus Lindsay's despatch confirmed that, in the view of Britain's long-serving – and suffering – Ambassador in Washington, Roosevelt I had indeed given way to Roosevelt II, and that cooperation with the United States would help to define the future character of American neutrality in as positive a way as possible.[24]

Canadian dimension

The desire for progress in the trade discussions at the impending Imperial Conference was no doubt one reason why Roosevelt invited Mackenzie King to Washington in March 1937. The Canadian Prime

Minister met with Hull, who showed himself to be deeply concerned by the European situation. He thought that a campaign of economic rehabilitation in Europe was vital and could be led only by Britain. But, Hull lamented, Runciman had admitted during his visit that the British Government had no such policy. Mackenzie King then met Roosevelt and they further discussed the possibility of the President organising a world conference, as well as a scheme whereby the League of Nations might be replaced by a new organisation that focused on economic and social issues, enabling the United States to become a member. As regards the Neutrality laws, Roosevelt said that he was sure the new legislation would favour Britain. 'In all he said, his sympathies were clearly with Britain in meeting the dangers of the European situation,' Mackenzie King wrote. While in Washington the Canadian also met Lindsay and told him about his talk with Roosevelt.

> To my mind [Lindsay wrote to Vansittart], the chief interest is that Roosevelt still has hankerings for a great conference and though this may be a nuisance to you if it breaks out badly at the wrong moment, I suppose there are conceivable circumstances in which it might be useful.[25]

Roosevelt's relationship with Canada was taken a stage further in April 1937 when Lord Tweedsmuir, the Governor General, made an official visit to Washington to return the President's visit to Quebec the previous year. The visit included a State Dinner at the White House for Tweedsmuir and his wife on 30 March, a trip to Mount Vernon, and an address to both houses of Congress on 3 April, when Tweedsmuir called for greater cooperation between Britain, Canada and the US. Tweedsmuir was 'most enthusiastic about the welcome accorded him', according to Mackenzie King. He had discussed the idea of a world conference with the President and, in contrast to Mackenzie King, had suggested it be held in the US rather than Geneva. Tweedsmuir also said that he thought FDR and Hull were anxious that Mackenzie King should help forward the whole movement for more liberal trade relations between the United States and Britain when in London for the Imperial Conference. Tweedsmuir later wrote to Chamberlain about his meeting with FDR, saying that he had 'long talks with the President about his scheme for a conference on the fundamental economic difficulties which are disquieting the world'. As regards a trade agreement, 'Hull has a crusading earnestness on this question which greatly impresses me', wrote Tweedsmuir, 'and the President, although he is a much looser thinker, has very much the same feeling.'[26]

Although revision of the Ottawa agreements was not on the agenda at the Imperial Conference in May 1937, unofficial talks took place on the side lines as to what trade concessions could be made to the US, despite Imperial Preference. Unsurprisingly, each Dominion insisted on compensation for any concession on the margins of preference – not least Canada, which was the Dominion most affected by the American 'essentials' list. 'We would be thought simpletons if we returned home after doing anything of the kind,' he told his British hosts. When he had talked to Roosevelt and Hull about the need for economic progress they had not mentioned the Anglo-American trade discussions directly but had spoken of the need for 'general economic appeasement' and 'a breaking down of the economic nationalism of European countries which was preventing Germany and other nations from expanding her trade, and other countries dealing with them'. He refused to make concessions to the American requests unless given full compensation and this fact, coupled with resistance from the other Dominions, meant that the opening of Anglo-American trade negotiations was bound to be delayed.[27]

Another initiative taken by Roosevelt at this time was the mission he assigned to Norman Davis, his Ambassador-at-Large, while the latter was due to attend the World Sugar Conference in London, scheduled to take place from 5 April to 6 May 1937. The attendance of Davis at the conference, at a time when Washington was abuzz with rumours that the President was contemplating a bold stroke in the field of foreign affairs, inevitably led to speculation in the American and British press that he had a 'secret mission' to discuss the formation of a peace conference of some kind with British and other officials – rumours that were robustly denied by the State Department and by Davis himself. In fact, the President had indeed asked Davis to discuss various issues while he was in London, especially with Eden and Chamberlain as well as other British, and European, officials. These issues included not only the idea of an international conference but also a scheme for the 'neutralisation of the Pacific' that he had mentioned to Runciman, and the possibility of transforming the League of Nations into an organisation dealing primarily with economic and social issues, which the United States could then join, as Roosevelt had discussed with Mackenzie King. By all accounts, Davis was listened to patiently, but very little headway was made on any of the suggestions he put forward.[28]

Neutrality revision

In the meantime, the Neutrality Act of May 1937 afforded further strong evidence of the Roosevelt Administration's friendly disposition towards Britain. Several bills had been introduced into Congress, including one by Key Pittman in the Senate and one by Sam McReynolds, the chairman of the House Committee on Foreign Affairs. Both of these bills included a 'cash and carry' clause – the brainchild of Bernard Baruch – by which American supplies could be bought in wartime by any foreign nation, provided it paid cash and took them away in its own ships. The House Bill gave the President more discretion by allowing him to enumerate articles of war, apart from arms and ammunition, and in making an exception of Canada from the Neutrality legislation. Stricter bills were also introduced by isolationists, notably Senator Gerald Nye and Representative Hamilton Fish. But it was the McReynolds Bill that emerged triumphant on 29 April and was signed by the President on 1 May.[29]

Lindsay was pleased with the outcome of the neutrality revision. 'Well informed comment by friendly members of the State Department', he reported, 'takes the line that in the event of a big European war the Act would never work and would be scrapped in twenty four hours.' Stress was also laid by the State Department on the exception in favour of trade with Canada, 'for which the Department privately take to themselves some credit'. Lindsay added that the general opinion in Washington was that the latitude given to the President ensured that he would apply the Act in such a way as to favour the democratic countries if they were attacked by the dictators. In particular, as raw materials such as oil were not considered 'implements of war', the 'cash-and-carry' clause would enable Britain to obtain them from the US in wartime and to deny them by means of a naval blockade to Germany. For this reason, even if the British Government was not completely satisfied with the new law, it would at least serve as a warning to potential aggressors, in line with US policy.[30]

However, the Admiralty did not agree that the new law would penalise Britain less than any potential enemy. It argued that some aspects of the legislation might conflict with belligerent rights such as the enumeration of contraband, and suggested representations to Washington. The Treasury was also of the opinion that the British position would be worse than in 1914 not only because of the Neutrality laws but also bearing in mind the Johnson Act. But the Foreign Office was opposed to further representations to Washington, although it recognised that there was still room for improvement. The main drawback continued to be the arms embargo: that is, the ban on the purchase during wartime of 'arms, ammunition and implements of war'. On the other hand, the 'cash-and-carry' clause clearly favoured Britain as the strongest financial power in Europe, with control of the Atlantic shipping routes and an ally in Canada. Much depended on the way in which the President used his discretionary powers and by May 1937 it was clear that he was anxious to use them on behalf of Britain and France.[31]

This was certainly the view of Winston Churchill, MP. 'No fact in the world situation is more hopeful or important than the excellent relations and understanding which have developed between the United States and the two Western democracies,' wrote Churchill in his regular newspaper column for the *Evening Standard* at the end of May. 'I cannot recall any period when the good will between the two main branches of the English-speaking peoples was so pronounced,' he continued. This good will, he argued, had resulted from 'an identity of outlook' towards international problems in both Europe and the Far East. As he wrote:

> Throughout the United States there is a keen abhorrence of the doctrines and practices both of Nazism and Fascism, and a strong current of sympathy with the countries great and small who are faithfully endeavouring to preserve their parliamentary institutions, and to maintain the conditions of law, freedom and peace.[32]

Churchill was a good friend of Bernard Baruch, the author of the 'cash-and-carry' concept, and he regarded the new Neutrality Act as a very positive sign of closer relations between the US, Britain and France. Like Lindsay, in his despatch of 22 March mentioned above, Churchill was careful to point out that this harmony in general outlook did not mean that Britain could rely on US intervention in the event of another world war. But he believed that the doctrine of 'cash and carry' had effectively revised the traditional American devotion to freedom of the seas. 'The arrangement certainly has the merit of rendering to superior sea power its full deserts. It avoids for Great Britain, if engaged in war, the danger of any dispute with the United States such as caused so much anxiety in 1914 and 1915', he argued. The 'growing moral association of ideas between the three great parliamentary democracies', he continued, also meant that the US, while maintaining a strict neutrality, was very unlikely to hamper Britain's traditional policy in time of war – 'the famous weapon of the blockade'.[33]

The view from Berlin

Before departing from Washington, Ambassador Hans Luther offered an analysis of the Neutrality laws, arguing that they had been drawn up largely with Europe in mind. 'Britain's decision to rearm has made such a lasting impression in America that one must, in some sense, regard this event as giving a lead to American foreign policy and even more to the emotional attitude of the Americans towards the situation in Europe.' The 'cash-and-carry' concept introduced in May 1937 meant that 'the neutrality legislation ... in a European theatre of war concedes all the advantages of American raw material supplies to Britain who commands the seas'. Roosevelt and the State Department would prefer no Neutrality legislation, as it limited American influence as a Great Power, but in the meantime the law would be implemented as far as possible for the benefit of Britain and France. As regards the Far East, although this was seen as a secondary issue, US public opinion was critical of the Anti-Comintern Pact between Germany and Japan as a potential cause of conflict. 'Thus the Far East, too, casts a shadow over German–American relations,' he said.[34]

When Hans Luther paid his farewell visit to FDR on 22 April 1937 the President's main theme was Germany's threatening conduct and the need for disarmament before any general financial or economic progress could be made. He told Luther that 'not only many Americans but people the world over dreaded especially Germany's aggressive intentions'. He also named Italy as the other country currently causing most concern in terms of its belligerence. He pointed out that 'the British regarded their own rearmament as defensive and insisted that, in his opinion, a first step must be to eliminate the fear of war'. Financial and commercial solutions would result from 'a calming of the atmosphere and the creation of a feeling of security'. He said that if he could meet Hitler, he was sure he could convince him of this. He had made the same argument to Bonnet, the French Ambassador, who felt that 'commercial and financial solutions' needed to come first. 'On the face of it', Luther remarked, the President's ideas appeared somewhat at variance with those of Hull. As regards taking some kind of initiative in the international field, Roosevelt told Luther that 'he would only hammer the peg home if he were certain that other States would hang up their hats on it'.[35]

Luther's warnings to Berlin about US support for the democracies were seconded by Hans Borchers, the German Consul General in New York. Referring to the German press campaign against Mayor La Guardia as counter-productive, following the Mayor's insults about Hitler at the American Jewish Congress in New York on 3 March 1937, his memo urged that German press, in responding to provocations such as the La Guardia speech, should focus criticism on the Mayor and not on the US more generally. Given the enormous financial and economic resources of the US, Germany needed to 'exert such influence on the sentiments of the American people as might avoid in times of crisis a repetition of the catastrophe on 1917'.

> I am deliberately referring to developments in German–American relations during the war, for I would regard it as a serious mistake if the lessons of those years were forgotten and the view were to be taken that because of the geographical distance or because of certain signs of decadence in American democracy it was not necessary nowadays to take the United States into account in our foreign policy.[36]

Such warnings were generally dismissed by Nazi Party officials in Berlin and this one was no exception. In May 1937 the reply to Borchers's cautionary message came from Alfred Ingemar-Berndt, the Director of Press Relations in the Ministry for Public Enlightenment and Propaganda, headed by Joseph Goebbels. Like Goebbels himself, Berndt was a fanatical Nazi. A refugee from Posen after the war, he joined the party, aged seventeen, in 1922 and when the Nazis came to power he was appointed to the Propaganda Ministry, whose mission was to promote Nazi Party ideology, including the cult of the Führer, and to rebut any opposing domestic or foreign propaganda. He therefore rejected Borchers's viewpoint and the idea that 'American susceptibilities must in all circumstances be respected'. He argued that the American press had 'attached so little importance to sparing German feelings that the need for a German riposte is merely the result of the attitude of that press'. There had been constant criticism of the German government and of social conditions in Germany and he did not believe that better relations with the US Government would result from letting 'the campaign of American agitation pass'.[37]

Notes

1. PREM/1/291, Runciman to Baldwin, 8 February 1937, enclosing 'Memorandum on Conversations with President Roosevelt and Mr Hull'. See also McCulloch, 'Runciman Visit', pp. 222–3.
2. See McCulloch, 'Runciman Visit', pp. 211–40 for detailed account of visit; also Harrison, 'Runciman Visit'; Hull, *Memoirs I*, pp. 524–6; Kottman, *Reciprocity*, pp. 159–60.
3. For American foreign policy background see Dallek, *FDR*, pp. 134–43.
4. For British policy see Bouverie, *Appeasing Hitler*, pp. 120–36; Parker, *Chamberlain and Appeasement*, pp. 58–79; Shen, *Age of Appeasement*, pp. 136–58.
5. McCulloch, 'Mackenzie King and the North Atlantic Triangle', pp. 5–8.
6. Murray papers, Box 8808, Roosevelt to Murray, 25 December 1936; Ibid., note of telephone conversation between Murray and Runciman, 26 December 1936; Ibid., Murray to Roosevelt, 26 December 1936.
7. PREM/1/291, Runciman to Baldwin, 8 February 1937, enclosing Runciman memo.
8. Ibid.
9. Ibid.
10. Ibid.
11. Ibid.
12. Ibid.
13. Ibid.
14. Ibid.; FO/371/20651, A666/38/45, Lindsay to Eden, 26 January 1937; Ibid., A1155/38/45, Eden to Lindsay, 18 February 1937; Harrison, 'Runciman Visit', pp. 217–39.
15. PREM/1/291, Runciman to Baldwin, 8 February 1937; Neville Chamberlain papers, NC 18/1/993, Neville Chamberlain to Hilda Chamberlain, 6 February 1937.
16. FO/371/20667, A2037/542/45, British Consul, New York, monthly report, 1 March 1937; FO/371/20659, A1326/228/45, Lindsay to Craigie, 3 February 1937; DGFP/C/VI, doc 159, Luther to GFM, 25 January 1937; FRUS/1937/II, doc 248, Hull memorandum, 25 January 1937.

17. Blum, *Morgenthau Diaries*, I, pp. 455–7; DBFP/2/XVIII, for Bewley message.
18. Ibid., pp. 456–9.
19. Blum, *Morgenthau Diaries I*, pp. 458–67; DBFP/2/XVII, doc 248, note 4; FO 371, C2138/3/18, Record by Bewley of conversation with Morgenthau on 11 February 1937; see also DBFP/2/XVIII, doc 268, JH Woods to OC Harvey, 11 March 1937; Ibid., doc 285, Eden to Chamberlain, 13 March 1937; Ibid., doc 290, Chamberlain to Eden, 15 March 1937; Minute by TK Bewley, 27 March 1937.
20. FO/371/20651, A1925/38/45, Eden to Lindsay, 20 March 1937.
21. Ibid.
22. FO/371/20659, A1704/228/45, Lindsay to Eden, 2 March 1937; Eden to Lindsay, 5 March 1937; SD 500.C1112/108: Hull to Grady, 7 March 1937. See also Kottman, *Reciprocity*, pp. 117–48.
23. FO/371/20651, A2378/38/45, Lindsay to Eden, 22 March 1937.
24. Ibid.
25. Mackenzie King Diary, conversations with Hull and FDR, 5 March 1937; FO/371/20670, A2082/2082/45, Lindsay to Vansittart, 8 March 1937.
26. <https://www.whitehousehistory.org/canada-visits-the-white-house> for State Dinner on 30 March 1937; see also Mackenzie King Diary, 2, 4, 23, 24 April 1937; Roosevelt papers, PSF: Canada, 1933–1937, Tweedsmuir to FDR, 8 April 1937; PREM/1/229, Tweedsmuir to Chamberlain, 25 October 1937.
27. Mackenzie King Diary, 7 June 1937; see also FO/371/20660, A4104/228/45, memo by Ashton-Gwatkin, 4 June 1937. For discussions with Dominion representatives see FO/371/20660/20661, file 228, 1937.
28. For World Sugar Conference see FRUS/1937/I, docs 923–942, especially doc 925, memorandum by Hull, 25 March 1937 and doc 927, Davis to Hull, 2 April 1937; for a detailed account of the conversations Davis had in London see Borg, *US and Far Eastern Crisis*, pp. 373–7; see also Dallek, *FDR*, pp. 138–9; Harrison, 'Presidential Demarche', pp. 267–8; Davis papers, memorandum of telephone conversation with FDR, 19 March 1937; Roosevelt papers, PSF: State Department, Davis to FDR, 13 April 1937.
29. FO/371/20666, A1895/448/45, Lindsay to Eden, 2 March 1937; Ibid., A2325/448/45, minute by W D Allen, 31 March 1937; Ibid. A3388/448/45: Lindsay to Eden, 4 May 1937; Divine, *Illusion of Neutrality*, pp. 162–99.
30. Ibid., A3191/448/45, Lindsay to Eden, 30 April 1937.
31. Ibid., A3392/448/45, S H Phillips (Admiralty) to Under-Secretary, Cadogan, FO, 3 June 1937; Ibid., A4631/448/45, R V Hopkins to Under-Secretary (FO), 28 June 1937; for NC and Treasury view, see

Hopkins memo, 28 June 1937; DBFP/2/XVIII, docs 332 and 333, FO memos by Fitzmaurice, 23 March 1937 (re US neutrality legislation); Ibid., A3392/448/45, minute by J Troutbeck, 22 June 1937.
32. Churchill, 31 May 1937 in *While England Slept*, pp. 89–91.
33. Ibid.; see also Churchill's speech in *Hansard*, House of Commons, 12 November 1936; also in Cannadine (ed.), *Winston Churchill*, pp. 114–28.
34. DGFP/C/VI, doc 306, Luther to GFM, 6 April 1937.
35. DGFP/C/VI, doc 338, Luther to GFM, 26 April 1937.
36. See *NYT*, 5 March 1937 for La Guardia speech; DGFP/C/VI, doc 267, Hans Borchers (New York) to Ministerial Director, Dieckhoff, 13 March 1937.
37. DGFP/C/VII, doc 556, Berndt, Ministry for Public Enlightenment and Propaganda, to GFM, 4 May 1937.

Part 2

Parallel Action, 1937–1938

4 Roosevelt and Chamberlain, May–September 1937

While in London for the World Sugar Conference, Roosevelt's Ambassador-at-Large, Norman Davis, raised with Anthony Eden the idea of a visit to Washington by him or Chamberlain. Eden was open to the suggestion, but Davis had also broached the idea to Chamberlain and gained the impression that the Prime Minister was willing to make the trip, given adequate preparation. When Davis returned to Washington in May he passed this information on to the President, who felt that a visit from Chamberlain would be preferable as it would not be so obviously associated with foreign affairs. On 10 June Davis wrote to Chamberlain, on the President's behalf, suggesting a visit at the end of September or early October, after Congress had adjourned. 'He believes, as I am sure you do, that world economic and financial stability and hence peace depend largely upon an enlightened policy of Anglo-American cooperation,' wrote Davis. If Chamberlain was unable to get away, Davis continued, Roosevelt wanted him to indicate another Cabinet member who could be invited to Washington.[1]

Chamberlain politely but firmly deflected the American invitation and made no attempt to nominate a member of the Cabinet to go to Washington in his stead. He simply replied that while he would welcome the opportunity to make the acquaintance of the President and explore common problems, he felt that the time had not yet come for such a meeting. Davis had suggested that the signing of an Anglo-American trade agreement would be a good occasion for a visit but, Chamberlain pointed out, the trade agreement discussions with the Dominions were by no means complete. The Van Zeeland mission on economic appeasement, entrusted to the Prime Minister of Belgium, had only just begun. Moreover, the situation in Europe and Germany's intentions were still uncertain. 'A meeting now would raise expectations which could hardly be fulfilled,' he said. 'I should therefore be grateful if you would express to the President my deep appreciation of his kind message and my earnest desire to take advantage of his suggestion as soon as conditions appear sufficiently favourable to warrant my doing so.'[2]

Advent of Chamberlain

The main aim of this chapter is to examine the Anglo-American relationship following the succession of Neville Chamberlain to the position of Prime Minister. His reply to Roosevelt's early invitation was perhaps not surprising, given that he had only just assumed his new role, but it was not especially helpful. At a meeting between Chamberlain, Eden and Bingham on 8 July it was subsequently agreed that the best time for a visit to Washington would be at the signing of an Anglo-American trade agreement. Roosevelt thereupon wrote to the Prime Minister at the end of July – via Bingham – confirming that he had hoped for a visit in the autumn and adding that he appreciated the need to make progress on other topics before such a visit could be arranged. 'I would be glad, however, to receive any suggestions you may have as to any additional preparatory steps that might be taken as between ourselves in the near future to expedite progress towards the goal desired,' wrote Roosevelt. The 'goal desired' by FDR was clearly to make further progress in moving the British and American governments closer together in a show of solidarity to head off what appeared to him to be an impending international catastrophe.[3]

Roosevelt's letter arrived in August while Chamberlain was on holiday in Scotland and he seems to have regarded it as another tiresome American missive. 'I don't think it necessary to do anything about suggestions to the President', he commented, 'but I suppose I should send an acknowledgement to the Ambassador.' Thus it was not until 28 September that Chamberlain sent a reply to the American President and by then the Sino-Japanese War was well under way and the Spanish Civil War was becoming increasingly bloody. In view of the uncertain international climate and the fact that the Anglo-American trade discussions were still in progress, Chamberlain told the President that he could not suggest any way in which the proposed meeting could be expedited, 'though I greatly regret this both on personal and official grounds'. The significance of Chamberlain's very tardy and ultimately negative reply is clear – a meeting with FDR was not high on his list of priorities, especially in view of the Neutrality laws and American isolationism. He had his own agenda for improving the international situation – one that involved a direct approach to Hitler to pave the way for a 'general settlement' of outstanding issues and the goal of European appeasement.[4]

Chamberlain's leadership was certainly appreciated by Mackenzie King, the Canadian Prime Minister, who had formed a very high opinion of him while in London for the Imperial Conference. On the evening of 15 June Chamberlain, Eden and Malcolm MacDonald discussed the European situation with the Dominion premiers. Mackenzie King was glad to note that Chamberlain recognised the value of economic appeasement and was not opposed to German expansion in the East, provided it was peaceful, or to colonial compensation to Germany. His support for appeasement increased yet further when he travelled to Berlin after the conference and met with Hitler and Neurath, the German Foreign Minister, Göring and Hitler himself – a trip arranged by Von Ribbentrop, the German Ambassador in London. Mackenzie King found the German leader to be utterly sincere and a friend of peace – an attitude that doubtless contributed to Hitler's view that the leaders of the British Empire were unlikely to fight Germany. Given FDR's desire to maintain a close relationship with his northern neighbour, the Canadian leader's support for appeasement was a significant factor in Anglo-American relations.[5]

Chamberlain arrives, Runciman departs

The advent of Chamberlain as Prime Minister at the end of May 1937 was, of course, an event of the first importance for the conduct of British foreign policy, not least in the field of Anglo-American relations. He did not have Baldwin's tolerance of the United States and he was not the best Prime Minister from the point of view of Anglo-American relations. Indeed, when Bingham informed Roosevelt back in November 1936 that Chamberlain was likely to be chosen as Baldwin's successor he said he thought this would be 'a great mistake' as 'he lives and breathes only for the atmosphere of the money-changers of the City'. Chamberlain was also a man with a mission and he had little confidence in the US as a potential ally, as had been shown during FDR's first term when he had been a leading critic of the 'Roosevelt bombshell' message in July 1933 and of the Johnson Act in April 1934. He had been quite ready to disregard American susceptibilities by coming to terms with Japan in the Far East but this had been blocked by the Cabinet and by Japanese intransigence. He consented to the Tripartite Currency Agreement of September 1936, but this was mainly the work of Morgenthau. When the US Secretary of the Treasury contacted him to discuss further cooperation to avert a European conflict, he could suggest little beyond revising the Neutrality laws.[6]

Further evidence of Chamberlain's disregard for American susceptibilities was provided by his Cabinet changes in May 1937, when he decided to send Oliver Stanley to the Board of Trade and he offered Walter Runciman the position of Lord Privy Seal instead. Chamberlain argued that as Runciman's translation to the Lords was imminent in view of his father's advanced age and ill-health, it would be best if he did not have charge of a department. There was a logic behind this view as Walter Runciman Sr, 1st Baron Runciman, was almost ninety and died in August 1937. However, Runciman Jr regarded the post of Lord Privy Seal as 'the poorest in the Cabinet' and therefore a demotion. He had hoped to move to the Treasury, but that post went to his long-time rival, Sir John Simon. Runciman believed that Chamberlain had been influenced by Tory Protectionists who were critical of his trade agreements, which they regarded as harmful to British agriculture. As a result, Runciman left the Cabinet unhappily and, like Baldwin, he became a viscount and went to the Lords.[7]

Runciman's departure from the Cabinet was a blow to Anglo-American relations and to Roosevelt's burgeoning personal diplomacy as, since his visit to Washington, he had become convinced of the value of close relations with the United States and the need for an Anglo-American trade agreement. He had also frequently been the chief opponent of Chamberlain in the Cabinet, especially on economic issues, and next to Baldwin, was the most senior politician in British government. 'I think you are a grievous loss', wrote Vansittart. Roosevelt himself wrote to Arthur Murray that he was sorry Runciman would no longer be in the Commons, but he added, optimistically, 'I am confident that the good work he started will go on.' In retrospect, it was, indeed, a pity that Runciman had not remained in office. His voice within the Cabinet on behalf of good relations with the United States, even as a National Liberal, would have been very useful at a time when Anglo-American relations were entering a critical phase.[8]

Roosevelt, Hull and Economic Appeasement

On 17 May 1937 FDR wrote to his old friend William Phillips, the recently appointed US Ambassador in Rome:

> The more I study the situation, the more I am convinced that an economic approach to peace is a pretty weak reed for Europe to lean on. It may postpone war but how can it ever avert war in the long run if the armament process continues at its present pace – or even for that matter at a slower pace? The answer they all give to any plea for reduction in armaments is that millions of workers would be thrown on the street. How do we make progress if England and France say we cannot help Germany and Italy to achieve economic security if they continue to arm and threaten, while simultaneously Germany and Italy say we must continue to arm and threaten because they will not give us economic security? . . . Anything, of course, that postpones war is that much to the good. The progress of the disease is slowed up, but the disease remains – and will probably prove fatal in the next few years.[9]

FDR's letter suggests that, well before his Quarantine speech in October 1937, he saw the growth of international lawlessness as a disease that needed to be confronted. It also suggests that, contrary to the view of some historians, he had little faith in the likelihood that 'economic appeasement', as it was termed, would be sufficient to pacify the ambitions of Hitler and Mussolini. As can be seen from his State of the Union message in January 1937, his main concern was the militarism in the 'dictator states' of Germany, Italy and Japan, and the danger to the democracies, including the United States, that this posed. Hence the Roosevelt Administration's desire to improve cooperation with Britain and Canada especially, during the first hundred days of FDR's second term, starting with the Runciman visit in January 1937, Morgenthau's secret message to Chamberlain, Bingham's meeting with Eden, and the visits of Mackenzie King and Tweedsmuir to Washington. As Runciman noted, the President was much less interested than Hull in the details of US trade policy and much more concerned with the risks of war in Europe.[10]

Like Morgenthau, FDR doubted that economic measures, including Hull's trade agreements programme, were sufficient by themselves to provide the immediate relief required to reduce tensions and avoid another war in Europe. As Lindsay pointed out to London, 'the President, while he esteems Mr Hull personally, appreciates the political importance of his policies, and supports them, he is bored by him. This is hardly surprising, because the sermons of a hot gospeller are indeed irksome to a busy man.' Hull was 'anything but a practical man', the Ambassador continued, and while William Phillips, the Under Secretary, had 'supplied a solid core' before he was moved to Rome, 'on the whole the Department lacks any real leadership'. In May 1937 Phillips was replaced by Sumner Welles, Assistant Secretary for Latin American Affairs and formerly US Ambassador to Cuba, who, like FDR, had attended Groton School and moved in similar circles. Welles provided the more energetic leadership the President was looking for in the State Department and he was to play an increasingly important role in US diplomacy during FDR's second term.[11]

Despite the scepticism of FDR and Morgenthau, Hull remained committed to the idea of economic appeasement through his trade agreements programme. Indeed, Hull's foreign policy depended partly on the conclusion of a trade agreement with Britain, to be followed, he believed, by a general movement of other countries away from economic nationalism and towards the promotion of international trade and harmony. Germany, Italy and Japan would then have no reason, or excuse, for their expansionist policies. Thus Hull envisaged a trade agreement with Britain as part of a broader 'world programme' based on the philosophy of 'economic appeasement', or 'economic disarmament' as he sometimes called it. However, the dictator states, especially Germany, were to be excluded from the benefits of this programme while they pursued restrictive and illiberal economic policies – unlike the appeasement of Germany and Italy by means of one-sided concessions that came to characterise British foreign policy under Chamberlain.[12]

Keen to follow up Morgenthau's initiative in February 1937, Hull and the State Department drew up a detailed statement on US foreign policy for the new British Prime Minister, which was handed to Lindsay on 1 June 1937. This 'informal memorandum' said that the US Government was 'deeply concerned over the absence of a trustworthy basis in international relations and the presence of a constant menace to peace' and it highlighted Hull's trade agreements programme. 'If this government emphasizes somewhat more than does Mr Chamberlain the economic aspects of the matters he discusses,' the memo read, 'it does so because it genuinely believes that if trade relations between nations can be broadened on lines and under conditions where it serves to advance economic welfare, existing political tensions would be thereby eased.' The memorandum also pointed out that the revised Neutrality Act gave the President more discretion, especially in terms of raw materials that might be useful in wartime and in deciding whether the Act's provisions should be invoked. It also allowed the President to make exceptions for neighbouring countries, meaning Canada.[13]

An important aspect of the document was its explanation of US foreign policy in the Far East and its reference to 'parallel action'. The United States, it said, based its policy towards the Far East on the principles to be found in the Washington Conference treaties of 1922, but in the event of aggression in the region the US could not state its exact response in advance. However, it preferred to proceed along 'parallel lines' with like-minded governments, following appropriate consultation. As regards a challenge to 'common or similar interests of the United States and of Great Britain', Washington 'would continue earnestly to desire that there may be found satisfactory means for collaboration as in the past between our two Governments'. More generally, the memo concluded that, despite the worsening international situation, the US Government believed that the maintenance of peace was still possible. 'In the achievement of this aim the Government of the United States is prepared to collaborate in every way compatible with its legitimate sphere of action. It is convinced that the British Government, actuated by the same desires, is equally concerned with the imperative need of exploring all possible avenues that may lead to the same end.'[14]

Hull regarded his informal memorandum as a very significant document, but Chamberlain called it 'singularly platitudinous'. It also caused much mirth in the British Treasury, which drew up a reply for Chamberlain to send. 'This is unusually long-winded even for an American,' commented Sir Warren Fisher, the Permanent Under Secretary. 'But the attitude is for the moment alright, and they like exchanging sweetly-worded nothings. When we come down to brass tacks, there is nothing much to take hold of.' Simon, the new Chancellor, added: 'This is typically American and very much à la Hull.' Chamberlain's reply to the Secretary of State declared his 'full agreement' with the general objectives set out in Hull's paper and said: 'In particular, it is my sincere desire that there should be the greatest possible measure of cooperation between our two countries.' While his reply was suitably diplomatic, the attitude behind it was rather typical of the British Treasury, if not the Foreign Office, in being somewhat dismissive and condescending towards US policy.[15]

Hull was not alone in thinking that economic appeasement could contribute to the lessening of international tensions, especially in Europe. In April 1937 it was announced that the Belgian Prime Minister, Paul Van Zeeland, would visit various countries at the request of the British and French governments to explore the possibility of a general reduction in trade obstacles. Taking as his starting point the Tripartite Currency Agreement of September 1936, Van Zeeland visited Washington in late June 1937 and had meetings with FDR, Hull and Sumner Welles. He received positive assurances about US willingness to cooperate in the limitation of armaments, trade expansion and financial stabilisation. He also proposed that the six governments that had signed up to the Tripartite Agreement – that is, including Belgium, Holland and Switzerland – should meet to discuss further moves. But he was told by Welles that informal discussions would be required before a US meeting to decide what steps could be taken at the meeting. In addition, the British Government would have to agree to join the American trade agreement programme. The Belgian Prime Minister was hopeful that Germany and Italy would engage with the outcome of such a conference if it contained constructive attempts at economic appeasement.[16]

Van Zeeland's mission was a reflection of the growing concern in European capitals about the deteriorating international situation, especially in Spain, and the hope that economic appeasement might reduce international tensions. Soon after the Belgian statesman's visit to Washington, Roosevelt was asked at a press conference about a suggestion by George Lansbury, the former Labour leader, that he should convene or chair an 'International Economic Conference'. The President commented that this idea came up 'all the time' and that 'all over Europe almost everybody, not only the members of governments over there but the man on the street, feels that in Europe they are up against a stone wall and that there is nobody in Europe that can solve it'. The rivalries and 'constant jealousies' in Europe meant that agreement seemed almost impossible, he continued. 'Therefore, it is a perfectly logical thing for them to look around for somebody outside of Europe to come forward with a hat and a rabbit in it and they think I got a hat with a rabbit in it. Well, that is about all there is to it. I haven't got a hat and I haven't got a rabbit in it.'[17]

Van Zeeland also met with Chamberlain and Eden in London in July. They told him that they agreed in general with the principles he expressed and suggested that the time had come when he should put his views in writing. In fact, van Zeeland did not circulate a draft of his report to London, Paris and Washington until December 1937. On 28 December Hull asked the US Embassy to ascertain the British view of van Zeeland's draft so Herschel Johnson, the US Chargé in London, arranged a meeting with Ashton-Gwatkin and Leith-Ross. 'I did not gather that Leith-Ross was optimistic about the practical results which would flow from the van Zeeland report,' reported Johnson. 'In fact at one point he expressed sympathy for van Zeeland for being burdened with this extremely difficult and uncomfortable task.' Leith-Ross felt that Britain had little to offer in the way of tariff reductions or changes to quotas. And while he was not against an economic conference, provided it was well prepared, he was opposed to van Zeeland's idea of setting up another organisation to encourage progress as various League committees were already fulfilling that role. Nor was there much enthusiasm in Paris. When van Zeeland's report was eventually published on 26 January 1938, it was very much a damp squib.[18]

Sino-Japanese War

By the time Chamberlain replied to Roosevelt's letter of July 1937 the situation in the Far East had taken a turn for the worse. The uneasy peace that had prevailed there since the signing of the Ho-Umezu agreement in June 1935 broke down on 7 July 1937 when clashes took place between Chinese and Japanese forces at the Marco Polo Bridge, ten miles south west of Beijing. Despite initial efforts to confine the fighting, the incident expanded into a large-scale conflict, much as the Mukden incident had done in September 1931. FDR decided not to invoke the Neutrality Act of May 1937 at the outset of the fighting as it was not clear at first whether it would escalate into a full-scale war. Cordell Hull was similarly guarded in his public approach at a press conference on 16 July and contented himself with the issuing of a general statement of principles based on the Eight Pillars of Peace he had announced at the Buenos Aires conference on 5 December 1936.

This reiterated US support for disarmament, more liberal trade and so on. 'We avoid entering into alliances or entangling commitments, but we believe in cooperative effort by peaceful and practicable means in support of these principles,' he said.[19]

Washington, London and Paris were all anxious to encourage a peaceful settlement of the dispute by appealing to both sides to show restraint and this resulted in a series of appeals to Chinese and Japanese embassy officials, in public and in private, to avoid any steps that might lead to an escalation of the dispute between the two governments. British and American officials regularly discussed the deteriorating situation, but their appeals were made separately rather than jointly. This suited the American preference for 'parallel action', taken independently and simultaneously, but Hull also made it clear to the Foreign Office that he welcomed a 'continuous and frank exchange of information and of views' as the situation developed. Eden, however, preferred joint action and an attempt at mediation. Washington was not prepared to do this. As Hornbeck explained, Washington wished to cooperate fully with London to try to persuade Tokyo and Nanking to avoid further hostilities but 'we felt that cooperation on parallel but independent lines would be more effective and less likely to have an effect the opposite of that desired than would joint or identical representations'.[20]

According to Bingham, Eden appeared to accept the US position. But on 20 July, Chamberlain 'suggested that a last effort might be made to avert war'. Hull was therefore asked if the US Government was willing to act with the British Government to make a 'joint approach' to the Japanese and Chinese governments and to ask them to agree to suspend hostilities to allow the US and Britain to put forward peace proposals. 'We appreciate that the chances of success may be slender', said the British proposal, but 'we consider the attempt should be made'. Not surprisingly, in view of his previous statements, Hull declined the British suggestion. The US Government fully concurred in the British desire to prevent the outbreak of major hostilities, he said. But 'we feel that the courses of action thus far pursued by our two Governments on parallel lines have been truly cooperative and that, in continuation of a common effort to avert hostilities, both Governments should again, each in its own way, urge upon the Japanese and the Chinese Governments the importance of maintaining peace'.[21]

Hull's response, which was no doubt motivated partly by the fear of arousing US public opinion and the isolationists, caused some resentment in London. When Eden reported on the episode to the Cabinet he said he had suggested joint action with the US Government 'with a view to averting war in the Far East' but this had been turned down by Hull as it might 'exacerbate the situation'. Chamberlain argued, somewhat erroneously, that 'joint action' had not been rejected on principle. He also 'expressed the view that joint representations by the British and United States Governments were likely to produce more results than simultaneous and parallel representations' and added that 'It would be deplorable if any major war were to develop.' Inevitably, Simon's mind went back to his disagreement with Stimson in 1931 and he 'recalled that at the time of the Shanghai affair the position had been reversed – the United States Government had made proposals to us for joint representations that did not commend themselves, and we had preferred to proceed independently'.[22]

'Parallel action'

Hull defended the US policy of 'parallel action' in his *Memoirs* and argued that there was no comparison with the British attitude during the Manchurian crisis as he was cooperating with Eden, unlike Simon's attitude towards Stimson's policy in 1931. He also pointed out that his informal memo of 1 June 1937 to Chamberlain (which the Prime Minister had largely dismissed) had made clear the US preference for parallel rather than joint action in the Far East. 'It is the traditional policy of this country not to enter into those types of agreement which constitute, or which suggest, alliance,' the memo had said.

> We feel that the governments principally interested in the Far East should endeavour constantly to exercise a wholesome and restraining influence toward conserving and safeguarding the rights and interests of all concerned, and toward preventing friction and development of tensions. We believe that consultation between and among the powers most interested, followed by procedure along parallel lines and concurrently, tends to promote the effectiveness of such efforts.

This policy was obviously guided by fears that 'joint action' might be seized upon by isolationists, especially in Congress, as evidence of a formal alliance. But it was also based on the premise that 'parallel action' still enabled significant cooperation, while avoiding greater exposure to isolationist attacks.[23]

Prior to the 1 June memo, the idea of 'parallel action' with Britain had been employed only occasionally by the State Department during Roosevelt's first term, usually in respect of the Far East. But during the Sino-Japanese War the concept of 'parallel action' began to be used more extensively. Given Japanese designs on China and the reluctance of London, as much as Washington, to threaten Tokyo with the use of force, it seems unlikely that 'joint action' would have been any more successful than 'parallel action' in deterring Japan. In any event, in August the conflict spread to Shanghai and Nanjing, where heavy fighting took place. At the end of August Japanese aircraft attacked a vehicle carrying the British Ambassador, Sir Hughe Knatchbull-Hugesson, who was seriously wounded. On 12 September, with Chinese forces in retreat, Chiang Kai-shek appealed to the League of Nations. The League set up a sub-committee 'to deal with the Far Eastern crisis', which Leland Harrison, the US Minister in Switzerland, was authorised to join. But at the same time Hull reiterated that US policy did not favour 'joint action' but rather it preferred 'spontaneous separate action on parallel lines'.[24]

Spanish Civil War

While the conflict between China and Japan escalated in the Far East, the Spanish Civil War continued to be the focus of bitter rivalries between the Great Powers in Europe. By July 1937 the civil war had lasted for a year and the Nationalist forces, supported by Italian and German 'volunteers', had gained the upper hand. In February they captured Málaga in the south from the Republicans and advanced towards Guadalajara, on the way to Madrid, where they were halted by the Republicans, with Soviet support. Meanwhile, in northern Spain, Bilbao fell to the Nationalists in June 1937. Appalling as the events of the Spanish Civil War were – not least the bombing of the Basque city of Guernica in April 1937 by German and Italian bombers that inspired Picasso's graphic depiction of the horrors of war – the impact of the conflict on the international situation and on domestic politics in France was no less a concern in both London and Washington.[25]

By July 1937 it had also become abundantly clear that the Non-Intervention Committee established in London was failing to prevent foreign intervention in the Spanish Civil War, on both land and sea. Naval patrols had been set up to control the supply of arms to both sides in the conflict, but various incidents had cast doubt on their effectiveness. In May two Soviet bombers had attacked the Nationalist port of Ibiza and – apparently by mistake – had bombed the German heavy cruiser *Deutschland*, which was anchored off Ibiza as part of the international patrol. In retaliation, a German naval force shelled Almería – held by the Republicans. Hull's approach was to support the non-intervention policy of Britain and France. FDR was less certain, although he kept in line with the State Department's policy. He was sympathetic to the Loyalists and concerned at the blatant intervention by Italy and Germany on behalf of Franco and the Nationalists, especially after the bombing of Guernica. He was also under some pressure domestically to extend the Neutrality Act to these two countries to prohibit the export of 'arms, ammunition and implements of war' to them. Hull therefore asked Bingham to ascertain whether there was any truth to press reports that suggested London was considering granting belligerent rights to the insurgents. Also, what effects might there be if the President felt obliged to declare an arms embargo against Italy and Germany?[26]

In his reply Bingham reported Eden as saying that the British and French governments were determined to maintain a 'stiff attitude' for the present and not to grant belligerent rights. Eden did not think that, technically, a state of war could be said to exist as long as the Non-Intervention Committee continued to function. Bingham pointed out to Washington that there had been intervention by the Soviet Union, and previously France, so any embargo against Italy and Germany might have to be widened. He felt that any departure from strict neutrality 'would be regarded by Europe as a gratuitous interference in continental affairs' and would also 'complicate the British Government's main object which is to foster a withdrawal of foreign interference in Spain so as to eliminate the danger of an extension of the conflict beyond the confines of Spain'. Eden had said that extending the arms embargo to Germany and Italy was, 'to say the least, premature' and would complicate his task.[27]

Phillips visit to Washington

FDR therefore did not pursue this line of policy; nor did he feel able to offer mediation, with or without the Pope – as had also been suggested to him. He was anxious to keep in step with the

British and French despite his own reservations about the war. For the same reasons he gave full support to Morgenthau's efforts to maintain the Tripartite Currency Agreement, which was being tested by pressure on the franc caused by the Spanish Civil War and the cost of the social reform programme of the Popular Front Government of Léon Blum. On 21 June Blum and Vincent Auriol (the Finance Minister) resigned. Blum was replaced by Chautemps and Georges Bonnet was recalled from London to become the Finance Minister. Once again, a crisis of the franc caused concern in London and Washington. Simon, the new Chancellor of the Exchequer, advised Morgenthau that he would be proposing an increase of £200 million in the size of the Exchange Equalisation Account established in 1932 to combat currency instability and Morgenthau was happy to agree. Simon was then able to inform the House of Commons that the increase was supported by the US Treasury.[28]

As always, Morgenthau was primarily concerned for the future of the Tripartite Agreement if France devalued again. He felt that 'the Pact had saved France temporarily from fascism.' Morgenthau therefore wanted to be supportive of the French and he telephoned Simon on 29 June to say that he felt that France must be kept in the Tripartite Pact. He followed this up with a cable to Simon urging that Britain and the US should act together to support the French and maintain the Tripartite Declaration. 'Simon immediately replied that he was sending Bonnet a message in the same terms Morgenthau had suggested.' The American Treasury therefore felt that it had helped to keep Simon loyal to the Tripartite Pact. 'Though not without friction', wrote the editor of Morgenthau's diaries, 'the treasuries of the three Western democracies were still working together, in part because Morgenthau had fortified Simon's faltering spirit.' On 1 July, following the parallel assurances from London and Washington, a decree was enacted by the new French Government removing the limits on the gold content of the franc. Divorced from gold, the 'floating' franc fell from 110 to 129 and then to 132 to the pound, but the markets then settled down awaiting Bonnet's reforms.[29]

Meanwhile, Eden was trying to achieve a compromise agreement regarding non-intervention patrols to keep the conflict in Spain from expanding into a general European war. In a survey of British policy after a year of the Civil War, Herschel Johnston at the US Embassy in London reported that there was a growing feeling in official circles that, especially since the fall of Bilbao, the Chamberlain Government needed to trim its sails and prepare for a Franco victory. But Johnson acknowledged 'from the beginning of the Spanish conflict, the sincere and open desire on the part of the British, paramount among various considerations, to keep the fighting strictly confined to the Spanish peninsula with a view to preserving European peace'. Even Claude Bowers, the US Ambassador in Spain, although critical of what he regarded as the British pretence that the non-intervention policy was working, felt that Britain was the only country, apart from the US, that was adhering to strict neutrality. Hull was therefore very pleased when Eden was able to arrange a conference at Nyon in September 1937 that led to an agreement to avoid further 'naval incidents' in the Mediterranean.[30]

Despite the Nyon agreement, a further run on the franc in September 1937 resulted in another substantial devaluation of the currency, which sank below the psychological figure of 150 to the pound. Unlike in September 1936 and July 1937, this was not a managed devaluation with the prior agreement of the British and US Treasuries but a unilateral action that was explained to London and Washington after it had been carried out. It was fortunate therefore that Sir Frederick Phillips, the Permanent Under Secretary at the British Treasury, had just arrived in Washington with the general aim of furthering financial cooperation between the US and Britain. Morgenthau had previously suggested to Bewley that 'it would be useful if a British Treasury expert such as Phillips could from time to time take a trip to the USA, with no special mission, but just to establish contact'. Following the French financial crisis in June, Simon took up Morgenthau's suggestion. Phillips was visiting Canada privately in September so it was agreed that he would visit Washington between 20 September and 7 October.[31]

'Austere, laconic, sometimes imperious, Phillips cultivated the reputation of a man of mystery,' according to the editor of the *Morgenthau Diaries*. The British official said that London expected the franc to fall gradually but they wanted to keep France within the Tripartite Pact unless the French imposed exchange controls. Morgenthau was also not keen on exchange controls, but his main priority was the continuation of the pact. Both governments therefore accepted the devaluation of the franc, which meant that the Tripartite Agreement continued to exist as a symbolic show of solidarity for the three Western democracies. But there was concern in

Paris that the Phillips conversations in Washington suggested cooperation with France was no longer so close and that 'the Tripartite Agreement was becoming bipartite'. This was not surprising as one of the outcomes of the September currency crisis was a strengthening of Anglo-American financial cooperation and confirmation of the view that France was becoming 'the sick man of Europe' – a view that Simon's positive remarks about the Tripartite Agreement in his Mansion House speech on 7 October could do nothing to hide.[32]

British support for the French devaluation and the future of the Tripartite Currency Agreement helped to reassure Morgenthau that Simon would be a reasonably cooperative partner, despite his reputation when he was Foreign Secretary. Indeed, at the end of September Simon sent his personal thanks to Morgenthau, via the British Embassy, 'for having kept so closely in touch with him' during this latest French currency crisis. 'It has been a great satisfaction to the Chancellor to feel that Mr Morgenthau's views and his own have so closely coincided.' Phillips also returned to London with a strong appreciation of Morgenthau's outlook and his attitude towards not only the Tripartite Currency Agreement but also the international situation more generally. This was very useful during the on-going crises in France over the next few years and was to prove invaluable when Britain itself faced an even worse crisis in May and June 1940 and Morgenthau asked Phillips to return to Washington for vital talks.[33]

The view from Berlin

Given the Roosevelt Administration's adherence to a doctrine of strict neutrality, there was little room for complaint in Berlin about US policy during the Spanish Civil War. US press comments were very negative about German and Italian policy but that was nothing new. Hull was anxious to support the Non-Intervention Committee and asked Dieckhoff to call on him following the *Deutschland* incident. After expressing sympathies for those who had been killed or injured, 'he expressed the hope that it might not be necessary for us to take further action and concluded with a friendly, rather vaguely phrased statement to the effect that Germany could presumably be counted upon to continue doing everything possible to preserve the peace'.

Dieckhoff defended the German reprisals after the attack and said that future policy would depend on the attitude of the Non-Intervention Committee and the Spanish Republican Government. In similar fashion, Hull's statement of principles on 16 July 1937 was delivered to the German Foreign Ministry by the US Ambassador, William Dodds, with an appeal for German support for the preservation of peace in the Far East.[34]

Of more concern to Berlin at this time than US policy towards the Spanish Civil War or in the Far East was the determination of the Roosevelt Administration to limit German influence in Latin America, both political and economic. One example of this which particularly exercised Berlin was American pressure on Brazil not to extend its trade agreement with Nazi Germany on the grounds that that it discriminated against the US. Brazilian products enjoyed most-favoured-nation treatment in the US and Brazil had an export surplus with the US of about $70 million per year so Washington was able to exert considerable leverage on the Brazilian Government. Dieckhoff was therefore asked to seek an urgent meeting with Welles to convey to him 'the astonishment and displeasure of the Reich Government at the unusual and strange interference of the USA in German–Brazilian economic relations'. Welles rejected the German claim and Hull 'expatiated in detail, in his customary manner', as Dieckhoff put it, on the principles of the American trade agreements programme. In the event, the German–Brazilian trade agreement survived until the outbreak of war in September 1939, when it came up against the British blockade.[35]

Notes

1. FO/371/20660, A3417/228/45, memo by Eden, 4 May 1937; Roosevelt papers, PSF, Box 52, Bingham to Roosevelt, 22 May 1937; Bingham papers, Box 25, Davis to Bingham, 10 June 1937; PREM/1/261, Davis to Chamberlain, 10 June 1937; see also Borg, *US and Far Eastern Crisis*, pp. 376–7.
2. PREM/1/261, Chamberlain to Davis, 8 July 1937.
3. FO/371/20661, A4881/228/45, FO minute, 8 July 1937; PREM/1/261, Roosevelt to Chamberlain, 28 July 1937; Dallek, *FDR*, pp. 144–9.
4. PREM/1/261, note by Chamberlain, 20 August 1937; Ibid., Chamberlain to Roosevelt, 28 September 1937; Bouverie, *Appeasing Hitler*, pp. 120–36.

5. Mackenzie King Diary, 27 May, 7 June, 15 June, 29 June 1937; DGFP/C/VI, doc 425, Ribbentrop to Neurath, 13 June 1937. See also Teigrob, *Four Days in Hitler's Germany*.
6. Bingham to FDR, 13 November 1936 in Nixon, *FDRFA/III*, p. 486; Kennedy, 'Neville Chamberlain and Strategic Relations with the US', pp. 95–120; Neilson, 'Defence Requirements Sub-Committee', pp. 651–84.
7. Runciman papers, Box 285, Chamberlain to Runciman, 10 May 1937; Runciman to Chamberlain, 7 May 1937; Runciman to 'an American observer' (unnamed), 21 June 1937.
8. Ibid., Vansittart to Runciman, 29 May 1937; Murray papers, Box 8809, Roosevelt to Murray, 17 June 1937.
9. FDR to Phillips, 17 May 1937, Elliott Roosevelt, *Roosevelt Letters*, III.
10. For a focus on American economic appeasement see MacDonald, *The United States, Britain and Appeasement*, pp. ix–xi and 1–15; MacDonald, 'Economic Appeasement', pp. 105–35; Schmitz, *The Sailor*, pp. 64–75.
11. DGFP/C/VI, Lindsay to Sargent, 30 March 1937; for Sumner Welles see Rofe, *Franklin Roosevelt's Foreign Policy and the Welles Mission*.
12. State Department, SD 600.0031 World Program/147: Hull to diplomatic and consular officers, 6 July 1937.
13. Hull, *Memoirs I*, pp. 532–3; see also FRUS/1937/I, doc 64, Welles to FDR, 27 May 1937, enclosing Informal Memorandum from the Department of State to the British Embassy (delivered on 1 June 1937).
14. Ibid.
15. FO/371/26660, A4165/228/45, Lindsay to Eden, 1 June 1937, enclosing memo from Hull (undated); PREM/1/261, note by Chamberlain, 29 June 1937; Ibid., minute by Sir W. Fisher, 2 July 1937; Ibid., minute by Sir J. Simon, 4 July 1937; Chamberlain to Hull, 30 July 1937. See also Hull, *Memoirs I*, p. 534.
16. For Van Zeeland mission see Toynbee, *Survey of International Affairs, 1937*, pp. 56–109. World Economic Affairs by Allan G. Fisher; FRUS/1937/I, docs 688–710 for VZ mission; doc 691, Dave H. Morris (Belgium) to Hull, 8 April 1937; doc 696, memo by Welles, 25 June 1937; FRUS/1937/I, doc 697, Joint statement of FDR and Van Zeeland, 29 June 1937.
17. FDR press conference, 13 July 1937, available on-line at Franklin Roosevelt Library.
18. FRUS/1937/I, doc 699, Bingham to Hull, 6 July 1937; doc 710, Johnson to Hull, 31 December 1937; FRUS/1938/I, doc 1, Bullitt to Hull, 4 January 1938.
19. Dallek, *FDR*, pp. 144–7; Borg, *Far Eastern Crisis*, pp. 276–317; Hull, *Memoirs I*, pp. 535–8.

20. FRUS/1937/III, doc 131, Hull to Bingham, 12 July 1937; doc 145, British Embassy to State Dept, 13 July 1937; doc 147, State Dept to British Embassy, 13 July 1937; doc 148, Hornbeck memo, 14 July 1937.
21. Ibid., doc 220, Bingham to Hull, 20 July 1937; doc 223, British Embassy to State Dept, 20 July 1937; DBFP/2/XXI, Eden to Lindsay, 20 July 1937; see also CAB 23, 31 (1937), item 3, 21 July 1937; FRUS/1937/I, doc 236, State Dept to British Embassy, 21 July 1937.
22. CAB 23, 32 (1937), item 5, 28 July 1937.
23. Hull memo of 1 June 1937. See also endnote 13.
24. Hull, *Memoirs I*, pp. 539–44.
25. Carr, *Arms, Autarky and Aggression*, p. 66.
26. For US policy and Spanish Civil War see Tierney, *FDR and Spanish Civil War*; Traina, *American Diplomacy and Spanish Civil War*; FRUS/1937/I, p. 344, Hull to Bingham, 30 June 1937.
27. FRUS/1937/I, pp. 353–5, Bingham to Hull, 6 July 1937.
28. Blum, *Morgenthau Diaries I*, pp. 473–8 and pp. 498–505; T177/35, FO to Lindsay 21/22/23 June 1937; *Hansard*, House of Common debates, 28 June 1937.
29. Blum, *Morgenthau Diaries I*, pp. 475–7; FO/371/20690, C5427/53/17, E. Rowe Dutton to S. D. Waley (Treasury) with memo 'The Financial Situation in France, June–July 1937', 23 July 1937.
30. FRUS/1937/I, pp. 374–6, Hershel Johnson (London) to Hull, 23 August 1937; Ibid., pp. 362–4, Claude Bowers to Hull, 20 July 1937; Hull, *Memoirs I*, pp. 504–17.
31. FO/371/20690, C6456/53/17, FO minute by Jebb, 16 September 1937; C6530/53/17, 17 September 1937, Minute by Waley (Treasury) for Sir R. Hopkins; C6591/53/17, 20 September 1937, note of conversation between French Ambassador Corbin and PM; C6605/53/17, speech by Bonnet on 20 September; see Treasury file T177/35 for details of Phillips visit. T177/35, Bewley memo, 14 April 1937; Ibid., Simon to Lindsay, T177/35, 28 June 1937.
32. Blum, *Morgenthau Diaries I*, p. 498; FO/371/20690, C6606, Mallet to FO from Phillips, 22 September 1937; C6630/53/17, 23 September 1937, Mallet (from Phillips) to FO; C6631/53/17, 23 September, Mallet to FO (Phillips for Treasury); C6629/53/17, 23 September 1937, FO to Mallet (for Phillips); 23 September 1937, memo by Waley on talk with Monick; 24 September 1937, record of conversation with Monick by Gladwyn Jebb with Leith-Ross in attendance; Mansion House speech on 7 October 1937, *The Times*, 8 October 1937.
33. Blum, *Morgenthau Diaries I*, p. 498; see T177/35 file for overview of Phillips visit, especially Eden to Mallet, 27 September 1937.

34. DGFP/D/III, doc 274, Dieckhoff to GFM, 31 May 1937; DGFP/C/VI, doc 481, memo by Hans Georg von Mackensen, State Secretary 20 July 1937.
35. DGFP/D/III, doc 428, Dieckhoff to GFM, 15 June 1937; doc 440, State Secretary (Mackensen) to German Embassy in US, 29 June 1937; doc 444, Dieckhoff to GFM, 30 June 1937; doc 488, Dieckhoff to GFM, 21 July 1937; February 1935 – US–Brazil trade agreement; see also Frank D. McCann Jr, *The Brazilian–American Alliance, 1937–45*.

5 Quarantine Speech, October–December 1937

On 5 October 1937, at the end of an 8,000-mile trip through the West and Mid-West, President Roosevelt arrived in Chicago to open a new bridge and to deliver what has become known as his 'Quarantine' speech:

> It seems to be unfortunately true that the epidemic of world lawlessness is spreading. When an epidemic of physical disease starts to spread, the community approves and joins in a quarantine of the patients in order to protect the health of the community against the spread of the disease.

Continuing with this metaphor he said: 'War is a contagion, whether it be declared or undeclared. It can engulf states and peoples remote from the original scene of hostilities.' American policy was to keep out of war, but it could not avoid 'the disastrous effects of war and the dangers of involvement'. The US was attempting to minimise its risk of involvement in war – a clear reference to the Neutrality laws – but complete protection was impossible 'in a world of disorder in which confidence and security have broken down'.[1]

FDR concluded his speech by saying: 'America hates war. America hopes for peace. Therefore, America actively engages in the search for peace.' Beyond the 'quarantine' metaphor, this was the most important theme of the speech. Having raised the question of how war could be avoided, FDR stated the internationalist viewpoint. 'Most important of all', he said, 'the will for peace on the part of peace-loving nations must express itself to the end that nations that may be tempted to violate their agreements and the rights of others will desist from such a course.' In other words, those countries that wanted peace must act together to contain the aggressor states. This sentiment was very much in line with the outlook of Roosevelt II. As the first hundred days of his second term had shown – from the Runciman visit to the revision of the Neutrality Act – the President felt that pre-emptive steps had to be taken by the democracies rather than just waiting upon events. 'There must be positive endeavours to preserve peace.'[2]

Significance of Quarantine speech

The primary aim of this chapter is to analyse the significance of FDR's Quarantine speech for Anglo-American relations in the late 1930s. Clearly, the speech – or rather the 'quarantine' reference – had a tremendous impact at the time, both domestically and in terms of US foreign policy and international relations. FDR reiterated the central message of the speech – active engagement – in his fireside chat on 12 October, the first one to feature foreign policy as a major theme. Pointing out that as a member of the Wilson Administration from 1913 to 1921, he was 'fairly close to world events', he said,

> I want our great democracy to be wise enough to realize that aloofness from war is not promoted by unawareness of war. In a world of mutual suspicions, peace must be affirmatively reached for. It cannot just be wished for. And it cannot just be waited for.

The Quarantine speech was also an appeal to the 'peace loving states' – that is, Britain, France and the other democracies – to take active steps to preserve peace. And, as with his previous speeches, its obvious criticism of the dictator states suggested that the President favoured a robust approach to Germany, Italy and Japan that opposed concessions without some quid pro quo in their attitude and conduct.[3]

While Chamberlain was sceptical in private (although not in public) about the Quarantine speech, Eden was more positive. Their differing attitudes to the role that the United States should play in British foreign policy was just one aspect of their diverging paths. Both Eden and Chamberlain were as anxious as Roosevelt to make progress in defusing the threat of war, and as the Prime Minister's speech at the Guildhall on 9 November suggested, he was keen to reach a closer understanding with the United States. But – as his reluctance to accept FDR's invitation to visit Washington had shown – his priority was coming to terms with Germany and Italy, if not Japan, so any understanding with the US would have to take cognisance of this fact. Hence the visit to Berlin in November 1937 of his trusted colleague, Lord Halifax, to try to ascertain the extent of Nazi Germany's ambitions – despite the strong reservations of Eden, Vansittart and other members of the Foreign Office that this approach would convey the impression of British indifference to German expansionism. Indeed, while in Berlin, Halifax let it be known that Britain would not oppose German expansion in the East, as long as it was achieved peacefully, and as part of a 'general settlement'.[4]

Roosevelt's Chicago speech, together with the deteriorating situation abroad, also helped to convince Mackenzie King of the need to act on the trade agreement question, even though he had been incensed during the summer at what he regarded as British and American pressure upon Canada to bear the brunt of the 'essentials' list. In late October both he and Tweedsmuir, the Governor General, met with Cordell Hull in Ottawa, and the Secretary of State urged them to help get the Anglo-American trade negotiations under way. Partly as a result, Canadian trade officials informed Washington that Canada was ready to make substantial concessions on Imperial Preference if the Canadian–American trade agreement of November 1935 could be renegotiated. This was a major breakthrough as the Canadians had at last made their position clear and the Americans were also prepared to hold simultaneous negotiations with Canada – a course they had previously resisted for fear of 'paying twice' for an Anglo-American trade agreement.[5]

FDR and 'active engagement'

On 12 September the Chinese Government appealed to the League of Nations, arguing that Japan had invaded China and invoking Articles 10, 11 and 17 of the Covenant. The escalating conflict between China and Japan was discussed at a US Cabinet meeting on 14 September 1937, at which FDR said he had 'no intention of making any warlike move' but he was very keen to defend democracy as a system against autocracy in his upcoming speech on the 150th anniversary of the Constitution. Hull suggested toning down some of his comments about autocracy – much to the annoyance of Harold Ickes, the Secretary of the Interior, who saw FDR later that day and pointed out that 'not only Germany but Italy is filling the world with propaganda against the democracies'. He also said that Hull was becoming 'altogether too timid'. According to Ickes's account,

> The President said I was right and that he had about come to the conclusion that he would have to take the ball in international relations from Hull. As I told him, he is the only one in the world who can mould or lead world public opinion for the democratic ideal. I believe that it is his duty to do so.[6]

FDR told Ickes he was thinking of contacting 'all the nations of the world, except possibly the "three bandit nations" [Germany, Italy and Japan], to suggest that, in the future, if any nation should invade the rights or threaten the liberties of any of the other nations, the peace-loving nations would isolate it. What he has in mind is to cut off all trade with any such nation and thus deny it raw materials.' FDR thought it was too late to do much in Spain or China but 'he wants to evolve a new policy for the future and, of course, if he should do this, it would be a warning to the nations that are today running amuck'. Ickes thought the idea was 'a good one' and he suggested that Roosevelt should make the dedication speech for the Outer Link Bridge in Chicago on 9 October. He also mentioned the quarantine analogy for dealing with a contagious disease, which FDR decided to use in his speech. 'His Chicago speech was by all odds the most important one on the international situation that he has ever made. Whatever the repercussions may be, it was a great speech.'[7]

At his regular press conference the day after the Quarantine speech the President was quizzed about the meaning of the speech, especially the 'quarantine' reference. He rejected the suggestion that it was, in the words of one journalist, 'a repudiation of the neutrality laws'. But he agreed that it was a step towards preparing the way for 'collaborative' measures and he underlined the significance of the last line of his speech: 'America hates war. America hopes for peace. Therefore, America actively engages in the search for peace.' He was unable to identify the actual methods to be used but he said he did not favour sanctions – 'they are out of the window' – or a conference – 'you never get anywhere with a conference'. Questioned about the London *Times* article describing the speech as 'an attitude without a program', he said: 'It is an attitude, and it does not outline a program; but it says we are looking for a program.' He refused to be drawn on whether the speech meant the US would be 'aligning' with 'the peace-loving nations', simply saying: 'There are a lot of methods in the world that have never been tried yet.'[8]

The day after FDR's Chicago speech, a League investigation found that the Japanese response to the original incident at the Marco Polo Bridge was out of all proportion to the incident itself. It could not be justified in terms of self-defence and contravened Japan's obligations under the Nine Power Treaty and the Kellogg Pact. The State Department then issued a statement declaring that Japan had acted in violation of Nine Power Treaty and the Kellogg Pact – thus aligning the US with the League of Nations. According to the *New York Times*, the Quarantine speech and the State Department's condemnation of Japan marked a radical departure in US foreign policy as they meant that 'President Roosevelt has made a dead letter of the American neutrality policy and is embarked on a new course of dealing actively with aggressor nations'. However, the overall reaction to the speech was mixed. While it was welcomed by internationalist opinion, it was severely criticised by isolationists such as Borah and Johnson. In his *Memoirs*, Hull said he felt that the 'quarantine' remark, by arousing isolationist fears of economic sanctions, had set back his own campaign to 'educate' American opinion by six months.[9]

The sentiments in FDR's speech received strong support from Henry Stimson, President Hoover's Secretary of State, in a letter to the *New York Times* published on 7 October. An accompanying editorial, entitled 'Our Policy in the East', praised the letter as 'an eloquent and important statement of the mounting opinion in this country which has prompted the President to declare that the United States must take its part in "concerted efforts" to maintain world peace, and caused the State Department to declare that the conclusions of our Government with respect to Japan's undeclared war in China are in general accord with those of the Assembly of the League of Nations'. The US was not abandoning 'the ways of peace', the editorial continued, but the American people were bound to be seriously concerned about the threat to peace in the Far East. 'We cannot, either with honour or with safety, play the role of the hermit in the modern world,' the editorial continued, so the Government was 'considering what can be done by peaceful means, in association with other nations, to uphold the sanctity of treaties and to safeguard international law'.[10]

However, the speech was criticised by isolationists in Congress and by various peace activists, who said the President was arousing a 'war spirit' and undermining the Neutrality Act while offering no constructive alternative. Several such groups held a meeting on 6 October in Washington, DC – the National Council for the Prevention of War, World Peaceways, the Women's International League for Peace and Freedom, the Emergency Peace Campaign and the Committee on Militarism in Education. In their joint press release they said that they agreed that the disease of war should be quarantined, but they felt that the only quarantine that would protect Americans was the implementation of the Neutrality laws. 'No quarantine will cure the disease for those who are suffering from it. The one cure that we have tried and know will not work is "war to end war".' They felt that the President's speech was pointing the American people down the road that had led to the World War. 'He offers the same reasons for advancing down that road now that were offered in 1917. They found instead war, fascism, communism, destruction and debt.'[11]

British reaction to the Quarantine speech

The British Embassy in Washington naturally took a different view. 'I have every reason to believe that the speech had been long contemplated, but the President was prepared to wait for the psychological moment for its delivery,' reported Victor Mallet, the British Chargé d'Affaires. Pointing out that FDR's arrival in Chicago coincided with the decision of the League of Nations to refer the conflict between Japan and China to the signatories of the Nine Power Treaty, Mallet said that the Quarantine speech showed that the President was trying to lead the United States towards cooperation with the European democracies. 'His approach to an objective he has long had at heart has so far been very careful and well-timed. He is above all an astute politician and he is unlikely to forget the fate of Mr Woodrow Wilson.' The speech marked a deliberate change in policy away from the Neutrality laws, said Mallet. 'The course has been carefully charted after long deliberation and the decision to proceed was announced in Mr Roosevelt's Chicago speech.'[12]

However, Roosevelt was looking for more from the democracies and he appears to have been disappointed with the immediate

British reaction to his speech. 'Strictly between ourselves, I did hope for a little more unselfish spine in your foreign office,' he wrote to Arthur Murray. This was no doubt because he wanted Britain to take the lead whereas he feared that the Foreign Office was trying to push him out ahead in confronting Japan, not appreciating that he had gone as far as he could. Indeed, Eden was anxious to make the most of the Chicago speech, as became clear during a discussion of the speech by the British Cabinet on 6 October, when he suggested that a meeting of the signatories of the Nine Power Treaty of 1922 would enable the American Government to give any cooperation it could. 'After President Roosevelt's speech it was hardly possible for the American Government to reject the suggestion,' Eden said. He had therefore asked the British Embassy in Washington to ascertain the meaning of the speech and 'to make some enquiries as to the American attitude towards the idea of action to bring an end to the conflict in China'.[13]

Chamberlain, ever mindful of domestic politics, thought that 'the speech introduced a new factor into the situation, and, whatever its real significance, it was likely to be made use of for political purposes by the Opposition Parties in this country'. He felt that the speech 'was so involved that it was difficult to discover its meaning' but that it would be important to avoid the impression that the US had offered to cooperate in economic sanctions and that the Government was standing in the way. Personally, he 'could not imagine anything more suicidal than to pick a quarrel with Japan at the present moment, when the European situation had become so serious. If this country were to become involved in the Far East the temptation to the Dictator States to take action, whether in Eastern Europe or in Spain, might be irresistible.' He therefore felt that the President had

> rather embarrassed the situation, but he did not under-rate the importance of his statement, especially as a warning to the Dictator Powers that there was a point beyond which the United States of America would not permit them to go. Consequently, if embarrassing today, the speech might prove useful later on.[14]

In public, bearing in mind the favourable reception that Roosevelt's words had received in Britain, Chamberlain very much welcomed FDR's speech. Addressing the annual Conservative Party conference at Scarborough on 8 October 1937, he said: 'Three days ago the attention of the world was arrested by a clarion call from the other side of the Atlantic, as welcome as it was timely in its utterance.' Chamberlain continued by saying that 'hitherto it has been assumed that the U.S.A., the most powerful country in the world, would remain content with a frankly isolationist policy. But President Roosevelt has seen that if what he calls the epidemic of world lawlessness is allowed to spread no country will be safe from attack.' The Prime Minister then associated himself with Roosevelt's words. 'In his declaration of the necessity for a return to a belief in the pledged word and the sanctity of treaties', he said, the President had 'voiced the convictions of this country as well as of his own, and in his call for a concerted effort in the cause of peace this Government will be wholeheartedly with him.' Eden also referred very positively to the President's Chicago address in a speech he made in Llandudno on 15 October 1937.[15]

Welles 'Armistice Day' plan

It soon became clear that FDR was not intending to take any immediate action specifically related to the Far East, especially in view of the opposition that his Chicago speech had aroused in the US. Sumner Welles informed Mallet on 12 October that the 'quarantine' idea was quite an abstract one. The President did not intend to suggest it as in any way an immediate policy. On the contrary, emphasis should be placed on the last sentence of the speech: 'America hates war. America hopes for peace. Therefore, America actively engages in the search for peace.' When speaking to Mallet about the President's Chicago speech, Welles made no reference to his own brainchild – the so-called Armistice Day peace initiative. On 6 October, the day after the Chicago speech, Welles had drawn up a memorandum suggesting that the time had come for the President to call a world conference to achieve common agreement on a number of problems – 'the basic principles of international relations and warfare; the rights and obligations of neutrals; and the right of freedom of access on the part of all peoples to raw materials'.[16]

In making this suggestion Welles was following up FDR's pet project of some kind of peace conference that would discuss the deteriorating international situation without directly involving the US in political issues that would alarm US public opinion, especially isolationists such as Borah and Johnson. Welles had been appointed Under Secretary of State in May 1937 to add some dynamism to the conduct of US foreign policy by supplementing the efforts of the ultra-cautious Hull and, at first, the President was very taken with the Welles plan, especially the idea that it should be announced on Armistice Day. However, the plan was delayed by discussions in the State Department as to its feasibility. Hull was scathing about Welles's 'somewhat pyrotechnical plan' in his *Memoirs* and he was able to persuade FDR to sound out the British Government regarding the idea, in view of the importance of Anglo-American relations at this time. When he did so, in January 1938, the so-called 'Roosevelt initiative' was to have far-reaching repercussions, even though it was not made public.[17]

On 12 October, the same day that Sumner Welles spoke to Mallet, the President and Hull met with Henry Wickham Steed, the former editor of *The Times*. An expert on Central and Eastern Europe, where he had spent time as a foreign correspondent for *The Times* before the First World War, Wickham Steed was now a lecturer in Central European History at King's College London. While in New York he was the guest of honour at two prestigious events, one organised by the Association of Foreign Press Correspondents and the other by the English Speaking Union. An early and vocal critic of Nazi Germany and British appeasement policy, he told his listeners that Fascism was 'infinitely more insidious than communism'. He also said that 'Britain should declare what she could and would do in the event of aggression by military dictatorships. A halt had to be called somewhere or Hitler and Mussolini would think democracies "were always on the run".' A firm advocate of Anglo-American friendship, he said he looked forward to the time when Britain and the United States would understand each other so well that they 'would pull together on the same rope for some big purpose'.[18]

Wickham Steed was therefore an obvious guest to meet FDR and Hull in the wake of the Quarantine speech. The President explained to his British visitor that his speech was intended to 'educate' American opinion about the threat posed by the 'aggressor states' and 'to show the world in which direction that opinion is running'. But Roosevelt emphasised that the process of 'education' was a slow one and that the British Government must not 'speak or think or act as though it were possible for me to be in any way an exponent of British Foreign Office policy'. A second important point for the British Government to note, said Roosevelt, was that 'it should never forget I cannot march ahead of our very difficult and restive public opinion'. Thirdly, he said: 'It must not try to push me in any way to the front or to thrust leadership upon me . . . I cannot and shall not try to impose anything on our people or the world. I will seek most earnestly to co-operate with all nations that are working for freedom and for peace.' Wickham Steed gave the Foreign Office a report of his meeting which Vansittart said was 'enlightening', while Holman commented: 'This shows very clearly that nothing concrete can be expected at the present time from the USA and that much harm may be done by the Press and public bodies trying to force the pace.'[19]

Brussels conference

Meanwhile, the Nine Power Treaty meeting proposed by the League of Nations began to take form as the Brussels conference, from 3 to 24 November 1937. At a Cabinet meeting on 13 October Eden said he hoped that the US delegates to the conference would stop off in London so as to confer regarding their respective viewpoints. He thought it was very unlikely that Japan would attend the conference – and this proved to be the case. Chamberlain also 'thought it very desirable that an understanding should be reached with the US representatives as to the line to be taken, as if a difference arose our position would be weakened'. He recalled that President Roosevelt had used the expression 'quarantine', which had been generally interpreted as a boycott. 'He himself had noticed, however, that the President's speech was so worded that he could escape from that interpretation.' If the Opposition parties interpreted the quarantine reference as an offer to impose economic sanctions, 'it might be necessary to come into the open'. Chamberlain said that he personally was very much opposed to sanctions.[20]

By the time of the next Cabinet meeting, on 20 October, Chamberlain was able to report – with some relief – 'that the situation had undergone considerable change. It was clear now that the Government of the United States of America had no intention of taking any decisive action in the Far East.' Indeed, in Brussels Davis and Hornbeck made it quite clear that the US would not support any offer of joint mediation with Great Britain in the dispute between Japan and China. However, despite differences in approach and an abundance of 'argument and counter-argument', relations between the US delegation and the British delegation, led by Malcolm MacDonald, remained good. Indeed, 'Davis said that he attached the greatest possible importance to Anglo-American cooperation in international affairs. In his view America had only one vital interest beyond her own shores, and that was the security of the British Empire.' He was disappointed American public opinion had not been more vocal about the situation in the Far East so as to give support for a stronger policy against Japan, as this had forced FDR to retreat from the expectations aroused by his Quarantine speech.[21]

On 24 November the British Cabinet was informed by MacDonald that 'the results of the Conference had been somewhat inglorious but there were at least some compensating features'. These included the fact that the Dominions delegates – including Canada – had kept in step with the United Kingdom delegates throughout. Indeed, Mackenzie King had not been happy with the Brussels conference as he would have preferred diplomatic channels to deal with the situation in the Far East. As regards Anglo-American relations, the Cabinet minutes noted that 'cordial relations and complete cooperation with the delegation of the United States of America had been and was still being maintained'. As a result, 'the door had been kept open for some possible future initiative by the United States and ourselves with a view to securing peace'. The Prime Minister, with the general concurrence of the Cabinet, felt that a difficult situation had been handled very effectively. 'The main lesson to be drawn', he concluded, 'was the difficulty of securing effective co-operation from the United States of America.'[22]

One obvious way of achieving this 'effective cooperation' with the United States was to secure the Anglo-American trade agreement that was one of Hull's main aims as Secretary of State. Hull made an important visit to Ottawa, on 20–22 October, during which he met Tweedsmuir and Mackenzie King and impressed upon them the need for progress in the trade talks between Britain and the Dominions over Imperial Preference and the American 'essentials' list. They also discussed the Brussels conference, which Mackenzie King was not happy about as he feared it could make the international situation worse by arousing expectations that could not easily be met. Hull then told him that 'the United States had found great embarrassment about the invitation extended by the League of Nations to them to participate in the Conference'. As regards Europe, both men felt that Hitler's aim was to absorb the German minorities in the East, peacefully if possible but by force if he was resisted. Mackenzie King, who had visited Hitler in Berlin after the Imperial Conference, was optimistic that Hitler's influence would be for peace. 'Mr Hull said he got many reports the same, and believed it was true but was very much afraid that if conditions went from bad to worse economically in Germany, that even Hitler could not prevent an outbreak.'[23]

Soon after Hull's visit, Tweedsmuir wrote to Chamberlain telling him about his meeting with FDR and Hull during his state visit to Washington in April 1937, and his more recent talk with Hull in which the Secretary of State reiterated the importance of 'economic appeasement'. Tweedsmuir reported Hull as believing that 'Germany has no immediate bellicose aims, even in the Near East', and that 'if the great democracies, led by Britain and America, would offer to her their help in getting her economic condition stable, she could be detached from her present alliance with Italy and Japan. . . . He believes that there is a solid and rational element in Germany with which we could work.'

Chamberlain did not agree. 'This shows how far USA is from appreciating German mentality which is shutting its eyes to economic difficulties and concentrating on prestige and ideology,' he commented. 'There is a rational element but it is not detachable.' The Prime Minister was obviously of the opinion that economic appeasement of the kind advocated by Hull would not work in Germany's case, and Roosevelt would not have dissented from this view. Indeed, his Chicago speech was partly the result of his frustration at the slow progress of Hull's trade agreement programme, as well as Chamberlain's own reluctance to follow up Runciman's visit to Washington with a visit of his own.[24]

Chamberlain, and his close adviser Sir Horace Wilson, felt that Tweedsmuir was moving outside his province. However, the Prime Minister replied in conciliatory fashion, 'You will doubtless have noticed that in recent speeches I have gone out of my way to encourage those sections of American opinion that seem to have welcomed the President's Chicago speech. Nevertheless, I am very conscious of the difficulties that have still to be overcome by the President before it can be said that he has his people behind him. His Chicago speech can be regarded, I think, as evidence that he recognises the need for the education of public opinion; but I should doubt whether such education can yet be said to have proceeded very far and it would seem likely that its development must take time.' In the meantime, the Government was doing its best to improve Anglo-American relations. There seemed little chance of a war debt settlement, as suggested by Tweedsmuir, but the trade agreement was still under discussion. 'We are striving hard to surmount the obstacles that still remain, realising to the full the advantage of enabling Cordell Hull and the President to add an Anglo-USA agreement to their list.'[25]

Indeed, on 27 October 1937 the issue of trade concessions to the United States was discussed at a meeting of the British Cabinet. The main opposition to substantial concessions came from Morrison, the Minister of Agriculture, who was worried about the effect on home agriculture of the American 'essentials' list and the political consequences that might follow. As a result, the final British list of possible concessions was some way from the requests made by the State Department. In fact, Lindsay was so alarmed that the British offers were not enough that he cabled to London urging that they be reconsidered. But the Board of Trade felt that there was little room for revision and suggested that if the State Department rejected the British reply, an appeal might be made to Roosevelt. In the event, Hull, although disappointed, would brook no more delay and accepted the British offers while warning that further American requests would be made in the future. An announcement of the opening of formal negotiations was made on 18 November.[26]

Progress towards an Anglo-American trade agreement was one of the few signs of encouragement for the democratic powers in the second half of 1937 but it was small comfort in the face of the obvious failure of the Brussels conference, and the enlargement of the Anti-Comintern Pact on 6 November beyond Germany and Japan to include Italy. In an editorial at the end of November the *New York Times* argued that 'the impotence of the Brussels conference' resulted from the fact that the US had lost its leadership in world affairs because 'treaty-breaking Governments and dictators have become convinced that for no cause short of actual invasion will the United States initiate or join in any effective movement to assure world peace'. FDR's Quarantine speech and the State Department's naming of Japan as the aggressor in China meant that 'a wholesome fear arose in certain capitals that the Neutrality

Act might not represent enduring policy for the United States'. But these steps had been undermined by pacifists and isolationists in and out of Congress.[27]

The remedy for this 'ostrich policy', according to the editorial, was for the US to react to the extension of the Anti-Comintern Pact by making 'a tangible expression of the determination of this country to stand by the democracies should the need arise'. An Anglo-American trade agreement would be a contribution to this end, but 'this should be supplemented by every possible kind of private and public cooperation between Britons and Americans and others who speak, if not the same language, at least the same spiritual tongue'. The 'enemies of peace' should be put on notice that 'the great democracies' were aware of what they were planning and would stand together to guard against it. 'The sure shadow of economic starvation' would be an effective deterrent 'without resort to the substance of sanctions or war'. If cooperation between the democracies was 'publicly revealed', the nation would rally behind the Administration and a clear warning would be sent to the dictators. Such a warning should be made sooner rather than later. In other words, what was required was not some kind of tacit understanding between Washington, London and Paris but an explicit show of solidarity.[28]

Panay crisis

The campaign being waged by the *New York Times* for a more active foreign policy was welcomed by Hull and other Administration officials and received added impetus with the onset of the *Panay* crisis, which renewed US criticism of Japan and revived the prospect of Anglo-American cooperation in the Far East. On 12 December 1937 the US gunboat *Panay* was attacked and sunk by Japanese planes and three Standard Oil Company tankers were destroyed on the Yangtze River, near Nanking. The planes also shot at the survivors, killing three of them. The *Panay* was then boarded by Japanese Army motorboats although the American markings on the ship were perfectly clear. Two British gunboats, HMS *Ladybird* and HMS *Bee*, also came under fire as they approached the scene, although they did not sustain serious damage and helped to pick up survivors from the *Panay*. The State Department made a strongly worded protest to the Japanese

Government and Roosevelt, 'deeply shocked', asked Morgenthau to 'find out what authority he needed as President to take possession of all the belongings of the Japanese Govt and its citizens in the US and hold them against payment for the damages the Japanese had done'.[29]

Morgenthau, impatient as ever with Hull and the State Department, was delighted when his trusted aide, Herman Oliphant, pointed out that a 1933 amendment to the Trading with the Enemy Act would allow the President to prohibit or restrict exchange transactions by Japan. He relayed this to Roosevelt and also telephoned Simon to share the idea with him. The President mentioned the Trading with the Enemy Act at his weekly Cabinet meeting on Friday, 17 December. When Vice President Garner said only military force would stop Japan, Roosevelt replied that he thought that economic sanctions ought to work. 'We don't call them economic sanctions; we call them quarantines,' he said. 'We want to develop a technique which will not lead to war. We want to be as smart as Japan and as Italy. We want to do it in a modern way.' According to Ickes, he had in mind a blockade of Japan by the US and Britain in the Pacific – west of the Hawaiian islands and north of the Philippines. 'Blocked thus, the President thinks that Japan could be brought to her knees within a year.' Ickes also noted: 'The President believes that between the three "bandit" nations, Germany, Italy, and Japan, there exists a secret agreement delimiting their spheres of influence'. These spheres comprised Central and Eastern Europe for Germany, North Africa and the Mediterranean for Italy, and Asia for Japan.[30]

The *Panay* crisis revived the possibility of closer Anglo-American cooperation against Japan, albeit still along 'parallel' lines. As Hull said to Lindsay: 'you may talk about parallel or similar action, or about constant or even close collaboration, but never use the word joint'. FDR acted quickly to arrange a secret meeting with Lindsay, after a White House reception on 16 December. He then raised the question of Anglo-American staff conversations. 'He wanted an arrangement such as prevailed from 1915 to 1917 . . . by which a systematic exchange of secret information had been established between the Admiralty and Navy Department,' reported Lindsay. FDR had been Assistant Secretary of the Navy at the time and felt that these conversations had been very effective. The officers concerned would have to be up to date regarding naval planning and it would probably be safest for the talks to take place in London.

The President then went into what Lindsay described as his 'worst inspirational mood', saying that the first object of staff conversations should be to arrange for a blockade or 'quarantine' of Japan. This blockade was to be shared by Britain and the US and its aim was to cut Japan off from raw materials. 'He denied that a blockade like this meant war,' added Lindsay, as under the US Neutrality laws, the President was able to decide whether or not there was actually a war.[31]

Roosevelt further suggested that a naval rendezvous, planned to begin at Hawaii in March 1938, might be brought forward by a couple of months and he agreed with Lindsay that a visit to Singapore would be a good idea. Lindsay said Britain might be able to commit some capital ships for a rendezvous, but the President thought it would be better for Britain to keep her best ships available for action in Europe. As Lindsay wrote to the Foreign Office,

> From the foregoing you may think that these are the utterances of a hare-brained statesman or of an amateur strategist, but I assure you that the chief impression left on my own mind was that I had been talking to a man who had done his best in the Great War to bring America in speedily on the side of the Allies and who now was equally anxious to be able to bring America in on the same side before it might be too late and if it should be necessary.

Lindsay added: 'The utmost friendliness was implicit in everything he said and I myself reciprocated with the utmost frankness.' The *Panay* crisis and the 'embitterment of American relations with Japan' had helped 'to bring us and America together', Lindsay concluded, 'and this is of inestimable value'.[32]

Parallel Action Revisited

The response of the Foreign Office to Lindsay's report of his meeting with Roosevelt was very typical of how the American President was regarded in London – rather mercurial and naïve but ultimately full of goodwill. 'If the Americans are to be induced to take a hand in anything, they have, I think, usually to be led in the first instance to formulate some idea which they can think of and represent to others as spontaneously conceived by themselves without any aid or prompting from anyone else. The plan sketched out by the President may be a fantastic chimera as it stands, but it has the supreme merit of being his, the President of the USA's own creation. With care and patience on our part it should not be impossible to preserve the lion's head while yet transforming the goaty body into something more congruous.' Cadogan, the Under Secretary at the Foreign Office, agreed. While FDR's plan seemed 'rather naïve if we wish to secure the President's cooperation (or rather "parallel" action), we should strike while the iron is hot and, while he is in this mood, try to keep him up to the mark'.[33]

Eden was pleased with Lindsay's report of his meeting with FDR, which 'seems at least to show the goodwill of the President, though it did not, and perhaps cannot at this stage, formulate any definite plan'. He asked Lindsay to tell the President that 'HMG are most gratified to find that his views on the international outlook are very similar to their own.' He said he would be delighted to receive the US naval emissary in London. In the meantime, he believed that 'some preparatory action by the two fleets now, even though such action were parallel and not joint, would be of the greatest advantage in restraining Japan'. He noted the warnings from the President and Hull about the danger of speaking of 'joint action' and said the Government 'would in all circumstances try to avoid that pitfall'. The Foreign Secretary concluded: 'It would I suppose, be better to represent any action that we each may be able to take as prompted by determination of each country to protect its own interests.' Thus Eden was now mindful of the need to avoid any impression of trying to entangle the US through 'joint' rather than 'parallel' action.[34]

This was the background to a significant debate in the House of Commons on 21 December 1937. Attlee, Sinclair and Churchill all spoke in favour of cooperation with the League and the US in the Far East and denied that this would lead to war with Japan. Chamberlain rejected this viewpoint – which was the same as the President's – although he was careful to stress the Government's cooperation with the US Administration. 'The Opposition are living in an unreal world,' he said. 'They are trying to put upon a mutilated League, duties which it is not able to perform as it is constituted at present.' He said the policy advocated by Labour and the Opposition was likely to lead to war. The Brussels conference had failed as Japan had refused to attend or cooperate. 'There was only one way in which the conflict could have been brought to an end, as it proved, and that was not by peace, but by force.' Although the outcome of the conference was disappointing, he added, 'we found ourselves in complete and harmonious agreement with the delegation of the United States of America on all the matters we discussed'.[35]

Eden was more conciliatory and agreed that it was necessary to work with the League. But his main emphasis was on cooperation with the US, which he said was a source of real satisfaction and which he referred to so warmly that his words later came to the attention of Borah and the isolationists in Congress. He stated:

> It is the fact that we are constantly and daily in close consultation with the Government of the United States. Over and over again we have taken either parallel or similar action, and that in itself is an indication of the closeness of such collaboration. I cannot say more on that subject to-night, but I would say this. It would be wrong, with the world as it is to-day, if we were to deny our own authority or belittle the firmness and the significance of our friendships. This country is not without friends in the world to-day.

There was 'no question of a treaty or of entanglement', Eden added, but there was 'a true community of outlook' which would prove 'an invaluable asset' in the maintenance of peace.[36]

Eden also gave an optimistic account of FDR's meeting with Lindsay to the Cabinet, including the President's proposals regarding the need for naval staff talks and moving the US fleet early to Hawaii, and visiting Singapore. 'It was clear that President Roosevelt was doing his best to mobilise his public opinion,' Eden said. There was unlikely to be any immediate action, but 'the President's attitude was an encouraging feature in the situation'. However, Chamberlain clearly saw FDR's attitude as being too close for comfort to the views of the Opposition, including Churchill. 'Our difficulty was not in President Roosevelt's good will, but in his failure to appreciate the needs of the situation,' he said. While any 'simultaneous demonstration of force by the United States and ourselves, whether in the Far East or even at a distance, would have a steadying influence', Roosevelt and Morgenthau 'were still contemplating the possibility of sanctions without war, and it was necessary to convince them that it was impossible to apply a blockade without being ready to support it by force, if necessary'. The Government's efforts, therefore, must be directed towards bringing home to the President 'the realities of the strategical position'. Thus whereas Eden viewed Roosevelt's attitude as full of promise, Chamberlain felt that the President – like Churchill and the Labour and Liberal Opposition – was being unrealistic.[37]

Eden was further encouraged in hoping for US support by the appearance of another significant editorial in the *New York Times*, on 24 December, which was sent to him by Lindsay as the end of the year. The editorial, apparently written by Walter Lippmann, the influential columnist, argued strongly in favour of 'parallel action' as an effective means of Anglo-American cooperation in the Far East. 'The two great democracies are moving in parallel lines in order to restore order, decency and safety in the world', it said. 'The parallel course is as sensible as it is strong. Self-interest automatically suggests it, and world peace requires it'. American politics and 'traditions' meant that the US could not engage in 'joint action', but 'parallel action' could be just as effective in acting as a warning to Japan, especially if other countries such as France and the Netherlands followed suit and advantage was taken of the democracies' control over credits and raw materials. However, dissension had to be avoided. British politicians who criticised the US government for declining joint action should recognise the faults of their own policies, while at the same time it had to be acknowledged that isolationism and pacificism in the United States had contributed to international lawlessness. It was therefore time for 'these two democracies to understand each other's difficulties and move sympathetically to surmount them'.[38]

The *New York Times* editorial was welcomed by most of the British press, both on the right and more especially on the left. The London *Times* argued that Japanese recklessness had brought the US and Britain closer together. The *Daily Telegraph* felt that the call for 'parallel action' would be welcomed in Britain because it suggested that the peaceful aims of the two democracies in the Far East were the same. The *Daily Herald* – traditionally supportive of the Labour Party – said that this spirit of Anglo-American cooperation in the US was a new development that 'any would-be aggressor must take into account'. But it added that this cooperation was 'easily capable of being killed' if the British Government did not respond positively to US desires for a trade agreement or if it failed to honour 'the principles and obligations of the covenant of the League'. The Liberal *News Chronicle*, like the *Daily Herald*, reproduced the *New York Times* editorial in full and entirely agreed with the argument that parallel or joint action between the democracies was the one thing that Japan and the fascist powers in Europe really feared. It also agreed that if the democracies cut off the supply of credits and raw materials to the militaristic states 'the bubble of aggression would be pricked'.[39]

The view from Berlin

In December 1937 Ambassador Dieckhoff sent a significant report to Berlin entitled 'American foreign policy – isolation or action?' Convinced that the *New York Times* editorial on 30 November was the 'opening shot' of a counter-attack by the interventionists and had been 'inspired by the State Department', he argued that while isolationism was still strong, isolationists and pacifists had no love for Germany, Italy or Japan. The internationalist thesis that 'the US could not remain unaffected by a future world conflict and that isolationism was therefore a utopia' had gained considerable ground since Roosevelt's Quarantine speech, he warned. 'We must not count on American isolationism as an axiom.' The US would continue to follow 'an essentially passive foreign policy as long as Britain is not prepared to become active herself, or as long as the US is not subjected to intolerable provocation, or values which vitally concern the US are not at stake', he said. However, 'should any of these occur, the US, despite all resistance within the country, will abandon its present passivity. In a conflict in which the existence of Great Britain is at stake America will put her weight on the scales on the side of the British.'[40]

On 20 December 1937 Dieckhoff sent another important despatch to Weizsächer, the Head of the Political Department at the German Foreign Ministry in Berlin. Looking back upon seven months in Washington, he reported that his interviews with the President had been 'frank and illuminating' and that, while Hull was 'an idealist who lives somewhat up in the clouds', he had a good formal relationship with the Secretary. He said he could also work 'harmoniously' with Sumner Welles. However, there had been no progress in improving relations between Germany and United States because US foreign policy was decided by public opinion and Germany was regarded as becoming an 'aggressor state' that constituted 'a constant threat to the peace of the world'. Interventionists in the United States were saying 'Wake up, America!' and British propaganda was working to the same effect.

There were very few voices raised on Germany's behalf. Dieckhoff also pointed out that ideological factors were coming to the fore – especially democracy versus totalitarianism, freedom versus despotism, and Christianity versus 'neopaganism'.[41]

Equally disturbing, Dieckhoff added, the impression had become prevalent in America that 'both Germany and Italy have given up their previous postulate that National Socialism and Fascism were not for export'. This impression had resulted partly from the activity of the German–American Bund 'and the suspicion that this activity is promoted by Germany'. Developments in Brazil and other South American countries had increased American fears that the ideology of Nazism and Fascism was spreading to the Western Hemisphere. 'Here, too', Dieckhoff said, 'the cry rings out: "Wake up, America!".' The departing Ambassador felt the situation was not yet hopeless, but the trend was clear and it was making Germany's position in the United States unfavourable. 'It may be argued that it is a matter of indifference to us what the American public thinks of Germany,' Dieckhoff said. 'But I believe that we should remember that once before, only 20 years ago, the development of unfavourable public opinion in America proved fateful for us.' Since then, Dieckhoff pointed out, the United States had 'grown even stronger and all rumours about social dangers, economic decline, etc., at least as far as the next few years are concerned, are pure fantasy. A conflict with this country would, therefore, be a very grave matter for us.'[42]

Dieckhoff's warning was one of many sent to Berlin from the Washington Embassy pointing out the direction of US foreign policy following the Quarantine speech. However, Hitler and the Nazi leadership also received alternative interpretations of US policy. Soon after the Quarantine speech the Foreign Ministry was sent a memo from the German Chancellery, enclosing a treatise by Baron von Rechenberg entitled 'Roosevelt – America – a Danger' for information. The accompanying note said that 'The Fuhrer and Chancellor has read this treatise with great interest. It is sent to you by his personal order.' Hitler evidently thought highly of the document, which accused Roosevelt of undermining American stability and being in the thrall of Jews and Communists, paving the way for Communism to take power in the USA. Needless to say, the German Foreign Ministry was highly critical of this document, which was contrary not only to the reports of the Washington Embassy but also to the impressions of Captain

Fritz Wiedemann, Hitler's personal adjutant, who had recently visited the United States with his wife. 'Apparently, however, their persuasive power was somewhat diminished by the R[echenberg] treatise,' Weizsächer lamented. Hitler continued largely to ignore the United States until the outbreak of war in September 1939.[43]

Notes

1. For text of Quarantine speech, 5 October 1937, see Miller Center collection: <https://millercenter.org/the-presidency/presidential-speeches/october-5-1937-quarantine-speech>.
2. Ibid.
3. Schmitz, *Triumph of Internationalism*, pp. 50–4; FO/371/20668, A7653/542/45, Mallet to Eden, 19 October 1937; for FDR fireside chat, 12 October 1937 see Miller Center: <https://millercenter.org/the-presidency/presidential-speeches/october-12-1937-fireside-chat-10-new-legislation>.
4. Chamberlain speech at Guildhall, *The Times*, 10 November 1937; for Halifax visit see Roberts, *Halifax*, pp. 64–75.
5. Mackenzie King Diary, 29 July 1937 and 20–21 October 1937; Hull, *Memoirs I*, visit to Ottawa, 20–22 October 1937; FO/371/20663, A7663/228/45, Mallet to Eden, 26 October 1937; FO/371/20663, A7664/228/45, minute by W.D. Allen, 27 October 1937.
6. See Dallek, *FDR*, pp. 145–8 for Sino-Japanese War; Ickes diary entry for 19 September 1937 (Ickes, *Diary*, II, pp. 209–14) – referring to Cabinet meeting on Tuesday, 14 September 1937.
7. Ickes, *Diary*, II, 9 October 1937, pp. 221–7.
8. FDR, Press Conference, <https://www.presidency.ucsb.edu/node/208847>.
9. *NYT*, 7 October 1937, Bertram D. Hulen; Hull, *Memoirs I*, p. 545.
10. *NYT*, 7 October 1937.
11. *NYT*, 6 October 1937.
12. FO/371/20668, A7186/7236/448/45, Mallet to Eden, 5 and 6 October 1937; Ibid., A7543/542/45, Mallet to Eden, 12 October 1937.
13. Murray papers, Box 8809, Roosevelt to Murray, 7 October 1937; CAB 23, 36 (1937), item 5, 6 October 1937.
14. Ibid.
15. Chamberlain and Eden speeches, *The Times*, 9 and 16 October 1937.
16. DBFP/2/XXI, doc 301, Mallet to Eden, 12 Oct 1937; Roosevelt papers, PSF, Box 95, Welles file, memo by Welles, 6 October 1937.
17. Hull, *Memoirs I*, pp. 546–9.
18. *NYT*, 7, 14 and 15 October 1937; also see Liebich, *Wickham Steed*.

19. FO/371/20663, A7441/228/45, Mallet to FO, 13 October 1937; FO minutes by Holman, 18 October, Vansittart, 14 October 1937. See also Ovendale, 'Appeasement', pp. 73–4.
20. DBFP/2/XXI, doc 304, 13 Oct 1937; CAB 23, 37 (1937), item 5, 13 October 1937.
21. CAB 23, 38 (1937), item 4, 20 October 1937; DBFP/2/XXI, doc 383, Sir R. Clive to Eden – from MacDonald, 22 November 1937.
22. CAB 23, 43 (1937), item 5, 24 November 1937; Mackenzie King Diary, 20–21 October 1937.
23. Mackenzie King Diary, 20 and 21 October 1937.
24. PREM/1/229, Tweedsmuir to Chamberlain, 25 October 1937; Ibid., comment in margin by Chamberlain (undated but probably 9 November 1937). See also MacDonald, 'Economic Appeasement and the German "Moderates"', pp. 105–35.
25. PREM/1/229, note by Sir Horace Wilson, 9 November 1937. Ibid., Chamberlain to Tweedsmuir, 19 November 1937.
26. CAB 23, 39 (1937), item 7, 27 October 1937; FO/371/20664, A7894/228/45, Lindsay to Eden, 3 November 1937; Ibid., A8000/228/45, Eden to Lindsay, 8 November 1937; Ibid., A8240/228/45, Lindsay to Eden, 16 November 1937; Kottman, *Reciprocity*, pp. 183–215.
27. *NYT* editorial, 30 November 1937.
28. Ibid.
29. *NYT*, 3 and 4 December 1937.
30. Blum, *Morgenthau Diaries I*, pp. 479–89; DBFP/2/XXI, doc 437, Simon to Chamberlain, 18 December 1937, with enclosures of Simon conversation with Morgenthau, 17 December 1937 and Eden to Chamberlain, 19 December 1937; Ickes, *Diary*, II, 18 December 1937, pp. 273–6.
31. DBFP/2/XXI, doc 433, Lindsay to Eden, 17 December 1937; FO/371/20665, A9142/228/45, Lindsay to Eden, 17 December 1937 for Hull quote.
32. DBFP/2/XX1, doc 402, Eden to Lindsay, 6 December 1937; doc 442, Lindsay to Eden, 22 December 1937; doc 445, Lindsay to Cadogan, 22 December 1937.
33. DBFP/2/XXI, doc 433, footnote 7, FO minutes by Ronald and Cadogan, 19 December 1937.
34. DBFP/2/XXI, doc 441, Eden to Lindsay, 20 December 1937.
35. Chamberlain speech, *Hansard*, House of Commons debate, 21 December 1937.
36. Ibid., Eden speech, 21 December 1937.
37. CAB 23, 48 (1937), item 5, 22 December 1937.
38. *NYT* editorial, 24 December 1937.
39. *NYT*, 28 December 1937, 'Parallel action praised in Britain'.

40. DGFP/D/I, doc 423, Dieckhoff to GFM, 7 December 1937.
41. Ibid., doc 427, Dieckhoff to GFM, 20 December 1937.
42. DGFP/D/I, Ibid.
43. DGFP/D/I, doc 416, State Secretary (Willuhn) to Foreign Minister and Reich Propaganda Minister, 15 October 1937; doc 417, memorandum by Davidsen, Berlin, 28 November 1937; doc 420, Dieckhoff to GFM, 24 November 1937; doc 427, Dieckhoff to GFM, 20 December 1937; doc 433, Weizsächer to Dieckhoff, 18 January 1938.

6 Roosevelt Initiatives, January–February 1938

On the evening of 11 January 1938, Sumner Welles gave Sir Ronald Lindsay a highly secret message from Roosevelt to Chamberlain. The President, 'being deeply impressed by the progressive deterioration of the international situation, proposed to take an initiative along the only lines which, in the state of public opinion in the U.S.A., were open to him'. This initiative was meant to be an action 'parallel to the efforts' of the British Government to maintain peace in Europe, he said. The proposal was being shared only with the British and no other government was to be informed about it. Roosevelt would proceed with the scheme only if he received Chamberlain's assurance – no later than 17 January – that it would meet with 'the cordial approval and wholehearted support of H.M.G'. In that case, on 20 January, he would alert the governments of France, Germany and Italy – as well as Britain – to the details of the scheme. Finally, on 22 January, Roosevelt would announce his plans to the diplomatic corps at an event that would take place at the White House.[1]

The so-called 'Roosevelt initiative' essentially consisted of a plan whereby the four European Great Powers would be asked to agree to a conference of neutral states in Washington that would discuss some of the basic issues affecting the current world situation. The conference would aim to put forward recommendations for all states, including these powers, to agree upon. The issues included the 'fundamental principles' governing international relations, disarmament, access to raw materials and the rights of neutrals in wartime. The neutral states suggested were Sweden, the Netherlands, Belgium, Switzerland, Hungary, Yugoslavia, Turkey and three Latin American countries. If the American plan proved acceptable, the President would be happy to cooperate in achieving 'the attainment of the objectives sought'. This rather convoluted scheme reflected several of the main themes in US foreign policy at this time. Firstly, it was communicated to the British Government, before any other, thereby demonstrating the primacy of London in US foreign policy. Secondly, it was in keeping with the American preference for 'parallel action' with Britain, as opposed to 'joint action'. Thirdly, the message referred to the initiative being shaped by 'the constraints of public opinion on US freedom of action'. Indeed, the conference was intended to focus on economic issues rather than political ones, which would have made Washington's role more controversial in the United States, but each issue had an obvious political dimension.[2]

Isolationism versus internationalism

The main aim of this chapter is to examine the significance of the 'Roosevelt initiative' in the context of isolationist fears of an Anglo-American 'tacit alliance' following the President's Quarantine speech. In fact, the proposed conference was but one of several American initiatives in the new year, both public and private, which, taken together, suggest that Roosevelt remained determined to exert whatever influence he could in heading off a major international conflict. His fear of such a conflict could be seen in his annual address to Congress on 3 January 1938, which was broadcast via the radio to the rest of the world. FDR reiterated his well-known view that 'world peace through international agreements is most safe in the hands of democratic representative governments' and said that in spite of America's determination for peace, the acts and policies of other countries had had far-reaching effects, not only on their neighbours but on the United States. Americans had been leaders in disarmament but, he added, with growing tension in the international situation 'we must keep ourselves adequately strong in self-defence'. This comment proved to be the prelude to a significant message on defence delivered later in the month.[3]

Lindsay pointed out that although the section in the address on foreign policy was short, it had come first. He then stressed the President's reference to peace being safest in the hands of the democracies. One Foreign Office official rather optimistically minuted that 'President Roosevelt's attitude of disapproval towards the totalitarian states cannot fail to exercise a check upon them.'

Lindsay also commented upon press coverage of the speech, especially in the *New York Times*, which, he said, was anxious to promote Anglo-American cooperation and therefore tended to play it up. On this occasion, the newspaper had said that the British had turned their attention from Europe to the American continent and so they were especially interested in the President's speech. Lindsay himself was worried that the economic recession that had gripped the US since late 1937 might hamper FDR's foreign policy and reduce his influence in maintaining world peace.[4]

The new year also found Mackenzie King contemplating the contribution that Canada might make to the preservation of world peace. The previous year, 1937, had been particularly significant for the Canadian Prime Minister, who was always aware of his heritage, especially the central part played by his grandfather, William Lyon Mackenzie, in the rebellions of 1837. Mackenzie King saw his meetings with leading statesmen in 1937 – including Roosevelt, Hull, Chamberlain and Hitler – as being part of his contribution to world peace, and he was anxious to follow up this 'annus mirabilis', as he termed it, by contributing to 'the goodwill of nations' in the new year. He saw 1938 as 'a new beginning'. Canada's mission was to lead the nations of the world 'into the paths of peace'. He thought that it ought to be possible to achieve international appeasement if the British Government pursued friendship with both Germany and Italy, and that London had 'missed chances of having Italy's friendship' because of the English sense of 'superiority'. Judging from his diary, while Mackenzie King was hopeful that economic appeasement as advocated by Hull would contribute to European peace, he clearly felt that the ball was in London's court as far as improving relations with Rome and Berlin was concerned.[5]

Shanghai incident

On 7 January two British policemen were assaulted by Japanese forces in Shanghai, reviving memories of the attack on the British Ambassador in August 1937. The 'Shanghai incident' led to renewed calls in London for further action against Japan. In Eden's absence on holiday, Cadogan conferred with Chamberlain and Lord Chatfield about the possibility of a strong naval demonstration as a warning to Japan. Lindsay was asked to check whether

Washington would take 'any parallel action', such as 'sending an advance force of cruisers, destroyers and submarines to Hawaii and the rest of the fleet to Pacific ports' to support a British move. Chamberlain apparently saw this as an initiative to spur the US Government into action in the Far East. As he wrote to his sister Hilda,

> I am trying to jolly them along with a view to making some sort of joint (or at least 'parallel') naval action. They are incredibly slow and have missed innumerable busses . . . I do wish the Japs would beat up an American or two! But of course, the little d—v—ls are too cunning for that, & we may eventually have to act alone & hope the Yanks will follow before it's too late.[6]

Cadogan accordingly asked Lindsay about the likelihood of Roosevelt declaring a 'state of emergency' as the prelude to a naval demonstration in the Far East, in the absence of a 'grave provocation'. He especially wanted to know how far any American action would be dependent on cooperation from Britain. Lindsay had already pointed out that Roosevelt was still 'educating' American public opinion. 'My impression is that the United States Government is at present a horse that will run best when the spur is not used,' he had told Eden. To Cadogan he replied that it was very unlikely that the US Government would declare a state of emergency without 'further grave provocation', which would have to affect 'American interests or honour'. If Washington took any action of a military nature, it would certainly expect similar and prior action by London. FDR was already ahead of public opinion – no more should be expected of him at this stage. The *Panay* crisis had made 'a profound impression which will not soon be forgotten' but American public opinion had moved on and was 'not likely to get excited over an assault on British policemen in Shanghai'.[7]

In fact, Washington was prepared to go a long way to meet the British request. On 10 January Welles told Lindsay that at a meeting between him, Hull and the President they had come up with the following plan. Firstly, FDR would announce that several cruisers on their way to Sydney would proceed to visit Singapore. Secondly, if the British Government issued a statement about naval preparations, the US would announce that vessels in the Pacific Fleet were 'scraping their bottoms': that is, taking preparatory action. Thirdly, the date for naval manœuvres in the

Pacific would be advanced to mid-February. When this plan was discussed by Cadogan, Chatfield and Chamberlain they decided not to proceed with a British naval demonstration. Chamberlain said he was against asking the Americans 'to commit themselves to any specific action in hypothetical circumstances and I am sure this would lead to nothing helpful. On our side I feel that this would be a most unfortunate moment to send the fleet away. . . .' Indeed, the Admiralty had earlier decided that it could not even spare ships to go to Sydney to meet the American ships there because of the situation in China and Europe. Thus it was clear that the British Government, no less than its American counterpart, was reluctant to commit its forces to the Far East at a time when the situation remained threatening in Europe.[8]

In the end, the Foreign Office sent a strong protest to Tokyo about the assault on the two policemen. Chamberlain also wrote to Lindsay, expressing gratitude for the President's earlier response. 'It is of great value to us to know what the US Government would be prepared to do in the event of our having to issue some statement,' he said. Welles replied that the State Department was happy to await the results of the protest to Japan before issuing its own statement. Washington would prefer to avoid simultaneous action, he explained, partly because of American public opinion and partly because it felt that the impression given to Japan was the same, regardless of whether the action was simultaneous or not. Despite this, Eden derived some satisfaction from the episode as he thought 'the fact that hostilities had not spread further south in China was due to an appreciation in Tokyo of the importance of growing cooperation between the US and UK'.[9]

Ingersoll naval mission

While Anglo-American cooperation improved in the Far East, an important step forward was being taken in London, in the form of the visit of Captain Royall Ingersoll, from the US naval planning department. In the wake of the *Panay* incident, and following Roosevelt's meeting with Lindsay on 16 December in which he proposed secret naval staff talks, Captain Ingersoll had been chosen for this sensitive task. FDR, Hull, Morgenthau and William Leahy, the US Chief of Naval Operations, met with Ingersoll at the White

House on 23 December 1937 and he left for England on the 26th, arriving in London on New Year's Eve. He had been given very little guidance from the President regarding the objectives of his mission beyond discussing naval plans with the British in the context of a possible conflict in the Far East, but Lindsay pointed out to London that the purpose of the staff talks was deliberately vague as the President wished to avoid 'any appearance of collusion or joint action'. He also pointed out that Roosevelt was largely influenced by his own personal recollection of Anglo-American naval talks prior to US entry into the Great War. These had begun with an exchange of naval information, but they had eventually included a wide range of intelligence. Lindsay thought that 'vagueness' might be an advantage as the British side could try to make the scope of the staff conversations 'as vast as possible'.[10]

When Eden and Cadogan met Ingersoll on 1 January the Foreign Secretary asked him to give more detail about the scope and purpose of his mission as set out by Roosevelt and Leahy. Ingersoll explained that he had no 'specific instructions' from the President or from Admiral Leahy but had been sent to 'exchange general information'. The American said that 'the President and Admiral Leahy thought we ought now to exchange information in order to coordinate our plans and would like to know what ours were. There were also a number of purely technical arrangements which should be made in advance of any cooperation in the Pacific.' He said that if his visit became known, 'which he hoped it would not, it had been arranged that it should be given out that he had come over in connexion with the Washington Naval Treaty'. Ingersoll's substantive discussions took place mainly with Admiralty staff, especially Captain Tom Phillips, who was also a planning officer and who he knew well from the London naval conference that took place in 1935–36.[11]

On 13 January Ingersoll and Phillips signed an agreed record of their conversations. The first part dealt with the composition, state of readiness and initial movement of the two fleets. Ingersoll provided a very detailed description of the US fleet and its state of readiness in terms of vessels in commission and personnel. He said it would be based at Honolulu and would be able to advance across the Pacific, although it was not envisaged that it would proceed immediately to Manila. Phillips said that the British Admiralty envisaged sending a large fleet to Singapore, although the base there would not be fully completed for another eighteen months. Both parties agreed that, as far as possible, the 'political and naval measures of each nation should be kept in step'; for example, the arrival of the British fleet at Singapore should be synchronised with that of the US fleet at Honolulu. It was assumed that all waters of the British Commonwealth, including the Dominions, would be available for US naval forces, and that all waters of the US, including the Philippines, would be available for the use of British naval forces.[12]

In the event of a blockade strategy against Japan, British naval forces were to look after the southern Pacific while US forces took care of the western Pacific up to the coast of North America. The US Navy would assume responsibility for the defence of the west coast of Canada. If Germany proved hostile, the British Navy would have to protect trade routes across the Atlantic. If Italy also became an enemy, the British Navy would have to hold the Suez Canal and Egypt to keep the Mediterranean trade routes open, while the French Navy patrolled the Western Mediterranean. In the event of a general European war, Britain would not be able to send a large fleet to the Far East and 'direct tactical cooperation between the US and British fleets' would be a necessity. In any case, arrangements for inter-communication between the British and US fleets would be required, such as the exchange of codes and re-cyphering tables between the two navies as well as liaison personnel, including naval officers who would be attached to the embassies in London and Washington 'for communication duties'.[13]

This record shows that the Ingersoll mission was of great importance in the evolution of Anglo-American cooperation in the late 1930s and the development of a 'tacit alliance', especially in naval strategy. The memorandum was naturally given a very limited circulation in London (the Prime Minister, Foreign Secretary and First Lord of the Admiralty) and Washington (the President and Admiral Leahy) in order to maintain top-level secrecy. Ingersoll expressed himself as very satisfied with his talks, and when he returned to Washington at the end of January Roosevelt and Leahy were also pleased with what had been accomplished. So too was Lord Chatfield, the First Sea Lord, although Eden would have preferred more immediate action on the part of the USA. Perhaps he should have been more careful what he wished for. Unbeknownst to the Foreign Secretary, a more immediate plan was being prepared in Washington, a plan that arrived in London on 11 January while he was on holiday in the South of France.[14]

Welles plan

The 'Roosevelt initiative' mentioned above, delivered by Welles to Lindsay on 11 January, was actually based on the 'Armistice Day' plan drawn up by Welles himself after the President's Quarantine speech. 'It is my belief', wrote Welles, 'that the proposal in itself will lend support and impetus to the effort of Great Britain, supported by France, to reach the bases for a practical understanding with Germany both on colonies and upon security, as well as upon European adjustments'. Indeed, the plan had a strong economic content and its reference to freedom of access to raw materials was in line with the work of the League and the Van Zeeland report, published in January 1938. But it was disliked by Hull on the grounds that its references to disarmament were unrealistic and that economic stability could best be promoted through his own trade agreements programme rather than through another world economic conference. Strong opposition from Hull was one of the reasons that the initiative was delayed until the new year. Indeed, Hull considered resigning at this time, according to his *Memoirs*, but decided to remain within the Administration. However, he insisted that the British Government should be consulted before any announcement in public was made.[15]

This was by no means the first time London had been informed by the Washington Embassy that Roosevelt was contemplating a conference and Chamberlain himself had been warned about this by the Foreign Office as long ago as November 1936. As before, Lindsay urged that the President's proposal should be adopted for the sake of Anglo-American relations. But, not surprisingly in view of his general outlook, the Prime Minister did not take to the American plan. He regarded it as a 'bomb' and feared that it might interfere with his moves to open up conversations with Berlin and Rome. He therefore replied to Roosevelt, without consulting Eden, welcoming the President's concern but saying that he would prefer the plan to be delayed while his own negotiations were proceeding, especially with Italy over the recognition of her conquest of Ethiopia. When Eden returned from his break in the South of France, he was mortified to learn that the Prime Minister had rejected Roosevelt's initiative. Chamberlain thereupon gave his rather grudging consent to the plan, but the President had already decided to postpone it and subsequent events – especially the *Anschluss* – overtook it.[16]

Roosevelt's reply to Chamberlain was, like the plan itself, drawn up by Welles. It thanked the Prime Minister for the information contained in his letter and agreed to defer the American initiative for a short while, pending the direct negotiations that Chamberlain intended to open with Italy and Germany. But it expressed concern at the idea of recognising the Italian conquest of Ethiopia, even though such a step might prove inevitable in due course. 'A surrender by His Majesty's Government of the principle of non-recognition at this time would have a serious effect upon public opinion in this country,' the American reply stated. It also asked that the President be kept informed of the negotiations with Italy and Germany. 'With regard to the political features of these negotiations, this Government of course has no connection.' But Washington wished to be kept informed about general issues related to 'the maintenance of international principles' and 'world appeasement', especially 'treaty rights and economic and financial questions'.[17]

Much has been written about the 'Roosevelt initiative'. Churchill declaimed: 'We must regard its rejection – and such it was – as the loss of the last frail chance to save the world from tyranny otherwise than by war.' On the other hand, Sir Samuel Hoare argued that FDR's postponement of the initiative showed he was not wedded to the plan. Indeed, had it gone into operation, Roosevelt would have encountered a great deal of opposition at home. The main casualty was Eden, who felt the American initiative should have been seized with both hands, and who resigned, partly for this reason, in February. This was a serious matter, but the initiative was not without positive results. It led to an arrangement, finalised between Welles and Lindsay on 25 January, that there should be a regular exchange of information and views regarding the European situation. As Lindsay reported, it was clear that the State Department was taking stock of the European crisis and was anxious to compare its own impressions with those of London. In the next few days, the Foreign Office supplied the American Embassy with information on Russia, the Anti-Comintern Pact, the Spanish Civil War and German policy towards Eastern Europe.[18]

The 'Roosevelt initiative' and the Ingersoll mission provide clear evidence of FDR's attempts to make American influence felt in both Europe and the Far East by following up his Quarantine speech behind the scenes. He also gave the go-ahead for a secret

French air mission to the US in January 1938. More overtly, on 28 January, he called for a 20 per cent increase in the size of the Navy as well as substantial increases in Army funding. In an effort to explain the Administration's foreign policy and, to some extent, his quarantine remark, FDR addressed Congress and said that while the US had sought disarmament for many years, armaments elsewhere were increasing at 'an unprecedented and alarming rate' while conflict was taking place in the Far East and in Europe. 'As Commander-in-Chief of the Army and Navy of the United States', he said, 'it is my constitutional duty to report to the Congress that our national defence is, in the light of the increasing armaments of other nations, inadequate for the purposes of national security and requires an increase for that reason.'[19]

In testimony before the House Naval Affairs Committee on 31 January 1938, Leahy argued that Germany, Italy and Japan, as well as Britain and France, were all engaged in rapid naval rearmament. The existence of 'an Italo-German-Japanese Anti-Communist Protocol', he said, had especially to be taken into account, because unless the Government embarked on a comparable increase in its Navy, the US would not be fully secure against attack from overseas. When asked about reports that 'an Anglo-American blockade of Japan was discussed earlier this month in London with British naval officers', Leahy said that the officer concerned, Captain Ingersoll, had gone to London for technical talks relating to the London naval agreement – which was the planned cover story in case news of the visit leaked out. Leahy played a very straight bat during most of his testimony but on Friday, 4 February, under sustained questioning from Republican senators, he agreed to make a statement in executive session, as long as absolute secrecy was maintained, because the matter was 'of vital importance to the interests and defence of the United States'. This naturally led to more questioning when he resumed his testimony on Monday, 7 February, and he was again forced to deny that there were any plans for joint action with Britain.[20]

'Tacit alliance' debate

FDR's defence message and Leahy's testimony sparked off a heated debate in the Senate on US foreign policy, especially in the Far East. On 1 February 1938 Senator William Borah, the leading isolationist in the Senate, accused the Roosevelt Administration of forming a 'tacit alliance' with the British Government. Borah made specific reference to Anthony Eden's comments in the House of Commons on 21 December, alluding to close consultation with the US regarding the threat from Japan to Western interests in the Far East. But he was also mindful of the President's defence message a few days before regarding a 20 per cent increase in the American Navy and reports that US and British representatives had held secret talks in London about Anglo-American naval cooperation in the Far East – a reference to the Ingersoll mission that Leahy was quizzed about. This circumstantial evidence aroused the suspicions of Borah, Johnson and their fellow isolationists that FDR's 'Quarantine' speech heralded a more interventionist policy by FDR and his Administration.[21]

Hiram Johnson also attacked the Administration when he called for a statement on US foreign policy in the light of the President's Quarantine speech, which, he said, had placed the US in a 'pusillanimous position' when the threat implied in the speech was not carried through at the Brussels conference. When Key Pittman, the Chair of the Senate Foreign Relations Committee, replied that there had been no change to the Administration's foreign policy, which was based on 'non-interference and non-intervention in the affairs of other governments', Johnson expressed scepticism and introduced a Senate resolution on 7 February, posing three questions: (a) 'whether or not any alliance, agreement, or understanding exists or is contemplated with Great Britain relating to war or the possibility of war'; (b) 'whether or not there is any understanding or agreement, express or implied, for the use of the navy of the United States in conjunction with any other nation'; (c) 'whether or not there is any understanding or agreement, express or implied, with any nation that the United States navy, or any part of it, should police, patrol or be transferred to any particular waters or any particular ocean'.[22]

FDR and Hull evaded answering these questions at their press conferences, but Hull wrote to Pittman on 8 February and said that the answer to each of Johnson's questions was an unequivocal 'no'. Thanking Hull for the prompt response to his resolution, Johnson replied:

> There were ugly rumours going about the Capitol and all through the country as to alliances, understandings, agreements and the like which might have been entered into by this country. We have now, in the way that is appropriate, the categorical and explicit denial of the Secretary of State in reference to all agreements, understandings and the like.

However, two days later the Senator was back on the offensive following the opening hearings on the Administration's Naval Bill, when there was further heated debate. Johnson said that new doubts had been raised and that he would ask Hull for 'a clear definition' of American policy and its objective as 'something the people were entitled to know'.[23]

This led to an important statement by Hull on US foreign policy in the form of an open letter to Congressman Louis Ludlow, who had proposed that a referendum should take place before war could be declared. Hull said that while the US had no intention of engaging in warfare it must use its influence 'to produce conditions of peace, order, and security in the world'. He said that it was common sense for nations that desired peace to cooperate in every practical way to achieve this end; otherwise, lawless nations would obviously be encouraged to disrupt the peace. Hull then stated the 'basic lines of action' underlining US foreign policy. 'This Government carefully avoids, on the one hand, extreme internationalism with its political entanglements, and, on the other hand, extreme isolation, with its tendency to cause other nations to believe that this nation is more or less afraid.' Beyond this, Hull said that US policy was to avoid 'any alliances or entangling commitments' but, where there were common interests with other countries, Washington would exchange information with the governments of those countries, confer with them, and, 'where practicable, proceed on parallel lines, while reserving freedom of action'.[24]

The 'puzzle of American foreign policy'

The debate on the existence or otherwise of a 'tacit alliance' with Britain was not confined to Congress and the State Department. The *New York Times*, a bastion of internationalism, also weighed in with an editorial that said that it was only sensible for the US and Britain to cooperate by taking 'parallel or similar action', as Eden had indicated on 21 December. This theme was taken up by the influential journalist Arthur Krock, writing in his regular column, 'In The Nation', that appeared weekly in the *New York Times*. Krock acknowledged that Pittman's answer to Johnson was 'not entirely consistent with FDR's quarantine speech'. Nor had the President challenged Anthony Eden's statement that the US had 'a particular relationship with the British nation'. Roosevelt had already 'disregarded the spirit of the so-called Neutrality law', he said, because abiding by it would mean that any quarantine would have to be applied equally to both 'treaty-breaking' and 'law-abiding' belligerents. In fact, Krock said, it was the existence of the Neutrality law, which was at odds with the Quarantine speech, that helped to explain 'the puzzle of American foreign policy' – a puzzle that had 'mystified more people than Mr Johnson, and was the basis for his question'.[25]

Arguing that the Neutrality laws were 'the handiwork of the powerful, if somewhat irreconcilable combination of isolationist and pacifist sentiment in the country, as reflected in Congress', Krock pointed out that this made it very difficult for the Administration 'to make a wholly candid statement of what our foreign policy really is'. He then put forward what he felt was 'a more explicit statement' of US policy. The starting point, he said, was FDR and Hull's fear that the current violation of treaties would lead to wars that were likely to involve the US. To avoid such involvement, the Administration had attempted to warn the 'treaty breakers' about the consequences of their actions – in the Quarantine speech, the US rearmament programme and 'the cautious diplomatic effort to move with Great Britain in parallel without adopting the course of joint action, perilous politically and in many other ways'. Krock therefore saw US policy as 'a mixture of practical measures and psychology, of executive action' that tried to work round the Neutrality Act but had to tread carefully as Congress was 'suspicious and pacifist' – a situation that was 'perfectly clear to the foreign nations which are the objects of the policy'.[26]

Krock continued this theme a week later, suggesting that Johnson and the isolationists wanted to make FDR 'watch his step in any dealings abroad'. According to Krock, they were 'suspicious of the President's aspiration to be a world statesman'. They thought he wanted to be seen by history as the statesman who had managed to avoid another world war 'when everybody else said it couldn't be done'. They did not think he could do this without 'involving the United States in dangerous commitments'. They did not want to make these commitments and feared they would lead to war rather than to peace. Nor did they think that FDR was 'as clever a diplomat as he thinks he is'. There was a suspicion in Congress, said Krock, that the Administration's naval programme contained 'more than the eye can see' and that American consultations with Britain and France – especially the former – had resulted in 'a firm prospect of parallel naval policy in the event of one of the only two wars the democracies can envisage at any time in the near future'.[27]

Krock felt that this suspicion was correct, and he hoped that it was. He said he was 'expertly informed that, should it at any time serve the common interests of the two great democracies, their navies would automatically complement each other in the Pacific'. Any such cooperation was likely to be based on 'a very private and common-sense understanding among experts and political realists'. Such an understanding would be 'hardly more than a wink or a nod' – a situation that irritated the isolationists and made them anxious, as they feared that 'to exchange even a wink with Great Britain' would involve the US in war. This suspicion, he said, was a legacy of the world war and the long-held view in the United States that 'British policy is always subtly selfish and British diplomacy is always superior to our own'. In addition, there was a 'strong belief in Congress that the President is a reckless adventurer in foreign affairs with a taste for dangerous histrionics'. As a consequence, he concluded, 'both the American people and Congress have a school-book distaste for cooperating with the British', even against dictators on behalf of democracy – a situation he thought the Fascist powers were doubtless aware of.[28]

Resignation of Eden

Krock had provided a masterly analysis of American policy towards Britain at the start of 1938 but this policy was thrown off course when the latent divisions on the British side came into the open with Eden's resignation on 20 February. Hull was clearly disturbed when the news broke that Eden had resigned, and laid down a strict 'no comment' rule for members of the State Department. At his usual press conference at noon on 21 February he said he was not yet in a position to make any comment – nor, indeed, on a speech by Hitler that occurred at the same time – a speech demanding the return of Germany's colonies, and rejecting the idea that she could be satisfied by financial loans from Britain or other countries. As it was Eden who had been named by Borah and Johnson as having told the House of Commons of an implied understanding between the US and Britain, there was naturally press speculation that this idea had been repudiated by Chamberlain. Eden's resignation also suggested that the isolationists' fear that London had been 'attempting to set up an anti-dictator bloc consisting of Britain, France and the United States' could now be allayed.[29]

Indeed, Eden's replacement as Foreign Secretary was Lord Halifax, a trusted colleague of the Prime Minister who had recently visited Göring in Germany to try to open up a dialogue with the Nazi leadership. Lindsay was asked to reassure the State Department that Eden's resignation had resulted from differences with Chamberlain over tactics rather than strategy, but he also confirmed that the appeasement of Germany was London's main priority. As Lindsay told Welles, 'the Prime Minister had determined to push actively for an understanding with Germany' and had instructed Sir Nevile Henderson, the British Ambassador in Berlin, to seek an interview with Hitler to ascertain the position regarding Germany's colonial ambitions and her attitude towards Central European appeasement. Lindsay added that the British Government would not be making any commitments at this time but merely wanted to understand the German point of view. Lindsay also said that any developments arising out of these conversations in Berlin would be reported to the US and that Washington would be kept fully informed as to what was going on. Nevertheless, the implication of an enhanced policy of appeasement was clear.[30]

From Paris, Bullitt reported that Chautemps, the French Prime Minister, believed that Hitler's speech of 20 February showed that he aimed to incorporate Austria and the Czech Sudetenland into the Reich and that the position of Austria was 'hopeless'. Chautemps said that Chamberlain had wanted to recognise the King of Italy as Emperor of Ethiopia in exchange for promises of good behaviour and a declaration regarding the withdrawal of volunteers in Spain, but Eden opposed this and therefore resigned. Chautemps thought Hitler's speech on 20 February made it clear that Germany and Italy would continue to support Franco and Chamberlain had been naïve in trusting Mussolini. Chamberlain had eliminated Eden, Vansittart and Cranborne (Eden's Parliamentary Under Secretary) from any influence in the Foreign Office, and it was therefore highly likely that Britain would be making significant concessions to Germany. Indeed, Bullitt reported that Chautemps believed 'Chamberlain contemplated with relative equanimity the control by Germany of Austria, Czechoslovakia, Hungary and Rumania'.[31]

Roosevelt's attitude to the European situation at this time can be seen from his reaction to Eden's resignation and the difference in policy between the Foreign Secretary and Prime Minister that led to it. John Cudahy, American Minister in Dublin, wrote to him on 1 March 1938 criticising Chamberlain's appeasement policy and saying that the Prime Minster was ready to make concessions to Mussolini before receiving anything in return, apart from promises, whereas Eden wanted specific benefits first. Chamberlain's policy therefore risked encouraging Mussolini – and Hitler – to demand more and more. Roosevelt complimented Cudahy on his analysis and repeated an analogy that had been put to him: 'If a Chief of Police makes a deal with the leading gangsters and the deal results in no more hold-ups, that Chief of Police will be called a great man – but if the gangsters do not live up to their word the Chief of Police will go to jail.' He then added: 'Some people are, I think, taking very long chances – don't you?'[32]

The view from Berlin

The German Foreign Ministry was fully aware that, whatever the view in London, there was growing hostility towards the Nazi regime in Washington. Luther's successor as ambassador to the United States, Hans-Heinrich Dieckhoff, reported that in his annual message 'the President stated again the propositions which he and Mr Hull have repeatedly expressed for months: that America could not remain unaffected by world events and hence could not pursue a policy of absolute isolationism'. The Ambassador continued: 'The familiar phrases about the need of maintaining and observing the fundamental principles of international law were likewise reiterated, as was the view that peace was chiefly threatened "by those nations where democracy has been discarded or has never been developed".' Dieckhoff argued that 'the foreign policy part of his speech with its sharp language – though less strong than his Chicago fanfare – has a double purpose – to create sentiment against the policy of absolute isolation and in favour of greater preparedness, especially a naval construction program'.[33]

In all his reports to Berlin Dieckhoff made it clear that relations between the US and Germany were deteriorating. 'Ideological differences have become even sharper. Jewish agitation goes on unchanged. Animosity in the liberal and Marxist camps has not diminished,' he said. In particular, the Church controversy in Germany had given many Americans the impression that the Government was attempting to solve religious problems through coercion. There was even a fear that Germany might turn away from Christianity – a course that would be regarded with 'apprehension and aversion' in the United States. 'Distrust and dislike of Germany have been intensified also by one-sided reports about German rearmament,' continued Dieckhoff, and the addition of Italy to the Anti-Comintern Pact between Germany and Japan in November 1937 had added to the growing sense of insecurity in the United States. Germany's partners were 'represented to the American people by the press here, day in and day out, as violators of treaties, disturbers of the peace, and aggressors', he pointed out.[34]

The activities of the German–American Bund added to anti-German sentiment, said Dieckhoff. In both Congress and the press, 'an ever louder alarm has been sounded against "Nazi activities" and against the "un-American activities" of the Bund'. These included 'uniformed parades, the use of the German flag, and summer camps', and there was a belief that these activities were being encouraged by Germany. As a result, American opinion believed that 'a systematic German attack on the American citadel is in progress, with the German element in the United States, or at least a part of it, playing the role of the Trojan Horse'. Thus the 'Nazintern' was being compared with the 'Comintern' and 'Berlin is said to be making use of the German–Americans' to undermine American democracy. Dieckhoff therefore warned Berlin that 'the danger of a change in American foreign policy from the former isolationism to a more active foreign policy – probably directed again, in the last analysis, against Germany – has of late grown greater, and we must therefore give redoubled consideration to discovering ways in which this danger can be met'.[35]

The Ambassador also reported to Berlin on the 'Tacit Alliance' debate in Congress. Referring to Hull's letter of 8 February to Pittman saying that no secret agreement existed between the American Government and the British or any other foreign government with regard to pursuing a common policy, he commented that 'hardly anyone here is under the illusion that this declaration, though perhaps literally true, means very much'. In 1917, he pointed out, 'there was in existence no agreement on the part of the American Government; nevertheless, the United States of America in due time joined the Allied Powers'. In Dieckhoff's view, despite 'the widespread indifference of the American people toward anything which does not directly concern America' and despite the opposition of the isolationists and pacifists, 'the American Government, should it so desire, will encounter no insuperable difficulties in again pushing this country into war at the psychological moment, just as quickly as in the World War, and perhaps even more quickly'.[36]

Berlin was naturally concerned about the trends identified by the Ambassador. The Foreign Ministry said it would act against the Bund and try to moderate the attitude of the German press to events in the US. Dieckhoff was subsequently able to inform Hull (on 28 February) that Reich Germans were not allowed to be members of the German–American Bund. In addition, Berlin would not allow any official or Party authorities to have links with the Bund and similar organisations, and the use of emblems of the German Reich would be prohibited to the Bund. As a result of these steps, the Foreign Ministry hoped that 'the American Government and the American public would now realise what great pains we were taking to improve the evidently unsatisfactory relations between Germany and the US'. Thus the Foreign Ministry in Berlin – fully aware of the danger for Germany of the enmity of US public opinion – was trying hard to mend fences with the United States. But, as so often, the efforts of German diplomats were to be undermined by disturbing events in Europe driven by the ambitions of the Nazi regime – including the decision to bring about an enforced union with Austria.[37]

Notes

1. CAB 23, 1 (1938), item 1, 24 January 1938.
2. Ibid.; see also Bennett, 'Roosevelt Peace Plan of January 1938', pp. 27–38.
3. FDR speech, 3 January 1938; *NYT*, 4 January 1938.
4. FO/371/21525, A519/64/45, Lindsay to Eden, 11 Jan 1938; FO/371/21527, A78/78/45, Lindsay to Eden, 3 January 1938; Ibid., A475/78/45, Lindsay to Eden, 11 January 1938; FO/371/21527, A298/78/45, Perth to Eden, 12 January 1938 – FO minute by Beith, 17 January 1938.
5. Mackenzie King Diary, 1 and 2 January 1938.
6. DBFP/2/XXI, doc 471, Eden to Lindsay, 7 January 1938; Neville Chamberlain papers, NC/18/1/1034, Neville Chamberlain to Hilda, 9 January 1938; Rock, *Chamberlain and Roosevelt*, p. 54.

7. DBFP/2/XXI, doc 471, Eden to Lindsay, 7 January 1938; doc 472, Lindsay to Eden, 8 January 1938; doc 463, Lindsay to Eden, 3 January 1938.
8. DBFP/2/XXI, doc 478, p. 645, Lindsay to Eden, 10 January 1938, plus notes 2 and 4; doc 480, Chamberlain minute, 11 January 1938; doc 467, Dominions Office to Australian High Commission, 4 January 1938.
9. DBFP/2/XXI, doc 481, p. 648, Eden to Lindsay, 12 January 1938; doc 482, pp. 648–9, Eden to Craigie (Tokyo), 12 January 1938; doc 485, pp. 650–1, Lindsay to Eden, 13 January 1938.
10. Leutze, *Bargaining*, pp. 22–8; DBFP/2/XXI, doc 463, Lindsay to Eden, 3 January 1938.
11. DBFP/2/XXI, doc 462, Eden to Lindsay, 1 January 1938.
12. DBFP/2/XXI, doc 486, pp. 651–6, Memorandum of agreed record of conversations between Ingersoll and Naval Staff at Admiralty, 13 January 1938.
13. Ibid.
14. Leutze, *Bargaining*, pp. 23–7; Reynolds, *Creation*, p. 60 and endnote 141; DBFP/2/XXI, doc 487, Eden to Lindsay, 14 January 1938; Pratt, 'Anglo-American Naval Conversations', pp. 754–63.
15. Roosevelt papers, PSF, Box 95, Welles file, memo by Welles, 10 January 1938; Hull, *Memoirs I*, pp. 546–8; for British reaction to Roosevelt initiative see Rock, *Chamberlain and Roosevelt*, pp. 55–77; McKercher, *Transition of Power*, pp. 253–6; Reynolds, *Creation*, pp. 31–3.
16. See Offner, *American Appeasement*, pp. 191–4, 218–32; Ovendale, '*Appeasement' and the English-Speaking World*, pp. 93–116; Feiling, *Neville Chamberlain*, p. 336; FRUS/1938/I, pp. 118–20, Chamberlain to Roosevelt, 14 January 1938.
17. FRUS/1938/I, pp. 120–2, Roosevelt to Chamberlain, 17 January 1938.
18. Churchill, *Gathering Storm*, p. 199; Templewood (Hoare), *Nine Troubled Years*, pp. 262–75; Earl of Avon (Eden), *Facing the Dictators*, pp. 586–606; FO/371/21525, A651/64/45, Lindsay to Eden, 26 January 1938; Ibid., minute by Sir A. Cadogan, 28 January 1938.
19. For FDR address see *NYT*, 29 January 1938.
20. *NYT*, 1 February 1938; *NYT*, 28 and 31 January; 1, 2, 3, 4, 7 February 1938.
21. See Chapter 1; *NYT*, 2 February 1938; FO/371/21525, A1081/64/45, Lindsay to Eden, 2 February 1938.
22. Senate debate; *NYT*, 2 and 8 February 1938; Hull, *Memoirs I*, pp. 574–5.
23. *NYT*, 9 and 11 February 1938.
24. Hull statement, 10 February 1938, *Memoirs I*, p. 574; *NYT,* 11 February 1938.

25. Editorial, *NYT*, 3 February 1938; Harold Hinton, *NYT*, 6 February; Arthur Krock, 'An Answer to Senator Johnson's Question', *NYT*, 3 February 1938.
26. Ibid.
27. *NYT*, Krock, 9 February 1938.
28. Ibid.
29. *NYT*, 22 February 1938; for Hitler's speech see <https://www.historycentral.com/HistoricalDocuments/Hitler'sSpeech.html>.
30. Roberts, *Halifax*, pp. 76–90; FRUS/1938/I, doc 12, Sumner Welles conversation with Lindsay, 3 March 1938.
31. FRUS/1938/I, doc 8, Bullitt to Hull, 21 February 1938.
32. Roosevelt papers, PSF: Ireland, Box 44, Cudahy to Roosevelt, 1 March 1938; Roosevelt to Cudahy, 9 March 1938; Rock, *Chamberlain and Roosevelt*, pp. 85–6.
33. DGFP/D/I, doc 429, Dieckhoff to GFM, 3 January 1938.
34. DGDP/D/I, doc 430, Dieckhoff to GFM, 7 January 1938.
35. Ibid.
36. DGFP/D/I, doc 440, Dieckhoff to GFM, 9 February 1938.
37. DGFP/D/I, doc 433, Weizsächer, Head of Political Dept, GFM, to Dieckhoff, 18 January 1938; Freytag (Counsellor of Legation), GFM memo, 24 February 1938. For Hitler's speech see note 29 above.

Part 3

Appeasement, 1938

7   *Anschluss*, March 1938–May 1938

'Hitler strikes again', declared the *New York Times* on 12 March 1938. Austria had fallen victim to 'a Germany in which democracy is dead and tyranny is master', it said. The suddenness of the *Anschluss*, the enforced 'union' of Austria with Germany, took most observers by surprise and brought the focus of international affairs back to Central Europe. It also confirmed the willingness of the Nazi regime to tear up existing agreements and to ignore international opinion. Enraged by the action of the Austrian Chancellor, Kurt von Schuschnigg, in calling a referendum to uphold his country's independence, Hitler ordered a Nazi takeover – a move that was aided by French political divisions and the British policy of appeasement. The London *Times* reaction to the *Anschluss* was not dissimilar to that of its New York cousin. The *Anschluss* was 'the latest and worst demonstration of the methods of German foreign policy', as it came at a time when there was the opportunity 'for a new approach to a settlement of Anglo-German relations'. It therefore dealt a blow to British policy 'by leaving it more than doubtful whether appeasement is possible in a continent exposed to the visitations of arbitrary force'.[1]

In Washington, all eyes were on British policy towards the *Anschluss* and Nazi Germany's future ambitions, which were likely to involve the German-speaking Sudetenland region of Czechoslovakia. But it soon became evident that Chamberlain and Halifax were prepared to accept the *Anschluss* as a fait accompli, although British policy towards the issue of the Sudetenland was less obvious. As Pierrepont Moffat put it, the 'British reaction . . . is, of course the key to the whole situation and with each day that passes it becomes clearer that England is willing to surrender Eastern Europe to German ambitions'. Indeed, on 12 March Lindsay informed the State Department that Britain would be accepting the *Anschluss*. Welles told Lindsay that FDR was 'revolted' by Germany's treatment of Austria and its leaders. But given the strength of isolationism in the US there was very little that he could do of a practical nature to aid Austria. Meanwhile, a statement by Halifax in the House of Lords on 16th March confirmed that Britain would not confront Hitler over the *Anschluss*.[2]

British appeasement

The primary aim of this chapter is to analyse the impact of the *Anschluss* on Anglo-American relations, especially its significance for the American policy of 'parallel action' and the British policy of appeasement. Coming so soon after Chamberlain had poured cold water on the President's proposal for a conference of neutrals, and Eden's resignation, the *Anschluss* provided an immediate test for the US policy of 'parallel action' – that is, aligning with Britain and France as far as possible. Borah, Johnson and other isolationists regarded this policy as tantamount to a 'tacit alliance' but 'parallel action' in Europe would be more difficult to justify to US public opinion than in the Far East, especially if British appeasement appeared to condone Nazi aggression. At a Cabinet meeting on 10 March Roosevelt had reported that Chamberlain's appeasement policy towards Germany was 'not going so happily', because of Hitler's demands for colonies. 'The President is of the opinion that if Hitler adheres to his position, Eden will be more than justified in his resignation and Great Britain will find itself in a difficult situation,' recorded Ickes. The *Anschluss* heightened the sense of crisis in Europe and presented problems for FDR, even though there could be no expectation that the US would intervene in European questions of a purely political character.[3]

Despite his disappointment – and annoyance – at the manner of the *Anschluss*, Chamberlain did not alter his conviction that the policy of appeasement was the correct one. He had only recently instructed Nevile Henderson, the British Ambassador in Berlin, to seek a personal interview with Hitler at which the Führer was informed of Britain's willingness to transfer some African colonies to Germany in return for reassurances such as a measure of disarmament, although nothing concrete had come out of the meeting. At an emergency meeting of the Cabinet on 12 March Chamberlain said he felt Schuschnigg had given Hitler an opportunity that he could not miss. However, 'the manner in which the German action in Austria had been brought about was most distressing and shocking to the world and was a typical illustration of power politics', he added. 'This made International appeasement much more difficult'. Chamberlain also observed 'how fortunate it was for President Roosevelt that he had held up the issue of his proposed message'. To his sister he wrote, 'What a fool Roosevelt would have looked had he launched his precious proposal. What would he have thought of us if we had encouraged him to publish it, as Anthony was so eager to do? And how we too would have made ourselves the laughing-stock of the world.'[4]

Chamberlain's policy of appeasement was fully supported by Mackenzie King, who felt that the German annexation of Austria constituted 'the darkest hour there has been in Europe since the Great War'. He feared that the *Anschluss* would lead to a European war if it was opposed by Britain and France, and was relieved that France was without a government at this time, which reduced the chance of a strong response by London. Nor did he think that the League had any useful role to play. In his opinion the League and the idea of 'collective security' had already wrought considerable mischief. 'It has been a millstone to bring down country after country who remains adhering with mere pretence to its Covenant.' He felt that Chamberlain had been right to move away from the League but that he had 'spoken out a little too late'. Mackenzie King took the view that for Britain to oppose Hitler over Austria or Eastern Europe was not worth the risk of a European war and the probable end of the British Empire. It was necessary to wait for the people in the countries with dictators to overthrow them – it could not be done from outside. The League was therefore based on a false premise as far as the Canadian Prime Minister was concerned.[5]

Chamberlain, Halifax and the *Anschluss*

In the days following the *Anschluss*, attention turned towards Czechoslovakia, which was now in the front line of German expansion eastwards, especially given the existence of the largely German-speaking Sudetenland. Chamberlain stated in a Commons debate on 14 March that the manner of the *Anschluss* was bound to prejudice relations with Germany and that the Government was reviewing its rearmament policy accordingly. But despite this the door was clearly left open for further appeasement as Chamberlain felt that his attempt to reach an understanding with Germany had been interrupted rather than abandoned. Rearmament was discussed at a regular meeting of the Cabinet on 14 March, prior to the Commons debate, and several ministers urged an acceleration of Britain's defence programme, including Hore-Belisha, Secretary for War, who quoted *Mein Kampf* and warned that Hitler's expansionist ambitions were clear for all to see. But other ministers such as Simon, the Chancellor of the Exchequer, saw no need for additional urgency. And Halifax said that 'the events of the last few days had not changed his own opinion as to the German attitude towards this country. He did not think it could be claimed that a new situation had arisen.'[6]

At a further Cabinet meeting on 22 March a report from the Chiefs of Staff made it clear that Britain and her potential allies could not save Czechoslovakia from certain defeat by Germany. The document made 'melancholy' reading, said Halifax. The idea of a guarantee to Czechoslovakia had seemed attractive but it would not save the Czechs and it would lead to a general war with Germany. France needed to be told this and public opinion needed to be prepared. It was also necessary to persuade the Czechs to come to terms with the Sudeten Germans. British air power was not yet sufficiently developed, and the state of the French Air Force and of Britain's anti-aircraft defences was 'deplorable'. Chamberlain added that Britain's existing plans for rearmament should be speeded up and an agreement with Italy obtained as quickly as possible. 'The conversations in Rome were proceeding with almost embarrassing ease and rapidity', he said, 'having regard to the statement to which the Government had committed itself over Spain.' However, the Civil War remained an issue, so 'the two Governments would have to trust one another'.[7]

As regards France, Chamberlain made a statement in the Commons on 24 March saying that, in the event of a conflict in Central Europe, it was 'well within the bounds of probability that other countries besides those which are parties to the original dispute' might become involved. This was taken in Paris as a pledge to come to the aid of France in the event of a war with Germany over Czechoslovakia – a step advocated by Churchill. This worried Halifax, who stated in Cabinet on 6 April that 'he had noticed, a tendency in France rather to over-rate the likelihood of our rendering assistance to that country in coming to the aid of Czechoslovakia'. He therefore intended to ask Sir Eric Phipps, the British Ambassador in Paris, to correct this view. At the next Cabinet, on 13 April, he said that 'the best policy appeared to be to discourage too broad an interpretation of the phrase' relating to British intervention when in Paris and Prague, 'while giving greater emphasis to it in Berlin'. By means of this policy of keeping both friends and foes guessing, he argued, 'it might be possible to bring both sides to reason'. Thus while the discussions in Cabinet suggested that the Government felt the need to avoid a clash over Czechoslovakia at almost any cost, in public its policy was very ambiguous.[8]

FDR, Hull and the *Anschluss*

According to Adolf Berle, an Assistant Secretary of State, the Department felt largely powerless in the wake of the *Anschluss*, especially in view of the British Government's rapid acceptance of the new status quo. 'The week has not produced much in Washington as we are practically confined to watching the course of European events without being able to affect their course,' noted Berle in his diary. 'The President wanted to issue some kind of statement at once; I gather a rather condemnatory statement. On Sumner's advice he withheld it for the time being.' According to Berle, 'The State Department is divided. About half of it is following a Wilsonian moral line which in my judgment would lead eventually to our entry into a war on the British side. The other half headed by Sumner and myself, is still endeavouring to steer matters into an ultimate conference,' which FDR had previously favoured. 'For the rest this job at the moment is a ringside seat at a slow movie watching Europe get ready to tear itself into pieces.' Berle evidently saw Welles, Moffat and himself as 'realists', in contrast to the Wilsonian 'idealists' led by Hull and no doubt including figures such as Norman Davis and George Messersmith, formerly US Ambassador to Austria and now an Assistant Secretary in the State Department. Both groups were vying for the President's attention.[9]

The immediate question for Washington after the *Anschluss* was whether to recognise the German annexation of Austria and how to register American displeasure. As well as the usual warnings from isolationists not to become involved in the affairs of Europe, there were calls by internationalist groups to invoke the Stimson doctrine of 1931 and not to recognise the takeover of Austria by Germany. If the new status of Austria was recognised, it would raise questions regarding the American recognition of Italy's conquest of Ethiopia and Japan's annexation of Manchuria. It might also allow German goods into the United States via Austria. However, non-recognition was not really practical, so instead the US Legation in Vienna was downgraded to a Consulate-General and most of the staff remained, including John Cooper Wiley, the American Chargé d'Affaires. In addition, the State Department removed Austria from the list of states receiving 'most favoured nation' status as from May 1938, in accordance with the Trade Agreements Act of 1934. An international conference was also organised at Evian, in Switzerland, to discuss how to aid the refugees – many of them Jewish – fleeing from Austria and Germany.[10]

Hull's statement on the *Anschluss*, at his regular press conference, was a masterpiece of under-statement. 'The extent to which the Austrian incident, or any similar incident, is calculated to endanger the maintenance of peace and the preservation of the principles in which this Government believes, is of course a matter of serious concern to the Government of the United States.' But he also made an important speech that was particularly welcomed by the Wilsonians in the Department, such as George Messersmith. No doubt with Chamberlain's rapid acceptance of the *Anschluss* in mind, Messersmith wrote to John Wiley in Vienna that, although the State Department was faced by some difficult decisions, 'you can take it that there will be no change in our policy no matter what may take place elsewhere'. Hull and the President were 'determined that we shall hold on to the line that we have taken. There will be no swerving from it in any detail.' Hull's speech 'should give all of our people abroad, as well as our people at home, a very clear conception of the broad lines of our policy to which we intend to adhere'.[11]

Hull's speech was delivered at the National Press Club in Washington on 17 March. It was approved in advance by the President, who wrote 'Grand!' on Hull's copy, and it was broadcast to a worldwide radio audience including Europe, South America and the British Empire. Hull's aim was clear – to repeat his warning to the dictator states that the United States might well become involved in any future conflict. Referring back to his early statements on American foreign policy, and especially the principles for peace that he had set out on 16 July 1937, he echoed the language of FDR's 'Quarantine' speech, pointing out 'how quickly the contagious scourge of treaty-breaking and armed violence spreads from one region to another'. In meeting this challenge, Hull said that the US Government was determined to steer 'a sound middle course' between the extremes of internationalism and isolationism. This meant proceeding along parallel lines with like-minded governments. In the Far East, the US had collaborated with other peace-seeking nations while avoiding alliances or involvement of any sort. 'The traditional US policy not to enter into entangling alliances or involvement with other countries had been maintained,' he said.[12]

At the end of his speech, Hull referred back to a key statement in Roosevelt's Quarantine speech. 'America hates war. America hopes for peace. Therefore, America actively engages in the search for peace.' The United States had to make a 'reasonable contribution' to 'a world order based on law' so as to uphold its own security. 'No other course would be worthy of our past, or of the potentialities of this great democracy of which we are all citizens and in whose affairs we all participate,' he said, clearly showing his Wilsonian outlook. 'Further than this speech we could not go,' Hull wrote in his *Memoirs*. He realised that the speech 'would not please an isolationist determined to confine us to our own shores'. Nor would it please the kind of internationalist who was 'determined to commit us to alliances'. But, he continued, the speech 'represented a positive foreign policy under which we could exert our influence, as well as our example, for peace, increase our strength, and render ourselves a factor that no aggressor could overlook in making his plans'.[13]

Hull's speech evidently pleased the internationalist *New York Times*, which took it as a sign that the President's idea of a defensive 'quarantine' against aggressor nations had not entirely disappeared from the Administration's foreign policy. 'No one knows today at what point Britain will draw the line of real resistance against an aggressive Germany,' it said in an editorial entitled 'Democracy and Dictatorship'. French opinion was divided and at home: 'the desire for peace is so compelling, and the belief that peace can be found through a policy of isolation is so widely shared, that the proposal for American participation in an international effort to uphold law and order – a proposal in which this paper has always believed and still believes – is at the moment out of the question'. Arthur Krock also commended Hull's speech and pointed out that nearly a week had passed since the Nazi takeover of Austria but pacifists and isolationists who had supported the Neutrality laws that 'tied the hands of the Administration' had remained silent while 'Hitler committed the grand larceny of Austria'.[14]

Hull's speech was also well received by the London *Times* and Halifax had the opportunity to comment on it when he spoke at the Pilgrims dinner, traditionally held in honour of the new US ambassador – in this case, Joseph Kennedy. According to the *Times*, Halifax said that the Secretary of State's words 'would find ready acceptance in the hearts of all English-speaking peoples'. It was a source of lively satisfaction to the people of Britain, he said, 'to know that on the other side of the Atlantic there remained a great and free nation with whom we shared many of the best things in life'. These things, Halifax continued, included 'that spirit of toleration which was won on both sides of the Atlantic after many a hard struggle'. It also included 'that firm belief in the ultimate responsibility of man to his own conscience'. Finally, it included 'that respect for justice both in relations with members of the same community and in the wider field of international relations' and 'a common agreement as to the foundations on which those wider relations between nations must be built'.[15]

In response, Joe Kennedy, the President's choice as ambassador following the death of Robert Bingham, adopted a more rugged style but the sentiments were similar. Saying that he favoured a 'frank and straightforward' exchange of views between the two countries, he added: 'I could talk to you for hours about the common heritage and the glorious heritage of the English-speaking peoples, but I believe we have come to take those things for granted.' He then continued, in more traditional style: 'Our two countries enjoy a relationship which is unique among the nations of the world. We should profit from that relationship. Few other nations can discuss their affairs without a mental reservation that war between them may one day be the deciding factor.'

Kennedy next made the point that the average American had two main fears at that time – the fear of losing a job and the fear that the US might become involved in war again. As regards the latter, FDR and Hull were trying to make the US position clear to the world. The United States would avoid entangling alliances, but it was not true to say that the US would never become involved in a future war or that the US was bound to become involved. The Administration hoped that war could be avoided but, if it came, 'the United States would decide its policy on the basis of its own national interests'.[16]

Anglo-Italian agreement

On 8 March, shortly before the *Anschluss*, the British Government opened discussions in Rome regarding the possibility of settling outstanding issues with Italy, including the conflict in Spain, in exchange for British recognition of the conquest of Ethiopia. This step had been advocated by the British Ambassador in Rome, Lord Perth, and Eden's opposition to negotiations with Italy or Germany until they had shown by their actions that they were serious about improving relations with Britain was one reason for his resignation in February. By contrast, his successor, Lord Halifax, agreed with the view that, as Britain would not be able to cope in a war against Germany, Italy and Japan, it was essential to lose no time in seeking a rapprochement with Italy. The talks mainly centred upon British concerns at Italian policy in the Middle East and the Mediterranean, while the subject of Spain was to be dealt with at a later date.[17]

After the *Anschluss* Chamberlain and Halifax hoped that it might be possible to win over Mussolini sufficiently from Hitler so that he might be prepared to act as a go-between and a restraining influence on the Führer. They also hoped for an endorsement from the President for this policy. On 15 April Halifax wrote to Hull and Welles, via Kennedy, saying that an agreement was likely to be signed in Rome by Perth and Ciano in the next day or two. It would consist of a protocol relating to various bilateral issues between Britain and Italy and an exchange of letters, one of which would commit Italy to the evacuation of its volunteers from Spain. In return, the British Government would put forward a proposal at the next League Council meeting to recognise Italian sovereignty over Ethiopia. Halifax was at pains to point out that the agreement would not enter into force until there was a 'satisfactory settlement' of the Spanish question. He argued that such an agreement would be 'a real contribution towards world appeasement' and added:

> Should the President share these views I need hardly say how grateful both the Prime Minister and myself would be should he feel able to give some public indication of his approval of the agreement itself and of the principles which have inspired it.[18]

Hull was, in his own words, 'strenuously opposed' to the US being associated with this agreement and there were rumours that he might resign over the issue. He argued that not only would it mean breaking with the US tradition, only recently upheld by Stimson in the case of Japan and Manchuria, of not recognising changes of status made by force but it would also encourage the dictators and undermine the League. And it was unlikely to win over Mussolini from his alliance with Germany. Nor was Roosevelt very keen on the agreement or on the direction of British policy since the resignation of Eden. In reply to a letter from Cudahy criticising Chamberlain's 'weak, vacillating, humiliating policy', he wrote that there was a pro-appeasement 'element' in Washington. 'They would really like me to be a Neville Chamberlain. . . . But if that were done, we would only be breeding far more serious trouble four or eight years from now.' However, he accepted Welles's 'realist' argument on behalf of the agreement and made a lukewarm statement at his next press conference that, while not attempting to pass judgement on its political features, 'this Government has seen the conclusion of an agreement with sympathetic interest because it is proof of the value of peaceful negotiations'.[19]

'Sympathetic interest' was some way short of 'joint action' or even 'parallel action' and the US never recognised the Italian conquest of Ethiopia, as Hull pointed out in his *Memoirs*. However, when the agreement came to be debated in the Commons, Chamberlain quoted the last part of Roosevelt's statement as signifying the President's support for the agreement, without mentioning that he was not commenting on the political aspects of the agreement. This enraged the Opposition, who accused him of distorting Roosevelt's words. Herbert Morrison, recently returned from a trip to the USA, declared that 'all good-thinking elements in America who want cooperation with Britain' despaired at the agreement with Italy and that Chamberlain had 'taken light liberty with the head of a very great nation with whom it is important that we should have no misunderstanding'. Indeed, there was some irritation in the State Department that Chamberlain had used the President's statement, in the words of Pierrepont Moffat, for 'partisan political gain'.[20]

British air mission

Even while British appeasement policy was gathering pace, there was also a growing concern on the part of the Chamberlain Government – and public opinion – to secure adequate rearmament for British defence, especially in relation to air power. FDR had raised this issue during the Runciman visit in January 1937 when he enquired about British aircraft production and was supplied with confidential figures by the Air Ministry. The question of defence was also discussed at the Imperial Conference of 1937, especially in relation to Canadian potential. Rearmament was under way, but relatively slowly compared with Germany, and only about 200 aircraft were being produced each month. A plan for increased aircraft production had been agreed by the Cabinet in February 1938 but the shock of the *Anschluss* and of the indiscriminate bombing of civilians in Spain and China led the Air Minister, Lord Swinton, to plead for a more ambitious plan, known as Plan K, involving extra spending on aircraft production and anti-aircraft defences. This met strong resistance from Simon, amongst others, and a decision was postponed. Simon's budget, to be delivered in April, was already likely to be unpopular, with tax rises to pay for rearmament.[21]

However, agreement was eventually reached on the idea of sending an air mission to visit the US and Canada, and the mission set sail in the middle of April. It was led by J. G. Weir, brother of Lord Weir, who was accompanied by a senior officer of the Royal Air Force and a test pilot. The mission, in the words of its official historian, resulted in 'two large contracts' for reconnaissance aircraft and trainers in the US. The first was for 250 Lockheed Hudson aircraft – transport aircraft to be converted into bombers – and the second for 200 North American Harvard trainers.' Halifax told the Cabinet that 'he had reason to believe that the Germans were impressed by the order' but no other contracts were placed in the US at this time. As in the case of Canada, the Air Ministry was aware of the great potential of the US in the production of military aircraft but, like the earlier French mission in January 1938, the Weir mission was disappointed with the quality of American output.[22]

Tripartite Currency Pact renewed

The *Anschluss* also had a significant effect on French politics, which were already beset with divisions between left and right and instability within parties and political groupings, including the Popular Front of left-wing parties nominally led by Léon Blum. The Blum Government had fallen in June 1937, but Blum returned as Prime Minister on 13 March, in the midst of the

Anschluss crisis. However, his Ministry was short-lived and on 10 April 1938 Edouard Daladier formed a centre-right government that remained in office until 21 March 1940, the eve of the German spring offensive – a government now chiefly associated with the Munich agreement of September 1938. The Daladier Ministry tried to maintain the level of the franc but on 2 May it informed London and Washington that it would allow the franc to fall to 175 to the pound. Morgenthau was disappointed at the French move but was not minded to revoke the Tripartite Currency Pact, especially when Simon, his British counterpart, indicated that he and Chamberlain would go along with the French devaluation, even though it was not in the spirit of the pact. They felt that, with Hitler in Rome, it would be disastrous if the Tripartite Currency Agreement were to collapse. Daladier was therefore assured on 4 May that the US Government regarded the Tripartite Accord as 'continuing in full operation'.[23]

However, it soon became clear that the Daladier Government was allowing the franc to fall lower than the rate agreed with the US and Britain. The US Treasury believed that a lower rate was unnecessary, and Morgenthau suspected that one of the reasons for this move was 'to assist and make effective certain private speculations of French banks and even of French officials'. He believed that the spirit of the Tripartite Pact had been broken by the French and demanded that the rate be moved up to 175 to the pound – a move supported by Hull and the State Department. Simon was also perturbed at the lower rate fixed by the French, although he was not as incensed as Morgenthau, who regarded the Pact as his project, to protect and uphold. The French Government subsequently agreed to bring the rate up to 175 to the pound. On 6 May Morgenthau wrote to Hull, saying 'I have just completed an extremely difficult week keeping the Tripartite Agreement alive' and thanking him for his 'sympathetic understanding'. Close cooperation between Washington and London had also helped to maintain the Pact but the French link was evidently becoming weaker and weaker.[24]

One reason for French weakness was the Civil War in Spain, where the Republicans, despite occasional victories against Franco's forces, had steadily lost ground since the start of the conflict. The Republican Government had initially been forced to move from Madrid to Valencia and in October 1937 it transferred to Barcelona. The city was subsequently bombed by Nationalist forces and by April 1938 the defeat of the Republican Government seemed to be a matter of time, especially when the Daladier Government came to power and reduced French aid. As regards the role of the other Great Powers, while the Nyon conference of September 1937, arranged by Eden, had been largely successful in reducing the number of incidents in the Mediterranean Sea, his proposal that foreign forces should be withdrawn, while agreed by all of the members of the Non-Intervention Committee sitting in London, had been very largely ignored. Italy and Germany continued to aid the Nationalists while the Soviet Union was providing most of the aid to the Republicans.[25]

Throughout the first few months of 1938 the Roosevelt Administration's policy towards Spain remained one of strict neutrality. Apart from foreign policy considerations, there were good domestic reasons for strict neutrality – not least the fierce debate between those who supported the Republican Government – mainly liberals, socialists and communists – and those who supported Franco and the Nationalists – mainly conservatives and Catholics. US policy might fairly be characterised as 'parallel action' with Britain, although the term was not used on the US side in the Spanish context. Washington justified its policy as being in line with the Non-Intervention Committee in London and there were also specific instances of parallel action with Britain when they could be divorced from the politics of the conflict. For example, the Foreign Office informed the US Embassy that Eden was to appeal to both sides in Spain to refrain from civilian bombing and asked the US to issue a public statement endorsing the British position and making a similar appeal. The State Department replied that Hull would be making a statement deploring bombardment from the air – but would do so independently, without reference to Britain. Indeed, the State Department made several statements along these lines during 1938.[26]

The decline in the fortune of the Loyalists, combined with the indiscriminate bombing used by the Nationalists and their Fascist allies, revived the impassioned debate about US policy towards the conflict, centring upon the arms embargo. On 2 May, Senator Gerald Nye, one of the original authors of the Neutrality laws, introduced a resolution calling for the end of the arms embargo on the grounds that it was unfair to deny weapons of self-defence to the legitimate government of Spain. The Nye resolution was supported by 100 prominent Americans from the churches, academia, the arts, business and labour. 'To continue the embargo against Spain', they said, 'means a further implementation of British policy, which today stands naked to the world as a policy of collaboration with predatory fascism.' At one stage it seemed as though the resolution might be carried, as Roosevelt was said to be in favour of it. But the continued opposition to aiding the Loyalists in Spain, especially from within the Catholic Church, and the opposition of Hull meant that the President withheld his support and the Senate decided to postpone consideration of Nye's resolution, pending a review of the Neutrality laws in the next session.[27]

This move was welcomed in London and there were suspicions that the Chamberlain Government had influenced Washington against removing the arms embargo in the case of Spain. This was not the case, but certainly US policy towards Spain continued to be helpful in most respects, as far as London was concerned. This is not to say that their policies were identical, and Washington continued to be opposed to joint action. For example, in June 1938, when the Foreign Office asked if the US Government would like to nominate a military officer to serve on an international commission to report on and publicise bombings of civilians in Spain, the State Department demurred. As Welles informed the apologetic Lindsay, the Department did not like receiving requests that had already been made public. Secondly, such a commission would find it very difficult to operate and was unlikely to remain apolitical. Overall, London could have few grounds for complaint about US policy towards Spain or the operation of the Neutrality laws in this case.[28]

Naval rearmament, May 1938

Another area of Anglo-American cooperation was naval rearmament. Although the President's defence message in January 1938 had met with vocal opposition from pacifist and isolationist critics and helped to spark off the 'Tacit Alliance' debate in the Senate, it had received strong support from the *New York Times* and internationalists. Even Borah and Johnson had not objected to it in principle, but only in as much as they thought it was too closely tied to British policy. The conflict between Japan and China had been the main focus of attention when Roosevelt's defence message was delivered but the *Anschluss* had returned Central Europe to the centre of the world stage and given renewed momentum to the Defence Bill. When the debate on the Bill began on 14 March the Administration had the upper hand, despite opposing testimony from Professor Charles Beard and the Coalition Against War, amongst others. The Bill emerged on 27 May 1938 as the Vinson Naval Act, authorising a 20 per cent increase in the size of the American Navy, including three new battleships and large numbers of cruisers, destroyers and submarines.[29]

While the debate on the Vinson Bill was proceeding, the chief signatories of the London Naval Agreement of March 1936 – Britain, the US and France – were coming to terms with Japan's refusal to discuss its naval building intentions, as requested in their simultaneous notes on 5 February 1938; here was another example of Anglo-American parallel action, this time joined by France. The US Navy wanted to escalate its own capability on a unilateral basis while Norman Davis, who had led the American delegation in the lead-up to the 1936 London agreement, wanted the US to announce its escalation at the same time as Britain. The French were not keen to escalate at all, partly for financial reasons and partly because they feared a naval race with Germany and Italy. Hull agreed with Davis that escalation should be simultaneous and concurrent, but he preferred any announcements to be in tandem with both Britain and France – not just the British. Negotiations regarding the maximum tonnage for warships, and so on, were conducted in London in a cooperative spirit, and the final Protocol announcing notice of escalation beyond the London agreement of March 1936 was signed in London by representatives of Great Britain, the US and France at the end of June.[30]

The view from Berlin

In Berlin, the shake-up in the German diplomatic system that followed Hitler's coup against the German Army leadership in February 1938 and the enforced retirement of von Neurath meant that the German Foreign Ministry was now beholden to Ribbentrop, formerly the German Ambassador in London. Ribbentrop was unlikely to act as a restraining influence on Hitler's ambitions, especially as he knew at first hand just how wedded the Prime Minister was to appeasement. However, the Washington Embassy continued much as before under the leadership of the Ambassador,

Hans Dieckhoff. Regular reports continued to flow from Washington warning of the dangers inherent in the growing antagonism in Washington towards the Nazi regime. In one such despatch, shortly after the *Anschluss*, the Ambassador wrote, 'I am perhaps becoming a bore in Berlin' because of his repeated warnings about the growing likelihood that the US would support Britain in the event of a conflict, but he said that he felt it was his duty to try to avoid 'unpleasant surprises' in the future. Weizsächer, the State Secretary in the Foreign Ministry, was quick to reassure him. 'Your warnings that we should have no illusions as to the American stand in the event of a world conflict are by all means valuable; it can do no harm if you point this out again and again.'[31]

The American reaction to the *Anschluss* was fully reported to Berlin by Ambassador Dieckhoff in Washington and taken on board by the German Foreign Ministry. The speeches by Hull and Kennedy after the *Anschluss* were regarded as clearly indicative of US policy. 'While Secretary Hull treats the problem with his usual academic and monotonous phraseology, Ambassador Kennedy does not shrink from employing an unmistakeable and resolute tone,' said Dieckhoff. But the message was the same – the US, while not wishing to obligate itself, refused to pursue an 'unconditional isolationist policy' and was 'prepared, if necessary, to take an active part in a conflict'. The Administration, aided by much of the press and by 'increasingly effective British propaganda', was pushing US public opinion towards support for the democracies – meaning primarily Britain. Opposition from isolationists was still strong but was likely to become steadily weaker. As Dieckhoff concluded:

> As things are today, the United States will not remain neutral in a great world conflict into which the British Empire is drawn, but, carried along by the vast propaganda painstakingly prepared and fostered by the Administration, will, when the Administration deems it advisable, come in on the British side.[32]

This despatch was followed by another that referred to 'a fantastic press campaign' in the US following the *Anschluss*. 'The President, who for a long time has not been very well-disposed towards us, is said to be greatly upset by the Austrian coup and to believe that the moment when the "democracies" must fight the "dictatorships" is not far off' wrote Dieckhoff. 'He is very systematically getting this country ready both in sentiment and in armament for that moment'. But, he continued, 'the key to the American attitude is in London. If England remains calm and accepts our increased strength and expansion, even if some circles here are not pleased, no action will be taken; after all, one cannot be more Catholic than the Pope. But if England decides to oppose us, and it comes to war, the United States will not hesitate very long to range itself on the British side'.[33]

Dieckhoff also reported that the *Anschluss* had brought renewed attention from internationalist opinion, especially the *New York Times*, to the Neutrality laws. The Roosevelt Administration was not happy with the Neutrality Act of May 1937, as it hampered the President's freedom of action and reduced US influence abroad. 'Even if the Act remains in force, there is no question of any real neutrality on the part of the United States,' said Dieckhoff. 'Moreover, the law can be repealed at any time, if necessary, by an act of Congress and a stroke of the President's pen.' The timing of US intervention was 'quite clearly intimated' in the speeches by Hull and Kennedy, he said, 'namely, when the great "democratic powers", especially Great Britain, become involved in a serious struggle and the "parallel" interests of the United States no longer permit her to stand on the side lines'. And he repeated his oft-expressed view that the Roosevelt Administration, aided by 'British propaganda', could galvanise US public opinion in favour of intervention when necessary.[34]

Copies of Dieckhoff's despatches were generally given a wide circulation in Berlin, including the Propaganda Ministry and the Nazi Foreign Affairs Bureau. The Ambassador had some influence – for example, Ribbentrop was dissuaded from the idea of Captain Wiedemann undertaking a 'goodwill tour' in the US in June and conducting unofficial conversations with prominent Americans, at least before the mid-term elections in November 1938. Hitler was also aware of this decision. But it is not clear how far the Ambassador's warnings registered within the Nazi Government, especially as it was taken for granted in Berlin that the key player was Britain and that Washington would take its lead from London and not go any further than the British themselves. As the British Government was determined to continue with its policy of appeasing Germany, not least via its Ambassador in Berlin, Sir Nevile Henderson, Anglo-American cooperation in 1938 would have to be on British terms and the impact of Roosevelt's hostility towards the Nazi regime was correspondingly reduced.[35]

Notes

1. *NYT*, 12 March 1938; *The Times*, 12 March 1938; Shen, *Age of Appeasement*, p. 166.
2. Hooker, *Moffat Papers*, p. 192; FRUS/1938/1/doc 465, Welles meeting with Lindsay, 16 March 1938; Rock, *Chamberlain and Roosevelt*, pp. 88–92.
3. Ickes, *Diary*, II, 12 March 1938, pp. 332–3; 30 March, p. 348.
4. CAB 23, 12 (1938), item 1, 12 March 1938; Neville Chamberlain papers, NC 18/1/1041, Neville Chamberlain to Hilda, 13 March 1938 (quoted in Rock, *Chamberlain and Roosevelt*, p. 89). For Henderson meeting with Hitler see DGFP/D/I, doc 138, Ribbentrop to Henderson, 4 March 1938, enclosing memorandum of conversation between Henderson and Hitler in presence of Ribbentrop, Berlin, 3 March 1938.
5. Mackenzie King Diary, 11 and 12 March 1938.
6. *The Times*, 15 March 1938.
7. CAB 23, 15 (1938), item 1, 22 March 1938; see also CAB 23, 16 (1938), item 1, 23 March 1938.
8. *Hansard*, House of Commons, 24 March 1938; CAB 23, 18 (1938), item 1, 6 April 1938; CAB 23, 19 (1938), item 2, 13 April 1938.
9. Berle and Jacobs, *Navigating the Rapids*, 19 March 1938, pp. 168–9.
10. *NYT*, 15 March 1938; FRUS/1938/II, doc 476, Hull to Wiley, 23 March 1938; Ibid., doc 401, German Embassy to State Dept, 14 April 1938; doc 402, State Dept to German Embassy, 29 April 1938 – rejecting protest; see also Dallek, *FDR*, p. 158.
11. FRUS/1938/I, doc 473, Hull to Wilson, 19 March 1938 – statement by Hull re Austria at press conference on 19 March; FRUS/1938/I, doc 468, Messersmith to Wiley, 16 March 1938.
12. For speech 'Our Foreign Policy', 17 March 1938, see Hull, *Memoirs I*, pp. 575–82; *NYT*, 18 March 1938.
13. Ibid.
14. *NYT* editorial, 18 March 1938; Arthur Krock, 'In The Nation', *NYT*, 18 March 1938.
15. *The Times*, 19 March 1938.
16. Ibid.
17. FRUS/1938/I, doc 86, Phillips to Hull, 8 March 1938 re Anglo-Italian negotiations; doc 87, Phillips to Hull, 10 March 1938 – Perth meeting with Ciano; doc 88, Phillips to Hull, 13 March 1938, Information from Perth re negotiations.
18. FRUS/1938/I, doc 89, Kennedy to Hull, 15 April 1938.
19. Hull, *Memoirs I*, pp. 579–80; Roosevelt papers, PSF: Ireland, Box 44; Cudahy to Roosevelt, 6 April 1938; Roosevelt to Cudahy, 16 April 1938; Rock, *Chamberlain and Roosevelt*, p. 92; FRUS/1938/I,

doc 93, pp. 147–8. Statement by President Roosevelt, 19 April 1938; for Hull resignation rumour see *The Times*, 13 May 1938.
20. *NYT*, 3 May 1938 for Morrison quote; Hooker, *Moffat Papers* for Moffat quote.
21. Hall, *North American Supply*, pp. 28–9; CAB 23, 13 (1938), item 3, 14 March 1938.
22. Hall, *North American Supply*, pp. 105–6; CAB 23, 19 (1938), item 8, 13 April 1938; CAB 23, 24 (1938), item 15, 18 May 1938; CAB 23, 25 (1938), item 6, 25 May 1938; CAB 23, 30 (1938), item 5, 29 June 1938.
23. FRUS/1938/II, doc 219, Wilson (Chargé in France) to Hull, 2 May 1938; doc 220, Feis to Hull, 4 May 1938; see also Blum, *Morgenthau Diaries*, I, pp. 502–5.
24. FRUS/1938/II, doc 223, Feis to Hull, 5 May 1938; doc 224, Wilson (Paris) to Hull, 6 May 1938; doc 225, Morgenthau to Hull, 6 May 1938.
25. See FRUS/1938/I, docs 95–171 for State Dept policy January–June 1938.
26. FRUS/1938/I, doc 101, Johnson (Chargé in London) to Hull; doc 104, Hull to Johnson, 2 February 1938; doc 115, statement by Hull criticising bombing of civilians, 21 March 1938.
27. *NYT*, 5, 6, 9, 14 May 1938.
28. *NYT*, 12 May 1938; FRUS/1938/I, doc 157, British Embassy memo for State Dept, 3 June 1938; doc 158, memo of conversation between Welles and Lindsay, 6 June 1938; doc 164, Hull memo of conversation with Lindsay, 10 June 1938; doc 168, memo by Pierrepont Moffat, 16 June 1938.
29. *NYT*, 15 March 1938 and 28 May 1938.
30. FRUS/1938/I, doc 869, Moffat memo, 4 March 1938; docs 865–92, especially docs 871, 873, 884–7.
31. DGFP/D/I, Dieckhoff to GFM, doc 445, 22 March 1938; ibid., doc 451, Weizsäcker, State Secretary in GFM, to Dieckhoff, 30 April 1938. For the background to von Neurath's replacement see Steiner, *Triumph of the Dark*, pp. 330–5.
32. DGFP/D/I, doc 444, Dieckhoff to Weizsäcker, 22 March 1938.
33. Ibid., doc 445, Dieckhoff to Weizsäcker, 22 March 1938.
34. Ibid., doc 447, Dieckhoff to GFM, 30 March 1938.
35. Ibid., doc 444, Dieckhoff to GFM, 22 March 1938; doc 446, Ribbentrop to Dieckhoff, 29 March 1938; doc 449, Dieckhoff to Ribbentrop, 14 April 1938.

8 Munich Crisis, May–September 1938

On 26 July 1938 Neville Chamberlain announced in the House of Commons that Lord Runciman – formerly Walter Runciman, the President of the Board of Trade – would be leading a mission to Prague in an attempt to mediate between the Czech Government and the German-speaking minority in the Sudetenland. Chamberlain said he hoped the mission would 'inform public opinion generally as to the real facts of the case', and, secondly, he hoped that it might mean that 'issues which hitherto have appeared intractable may prove, under the influence of such a mediator to be less obstinate than we have thought'. It is clear from the Cabinet and Foreign Office papers at this time that American opinion was an important factor in the British Government's thinking about the Runciman mission. At a Cabinet meeting on 28 July 1938, it was agreed that an approach should be made to Roosevelt to support the mission to Czechoslovakia. As Halifax later put it, 'the Cabinet hoped (as I do) that we might be able to get some commendatory message out of Roosevelt about Runciman'.[1]

On 29 July the American Embassy was given a message about the Runciman mission and the background was explained in some detail.

> The Foreign Office said that should the President or the Secretary feel that he could make some public statement expressing approval of Lord Runciman's mission this would have a favourable effect on world opinion and Lord Halifax would naturally be much gratified.

At the same time as this official overture, Runciman himself wrote a private letter to Roosevelt, with whom he had had little contact since his visit to Washington in January 1937. 'I am now about to set afloat in an open boat in the treacherous ocean, independent of this or any other Government,' he said. The aim of the mission was 'to reduce the points of friction between the Czechs and the Sudeten Germans and to guide that unhappy country into smooth waters. As we stand at present war is far too easily excused and may spring on the old world at any moment appropriate to the aggressor.'[2]

Runciman mission

The aim of this chapter is to examine the events leading to the Munich crisis at the end of September 1938, especially the Runciman mission, in terms of Anglo-American relations, and to show why the British Government was so keen to obtain an endorsement from Roosevelt for the mission and, indeed, for the wider policy of appeasement as implemented by Chamberlain and Halifax. The President was on holiday, cruising in the Caribbean on the USS *Houston*, when the Runciman mission was announced, although he was informed about it while at sea. Hull and the State Department were opposed to any American endorsement of Runciman's mission. Pierrepont Moffat, the Chief of the Division of European Affairs – who was generally unsympathetic towards the British Government – felt that the President's 'approval' of the Anglo-Italian Agreement in April 1938 had been used 'for partisan purposes by Chamberlain in the House of Commons and for the diplomatic purposes by Halifax at the League of Nations'. Hull and the State Department were anxious to avoid being drawn into any British plan for solving the Sudetenland crisis on Hitler's terms, especially before the outcome of the Runciman mission could be known.[3]

In London, Chamberlain and Halifax were anxious to obtain a public statement of support for the mission from the President for reasons of both foreign and domestic policy. They hoped that American support would strengthen Britain's hands in negotiations with Germany over the fate of the Sudetenland. And, mindful of the experience of the Ethiopian crisis, and the shock to domestic and world opinion caused by the Hoare–Laval pact, they wanted to 'educate' public opinion both at home and abroad – especially in the US – to the benefits of their appeasement policy before a dangerous crisis over the Sudetenland arose. An endorsement from Roosevelt would be especially valuable. Not only would it help to garner American support for appeasement, but it could also be expected to have a positive influence on British opinion, especially liberal opinion, as the President was seen by many in the Liberal and Labour parties, as well as those on the right such as Eden and Churchill, as the great spokesman for Western democracy.[4]

The Canadian Prime Minister remained a strong supporter of Chamberlain's appeasement policy and Roosevelt could not be unmindful of this fact in view of his desire for closer American–Canadian cooperation. Mackenzie King welcomed the Runciman mission, writing in his diary:

> I have found tremendous enjoyment and peace of mind in the appointment of Runciman as mediator to Czechoslovakia. . . . It looks to me as though the whole situation is developing, as I hoped it would, and that we shall see the world saved, and Germany and Britain closer together in the preservation of world peace.

The Canadian found Chamberlain's appeasement policy very comforting and gave it his support during a speech in Toronto on 30 July. 'I am sure that Britain will never go to war unless she is driven to it to save herself and civilisation,' he confided to his diary. He also sent a private telegram to Runciman, in which he offered his best wishes 'for the outcome of your efforts which I feel sure will be of the greatest benefit to all'.[5]

Czech crisis

Following the annexation of Austria in March 1938, Hitler's attention turned to Czechoslovakia, which had a large German-speaking population in the Sudetenland region. The Czech Government had alliances with France and the Soviet Union, as well as strong defences, but the *Anschluss* of 12 March 1938 put enormous pressure on the Czech state, which was regarded by Hitler as a 'dagger' pointing at the heart of the new Germany. The chief aim of Chamberlain and Halifax was to avoid war in Europe over the Sudetenland. The main danger to peace, as they saw it, was the fact that Czechoslovakia had an alliance with France, which might therefore become involved in a conflict with Germany and, in turn, involve Britain. French policy had been to use Czechoslovakia as a counterbalance to the power of Germany but Chamberlain and Halifax did not believe that the Czech state was strong enough militarily to stand up to Germany or that British public opinion would support a war to defend the Czechs, with their large German minority. German expansion in Eastern Europe might even be useful in diverting Hitler away from the British Empire and in containing expansion by the Soviet Union.[6]

In April 1938, emboldened by events in Austria, Konrad Henlein, the leader of the Sudeten Nazi Party, put forward the so-called Carlsbad points, which sought virtual autonomy for the German Sudetenland within Czechoslovakia. These demands were rejected by the Czech Government, which offered instead a Nationalities Statute to address the concerns of the Germans and other minority groups in Czechoslovakia – the Poles and Hungarians in particular. On 21 May there were rumours of a German invasion and this was met by a partial mobilisation of the Czech armed forces. This in turn led to warnings from London and Paris that an invasion of Czechoslovakia could lead to war. This *démarche* seemed to work in the short term, but Chamberlain and Halifax were now even more convinced of the need to avoid war with Germany by pressuring the Czechs to come to terms with the Sudeten Germans. They had met in London with their French counterparts, Daladier and Bonnet, at the end of April to agree a common strategy towards Germany and Italy. One aspect of this strategy was to keep Berlin 'guessing' regarding Anglo-French military support for Prague but the signals emanating from London and Paris suggested appeasement rather than deterrence.[7]

The Czech Government believed that Germany was using the Sudetenland issue to divide Czechoslovakia from France and Britain with the aim of destroying the country and using it as bridge to eastward expansion. It was also clear that the French Government felt totally unprepared for war because of its great lack of air power and anti-aircraft defences. The Chamberlain Government was also against a war over the Sudetenland issue. As regards the May crisis, Adolf Berle was scathing of British policy, believing that not only was there no evidence of an imminent German move being planned against the Czechs but also that the British had made 'foolish moves', 'urging the Czechs "to be reasonable", which was 'simply ridiculous', as 'when you want to make the lion lie down with the lamb, there is not much point in beating the lamb'. He was deeply suspicious of the Chamberlain Government. 'The British keep making moves, all of them designed merely to bring the United States into an understanding with them, which actually would probably result in our entering the probable war on the British side,' he wrote in his diary. 'But there is no Colonel House in this Administration to make understandings of that kind behind the back of the State Department and the President. We may have to go to war, but if we do, it will be our decision and not someone else's.'[8]

Runciman and Roosevelt

Following the May crisis, Chamberlain and Halifax were more convinced than ever of the need to avoid war with Germany by pressuring the Czechs to come to terms with the Sudeten Germans. Accordingly, they sought a way to intervene in the dispute and the Foreign Office eventually decided upon the idea of a British adviser or mediator who would go to Prague and bring the negotiations back on track. This would obviously involve Britain more directly in the dispute, but Halifax agreed that, as a last resort, 'we ought to be prepared to act alone – to try and resolve the deadlock'. He then began the process of trying to come up with a suitable candidate for the position of mediator. The first name he suggested was that of Lord Lothian – later Ambassador to Washington, but eventually the trail led to Walter Runciman, who had resigned from the Cabinet in May 1937. At the end of June Runciman was asked if he would accept the task. He initially rejected the idea but, ultimately, he agreed to lead the mission on the understanding that he would be independent of the British Government and a 'mediator' rather than an 'arbitrator'.[9]

The Foreign Office files do not include a definitive statement of the reasons for the choice of Runciman as the British 'mediator' in Prague, but the circumstantial evidence suggests that one factor was the hope that his visit to Washington in January 1937 and his personal acquaintance with Roosevelt would elicit the sympathy of the President and help to keep the State Department 'on side'. Not only did Halifax and the Foreign Office pursue Runciman quite relentlessly, even after he had originally turned down the mission, but after his appointment every opportunity was taken to seek an endorsement from Roosevelt and the State Department for Runciman's mission to Prague. Runciman had other qualifications for the mission, including his experience of negotiations while at the Board of Trade and his sympathy for the policy of appeasement. But he was now sixty-seven years old, of delicate health, and in retirement. Arthur Murray, for one, was delighted at Runciman's mission and was sure that Roosevelt would be. 'The "contact" you established with him may well be not unhelpful at this juncture,' he wrote to Runciman.[10]

Relations with the United States also featured prominently in the House of Commons debate on 26 July when Chamberlain announced the Runciman mission. The Liberal leader, Sir Archibald Sinclair, began by expressing some surprise that Runciman should wish to take on such an assignment. Later, referring to the dangerous world situation, Sinclair stressed the need for good Anglo-American relations and urged the Government to take the opportunity of Roosevelt's move away from isolationism. The Prime Minister should 'strike in his speeches the same note as President Roosevelt and Cordell Hull do in theirs': that is, freedom, democracy and so on. There should also be a move towards an Anglo-American trade agreement. Whatever his private doubts, Chamberlain was anxious to be positive about the United States in public. 'I agree very much with the right hon. Gentleman in the value that he attaches to our relations with the United States of America. I am happy to think they have never been better than they are at the present moment.'[11]

At the same time as cultivating American opinion, Chamberlain was appeasing Nazi Germany. When the Runciman mission was notified to Berlin, Weizsäcker, the State Secretary, felt that the explanation of the mission by the British Ambassador, Sir Nevile Henderson, 'proved above all that the British Government, in their anxiety over the further development of the Sudeten German affair, now think that they can no longer withhold their influence in shaping the matter, even in minute details'. He also discerned that the British hoped to find in Runciman 'a pliable go-between, in order not to have to bear the responsibility themselves for individual proposals, a responsibility which hitherto they have always declined'. The German Foreign Ministry was fully informed of Chamberlain's anxiety for an agreement with Hitler not only by Henderson in Berlin but by the German ambassador in London, who was told by Chamberlain that his statement in the House of Commons on 23 March criticising the *Anschluss* was not meant to end negotiations with Germany but rather to suspend them until a more propitious moment arrived.[12]

The Foreign Office plan to obtain an endorsement of the Runciman mission met with some success, indirectly at least. On 16 August Hull gave a radio address entitled 'International Relations and the Foreign Policy of the United States', in which he said that in a world that was increasingly confronted by the choice between peace and 'international lawlessness' the United States supported peace. He also made a statement on the tenth anniversary of the Kellogg Pact on 27 August 1938, calling for world peace. Both of these statements could be taken as giving general support for appeasement, although Hull was primarily interested in 'economic appeasement'. His main concern, as he told Lindsay, was the slow progress of the trade negotiations with Britain because he saw an Anglo-American trade agreement as being fundamental to improved international relations. Hull had not got on well with Runciman when they met in Washington in January 1937 but Roosevelt's attitude towards Runciman and his mission was more appreciative. Apart from the fact that he had personally invited Runciman to meet him in Washington, the President was open to a wider range of influences than Hull and, as we have seen, was becoming impatient of Hull's obsession with trade issues and 'economic appeasement'.[13]

FDR'S Kingston speech

After his cruise on the USS *Houston*, Roosevelt spent most of August at home in Hyde Park. But on 18 August he took the short trip north to Canada to meet Mackenzie King for the dedication of the Thousand Islands Bridge across the St Lawrence River. After FDR greeted the Canadian Prime Minister in his usual fashion as 'Mackenzie', the two leaders enjoyed a long conversation during which FDR invited the Canadian to Hyde Park for the signing of the Anglo-American trade agreement, once it had been finalised. They also talked about the visit of George VI and Queen Elizabeth to Canada that was scheduled to take place in the summer of 1939. Later the same day, Roosevelt gave an address at Queens University in Kingston, Ontario, where he was awarded an honorary degree. In a speech that reviewed the international situation he referred indirectly to Czechoslovakia. 'The theory of the speech is an endeavour to create a certain amount of doubt abroad as to what our intentions may be,' noted Adolf Berle, Assistant Secretary of State. 'This, it is thought, may have a moderating effect.'[14]

In his conversation with Mackenzie King, the President had made it clear that he regarded Germany under Hitler as especially dangerous because of the Führer's belief in his personal destiny. He also thought that Germany might try to provoke a revolution in Brazil, where there were many Germans and Italians living. These concerns came through in his acceptance speech at Queen's University.

> We in the Americas are no longer a faraway continent, to which the eddies of controversies beyond the seas could bring no interest or harm. Instead, we in the Americas have become a consideration to every propaganda office and to every general staff beyond the seas. The vast amount of our resources, the vigour of our commerce and the strength of our men have made us vital factors in world peace whether we choose or not.

And he continued: 'The Dominion of Canada is part of the sisterhood of the British Empire. I give to you assurance that the people of the United States will not stand idly by if domination of Canadian soil is threatened by any other Empire.'[15]

This was a significant speech in several respects. Not only did it commit the US to the defence of Canada if that country was openly threatened by Germany or any other hostile nation, but it was also, as Lindsay pointed out, an acknowledgement of American influence on the international situation – influence that was of interest, as Roosevelt put it, 'to every propaganda office and to every general staff beyond the seas'. Mackenzie King responded to FDR's speech in a speech of his own at North York on 20 August. 'I took the position that Roosevelt's assurance only added to our responsibilities,' he noted in his diary. The Ottawa Government would have to ensure that Canada's coasts were secure and that no enemy forces could operate from Canadian territory against the United States. 'This I know is what will please the Americans above all else and is right.' He envisaged 'Good neighbours on one side; partners within the Empire on the other' and a 'readiness to meet all joint emergencies'. Indeed, this understanding led to the Ogdensburg agreement of August 1940 and the establishment of the Permanent Joint Board of Defence between the US and Canada, referred to by Churchill in his Fulton speech as a model for the Anglo-American 'special relationship'.[16]

While by no means a direct endorsement of the Runciman mission, the speeches by Hull and especially Roosevelt were regarded in London as being quite helpful. On 27 August Sir John Simon, the Chancellor of the Exchequer (and a former Foreign Secretary), spoke at Lanark and set out the British position, which he described as 'a positive policy of peace'. The efforts of the British Government aimed 'to reduce tension and to promote appeasement', he said. 'This very case of Czechoslovakia may be so critical for the future of Europe that it would be impossible to assume a limit to the disturbance that a conflict might involve, and everyone in every country who considers the consequences has to bear that in mind.' He then referred to the speeches by Hull and Roosevelt which he said 'must waken a responsive echo in many British hearts'. Halifax also spoke warmly of the speeches by FDR and Hull when he discussed the Czech situation with Herschel Johnson from the American Embassy, and he added that further speeches along the same lines before the Nazi Congress met in Nuremberg 'might have a wholesome effect in restraining Hitler'.[17]

On 30 August Kennedy met with Chamberlain, who said he was very disturbed about the Czech situation. The general view he was receiving was that 'Hitler has made up his mind to take Czechoslovakia peacefully if possible but with arms if necessary.' Hitler believed that France was not ready to fight and England did not want to go in. 'Runciman feels that if the matter were one just to be decided between the Sudetens and the Czechs it could be settled amicably but unfortunately it rests with Hitler.' Despite everything, Chamberlain was still hopeful that war could be averted, as opposition to Hitler was gathering. 'The *Anschluss* lost Hitler a great deal of public opinion in the United States,' Chamberlain said. He also felt that British 'public opinion is definitely against going to war for Czechoslovakia' unless France became involved. Kennedy asked him if he thought Hitler was affected by the speeches from America. 'He said he thought that psychologically the two speeches in America – the President's and the Secretary's – and Simon's had had an excellent effect, but he is advised that very little of the proper information, so far as world peace is concerned, gets to Hitler any more.'[18]

Kennedy also saw Halifax the next day, 31 August. Halifax repeated the view that public opinion in Britain was against going to war for Czechoslovakia and that the French did not want to fight either. He asked Kennedy what the reaction would be in the United States if Germany invaded Czechoslovakia and Britain stood aside. 'I told him a great deal would depend on the attitude the President would take as to whether he thought England should be encouraged to fight or whether he would contend that they should stay out of war until the last possible minute.' Kennedy then cabled Hull for some guidance on this point, but he received no further details from the Secretary of State. 'The recent public speeches and public statements of the President and myself, which were prepared with great care, accurately reflect the attitude of this Government toward the European and world situation,' Hull replied. 'It would not be practicable to be more specific as to our reaction in hypothetical circumstances.'[19]

Thus the mid-August speeches were as far as Hull and Roosevelt were prepared to go in commenting officially upon the Czech situation at this stage. They had not directly referred to the Runciman mission, but their speeches were clearly designed to support efforts for peace and to warn Germany against the consequences of a war over the Sudetenland. In one sense at least, American policy was similar to British policy, which was to keep Berlin 'guessing' by pointing out that if war began, it might be impossible to contain it to the Czech state and that other countries – probably Britain and possibly even the United States – might become involved, as had happened during the First World War. Just how effective these speeches were in influencing German policy towards Czechoslovakia was, of course, open to debate. According to Ambassador Hugh Wilson in Berlin, German officials were very interested in the American viewpoint. Similarly, Ambassador Biddle reported from Warsaw that the Polish Government felt that Roosevelt and Hull's speeches 'had undoubtedly had a sobering effect' in Berlin. But Hitler was a law unto himself.[20]

Meanwhile the Runciman mission was making little progress in Prague. Whatever concessions were reluctantly made by the Beneš Government, the Sudeten German Party wanted more. Fearful that Hitler might reject any agreement negotiated in Prague, Halifax urged Runciman, on 25 August, to offer to meet the German Führer in person. The Foreign Office went so far as to provide Runciman with the draft of a telegram to send Hitler, requesting a personal meeting. But Runciman refused to follow up this suggestion, arguing that whatever progress he had achieved in Prague had resulted from his role as an independent mediator and that to broaden his task by including a visit to Germany would be a mistake. Despite coming under increasing pressure from Halifax and the Foreign Office to publish new proposals of his own, Runciman remained convinced that his usefulness, such as it was, depended on his being a mediator rather than an arbitrator.[21]

In these circumstances Halifax stepped up his efforts to keep Hull and Roosevelt informed about British efforts to defuse the Czech situation in the days before Hitler's speech, with almost daily meetings between British and American officials in London and Washington. On 3 September Lindsay delivered a detailed *aide-mémoire* to Hull on the progress made by the Runciman mission and another memo followed soon after. As Moffat noted, it was clear that the Czechs were being urged to make concessions to the Sudeten Germans that at least satisfied the Carlsbad points. In London, Kennedy met with Halifax on 10 and 11 September. Halifax said that secret information reaching the British Government suggested that Hitler was fully prepared to march on Czechoslovakia. He asked what America's reaction would be and Kennedy replied that the US would certainly want to keep out of war. Halifax then asked why Britain should be 'the defender of the ideals and morals of the democracies' rather than the United States, to which Kennedy replied that Britain 'had made the Czechoslovak incident part of their business', whereas US opinion did not feel directly involved.[22]

Hitler's Nuremberg speech

On the evening of 12 September Hitler made his long-awaited speech at the Nuremberg rally. The speech was very outspoken and attacked the Czech Government, and particularly Beneš, for the alleged mistreatment of the Sudeten Germans. Despite this, the initial reaction of the British and French governments was that the speech was not as extreme as they had feared and that it had not made war over the Sudetenland inevitable. Speaking to Kennedy the next day, Sir Samuel Hoare, the Home Secretary – and another former Foreign Secretary – felt that the door had not yet been closed on peace. However, following the speech there were demonstrations and outbreaks of violence in the Sudeten region, including serious incidents at Eger and Aussig where several Sudeten Germans and at least one Czech citizen were killed. Serious injuries to Czechs were also reported from other areas. This led the Czech Government to declare martial law in the Sudetenland and the Sudeten negotiators then broke off talks with the Czechs.[23]

It was against this background, and Runciman's continued reluctance to issue proposals of his own for a settlement, that Chamberlain made his unexpected offer to meet Hitler at Berchtesgaden, the Führer's mountain-top retreat near Munich – Plan Z. In one sense, Chamberlain's meeting with Hitler at Berchtesgaden on 15 September marked the end of the Runciman mission. Lord Runciman and his team left Prague on the same day, never to return. However, in another sense, Chamberlain's flight to Berchtesgaden was a continuation of the mission to reach a peaceful solution of the Czech crisis while keeping Washington fully informed. Prior to 15 September the United States Government was already very well informed as to the situation in Berlin and Prague, thanks to the Foreign Office and the British Embassy as well as its own sources. During the period of Chamberlain's dramatic flight to Berchtesgaden on 15 September and his subsequent trips to Godesberg (22/23 September) and Munich (29/30 September), the campaign to keep Roosevelt and the State Department 'on side' remained an important part of British policy.[24]

The threatening situation in Europe was discussed at the usual Friday US Cabinet meeting on 16 September. According to Ickes, FDR said that 'Chamberlain is for peace at any price,' including the cessation of the Sudetenland to Germany, although he thought there was opposition in the British Cabinet. If the Czechs did not agree and chose to fight, they would be abandoned by Britain and France. 'In the President's graphic language, England and France, during and after this international outrage, will "wash the blood from their Judas Iscariot hands" by arguing that the Czechs had not listened to reason.' Roosevelt thought that British public opinion in general, as well as Labour, the Liberals and some Tories, might well rebel against such a policy if the Czechs did decide to go to war on their own. However, if Germany was prepared to accept the principle of 'national hegemony' and to limit its gains to the German-speaking area of Czechoslovakia, war might be avoided, although Hungary and Poland would move to acquire the areas of the country that had minorities that looked to them for support.[25]

FDR also shared with the Cabinet his views as to how a war could be conducted from the democracies' perspective. According to Ickes, the President did not think France could break through the German frontier, or that Germany could breach the Maginot Line. If he was conducting this war, he would tell the Germans that their sovereignty was not under threat, but he would also impose a tight blockade of the country. He thought that the British fleet would be able to 'bottle up' the German fleet and that supplies to the neutrals surrounding Germany should be rationed if they would not voluntarily join an alliance against Germany, so as to prevent excess supplies getting through the blockade. He also thought the war should be fought mainly from the air, and that the morale of the German people would crack before that of Britain and France. He told the Cabinet that, in his opinion, 'this kind of war would cost less money, would mean comparatively fewer casualties, and would be more likely to succeed than a traditional war'.[26]

Roosevelt's views were not very different from the strategy that the British and French actually employed at the outset of the war, although the President had assumed that the Soviet Union would be on the side of the Allies rather than in a non-aggression pact with Germany. FDR also envisaged a more robust policy towards the neutral countries that were neighbours of Germany if they did not join in an alliance against her. At the next Cabinet on 23 September the President elaborated upon his idea of a strictly defensive war, especially the issue of military supplies to Britain. He estimated Britain's private investments in the US at about $7 billion, which, in the event of war, could be taken over and used for purchasing supplies and munitions, in addition to those that would be obtained from Canada. Roosevelt also said that even if the Neutrality laws had to be enforced, there would be ways for munitions to reach Britain and France via Canada and other methods. Non-military items such as pipes could also be purchased in the US and used to make shells, for example. 'In carrying out our neutrality laws', Ickes recorded the President as saying, 'we would resolve all doubts in favour of the democratic countries.'[27]

FDR and the Munich crisis

Thus, despite his reservations about Chamberlain's policy, Roosevelt was ready to support Britain and France in the event of war. He also felt unable to stand aside as the Czech crisis reached its climax during the second half of September. On the evening of 19 September, he arranged a secret meeting with Sir Ronald Lindsay, the British Ambassador. The President indicated to Lindsay that their meeting was absolutely confidential. 'Nobody must know I had seen him and he himself would tell nobody of the interview. I gathered not even the State Department.' Roosevelt told Lindsay that the sacrifice being asked of Czechoslovakia 'would provoke a highly unfavourable reaction in America'. But he understood the difficulties of the British and French governments and, if their policy proved to be successful, he would be the first to cheer. 'He would like to do or say something to help, but was at a loss to know what. He had no illusions as to the effect in Europe of his previous statements.'[28]

On 26 September, after the Godesberg conference ended in disagreement and war seemed likely, Roosevelt sent a message to Hitler, Beneš, Daladier and Chamberlain, appealing to them not to break off negotiations. Following this appeal, Hitler gave an hour-long speech in the Berlin *Sportpalast* saying that his patience was exhausted and threatening the Czechs with war. On 27 September Chamberlain made a short radio broadcast, in which he said that the British Empire would not go to war with Germany over Czechoslovakia alone. 'If we have to fight it must be on larger issues than that.' A similar message came from Paris. Later that day, following a special Cabinet meeting, Roosevelt sent Hitler a second message in which he argued that agreement in principle over the Sudetenland had already been reached and urged continuation of the negotiations. While reiterating that the United States had 'no political involvements in Europe', Roosevelt declared: 'The conscience and the impelling desire of the people of my country demand that the voice of their government be raised again and yet again to avert and to avoid war.' A message was also sent to Mussolini asking him to use his good offices.[29]

On 28 September Hitler announced his consent to a conference in Munich to resolve the Czech crisis, consisting of Germany, Italy, Britain and France. The Czechs were not invited and nor was the Soviet Union. The ensuing Munich agreement resulted in the transfer of the Sudetenland region to Germany, while the rest of the Czech state was to be guaranteed by the four powers – although Teschen was soon annexed by Poland and Hungary also made territorial demands. According to Ickes's account of the Cabinet meeting held on 27 September, when it was not clear whether the Czech crisis would end peacefully or in war, the entire Cabinet was in favour of aiding the democracies, short of actual participation in the war. FDR was optimistic that, in the event of war, Italy would soon be defeated if she joined in, while Germany would eventually succumb to the combined forces of Britain, France, Russia and an anti-German coalition. Ickes thought that Roosevelt had been very influential during the Czech crisis and recorded that the President had told him that he wanted to avoid the mistake of Woodrow Wilson in 1914, who, he felt, had not used his influence to avert the war.[30]

Whatever the significance of Roosevelt's role in facilitating the Munich conference, there can be no doubt that his intervention was exactly the kind of backing Chamberlain and Halifax had been looking for from the President since the outset of the Runciman mission because of the support it had given to the policy of continuing negotiations with Germany and the consequent effect on British and world opinion. Chamberlain also received FDR's short, but eloquent, 'Good Man' telegram, sent to him on 28 September after Chamberlain had accepted the invitation to Munich. Hoare later wrote that Chamberlain greatly appreciated Roosevelt's brief message and added: 'What two words could better show his full approval of Chamberlain's efforts?' This was somewhat misleading – while FDR admired Chamberlain's dogged pursuit of peace at the end of September 1938 the evidence shows that he was also highly critical of prior British policy, which had resulted in the dilemma facing the democracies at Munich of either abandoning the Czechs or risking a war with Germany for which the democracies were not prepared.[31]

'One other power'

Not surprisingly, the Prime Minister referred to Roosevelt's role during the Munich crisis in his speech to the House of Commons on 3 October. This speech, especially when compared with the views he put forward in the Commons on 26 July, neatly conveys Chamberlain's interpretation of events. The strongest force in favour of peace, he said, was public opinion – 'the unmistakable sense of unanimity among the peoples of the world that war somehow must be averted'. At Munich the leaders of Germany, Italy, France and Britain had all played their part, he said. He then continued:

> There is one other Power which was not represented at the Conference and which nevertheless we felt to be exercising constantly increasing influence – I refer, of course, to the United States of America. Those messages of President Roosevelt, so firmly and yet so persuasively framed, showed how the voice of the most powerful nation in the world could make itself heard across 3,000 miles of ocean and sway the minds of men in Europe.[32]

The Chamberlain–Halifax policy during the Sudetenland crisis shows that, despite their reservations about the role of the United States in international affairs, the two men felt the President had a useful part to play in the diplomacy of Europe, provided that he was kept 'on side'. While Chamberlain had no time for 'bombshells' like the Roosevelt initiative of January 1938 that might complicate his attempt to come to terms with the dictators, he was very happy to receive the President's 'endorsement' of the Anglo-Italian agreement of April 1938 and to seek similar support for the Runciman mission and British policy towards the Sudeten German problem. Looked at in this light, his oft-quoted comment that 'it is always best and safest to count on nothing from the Americans except words' takes on a somewhat different meaning. Supportive American words – as opposed to disconcerting American actions – could be very useful in enlisting public opinion behind British appeasement while reminding the German Government that, if war came, the United States might eventually become involved on the British side.[33]

Clearly, Roosevelt had his doubts about Chamberlain's policy and the likelihood that the appeasement of Germany would be successful in the long run, and he had no desire to be openly associated with the Runciman mission and British pressure on Czechoslovakia. But whereas Hull took refuge, throughout the Sudeten crisis, in generalities about international morality and world peace, Roosevelt could not refrain from becoming directly involved. As he had said to Runciman in January 1937, he saw the Parliamentary countries as the best hope to avoid war and, as the European situation worsened in 1938, he went as far as he could to support British policy. This can be seen in his Kingston speech and his meeting with Lindsay on 19 September, following the failure of Runciman's attempts at mediation and Chamberlain's flight to Berchtesgaden. Above all, it can be seen in his messages at the time of the Munich crisis. But once the crisis was over, he redoubled his efforts to bolster the democracies against further intimidation by Nazi Germany, especially after the *Kristallnacht* pogrom in November 1938, while Chamberlain's faltering appeasement policy meant that he became increasingly dependent in the new year on the President's goodwill.[34]

The view from Berlin

During the critical period leading up to the Munich agreement in September 1938 the German embassy in Washington took the view that the Roosevelt Administration would provide 'moral' – that is, diplomatic – support for British attempts to find a peaceful solution to the Czech crisis and that, if it came to war, the US would assist Britain and France in any way that it could, including the repeal or modification of the Neutrality laws. Indeed, the ideological affinity between the three great democracies of the US, Britain and France was regularly referred to in the American press, and the visit of George VI and Queen Elizabeth to Paris in late July 1938 was the occasion for similar sentiments in Britain and France. 'The "Entente Cordiale" was approved and sealed with the enthusiastic acclamation of press and people with practically no opposition,' reported Count Johannes von Welczeck, the German Ambassador in France. 'The common ideals of democracy, the identical conception of human values and the benefits of individual freedom' were all emphasised during the visit, he added, as were 'the preservation of peace by means of international agreements' and 'by respect for international laws'.[35]

From Washington, Thomsen pointed out that the Neutrality Act masked the real attitude of the Roosevelt Administration towards a European conflict. The fact that 'America has consciously waived the rights of a neutral and conceded to England unrestricted control of the seas' also revealed 'the solidarity of Anglo-American interests'. Indeed, he continued, 'the history of Anglo-American relations since 1914 teaches us that in normal times they occasionally become strained, but that in a crisis solidarity is forthwith adopted'. This was clear from 'the parallelism of Anglo-American policy in recent years', he said, one example of which was the upcoming trade agreement, which had much more than just economic significance. As Thomsen argued,

> If England is involved in a life-and-death struggle, America will, as in 1917, seek by every possible means to prevent the defeat of England, because this would result in a shifting of the balance of power in Europe and Asia, which would directly affect America.

'Herein lies America's vital interest', he said, 'which she already feels to be threatened by the urge toward expansion and the desire for power of the totalitarian states.'[36]

While the Runciman mission undertook its mediation talks in Prague there remained some hope that a deeper crisis leading to war could be avoided. In Berlin, Weizsächer believed that there was no need for a war over the Sudetenland as German aims towards Czechoslovakia could be achieved by diplomacy, and he put this view to Ribbentrop in person, and quite forcefully, at the end of July. The signals emanating from Britain and France appeared to bear out this viewpoint. The British Ambassador in Berlin, Henderson, made it clear that London was doing its best to force Beneš to come to terms with the Sudeten German leaders. There was even less appetite in Paris for a conflict with Germany and reports from Rome suggested that it was 'out of the question that Italy would take an active part in a war breaking out now'. From Washington, Thomsen reported that FDR was 'striving . . . to quell the war psychosis existing there' by denying at a press conference on 9 September that 'a kind of alliance existed between America and the democracies "to stop Hitler"'.[37]

'Chamberlain's radio broadcast on the eve of Munich made a deep impression everywhere here,' reported Ambassador Dieckhoff. 'Comments are all to the effect that it is no longer a matter of the justification or non-justification of the German point of view in the Sudeten question, but the fundamental question of force or peaceful negotiation,' he said. If Hitler accepted the peaceful resolution of the crisis offered by Chamberlain, then this would suggest that he was genuinely concerned only with the Sudeten German question. But if he resorted to force, it would show that he really had a programme of conquest and that he had to be stopped. 'There is reason to assume that this view is also the view of the American Government, who are doing everything to suppress the existing but decreasing isolationist tendency among the American people, so that, when the moment comes, the whole weight of the US can be thrown into the scale on the side of Britain,' Dieckhoff continued, before adding, 'I consider it my duty to emphasise this very strongly.'[38]

In the event, the Munich agreement averted war in September 1938, and the German Embassy in Washington was optimistic that a corner had been turned in relations with the United States. 'Germany's brilliant diplomatic success at the Munich conference is generally acknowledged here today,' Dieckhoff enthused, adding that 'as the eyes of America are always particularly directed upon London', the joint declaration between Hitler and Chamberlain on Anglo-German relations was being given special attention. There were still 'numerous antagonists' in the US who could not accept 'this enormous German success', he continued, especially 'Jews and pacifists'. But he thought 'the vast majority of the American people' were grateful that war had been avoided. However, the Ambassador, like Berlin's other diplomats, was at the mercy of events – not least the *Kristallnacht* pogrom in November 1938, which cut the ground from under whatever supporters the Reich had in Washington.[39]

Notes

1. Chamberlain, *Hansard*, House of Commons, 26 July 1938; CAB 36 (38), item 1, 28 July 1938; FO/371/21730, C7757/1941/18, FO minute by Halifax, 29 July 1938; MacDonald, *US, Britain and Appeasement*, pp. 89–91.
2. FRUS/1938/I, Kennedy to Hull, 29 July 1938, pp. 537–9; Runciman to Roosevelt, 28 July 1938 in Schewe, *FDRFA*, Vol. 6, doc 1208.
3. Hull to FDR, 26 July 1938; Hooker, *Moffat Papers*, 12 May 1938, quoted in MacDonald, *US, Britain and Appeasement*, p. 90.
4. See McCulloch, 'FDR and Runciman Mission', pp. 152–9, for the motives behind the mission.
5. Mackenzie King Diary, 28, 29, 30 July and 18 August 1938.
6. For origins of Czech crisis see Shen, *Age of Appeasement*, pp. 173–93; Bouverie, *Appeasing Hitler*, pp. 192–210.
7. For May 1938 crisis see also Watt, 'Hitler's Visit to Rome and the May Weekend Crisis', pp. 23–32.
8. Dallek, *FDR*, pp. 161–8 for origins of Czech crisis; FRUS/1938/I, docs 493–521 (14 March–31 May 1938) for State Department correspondence; Berle diary, 26 May 1938, p. 177.
9. Watt, *How War Came*, pp. 27–8. Farnham, *Roosevelt and Munich Crisis*; Vysny, *Runciman Mission*; McCulloch, 'FDR and Runciman Mission', pp. 154–5.
10. Runciman papers, Box 284, Murray to Runciman, 27 July 1938.
11. *Hansard*, House of Commons debates, Sinclair and Chamberlain, 26 July 1938.
12. DGFP/D/I, doc 313, minute by Weizsäcker for Ribbentrop, 25 July 1938.
13. *NYT*, 17 August and 28 August 1938; Schewe, *FDRFA*, Vol. 6, doc 1211, Murray to Roosevelt, 30 July 1938.
14. Mackenzie King Diary, 18 August 1938; Schewe, *FDRFA*, Vol. 6, doc 1225, memo by A. Berle for FDR, 15 August 1938.
15. Mackenzie King Diary, 18 August 1938; Schewe, *FDRFA*, Vol. 6, doc 1234, Speech by Roosevelt, Queen's University, 18 August 1938.
16. FO/371/21526, A6491/64/45, Lindsay to Halifax, 18 August 1938; minute by Perowne, 21 August; Mackenzie King Diary, 20 August 1938; see Perras, *Origins of Canadian–American Security Alliance*, for the Ogdensburg agreement.

17. *The Times*, 28 August 1938; DBFP/3/II, doc 704, Halifax to Newton, 27 August 1938; FRUS/1938/I, pp. 549–51, Johnson to Hull, 24 August 1938; DBFP/3/II, doc 679, Halifax to Lindsay, 24 August 1938.
18. FRUS/1938/I, pp. 560–1, Kennedy to Hull, 30 August 1938.
19. FRUS/1938/I, pp. 568–9, Kennedy to Hull, 31 August 1938; Hull to Kennedy, 1 September 1938.
20. FRUS/1938/I, pp. 566–7, Wilson to Hull, 1 September 1938; Ibid., pp. 576–7, Biddle to Hull, 5 September 1938.
21. DBFP/3/II, docs 686 and 687, Halifax to Newton, 25 August 1938; DBFP/3/II, doc 695, Newton to Halifax, 26 August 1938; DBFP/3/II, 1938, doc 723, Runciman to Halifax, 30 August 1938.
22. DBFP/3/II, 1938, doc 741, Halifax to Lindsay, 2 September 1938; FRUS/1938/I, pp. 574–6, aide memoire, Lindsay to Hull, 3 September 1938; DBFP/3/II, 1938, doc 79; Halifax to Lindsay, 6 September 1938; FRUS/1938/I, pp. 580–1, memorandum by Moffat, 7 September 1938; Ibid., pp. 584–5, Kennedy to Hull, 9 September 1938; Ibid., pp. 584–6, Kennedy to Hull, 10 September 1938; Ibid., pp. 587–8, Kennedy to Hull, 11 September 1938.
23. *The Times*, 13 September 1938 for Hitler's speech; FRUS/1938/I, p.591, Kennedy to Hull, 12 September 1938; FRUS/1938/I, p. 592, Kennedy to Hull, 13 September 1938; FRUS/1938/I, p. 593, Carr to Hull, 13 September 1938.
24. FRUS/1938/I, pp. 605–6, Carr to Hull, 16 September 1938; Runciman papers, Box 354, memo by Robert Stopford on the Runciman mission (1968).
25. Ickes, *Diary*, II, 18 September 1938, pp. 467–9.
26. Ibid., pp. 469–70.
27. Ickes, *Diary*, II, 24 September 1938, pp. 472–4.
28. Farnham, *Roosevelt and the Munich Crisis*, pp. 106–7; DBFP/3/VII, pp. 627–9, Lindsay to Halifax, 20 September 1938; Hooker, *Moffat Papers*, 16 September 1938.
29. Haight, *American Aid to France*, pp. 19–21; Schewe; *FDRFA*, Vol. 7, doc 1303, Roosevelt to Hitler, 27 September 1938; Farnham, *Roosevelt and the Munich Crisis*, pp. 108–36.
30. See Ickes, *Diary*, II, 30 September 1938, pp. 476–81.
31. FRUS/1938/I, p. 688, FDR to Chamberlain, 28 September 1938; Haight, *American Aid to France*, pp. 21–2; Templewood, *Nine Troubled Years*, pp. 325–6; Rock, *Chamberlain and Roosevelt*, p. 125.
32. *Hansard*, House of Commons, Chamberlain, 3 October 1938.
33. Feiling, *Chamberlain*, p. 325.
34. McCulloch, 'FDR and Runciman Mission', pp. 170–1.
35. DGFP/D/I, doc 308, Welczeck to GFM (DAA), 22 July 1938.
36. DGFP/D/I, doc 462, Thomsen to GFM, 12 September 1938.

37. DGFP/D/I, doc 329, memorandum by Weizsächer, 31 July 1938; doc 331, memorandum by Weizsächer of a conversation with Ribbentrop; doc 419, minute by Weizsächer to Ribbentrop, 1 September 1938; doc 421, Thomsen to GFM, 2 September 1938; doc 453, Thomsen to GFM, 10 September 1938.
38. DGFP/D/I, doc 651, Dieckhoff to GFM, 27 September 1938.
39. DGFP/D/IV, doc 497, Dieckhoff to GFM, 30 September 1938.

9 'Unspoken Alliance', October–December 1938

Shortly after the Munich agreement the British author and travel writer Robert Byron visited America and spent several weeks gauging US public opinion in the wake of the Czech crisis. He later wrote to a member of the Foreign Office:

> If the impact of Munich has made the average American realise the extent to which he has depended all these years on the British Fleet for the security of the Atlantic seaboard, if he now believes that he can depend on the British Fleet no longer and if, in consequence, his Government decides to provide him with new bases and fortifications extending to the Gulf of Mexico, the Munich Agreement may well be celebrated by the future historian as the event which transformed the Unspoken Alliance from an abstraction to a political fact.

But, he cautioned, the impression of British weakness should not be allowed to go too far. 'If one partner believes, however untruly, that the other is not pulling its weight, he will be disinclined to accept responsibility for the other's commitments.' Americans were 'puzzled out of their wits' by Munich and so their faith needed to be restored in British power, especially the Navy, which was still the strongest in the world.[1]

Byron, a strong critic of Chamberlain and British appeasement, was in the United States from 25 October to 10 December 1938. He had been dismayed by the Prime Minister's reaction to the *Anschluss* and even more so by the Munich agreement, and on his return from the US he produced a paper on American opinion in the wake of the Munich crisis which, through the historian G. M. Young, was passed to King George VI's private secretary as being of possible use for the upcoming Royal Visit to America. Young later commented to Byron: 'Wherever the K**g turns someone respectfully tenders him a copy of your memorandum.' Byron's paper, which was sent to the Foreign Office as well as to the King, was entitled 'Unspoken Alliance' and, after stating that 'England occupies quite a different place in the American mind from any other country', argued that an emphasis on common ideals of democracy and the rule of law was the best way of winning American 'hearts and minds' to support Britain (and France) against Nazi Germany and the dictator states.[2]

Munich aftermath

The aim of this chapter is to examine the impact of the Munich crisis on Anglo-American relations and to show how American opinion – and not least FDR himself – while relieved that the Czech crisis had not led to war, soon came to believe that the Munich agreement had by no means brought about 'peace in our time', as Chamberlain had claimed. Indeed, the months immediately following the Munich crisis provide clear evidence of Roosevelt and his Administration taking urgent steps to aid the democracies, bolster British resolve and deter the dictator states. These steps included the President's efforts regarding US aircraft production, the Anglo-American trade agreement signed in November 1938, the strong reaction to the *Kristallnacht* pogrom, and the confidential message given to Arthur Murray for Neville Chamberlain, regarding the industrial resources of the United States, that was delivered to the Prime Minister in December 1938. These examples of US support for Britain and France provide the background to Roosevelt's State of Union address in January 1939, with its reference to 'methods short of war, but stronger than mere words' to oppose aggression.[3]

However, as some historians have pointed out, Chamberlain did not readily abandon his hope that Munich would lead to a long-term peace. While some members of the Government, such as Duff Cooper, resigned from the Cabinet in protest and others – including Halifax – realised that Hitler and Nazi Germany were now all the stronger, Chamberlain clung on to the policy of appeasement, even going so far as to authorise secret talks with the Nazi regime. On 23 November 1938 Sir Horace Wilson held a secret meeting with Fritz Hesse at the German Embassy – soon after *Kristallnacht* – to appeal to Hitler to help improve the attitude of British public opinion towards Germany. Recently declassified papers 'reveal Chamberlain told Hitler that it would have "the greatest effect on public opinion in England" if, in the event of war, they had a pact in place not to use poison gas, not to bomb each other's civilians and to spare cities with cultural treasures'. The meeting took place without the knowledge of the Cabinet or even Halifax, the Foreign Secretary, but it came to the notice of MI5, who passed the details on to Cadogan. The Under Secretary informed his superior but when Halifax confronted Chamberlain with the facts the Prime Minister denied any foreknowledge of the meeting – a very unlikely defence.[4]

Mackenzie King was also reluctant to abandon appeasement. He found Chamberlain's speech on 27 September 'deeply moving' and 'very chivalrous' and later issued a statement supporting Chamberlain's views. He was also pleased with FDR's appeals. 'Roosevelt has done well in the manner in which he has spoken out, though political conditions compel him to avoid commitments. The moral influence is there and would mean ultimately active participation by the US.' News of Hitler's decision to attend a conference in Munich was 'an immense relief' and when, on 29 September, word came that an agreement had been reached he went to his library, knelt down and thanked God 'for the peace that had been preserved to the world'. But like that of many others, his relief was short-lived, especially following *Kristallnacht*. 'The way the Germans have allowed their younger men to destroy Jewish property and others siding with the government to deal with Jews in higher positions is appalling,' he wrote on 12 November. 'We are facing an era of barbarism.' Two days later he wrote: 'I loathe expenditure for military purposes, but we are dealing with gangster nations, especially in the case of Germany and Japan.[5]

Churchill and America

Byron was a man of the left, as well as a man of letters. He was also well informed and had attended the Nuremberg rally and Hitler's speech on 12 September on behalf of British Intelligence before his American trip. His memorandum on the 'Unspoken Alliance' shows that Churchill was not the only Englishman at this time who believed that Anglo-American relations had a special character, based on a common heritage and belief in democracy as well as the strategic relationship between the two countries. Byron was also a founding member of the Federal Union Club, an idea based on Clarence Streit's book, *Union Now*, that advocated a federal organisation, more effective than the League of Nations, 'to override the selfish policies of individual states'. Lord Lothian was also a supporter of 'Federal Union', while others on the liberal side of British politics, such as the Labour MP Colonel Josiah Wedgwood, and Arthur Murray, the former Scottish Liberal MP and friend of Roosevelt and Runciman, were tireless advocates of closer Anglo-American relations despite the continuing strength of isolationism in the United States. So too was Henry Wickham Steed, the journalist and former editor of *The Times*, which ran a series of articles in June 1938 on 'The America of Roosevelt'.[6]

The best-known advocate of what he later referred to as the 'special relationship' was, of course, Winston Churchill. In July 1938 Churchill wrote to his wife that, according to Bernard Baruch, 'the President is breast-high on our side and will do everything in his power to help. . . . Opinion in the States had never been so friendly to us.' It was therefore 'a great pity', Churchill continued, that 'matters cannot be carried further now. Apparently, you always have to have a disaster before anything sensible can be done which would prevent it.' Writing in the *Daily Telegraph* soon after, he posed the question:

> Will the United States throw their weight into the scales of peace and law and freedom while time remains, or will they remain spectators until the disaster has occurred; and then, with infinite cost and labour, build up what need not have been cast down?

This was, Churchill opined, 'the riddle of a Sphinx who under the mask of loquacity, affability, sentimentality, hard business, machine-made politics, wrong-feeling, right-feeling, vigour and weakness, efficiency and muddle, still preserves the power to pronounce a solemn and formidable word'.[7]

Shortly after denouncing the Munich agreement in the House of Commons as 'a total and unmitigated defeat', Churchill delivered a major radio broadcast in which he argued that a joint declaration by Britain, France and Russia on behalf of Czechoslovakia would have been sufficient to deter Hitler from invading Czechoslovakia. Echoing Sir Edward Grey in 1914, he said: 'The lights are going out. But there is still time for those to whom freedom and parliamentary government mean something to consult together.' There was no doubt where American sympathies lay, he continued. 'But would they wait until British freedom and independence succumbed, and then take up the cause when it was three-quarters ruined?' The British Government, for its part, needed to demonstrate the contrast between Nazism and democracy. 'The resolute and sober acceptance of their duty by the English-speaking peoples and by all the nations, great and small, who wish to walk with them' was 'the sole guarantee of peace', he maintained, and their 'faithful and zealous comradeship' would be able to deter the Nazi threat. It was no doubt sentiments like this that led Hitler to attack Churchill in his speech at Saarbrücken on 9 October, when he criticised Britain for interfering in German affairs and added that if Churchill, Eden or Duff Cooper were to join the British Government, 'their aim would be immediate war with Germany'.[8]

FDR and air power

Behind the scenes, the Roosevelt Administration was redoubling its efforts to bolster Britain and France in standing up to Nazi Germany. While the President was far from happy with the Munich agreement, he had felt the need to go along with British and French efforts to avoid a war over the Sudetenland, even at the expense of the Czechs. He was well aware of the deficiencies in the British, and especially the French, air forces in comparison with Germany – not only from a first-hand report by Colonel Charles Lindberg, who had toured the front-line countries in September 1938, but from other American observers in Europe. He was also very aware of US shortcomings in military aircraft production which made it impossible to bridge the gap in air power between Germany and the democracies overnight. Following Hitler's Nuremberg speech on 12 September, Roosevelt had asked Harry Hopkins, the head of the Works Progress Administration (WPA), to undertake a survey of the aircraft industry on the west coast and to make recommendations as to how WPA funds could be used to build new plants there, on the basis of reducing unemployment.[9]

An indication of FDR's thinking in the wake of the Munich crisis can be seen in a report sent to London by the British air attaché in Washington on 29 September that, as Haight has noted, was very similar to the President's views as expressed at the US Cabinet meeting on 23 September. According to the attaché, Roosevelt said that he believed the Munich agreement was forced on Britain and France because of their weakness in terms of air power and he was determined that the United States would never find itself in that position. The President had instigated a survey of plane production in the United States with the aim of outdoing German production as soon as possible, so that if Germany was producing 30,000 planes per year, the US would produce 40,000. Indeed, by 1941 – before Pearl Harbor – US annual production of aircraft was greater than Germany's and not far behind Britain's. As regards the Neutrality Act, especially the arms embargo, Roosevelt pointed out that the US could supply Britain and France with partly finished basic materials such as 'fabricated aluminium, tubing, steel castings, magnetos, and other accessories', which would enable them to 'build aircraft far in excess of German production'. He also said that Canada could build factories to assemble aircraft using parts imported from the United States.[10]

FDR's concern over the deficiencies in the air power of the democracies was not new. The issue had been raised during the Runciman visit in January 1937 and the President had requested then – and received – confidential information from the Air Ministry regarding aircraft production. The *Anschluss* in March 1938 had aroused fears that both France and Britain had fallen far behind Germany, and both governments had sent air missions to the US in May 1938. These missions discovered that the US military aircraft industry was far from advanced but both governments had placed small orders in the US. The Munich crisis brought to the fore the weaknesses in the air of the democracies and the Air Ministry decided to order an additional 200 Harvards from the United States. The French position regarding air power was even worse than Britain's, as Bullitt discovered during a lunch meeting with Daladier, Guy La Chambre and Monnet on 3 October. Bullitt immediately returned to Washington to brief the President, who agreed that Monnet should also come to the US to discuss the situation and how US manufacturers could help.[11]

On 12 October Roosevelt received a report from Bernard Baruch dealing with the rearmament problems of the European democracies and the need for the US to build its defences in the face of Germany's call for rearmament. The President then requested that the US Air Corps prepare plans for rapid expansion of American aircraft production and asked the State Department to draw up a strategy for the removal of the arms embargo. On 14 October FDR met with Louis Johnson, the Assistant Secretary of War, in charge of procurement, to discuss aircraft production. At his weekly press conference on the same day, the President announced what he called 'a complete restudy of American national defence'. He said he was aiming for this review to be completed by 3 January 1939, which was the day before the State of Union message. When asked why it was necessary to reorganise 'the whole national defence picture', he replied that 'events, developments and information received within the past month' had brought matters to a head: in other words, the reports from Bullitt and Baruch about the lack of modern planes and equipment that had weakened the British and French position during the Czech crisis and culminated in the Munich settlement.[12]

Murray visit

FDR then left for a stay at Hyde Park, from 16 to 24 October, that included talks with Morgenthau, Bullitt and Monnet about the French Government obtaining American planes. Monnet left for France on 30 October and reported to Daladier. On 9 December – after discussions in the French Cabinet – Daladier announced that France would order 1,000 planes from the US for delivery by July 1939. Another visitor to Hyde Park at this time was Arthur Murray, who had arranged the visit of Walter Runciman to Washington in January 1937. Murray had been Assistant Military Attaché in Washington, 1917–18, when Roosevelt was Assistant Secretary of the Navy. He had resumed his friendship when Roosevelt was running for President and Murray and his wife stayed at the White House in May 1935. Murray had been involved in British intelligence operations during the First World War, passing highly confidential information between Washington and London, so he was well used to the need for secrecy as well as being a good friend of the President and Eleanor Roosevelt. During his stay at Hyde Park Murray discussed the European situation with Roosevelt, who again laid particular emphasis on the need for the democracies to improve their air power.[13]

On 21 October Roosevelt talked with Murray about the German air programme and suggested that, in the event of war and the United States being neutral, he would still be able to help the democracies. 'The President asked me to convey his very sincere greetings and best wishes to the Prime Minister, and an assurance of his desire to help in every way in his power,' recorded

Murray. 'I will help all I can,' he said, and he wanted Murray to tell the Prime Minister that, insofar as Roosevelt was able to do so, he would put 'the industrial resources of the American nation behind him in the event of war with the dictatorships'. He did not want Chamberlain to use this phrase in public but he agreed that the Prime Minister could say, whenever he thought fit, that 'Great Britain, in the event of war, could rely upon obtaining raw materials from the democracies of the world.' What he had in mind was to provide partly finished basic materials that were not included in the Neutrality law's arms embargo, such as plates for wings and steel castings for engines. Roosevelt added that people in America were at last beginning to realise that the aims of the dictators were not limited to Europe and that Germany had definite designs on South America.[14]

Roosevelt had another talk with Murray on 23 October and he asked him to convey the plans they had discussed to Lord Tweedsmuir, Governor General of Canada, and to advise him to suggest to Mackenzie King that liaison officers be appointed to facilitate cooperation between the US and Canada and 'to obviate any undue rise in contract prices'. The President said he believed that 'through the liaison thus established, it would be possible for information as regards design, engines and other aspects of aeroplane manufacture, to pass confidentially between the US, Canadian and British Governments to the extent that each thought fit'. But, as his comments were 'entirely sub-rosa', he warned that 'existing official channels . . . should not for various reasons be used for this purpose'. Roosevelt asked Murray to pass this message on to Mackenzie King when he visited Canada after his stay at Hyde Park. Murray was, indeed, able to pass on the message via Tweedsmuir to Mackenzie King, who discussed these issues with Roosevelt in Washington in November 1938 when the Anglo-American trade agreement was finally signed, alongside a Canadian–American trade agreement.[15]

Kristallnacht

Roosevelt's talks with Murray and his messages to Chamberlain afford evidence that – like Churchill and other critics of the Prime Minister's appeasement policy – the President did not expect the peace obtained at Munich to last for long. Clearly, he was planning in October to increase his material, as distinct from his moral, support of the European democracies. He was doubtless strengthened in this resolve by events in Germany which suggested that Hitler's regime had no desire to mend its ways. In particular, a massive pogrom on the night of 9/10 November – generally known as *Kristallnacht* – led the President to recall the American Ambassador, Hugh Wilson, who had only recently replaced Dodd in Berlin. He announced this move in a statement from the White House which was a stronger version of one that had been prepared in the State Department. 'The news of the past few days from Germany has deeply shocked public opinion in the United States,' read the President's statement. 'I myself could scarcely believe that such things could occur in a twentieth century civilisation.'[16]

Wilson's recall from Berlin was a major setback for relations between the US and Germany, which he had been striving hard to improve following the departure of Dodd, and his more positive attitude was appreciated by the German Foreign Ministry. He was not formally withdrawn in November, but he never returned to Berlin. The German Government retaliated by recalling Dieckhoff from Washington for consultation on 18 November 1938. Dieckhoff continued in his post as ambassador until 11 December 1941, when Germany declared war on the US after Pearl Harbor, but he was resident in Berlin and, like Wilson, he never returned to his post. In his absence the management of the German Embassy in Washington was overseen by the Chargé d'Affaires, Hans Thomsen. Nevile Henderson, the British Ambassador, had gone on sick leave in October 1938 but returned to Berlin in February 1939 and was not withdrawn until the outbreak of war – even remaining in post after the German annexation of Prague in March 1939.[17]

At what John Morton Blum described as 'a momentous White House meeting' on 14 November 1938, the President met with Henry Morgenthau and officials from the Treasury, Justice and War Departments, together with senior Army and Navy officers, to review his plans for American defence, particularly those for aircraft production. Roosevelt began by revealing the latest information he had received about the air situation in Europe – France had about 600 air-worthy planes and Britain had between 1,500 and 2,200, while Germany could call on 5,500–6,500 first-line and 1,000 second-line planes. Furthermore, the gap between the democracies and the dictatorships was growing bigger as French production was very low and British production was not much better. 'The President then pointed out that the recrudescence of German power at Munich had completely reoriented our own international relations,' noted Morgenthau. 'For the first time since the Holy Alliance in 1818 the United States now faced the possibility of an attack on the Atlantic side in both the Northern and Southern Hemispheres.' The President argued that this situation required rapid action to provide 'a huge air force so that we do not need to have a huge army to follow that air force. He considered that sending a large army abroad was undesirable and politically out of the question.'[18]

Roosevelt also pointed out that in 1917 it required more than a year after the declaration of war to start sending planes to Europe. In the event of another war it would be necessary to act much more quickly. 'I am not sure now that I am proud of what I wrote to Hitler in urging that he sit down around the table and make peace,' Morgenthau remembered the President as saying. Roosevelt continued:

> When I write to foreign countries I must have something to back up my words. Had we had this summer 5000 planes and the capacity immediately to produce 10,000 per year, even though I might have had to ask Congress for authority to sell or lend them to the countries in Europe, Hitler would not have dared to take the stand he did.

Although the Army and Navy representatives did not endorse FDR's single-minded emphasis on air power, they supported his proposal for a greatly enlarged industrial capacity to enable the US to produce 10,000–20,000 planes per year and, together with the Treasury, they worked out the details of the defence programme he presented to Congress in January 1939, shortly after his State of the Union address.[19]

Trade agreement

The Anglo-American trade agreement, after long and arduous negotiations, was eventually concluded six weeks after Munich, in November 1938. This agreement was central to Hull's trade policy and to his world programme of 'economic disarmament'. Ever since the passage of the Reciprocal Trade Agreements Act in June 1934, the Secretary had set his sights on an agreement with

Britain. 'It seemed to me that our trade agreements programme could not be considered complete until the United Kingdom was inserted as the apex of the arch,' he later wrote. But to maximise the political value of the agreement he felt he needed significant British concessions, especially on agricultural items important to the South. In a formal note of 5 October 1938, he submitted the final American requests to Lindsay and said: 'I am not prepared to sign an agreement which does not include more comprehensive concessions on the part of your Government.' He recognised that Imperial Preference limited the scope for British concessions, but he maintained that there were other items, not affected by the Ottawa agreements, on which further concessions could be made. Lindsay urged London to accept Hull's final requests and argued that a trade agreement was still of great political importance.[20]

On 19 October the Cabinet discussed the final American requests. Halifax stressed the great diplomatic importance of securing a trade agreement, while Chamberlain pointed out that a breakdown in negotiations would be very serious. 'He had never hoped that we should obtain any great economic or political support from the United States as a result of making this Agreement,' ran the minutes. 'The advantages to be derived were of a somewhat negative kind. It was clear that if after months of negotiations no Agreement was reached, hard things would be said.' Eventually, the Cabinet decided to allow further concessions on lard and maize but not on the other American requests. On 25 October Lindsay gave Hull the British reply. The Secretary expressed his disappointment but said that he would seek Roosevelt's approval to accept the final concessions from London. Roosevelt was in favour of action, having remarked to Henry Morgenthau in October 1938 that the trade agreement programme was 'just too goddamned slow. The world is marching too fast.' Roosevelt also told his Cabinet that 'it bordered on the ridiculous to think that America could improve the international situation merely by selling a few barrels of apples here and a couple of automobiles there'.[21]

On 4 November, Sayre informed Lindsay officially of the US acceptance of the remaining British concessions. The Anglo-American trade agreement was finally signed in the East Room of the White House on 17 November 1938, one week after the Congressional elections. The main participants were the President, Lindsay, Hull, Mackenzie King, who signed a Canadian–American trade agreement, and Arnold Overton, the head of the British trade delegation. But the man of the hour was Cordell Hull. 'Today was the big day in Mr Hull's career,' noted Moffat, who was again head of the European Division of the State Department. Mackenzie King also recorded Hull's sense of achievement. 'Mr Hull was greatly delighted with the conclusion of the Trade Agreements and could not be too friendly. If I had been a long-lost brother, I could not have received a warmer welcome,' he noted. 'He spoke almost immediately of how pleasant the negotiations had been between Canada and the United States and indicated there had been a good deal of difficulty in the other negotiations.'[22]

While in Washington Mackenzie King spoke to Roosevelt, Hull and Welles about the European situation. Roosevelt said he thought that Germany was seeking to gain a strong foothold in South America and that the US must be prepared to defend itself, because with the advent of air power it was no longer beyond reach. He developed this point with Mackenzie King later and complained that Britain and France had been 'appallingly blind' over air defence and had let Germany get too far ahead. He said that he had made his appeal to Hitler after he and the Cabinet had listened to Chamberlain's address on the radio on 27 September and had been much moved by it. But he pointed out that Chamberlain was now very unpopular in the United States because of the reaction against Munich – a point made by Byron in his 'Unspoken Alliance' memorandum. Mackenzie King had urged Chamberlain to attend the signing of the trade agreement, but he was exhausted after Munich, as he confided to Baldwin.[23]

It is difficult to say who got the better of the trade agreement between Britain and the United States in economic terms. Taking 1936 as the basis of comparison, duties were reduced on 27 per cent of British exports to the United States and on 11 per cent of American exports to Britain. On the other hand, the United States did have a substantial trade surplus with Britain, and this did not change after the agreement. Nor had the agreement brought the end of Imperial Preference and, at most, it made but a small dent in the Ottawa agreements. The trade agreements were generally well received by the press in London, Ottawa and Washington. The main criticism in America came, not surprisingly, from the isolationist Hearst press, which launched a strong attack on the agreements and on Hull's trade policy in general. But the influential radio commentator, Raymond Gram Swing, emphasised the contribution of the Anglo-American trade agreement in helping to counter the bad impression made by the Munich settlement. 'The emotional distance between Britain and the United States was widening and signing this agreement just at this time has suddenly wiped out most of that distance,' he said.[24]

In diplomatic terms, Francis Sayre, the Assistant Secretary of State in charge of the trade agreements programme, described the agreement as 'the effective reply to the defeatism which appeared in some quarters after the Munich settlement'. This was its short-term significance – an indication that, after Munich, Anglo-American relations were still close. Nor should the consequences of the trade agreement not materialising be forgotten. If, after months of negotiations, the two sides had not reached agreement, this would have been a tremendous setback. It would not only have undermined Hull's economic programme for world peace and possibly have alienated him from the British Government, it would also have represented great problems for Roosevelt's own attempts to cement relations with Britain. For example, it would probably have made it more difficult to modify the Neutrality laws against the opposition of the isolationists. However, an agreement was signed, and the Roosevelt Administration could now move on to other things.[25]

It may not have been a bad thing that Chamberlain was unable to attend the signing of the trade agreement, as a more popular British representative, Anthony Eden, made the trip across the Atlantic in the following month. His speech in New York on 9 December to the National Association of American Manufacturers was broadcast on radio and was a moderate defence of British foreign policy, including an early reference to the recent trade agreement as a sign of good relations between Britain and the United States. It was fortunate for Chamberlain that Roosevelt was committed to aiding Britain, as American public opinion after Munich was largely hostile to the National Government. Eden received a hero's welcome, which contrasted with the decline in popularity of Chamberlain himself. 'I was horrified at the atmosphere I found,' Eden wrote to Baldwin, who, with Kennedy, had been largely responsible for the visit. He added that

> 90% of the U.S. is firmly persuaded that you and I are the only two Tories who are not Fascists in disguise. Certainly, HMG have contrived to lose American sympathy utterly ... most of my time was spent in asserting that Neville was not a Fascist, nor John Simon always a 'double-crosser'.[26]

Murray and Chamberlain

After his visit to Hyde Park Murray returned to London on 20 November and wrote to Halifax, asking to see Chamberlain in person so as to convey the messages from Roosevelt. Halifax invited Murray to see him at the Foreign Office on 29 November. Next day he reported the conversation to the Prime Minister, who, apparently, had not been keen to meet Murray. 'When I saw Arthur Murray yesterday, I failed to ride him off seeing you,' wrote Halifax. 'He was especially charged to give you personal messages from the President – & would feel unhappy if he could not say he had seen you.' The Foreign Secretary felt that a meeting would be well worthwhile, especially in view of Murray's message from Roosevelt that Britain could count upon American raw materials in the event of war. 'I told him that if we could get something out of the President about war potential, it would be really valuable, & he did not think that this was at all out of the realm of possibility,' Halifax continued. 'But I do think it would be worth your seeing him. He is evidently very close to F.R.'[27]

Eventually, a meeting was arranged with Chamberlain at the House of Commons on 14 December and Murray reported on his talks with FDR in October. According to Murray, the Prime Minister felt it was 'very encouraging indeed' to have the President's private assurance that Britain 'would have the industrial resources of the American nation behind him'. As regards Roosevelt's statement that Great Britain could rely upon receiving raw materials from the democracies of the world, Chamberlain commented: 'It might be most important. There is no question but that in certain circumstances a statement, which really brought it home that the vast resources of the United States would be behind Great Britain, might have a properly deterrent effect.' Chamberlain was not sure that it would influence Hitler but, as he said to Murray, 'at any rate, a statement of this kind might certainly have a powerfully deterrent effect on the rest of them and on the Army and make them do their best to put a brake on Hitler if his idea looked like bursting out'.[28]

Having successfully accomplished his mission, Murray wrote once more to Roosevelt. He said that Chamberlain deeply appreciated the messages and was certainly encouraged by them. 'He asked me to tell you that he was immensely grateful to you for all that you had done and were doing, not only by your very powerful messages to Hitler at the time of the crisis, but generally by your exceedingly sympathetic and helpful attitude throughout these trying times.' Murray had also conveyed to Chamberlain the President's views on the German air programme and the issue of Palestine, which was coming to the fore. In addition, Murray passed on Roosevelt's aims concerning aircraft construction to Sir Kingsley Wood, the Secretary of State for Air. Chamberlain was to use FDR's message in the new year, especially in his Birmingham speech on 28 January 1939 when he stated that 'any aggressor who tried to win world power by war would find the great democracies lined up against him'.[29]

The view from Berlin

The optimism of the German Embassy in Washington that the Munich agreement would usher in a period of conciliation between Germany and the US was completely undermined by *Kristallnacht*. 'At the moment a hurricane is raging here which renders steady work impossible,' Dieckhoff reported after the pogrom. 'The outcry comes not only from Jews but in equal strength from all camps and classes, including the German–American camp.' Even 'the respectable patriotic circles, which are thoroughly anti-Communist and, for the greater part, anti-Semitic in their outlook, also begin to turn away from us'. Thus 'the argument which we have hitherto put forward against the American propaganda campaign and their peace sabotage, that the Europeans, since Munich, are on the threshold of jointly building up a new peaceful Europe, is reduced ad absurdum or at any rate largely discredited'. Dieckhoff wrote in similar vein to Weizsäcker, saying that the American press, always critical of Germany, was now even more hostile than before. The situation was further exacerbated by the outcry in Britain, which had resulted in 'increased obstacles' to cooperation between London and Berlin – 'a fact which – as I have always reported – is immediately noted here and poisons the atmosphere'.[30]

The German Foreign Ministry was especially concerned that the withdrawal of Wilson and Dieckhoff as ambassadors might lead to a complete rupture in relations with Washington. Ernst Woermann, the Director of the Political Department, felt that a rupture would be a logical conclusion of the anti-German campaign that had been waged by the Administration and much of the American press, and would give Roosevelt even more scope for attacking Germany. Ever since his re-election, Woermann argued, Roosevelt had orchestrated a 'campaign of incitement against Germany' and had 'created in the minds of the American people a psychological receptiveness to any anti-German measures even though these might in the end involve America in war'. He thought that a rupture would have serious consequences for Germany in Latin America, where 'American propaganda and economic pressure' were already at work, especially in Brazil, Argentina and Chile. Roosevelt would also attempt 'to align the big European democracies with the anti-dictatorship front. Even as Wilson had, Roosevelt has also his saviour complex,' he argued. 'Whereas Wilson wanted to make the world safe for "democracy", Roosevelt wishes to overthrow the dictatorships and to restore the world authority of liberalism, the one and only true political creed.'[31]

On 14 December Washington officially protested against a post-*Kristallnacht* decree that excluded Jews, including those who possessed foreign citizenship, from the German economy. Thomsen warned Berlin that relations between the US and Germany had 'entered a decisive phase' and that Roosevelt might employ reprisals against Germany, especially by raising duties on German goods. Dieckhoff, now back in Germany, agreed and urged Weizsäcker to make a positive reply to the American note. 'I consider a breach to be politically and economically so grave a matter that we must avoid it under any circumstances as long as we possibly can,' he said. Heeding this advice, the German reply to the American Note was quite conciliatory, stating that existing treaty rights with the United States would be respected and asking to be informed of any problem cases so that they could be examined. In its reply, Washington reiterated its position that US citizens must not be subject to discrimination in Germany but accepted the procedure put forward by Berlin, whereby any individual cases that appeared to breach existing treaties between the US and Germany would be submitted to the German Foreign Ministry for review.[32]

It is clear from the above that Berlin officials were anxious to avoid a breach with Washington in the wake of *Kristallnacht*. Not only were they conciliatory regarding the treatment of American Jews but they were also very circumspect about other potentially controversial issues. For example, they continued to monitor the activities of the German–American Bund, led by Fritz Kuhn, and did their best to curtail its support from prominent German figures. They also persuaded Berlin to cancel the mission to America of a high-ranking minister, Herr Kiep, to advance plans for skilled German nationals to be repatriated to Germany. The German Consul General in New York, Dr Hans Heinrich Borchers, was given the job instead. Last, but not least, permission from Berlin was sought and supplied for the removal of sensitive political files from the German Embassy in Washington, in case they were seized by the US authorities – an eventuality that became all the more likely in 1939 as relations between Washington and Berlin deteriorated yet further.[33]

Notes

1. Byron papers, Beinecke files, GEN MSS 605, Box 37, folder 593, 'Unspoken Alliance', pp. 25–6; 22 January 1939. See also FO/371/22827, A1143/1143/45, FO minute, David Scott, 7 February 1939.
2. Byron, 'Unspoken Alliance', p. 12; Knox, *Byron*, especially pp. 405–11; Butler, *Byron, Letters Home*, especially pp. 288–305 – Young quote on p. 292.
3. Dallek, *FDR*, pp. 171–9; MacDonald, *US, Britain and Appeasement*, pp. 106–23.
4. Bouverie, *Appeasing Hitler*, pp. 311–13; Phillips, *Fighting Churchill, Appeasing Hitler*, pp. 219–26.
5. Mackenzie Diary, 27, 28, 29 September and 12, 14 November 1938.
6. For Byron see Knox, *Byron*; Butler, *Byron: Letters Home*; see also McCulloch, *Arthur Murray*; Liebich, *Wickham Steed*; Adams, *Wedgewood and Ickes*; *The Times*, 27, 28 and 29 June 1938.
7. Gilbert, *Churchill and America*, p. 166 for letter from Churchill to Clementine, 8 July 1938; 'The United States and Europe', 4 August 1938, in Churchill, *While England Slept*, pp. 201–3.
8. *Hansard*, House of Commons, Churchill speech, 5 October 1938; Churchill broadcast, 16 October 1938, in *The Times* and *NYT*, 17 October 1938. For Hitler's speech on 9 October see *The Times* and *NYT*, 10 October 1938.
9. Haight, *American Aid to France*, pp. 14–17; Sherwood, *Roosevelt and Hopkins*, pp. 99–100.
10. See p. 160 for US Cabinet meeting on 23 September 1938; Haight, *American Aid to France*, pp. 19–28; see also Hall, *North American Supply*, p. 106; for the role of US aircraft production in British air power see Bailey, *Arsenal of Democracy*.

11. See Chapter 3 for Runciman visit, January 1937; Haight, *American Aid to France*, pp. 28–47; Hall, *North American Supply*, pp. 106–8.
12. Haight, *American Aid to France*, p. 48; see FRUS/1938/I, pp. 711–12 for Bullitt message, 3 October 1938; FDR press conference, 14 October 1938.
13. Murray, 'Franklin Roosevelt: Friend of Britain', pp. 362–8; Haight, *American Aid to France*, pp. 37–47.
14. Murray papers, Box 8809, Note of certain conversations between Roosevelt and Murray, 16–24 October 1938. See also Haight, *American Aid to France*, pp. 30–2.
15. Murray papers, Box 8809, Note of conversation between Roosevelt and Murray, 23 October 1938; Murray to FDR, 30 October, reporting on conversation with Tweedsmuir, who was 'entirely gratified'. See also Mackenzie King Diary, 17 November 1938.
16. MacDonald, *US, Britain and Appeasement*, pp. 113–23; Hull, *Memoirs I*, p. 599; *NYT*, 11 November 1938; Krock, *In the Nation*, pp. 70–1.
17. See Kimball, 'Dieckhoff and America', pp. 218–43.
18. Mackenzie King Diary, p. 48.
19. Mackenzie King Diary, pp. 48–50.
20. Kottman, *Reciprocity*, pp. 219–71; Kreider, *Anglo-American Trade Agreement*; Hull, *Memoirs I*, p. 520; State Department, SD 611.4131/1807a: Hull to Lindsay, 5 October 1938; FO/371/21506, A7645/1/45, Lindsay to Halifax, 8 October 1938.
21. CAB 23, 49 (1938) item 9, 19 October 1938; SD 611.4131/1855: memo by Hull, 25 October 1938; SD 611.4131/1805, Kennedy to Hull, 7 October 1938; Blum, *Morgenthau Diaries I*, p. 524; Ickes, *Diaries II*, p. 568; SD 611.4131/1855a: Hull to Kennedy, 3 November 1938; FO/371/21507, A8305/1/45, Lindsay to Halifax, 4 November 1938.
22. Burns, *Roosevelt: The Lion and the Fox*, pp. 365–6; Leuchtenburg, *Roosevelt and the New Deal*, pp. 271–4, for election results; Hooker, *Moffat Papers*, p. 141, 17 November 1938; Mackenzie King Diary, 17 November 1938.
23. Mackenzie King Diary, 17 November 1938; Baldwin papers, Vol. 124, Chamberlain to Baldwin, 2 October 1938, pp. 138–9.
24. Toynbee, *Survey of International Affairs*, 1938, pp. 21–2, based on British White Paper on Anglo-American Trade Agreement, 1938; Hull, *Memoirs I*, p. 530; Kottman, *Reciprocity*, pp. 266–71; FO/371/21510, A9228/1/45, Lindsay to Halifax, 30 November 1938; FO/371/21509, A8917/1/45, commentary by Raymond Gram Swing, 19 November 1939.
25. *NYT*, 13 December 1938.

26. *NYT*, 10 December 1938 for Eden speech; see FO/371/21548, file 9029, for Eden visit; Baldwin papers, Vol. 124, Eden to Baldwin, 19 December 1938, pp. 155–7.
27. Murray papers, Box 8809, Murray to Halifax, 20 November 1938; Halifax to Murray, 22 November 1938; PREM/I/367, note by Halifax in pencil, undated (30 November 1938).
28. Murray papers, Box 8809, Note of certain conversations between Roosevelt and Murray, 16–24 October 1938. With comment by Chamberlain, 14 December 1938.
29. Murray papers, Box 8809, Murray to Roosevelt, 15 December 1938; Murray to Kingsley Wood, 15 December 1938; Murray to Roosevelt, 15 December 1938; Murray, 'Franklin Roosevelt: Friend of Britain', pp. 362–8; Haight, *American Aid to France*, pp. 67–8; *NYT*, 29 January 1939.
30. DGFP/D/IV, doc 501, Dieckhoff to GFM, 14 November 1939; DGFP/D/IV, doc 502, Dieckhoff to Weizsächer, 15 November 1938.
31. DGFP/D/IV, doc 504, 22 November 1938 – Woermann to Ribbentrop, Memorandum on political implications of diplomatic rupture between US and Germany, 20 November 1938.
32. DGFP/D/IV, doc 506, Note Verbale to American Embassy, 10 December 1938; doc 507, Note from the American Embassy, 14 December 1938; doc 512, Thomsen to GFM, 17 December 1939; doc 516, Dieckhoff to Weizsächer, 21 December 1938. See also doc 517, Memo by Director of Economic Policy Department, 19 December 1938 – 'Opportunities for US Economic Reprisals against Germany and the Possible Consequences'; doc 518, Note to American Embassy, 30 December 1938, from Weizsächer; doc 522, memorandum by Woermann, 11 January 1938.
33. DGFP/D/IV, doc 509, memo by State Secretary Weizsächer, 16 December 1938 re Bund; doc 525, memo by Weizsächer, 13 January 1939 re Kiep mission; doc 505, Thomsen to GFM, 30 November 1938 re confidential files.

Part 4

Peace Front, 1939

10 'Methods Short of War', January–April 1939

Roosevelt's attitude to the worsening international situation – and the greater influence he hoped to exercise – were clearly apparent in his annual address to Congress at the start of 1939. In an early reference to Munich he said: 'A war which threatened to envelope the world in flames has been averted: but it had become increasingly clear that peace is not assured.' Rearmament, military and economic, was growing and there were threats of new aggression, he continued. 'Storms from abroad' directly challenged 'three institutions indispensable to Americans – 'religion, . . . democracy and international good faith'. No country was now safe from war and America must concentrate her resources on self-defence. He warned against the 'illusion of neutrality' by legislation and said that the United States could not be indifferent to aggression abroad. And in a memorable and highly significant phrase he declared: 'There are many methods short of war, but stronger and more effective than mere words, of bringing home to aggressor governments the aggregate sentiments of our own people.'[1]

The *New York Times* felt that the President's message to Congress marked a turning point in the Administration's foreign policy, as he had said that the period of controversial reform under the New Deal was over – the priority now was the international situation and the need to strengthen national defence. 'The tremendous emphasis which Mr Roosevelt laid in his speech upon the need for defence organisation and preparedness for war is an indication of how strong is his alarm at the present state of affairs in Europe and Asia,' wrote Mallet from the British Embassy in Washington. 'I understand that he talks quite openly with his intimates about the probability of war in Europe this Spring.' The British Chargé reasoned that Roosevelt's main aim was to 'educate' the American people away from isolationism. 'He began the process at Chicago in the Autumn of 1937, but in spite of the "Panay" incident he met with very little success,' continued Mallet. 'The shock of events in Europe last September has made his hearers more receptive, but the Munich settlement is not popular and the President's part in it has been rather played down of late.'[2]

State of the Union

The main aim of this chapter is to show that FDR's State of the Union address reflected the fact that US opinion – as Byron had argued in his 'Unspoken Alliance' paper – had been profoundly shocked by the Munich crisis and alarmed by the threat that Nazi Germany appeared to pose to American security. This meant that, even before the German annexation of Prague in March 1939, Roosevelt was in a better position to support Britain and France if they took a stronger line against Hitler. This was clearly seen in his State of the Union address and in his far-reaching defence message to Congress on 12 January, which set out America's requirements along the lines of his discussions with Morgenthau, Bullitt and Monnet in October 1938. He denied that he was yielding to war hysteria, reported Mallet, but said that America had been unprepared during the Great War. While he had no intention that the United States should join any war in Europe, she was now more vulnerable than in 1914. He therefore recommended an appropriation of $525 million, of which $210 million was to be spent by June 1940 and $300 million was earmarked for expanding the Air Force.[3]

The day after FDR's State of the Union speech Chamberlain made a significant statement, welcoming his 'solemn words' and saying:

> In these islands, where there is so clear a realization that only through freedom and peace can we hope to maintain and develop for ourselves and those that come after us the benefits for which we have laboured for generations, the sentiments expressed by the President will be welcomed as yet another indication of the vital role of democracy in world affairs and its devotion to the ideal of ordered human progress.

Arthur Murray told a member of the Foreign Office that he thought Chamberlain's statement would have 'the happiest effect' in the

United States, 'where there had been, in circles friendly to us, discouragement at the circumstances that previous Presidential utterances of this kind had seemed to evoke no official response or even interest here'. So warm was Chamberlain's praise for Roosevelt's annual address, Phipps reported from Paris, that the semi-official *Le Temps* had suggested that, following the trade agreement signed in November, there was now an 'Anglo-American rapprochement' in both Europe and the Far East.[4]

Mackenzie King was greatly impressed by FDR's State of the Union message, despite its incompatibility with appeasement. 'It was, I think, the finest thing I have heard anywhere at any time, in the way of a political utterance – fearless, comprehensive, constructive.' The Canadian equivalent – the Speech from the Throne, delivered by Lord Tweedsmuir, the Governor General – took place on 12 January, and while not as dramatic, it expressed similar concern at 'aggressive policies being pursued in other continents'. Despite the Munich agreement, tensions remained, he said, and Canada must strengthen its defences and increase the rearmament programme begun two years before. As part of the follow-up to this declaration, Mackenzie King instituted a significant discussion within the Cabinet about the Canadian position in the event of another great war. In particular, Sir Wilfrid Laurier's much-quoted phrase before the First World War – 'If Britain is at war, Canada is at war' – needed to be considered. The Cabinet agreed that in current circumstances the Government would recommend that Canada would join a European war if Britain was at war, although it would be up to Parliament to decide on the nature of the Canadian contribution.[5]

Chamberlain echoes Roosevelt

Just how far Chamberlain's statement represented his real attitude towards FDR's annual address has been debated by historians, as the Prime Minister simply issued a short text that had been prepared in the Foreign Office. However, the most significant point is that he issued the statement at all, even though he had not yet abandoned his hopes for European appeasement, as his upcoming visit to Rome in mid-January clearly demonstrated, not to mention his desire to maintain channels of communication with Berlin. The possibility of greater US involvement in international affairs was, to some extent, a useful weapon for Halifax and Chamberlain in their dealings with the dictators, as long as the President could be kept 'on side'. But, as Ferdinand Kuhn, the *New York Times* correspondent in London, suggested, there was probably another reason for Chamberlain's 'almost unprecedented step of issuing a personal statement expressing his appreciation of the President's message' – the pressure of public opinion both in the United States, where he was 'generally regarded as a fascist sympathiser', and in Britain, where there was growing scepticism about the policy of appeasement.[6]

Labour and Liberal criticisms that the Chamberlain Government was not speaking up for freedom and democracy along the lines of Roosevelt's addresses were especially strong. The President's ringing declaration against 'dictatorships' was contrasted with Chamberlain's 'timid exercises in the same field' by the liberal *Manchester Guardian*. 'Most English men and women, when they listened to President Roosevelt, must have wished sadly that it was the head of their own government who was saying these things,' the *Guardian* said in its editorial. In listening to the President's stirring defence of democracy, the British people 'must have recalled with shame' the Prime Minister's 'naïve confession' that, although he was not a supporter of Fascism in Britain, he 'could not get up much excitement over different systems of government'. Furthermore, the editorial continued, 'they must have regretted that it has been left to an American President to state the British (as it is also the American) way of life without apologizing for it. The contrast is painful and need not be pursued.'[7]

There was also growing criticism of Chamberlain's policy within the Tory Party, including a minor revolt at the end of 1938 when several Tory MPs, including Parliamentary private secretaries, expressed dissatisfaction with the record of Leslie Hore-Belisha, the Secretary of State for War, in terms of his record in pushing for British rearmament, although this fizzled out in the new year. A small group of the Government's critics, including Churchill, Duff Cooper, who had resigned in protest at the Munich agreement, and Amery, a former Secretary for the Colonies and Dominions, was also calling for speedier rearmament and a stronger foreign policy. However, probably of more concern to Chamberlain was the growing criticism amongst grassroots Tories in the country at large. The Federation of Conservative Associations defeated a resolution supporting Mr Chamberlain's foreign policy 'and in particular the policy of renewing friendship with Italy', while the *Birmingham Post*, in Chamberlain's own city, expressed concern over his policy while praising Roosevelt's speech and his warning to the dictators. 'It is the biggest departure from traditional isolation that any American President has ever made; the strongest appeal that any American President has ever made to Britain to cooperate in a world "peace and prosperity" system.' Roosevelt's message was, the *Post* declared, 'a definite appeal to Britain'.[8]

On 10 January Chamberlain and Halifax met with their French counterparts, Edouard Daladier and Georges Bonnet, in Paris, before embarking on a trip to Rome for talks with Mussolini and Ciano. While heartened by his warm reception by the crowds in Italy, Chamberlain made little progress in trying to persuade the Italian dictator to engage in diplomacy rather than force to gain his ends. Upon his return to London, on 28 January, he carried out a Cabinet reshuffle, in which Admiral of the Fleet Lord Chatfield, who was credited with rebuilding the British Navy in the previous few years, was appointed as the new Minister for the Co-ordination of Defence. He replaced Sir Thomas Inskip, who moved to the Dominions Office in place of Malcolm MacDonald, leaving MacDonald free to focus on the affairs of the Colonial Office and especially the difficult issue of Palestine. The Prime Minister then followed up his Cabinet changes with a significant speech on his home turf in Birmingham.[9]

Clearly trying to balance appeasement with deterrence, Chamberlain went out of his way to show cordiality to Italy in the wake of his recent trip to Rome and he expressed his desire for international peace. But he also stressed the growing strength of British rearmament and he again referred to FDR's State of the Union address and warned that 'any aggressor who tried to win world power by war would find the great democracies lined up against him'. He commented that 'the air is full of rumours and suspicions which ought not to exist' and quoted Roosevelt as saying that peace would be endangered if any country demanded domination by force. 'That would be a demand', he continued, 'which, as the President indicated and I myself have plainly declared already, the democracies must inevitably resist.' This was a powerful statement that was apparently linked to FDR's confidential message to Chamberlain via Arthur Murray the previous month. As Kuhn pointed out in the *New York Times*: 'The obvious intention behind these words was to hint that an aggressor might find the United States as well as Great Britain and France among his enemies.'[10]

'Frontier on the Rhine'

For isolationists, such comments were likely to act as the proverbial red rag to the bull but even more alarming for them was the news that the Roosevelt was facilitating the sale of military aircraft to France, following a French air mission to Washington, DC, in December 1938. This was discovered by accident when a Douglas bomber crashed with a member of the French air mission on board and created a stir in the press and in Congress, where accusations were made that the French mission had been unduly favoured and given access to secret American aircraft and equipment. Senator Gerald Nye, a prominent isolationist, argued that the incident showed that there was practically an alliance between the United States and France. On 31 January the President summoned members of the Senate Military Affairs Committee to a private meeting at the White House, at which he was alleged to have said that, if war broke out in Europe, 'the frontiers of the United States would be in France'. Next day, the Senate debated the French air mission. 'All the best-known isolationists are in full cry', reported Mallet, 'and much will be heard of the President's secret diplomacy and attempts to entangle the nation in the affairs of Europe.'[11]

Roosevelt gave his version of the alleged 'frontier on the Rhine' statement to John Cudahy, the American Ambassador in Dublin. 'The howls and curses that have continued to come from Berlin and Rome convinces me that the general result has been good even if a few silly Senators reported the conversation in a wholly untruthful way,' he wrote. Clearly, the President wished to take a strong line against the dictators and, equally, he looked to Britain and France to take the lead. On 1 February he gave an interview to Jacques Kayser, a close friend of Daladier, the French Premier. According to a British report of this conversation, the President told Kayser that 'he might assure the French Prime Minister that the United States would send Britain and France all the aeroplanes they require, impressing on him however the urgency of those two countries without delay reaching a production of a minimum of 6,000 planes themselves'. Roosevelt was also reported as saying once again that he expected war to break out in the spring.[12]

Hitler's speech to the Reichstag on 30 January 1939 to mark the sixth anniversary of his appointment as the German Chancellor did little to reassure the democracies about the future direction of German foreign policy. It was also significant for the attention Hitler devoted to the US, which he clearly viewed as an ally of Britain and

France. Declaring that Germany 'would not stand for the Western states meddling in certain affairs', the most important of which was evidently the need for '*Lebensraum*', he attacked the 'campaign of hatred pursued by certain British apostles of war', amongst whom he named Churchill, Eden and Duff Cooper. This campaign could not simply be ignored as, 'within a few months' time, the most notorious of these warmongers may actually have emerged as the leaders of their government'. He also included Ickes on his list of 'warmongers' and dismissed 'the libelous claim' that Germany would attack America. 'The German Volk harbours no hatred for England, America, or France', he said, 'and desires nothing other than to live calmly and peacefully.' He especially blamed Jews, 'under the cover of press, film, radio, theater, and literature, which are all in their hands', for stirring up animosity against Germany and warned that if 'international Jewry' succeeded, both within and beyond Europe, in plunging mankind into yet another world war, then the result will be . . . the annihilation of the Jewish race in Europe'.[13]

Despite Hitler's diatribe about the Jews, Chamberlain, speaking in the Commons the next day, commented that it did not seem to him to be 'the speech of a man who was preparing to throw Europe into another crisis'. The Prime Minister's optimism was also evident in his correspondence with Arthur Murray, who had written to him to say that Roosevelt had mentioned that he had a 'real friendship' for the Prime Minister. Replying to Murray's note, Chamberlain wrote: 'I am very grateful for its terms, and while it looks as if the immediate danger has been averted I am sure that the reports of his communication to the Senate will have a very powerful effect in Europe.' Murray passed on Chamberlain's comment to Roosevelt and mentioned that Walter Tyrrell, the former British Ambassador in Paris and an old friend, was also less anxious about the immediate situation in Europe than he had been. 'Reports that reach him tend to indicate that Hitler is not quite "the law unto himself" that he was six months ago,' wrote Murray, largely owing to British and French rearmament and fear of the United States.[14]

Haldane mission

However, while Chamberlain remained optimistic after Munich, 'preparedness for war' was being stepped up in the US, especially industrial mobilisation. As FDR had said to Murray at the end of 1938, he was intending to put the industrial resources of the US behind the democracies. He had appointed Louis Johnson to the key post of Assistant Secretary of War in 1937, shortly after the Presidential election. The Assistant Secretary had a statutory duty to manage industrial mobilisation and Johnson took this very seriously, as can be seen from the annual reports on US industrial mobilisation that plot the increasing sophistication of American preparations. The US 1937–38 report (year ending 30 June 1938) was summarised by the Industrial Intelligence Centre in Britain under Douglas Morton and sent to the various Whitehall departments, including the Foreign Office, in December 1938. Sir John Anderson, the Lord Privy Seal, who was in charge of civil defence in Britain, thereupon sought an assessment of US industrial mobilisation in the event of war. This led to a significant appraisal of the Roosevelt Administration's defence policy at this time by a British industrial consultant, Graham Haldane.[15]

While in the United States on a business trip Haldane had private discussions with the President at Hyde Park. Roosevelt also arranged meetings for Haldane with other members of the Administration, including Louis Johnson. Haldane reported: 'I have little doubt that the President would like to intervene in European and world problems and to cooperate with the democracies to a much greater extent than is politically expedient at the present moment.' From his travels around the United States, Haldane detected great anti-Nazi and anti-Fascist feeling and he felt that US opinion was more hostile towards the German Government than in 1917. He also believed that FDR's speeches reflected the attitude of US public opinion in arguing that the defence of democracy and isolationism were incompatible. But, Haldane continued, 'isolationist opinion in America will be strengthened in the future if Great Britain pursues a weak and negative foreign policy; similarly it is likely to be weakened if our policy is definite and positive and appeals to idealism'. It was necessary, therefore, for the British Government itself to provide an example of positive leadership.[16]

'The Administration are ... tackling the problem of national defence with great vigour,' reported Haldane. 'The American Defence Plan is largely concerned with the organisation of industry so that it can be put on a war footing in the shortest possible time.' A rapid expansion of American defence forces was also in progress, Haldane said, 'but I think it would be true to say that the primary idea behind American defence is the effective use of her economic, industrial and financial strength'. He thought that the United States might be able to exercise great pressure on Germany, Italy and Japan by controlling the exports of certain materials to them, such as phosphates to Germany, provided that Britain, France and Russia cooperated. 'Industrially the US Administration contemplates America acting as the warehouse and munition factory for all the democracies who may be involved with the Nazi and Fascist countries,' Haldane concluded. 'The whole approach to the defence problems seemed to me to be very vigorous in its character and I think this is due, to a considerable extent, to the personality and driving power of Mr Louis A Johnson – Assistant Secretary of War.'[17]

Lothian and Willert visits

While Roosevelt was busily strengthening America's own forces he was also concerned about the strength of British resolve, as was illustrated by the fallout from his meeting with Lord Lothian in January 1939. Lothian had recanted his earlier view of Hitler as someone who could be reasoned with, but he also believed that only the intervention of the USA could prevent war from breaking out and destroying Europe. Roosevelt felt that Lothian's views were symptomatic of a lack of self-confidence in London and told an American friend that he was 'getting sick and tired of this *moritari te salutamus* attitude of the British'. Talk of yielding up the sceptre to the US had the opposite effect of what was intended, as far as the President was concerned. 'I got so wild with Lothian who came to see me and spoke like this that I could hardly listen to him,' he said. If the British wanted cooperation, they should make the US believe they had backbone. 'What the British need today is a good stiff grog, inducing not only the desire to save civilisation but the continued belief that they can do it. In such an event they will a lot more support from their American cousins.' Roosevelt's comments reached the American Department of the Foreign Office, where one official remarked that he was never so well disposed to the French entente as when the French said that they would not need an expeditionary force.[18]

The President expressed similar views to an old friend from the Great War – Sir Arthur Willert – who visited him in March 1939, at the end of an American lecture tour. FDR told Willert that a reliable source had said to him that Hitler was encouraged by the weakness of British policy since Munich and planned to take his opponents one by one. Roosevelt favoured the stronger line taken by Chamberlain in his Birmingham speech but felt that the British Government was not doing enough to deter Hitler by means of propaganda – for example, leaking stories about preparations to bomb Germany. He also spelled out to Willert very clearly his 'tacit alliance' strategy, telling him that he was trying to give the impression to the dictators that, if war broke out, they would face the hostility of the United States in support of Britain and France. In the event of war, he would exercise 'the most beneficent neutrality possible' towards Britain and was confident that the arms embargo would be replaced by a system of 'cash and carry', which would favour Britain because of her superior naval and financial resources. 'The President brushed aside the Johnson Act as not mattering owing to the way in which money seeps through barriers.'[19]

Polish guarantee

While Willert was in the USA the uneasy peace following the Munich agreement was shattered when German forces occupied Prague on 15 March and Hitler proclaimed a protectorate over Bohemia and Moravia. Chamberlain's response in the Commons was regarded as very weak in comparison to his Birmingham speech at the end of January. Public opinion was in favour of a strong stand after 'the humiliation of Prague' so trade talks planned to take place between Robert Hudson, the Trade Minister, and Helmuth Wohltat, his German opposite number, were postponed (until July) and Nevile Henderson was withdrawn from Berlin for consultation. On 17 March Chamberlain attempted to make amends with a strongly worded speech in Birmingham, broadcast throughout the Empire and the US, in which he denounced the German move against Czechoslovakia and declared that any attempt to dominate the world by force would be resisted. He was prepared to sacrifice almost anything for peace, he said, but he would not sacrifice 'the liberty we have enjoyed for hundreds of years and which we will never surrender'. The British people would rise to the challenge with the support of 'the whole British Empire and of other nations who value peace indeed but who value freedom even more' – a clear reference to the United

States, couched in language that was felt likely to appeal to Americans.[20]

Following the German annexation of Prague, Sumner Welles issued a statement on 17 March with the President's approval, condemning the German move as one of military aggression. 'It was one of the sternest denunciations of another government by the United States for many years', according to the *New York Times*. The statement referred to 'the temporary extinguishment of the liberties of a free and independent people' and said that the United States was, by contrast, dedicated to the principles of human liberty and democracy and was opposed to military aggression. The State Department also dropped its opposition to Morgenthau's desire to introduce 'countervailing duties' of 25 per cent on imports from Germany, in accordance with the 1930 Tariff Act, on the grounds that German exports to the US were heavily subsidised. Meanwhile, the President took advantage of the reception of a new Italian ambassador, on 22 March 1939, to warn Rome that the US might become involved if a European conflict broke out. Shortly afterwards, Roosevelt's National Defence Bill – introduced in January 1939 – was passed by both houses of Congress, envisaging an expansion of the American Air Force to 6,000 planes.[21]

At the same time, a joint resolution was introduced into the Senate by Pittman to amend the Neutrality laws by permitting the sale of arms and ammunition in wartime on a 'cash and carry' basis, thereby repealing the arms embargo that had been the focus of so much criticism by British Government ministers and officials. Pittman frankly admitted that the Bill was intended to favour the democracies in any struggle with the dictators, although the Administration's primary strategy was to argue that the arms embargo discriminated against 'peace loving' countries rather than saying it was calculated to aid Britain especially. Roosevelt and Hull would have preferred the complete repeal of the Neutrality Acts but Pittman told them that the Senate would never allow this. Indeed, the isolationists in Congress argued that the 'democracies' of Britain and France were really no better than the dictators, as had been shown at Munich. Borah, for example, said that if war broke out in Europe, 'a more sordid, imperialistic war could hardly be imagined'.[22]

On 18 March Kennedy informed Halifax that he warmly applauded the Prime Minister's Birmingham speech of the day before and pointed out that it suggested that Britain would henceforth take a strong stand against German aggression. Evidence of further German moves was not long in coming, with reports of German threats against Romania and, on 22 March, the cession of Memel to Germany under threat of invasion. Fearing further German moves, especially against Poland and Romania, the Chamberlain Government took the unprecedented step of issuing a guarantee of the territorial integrity of Poland. With the invasion of Albania by Italy early in April further guarantees were given to Greece and Romania. While the Opposition parties supported moves towards an anti-aggression pact, they were critical of Chamberlain's general handling of foreign policy, especially his refusal to abandon the Anglo-Italian agreement after the invasion of Albania and his apparent reluctance to pursue an alliance with Russia. They also wanted him to do more to enlist American support, although it was recognised that the Administration was already ahead of US public opinion. Quintin Hogg, on the Government benches, cautioned against too open appeals to US opinion. 'You never get anywhere with the American people by suggesting an alliance between Great Britain and America,' he said. 'It only makes them suspicious.'[23]

In fact, the Government had kept Washington, as well as Ottawa and the other Dominion governments, informed of its thinking regarding the guarantee to Poland by sending them copies of diplomatic documents. Further evidence of American influence was on show during a meeting of the Foreign Policy Committee on 27 March 1939. Halifax said that he recognised that Britain and France could not prevent Poland from being overrun by Germany. 'We were faced with the dilemma of doing nothing or entering into a devastating war,' the Foreign Secretary said. 'If we did nothing this in itself would mean a great accession to Germany's strength and a great loss to ourselves of sympathy and support in the United States, in the Balkan countries, and in other parts of the world.' In those circumstances, he said, he favoured going to war. He was therefore gratified to receive support from Washington for the anti-aggression front against Germany when Kennedy told him that 'the President thought the statement was excellent and said that in his judgement it would have a very great effect. The United States, he thought, would consider that war was imminent, but the President did not think that this would do any harm.'[24]

The guarantees were a clear reversal of British policy in Central and Eastern Europe in the 1930s. Mackenzie King called the move 'a curious sudden shift', while Cadogan, in the Foreign Office, was unhappy at American moral pressure for a strong British stand in Europe. 'What I want to know more about is the practical reaction in America,' he minuted. 'I am sure they are frightfully keen that we should "fight for the right", and I know it is unfair – and useless – to ask them what they are going to do. But with much more talk about "moral" issues it will begin to be a fair question.' The American Department, on the other the other hand, felt that it was vital to maintain American confidence as a deterrent to Germany. Vansittart was also a firm advocate of cooperation with America, in contrast to his earlier attitude. 'I think they will not only talk but do a great deal, and do it quickly, if we have no more Munichs,' he wrote. 'We nearly lost the USA over that; but if we now make it clear that henceforth we really are going to stand up, we can have much confidence in the attitude of the USA. Anyhow it is our only chance.'[25]

FDR'S peace appeal and Hitler's response

Following the British and French guarantees to Poland, Greece and Romania, FDR decided to make another move. On 14 April he sent a public appeal to Hitler, stating that the US was prepared to take part in an international conference, provided that Germany would give assurance that it would not attack any one of thirty-one named countries in Europe and Middle East for at least ten years and that these countries gave similar assurances to Germany. This was intended to create peaceful conditions for discussing 'two essential problems' – firstly, the need for 'the peoples of the world' to obtain 'progressive relief from the crushing burden of armament which is each day bringing them more closely to the brink of economic disaster', and, secondly, the most practical way of 'opening up avenues of international trade' on equal terms and to enable states to obtain the raw materials and so on that they required. At the same time, those governments other than the US that were directly interested 'could undertake such political discussions as they may consider necessary or desirable'. A similar message was sent to Mussolini.[26]

Ickes thought that 'this was not only a brilliant move on the President's part, it was an act of striking statesmanship'. Both Hitler and Mussolini had been 'put in a hole' so that 'if war now comes the whole world will know who is responsible'. He also thought that the President's move would 'stiffen further the backbones of England and France and give them further time, if only a short one, within which to strengthen their diplomatic lines and to put their defences in order'. In fact, the proposal was, to some extent, a revival of the Welles plan put to Chamberlain by Roosevelt in January 1938. But it is notable that, on this occasion, Chamberlain and the Foreign Office do not appear to have been warned in advance. However, it was welcomed – in public at least – by Chamberlain, who, responding to a question from Attlee in the House of Commons on 18 April, expressed 'the great satisfaction' with which the Government had welcomed the President's initiative'. It was not discussed by the Cabinet, however, probably because it stood no chance of success.[27]

Hitler delayed his formal reply until his speech to the Reichstag on 28 April, during which he mocked Roosevelt's peace appeal, especially the list of thirty-one countries that Germany had been asked to refrain from attacking. He claimed that they had all been asked by the German Foreign Ministry whether they felt threatened by Germany and had replied in the negative. He also announced that he no longer regarded the 1934 German–Polish Peace Declaration or the 1935 Anglo-German Naval Agreement as being in effect and he demanded once more the return of German colonies. Ickes referred to it as 'a truculent speech not at all calculated to allay international uneasiness'. Indeed, it raised very clearly the growing tensions between Nazi Germany and Poland, especially over the issue of Danzig, and between Berlin, London and Paris following the Anglo-French guarantee to Poland. However, Halifax said he did not think that the speech was especially aggressive. He assumed that the attacks on democracy were mainly for domestic reasons and he believed that Hitler had kept the door open for negotiations both on Danzig and relations with Poland and on a revised Anglo-German naval agreement.[28]

As regards the 'stiffening of England's backbone' referred to by Ickes, it is clear from the discussions of the British Cabinet at this time that the emphasis of British policy towards Germany had moved from 'appeasement' to 'deterrence' – although it had been decided that Sir Nevile Henderson should return to Berlin and it was still felt that Mussolini was worth cultivating so that Italy could be kept on friendly terms. The main change to British policy was the idea of a 'common front' with Poland, Romania and neighbouring states to act as a buffer to German expansionism – a move that accorded well with FDR's call in his Quarantine speech and his annual address for 'peace-loving nations' to stand up to 'aggressor states'. The idea of a 'common front', or a 'Peace Front' as it was later called, was discussed by the British Cabinet at several meetings in the second half of March and regularly thereafter until the outbreak of war in September. A major issue was the desirability, or otherwise, of including Russia in this common front, which the Polish Government, amongst others (including Mackenzie King), was nervous about doing. Chamberlain and Halifax also had reservations about including Russia, except on a limited basis, whereas Churchill was very much in favour of a triple alliance, as was Roosevelt.[29]

Although the US was not officially part of this 'Peace Front', it was clearly a development that FDR had encouraged both through his speeches and through American diplomacy. US influence was certainly being felt in London, as can be seen in British Cabinet discussions and the records of the Foreign Office. As well as the guarantees to Poland, Greece and Romania and a sizeable increase in the British defence budget to £630 million, Chamberlain announced on 27 April a modest conscription bill designed to bolster the deterrence aspect of British policy while not alarming the trade unions or disrupting the position of the Territorial Army. In explaining the policy to the Cabinet, he said that there had been great pressure to introduce some scheme of compulsory military training, 'not only from France but also from the United States'. There was also continuing naval cooperation. Concerned that Japan might try to exploit the European crisis, Halifax told the Cabinet on 22 March that he had suggested to Kennedy that moving the US fleet to Honolulu would be a great help. The Ambassador said he would take it up with the President and on 16 April, the day after Roosevelt's appeal to Hitler, it was announced that the American fleet was shortly to be moved to San Diego – which was a stepping-stone to Hawaii and Pearl Harbor.[30]

The view from Berlin

The German press attacked Roosevelt's State of the Union address and accused the President of being dependent on 'Jewish high finance' and of stirring up international tensions to divert attention away from his domestic problems and to secure a third term.

The German Embassy in Washington, now led by the Chargé d'Affaires, Hans Thomsen, regarded FDR's message as typical of his hostile attitude towards Nazi Germany. While claiming that the US was against entangling alliances and was not thinking of participation in European wars, FDR's foreign policy was, in fact, 'characterised by support of the democratic front by all possible means and simultaneous injury to totalitarian powers as far as opportunities for this are presented to the United States'. The isolationists feared that Roosevelt was 'arbitrarily, and without reference to Congress, manoeuvring America into a position similar to that of 1917' but it was not certain that they had the strength to contest the policy, 'which, by virtue of the wide powers conferred upon him, he is carrying through'.[31]

The events of March 1939 were a major setback for efforts by the German Embassy in Washington to repair relations between the US Government and the Nazi regime. As Thomsen reported, the occupation of Czech territory was regarded as 'a breach of the letter and spirit of the Munich agreement and evidence that the Führer's declaration that Germany had no further territorial claims in Europe was not true'. This view was strengthened, he said, by Chamberlain's Birmingham speech on 17 March, which was broadcast in North America and 'commanded great attention' in the US, being 'welcomed, in conjunction with Sumner Welles' statement as the joint expression of Anglo-American disapproval'. As a result, 'the greater part of the press is advocating support of the democracies in Europe even more vigorously than before', he said. 'There is practical unanimity of opinion today that, as a result of the new situation, America is more than ever obliged to make the Western Hemisphere safe against totalitarian Powers.' Thomsen argued that the US imposition of countervailing duties on German goods was 'purely a political move', resulting from the Prague occupation. But he recommended that any counter-measures should be unobtrusive so as to avoid further US retaliation.[32]

According to Thomsen, Roosevelt was

> inwardly convinced that Germany is the enemy who must be crushed, because she has so upset the balance of power and the status quo, that America also will feel the consequences should she fail to get in first. . . . He does not believe in the possibility of maintaining peace and reckons on a trial of strength between the totalitarian Powers and the democracies. These are America's first line of defence: should this fail America's role as a Great Power would, in Roosevelt's view, be finished.

He therefore wanted to make sure that, unlike in the Great War, American aid would not be delayed. That conflict had showed that 'years are necessary in order to place America's industry on a war footing'. Hence FDR was aiming to make sure that American war potential was organised in time for the outbreak of a war involving the democracies and Germany. There were no plans for sending American troops abroad, Thomsen said, as public opinion was clearly against this, but the President was prepared to make 'the whole of America's economic might . . . available in good time'.[33]

Thomsen reported that the US Government and 'a large part of the press' fully supported the Anglo-French guarantees offered to Poland and other states as a means of combating Germany. He also noted that FDR's 'so-called peace appeal' on 15 April was received by the US press and public opinion with general approval, 'which can be explained by the Americans' predilection for such missionary ideas'. The peace appeal was especially well received by Roosevelt's supporters 'as an opportune attempt by the President to assume the leadership of the anti-totalitarian front, and thereby support the efforts of the Western Powers to encircle the "dictatorships", and to stem their expansion'. According to Thomsen, 'these circles see in the appeal the expression of Roosevelt's consistent attitude which, from the well-known Chicago speech in October 1937, in which he spoke of the quarantine of aggressor nations, to this latest step, presents a uniform policy'. Roosevelt was, in effect, compelling the leaders of Germany and Italy 'to show their hand and clearly state their aims'. However, Hitler's speech, which had been broadcast across America, had made 'a great impression', and had taken some of the wind out of the President's sails.[34]

Roosevelt's policy at this time, especially his peace appeal, has been criticised for sending mixed messages to Berlin. But the German Foreign Ministry clearly did not consider FDR in these terms. Dieckhoff, for example, now resident in Berlin, believed that 'Roosevelt will, if need be, act in exactly the same way as Wilson did. At first Wilson also declared that he did not wish to enter any war, and then he did do so with the entire might of the US – expeditionary force, fleet, etc.' Dieckhoff was convinced that 'Roosevelt intends, if necessary, to act in the same way, and I do not believe that there are elements in the USA which have courage enough or are strong enough to prevent this.' Karl von Wiegand, the Hearst press correspondent in Berlin, issued an even stronger warning to Berlin, telling Captain Wiedemann, Hitler's former adjutant:

> The Führer must clearly understand that President Roosevelt is his most dangerous opponent. President Roosevelt fights for his democratic aims with the same fanatic idealism as does the Führer for National Socialism. Britain and France are no longer dragging America behind them: today America is driving them both before her.[35]

Notes

1. Franklin Roosevelt, Annual Message to Congress, 4 January 1939, available at: <www.presidency.ucsb.edu/documents/annual-message-congress>.
2. *NYT*, 5 January 1939; FO/371/22812, A660/98/45, Mallet to Halifax, 10 January 1939.
3. FO/371/22812, A339/98/45, Mallet to Halifax, 12 January 1939.
4. *The Times*, 6 January 1939; FO/371/22812, A114/98/45: minute by J. V. Perowne, 6 January 1939 for Murray comment; FO/371/22812, A166/98/45, Sir Eric Phipps to Halifax, 6 January 1939.
5. Mackenzie King Diary, 4 January 1939; *The Times*, 13 January 1939 for Canadian Speech from the Throne.
6. See MacDonald, *US, Britain and Appeasement*, p. 122; Reynolds, *Creation*, p. 47; and especially Smith, 'Thompson–Claude Bowers Correspondence', pp. 839–64; *NYT*, 6 January 1939.
7. *NYT*, 6 January 1939, commenting on British press reporting of Roosevelt's annual address.
8. Ibid.
9. *The Times*, 28 January 1939; *NYT*, Kuhn report, 29 January 1939.
10. Chamberlain speech, *The Times*, 29 January 1939; *NYT*, Kuhn report, 29 January 1939.
11. FO/371/22812, A1272/98/45, Mallet to Halifax, 3 February 1939. See Chapter 9 for background of US support for purchase of planes by France, pp. 173–5.
12. *Roosevelt Letters*, III, Roosevelt to Cudahy, 4 March 1939, pp. 256–7; FO/371/22813, A1321/98/45, Haggard to Mallet, 2 February 1939.
13. Hitler speech to Reichstag, 30 January 1939, Wikisource.
14. Chamberlain speech in Commons, 31 January 1939; Murray papers, Box 9809, Murray to Chamberlain, 1 February 1939; Chamberlain to Murray, 2 February 1939; Murray to Roosevelt, 10 February 1939.
15. McFarlane and Roll, *Louis Johnson and the Arming of America*.

16. FO/371/22813, A1378/98/45, memo on 'USA National Defence' by Haldane, February 1939.
17. Ibid.
18. FO/371/22827, A1143/1143/45, Mallet to Scott, 26 January 1939; Vyvyan to Strang, 4 March 1939, commenting on FDR to Professor Roger B. Merriman, 15 February 1939, also to be found in Roosevelt papers, PSF 46, Great Britain, 1939; see also Reynolds, *Creation*, pp. 43–4 and Rock, *Chamberlain and Roosevelt*, pp. 143–7.
19. FO/371/22829, A2907/1292/45, memo of conversations between Willert and Roosevelt, 25 and 26 March 1939.
20. DGFP/D/VI, doc 35, 18 March 1939, Dirksen to GFM; Neville Chamberlain speech, 17 March 1939 in *The Times*, 18 March 1939.
21. Welles statement, 17 March 1939 in *NYT*, 18 March 1939; Blum, *Morgenthau Diaries II*, pp. 78–82; *NYT*, 19 March 1939; National Defence Act, 3 April 1939.
22. FO/371/22813, A2440/98/45, Lindsay to Halifax, 23 March 1939; Ibid., A2982/98/45: Lindsay to Halifax, 14 April 1939; see also Hull, *Memoirs I*, p. 641.
23. See CAB/23/12(1939), item 1, 18 March 1939, for a key discussion by Chamberlain, Halifax and other members of Cabinet regarding Britain's response to further German expansion; *Hansard*, House of Commons debate, Quintin Hogg, 13 April 1939.
24. CAB/24/CP/74/59, Conclusions of Foreign Policy Committee, 27 March 1939, for reference at Cabinet meeting, CAB/23, 15 (1939), item 2, on 29 March 1939; DBFP/3/IV, doc 586, Halifax to Lindsay, 31 March 1939 re FDR's support for British policy.
25. Mackenzie King Diary, 31 March 1939; FO/371/22829, A2693/1292/45, minute by Scott, 6 April 1939; minute by Cadogan, 7 April 1939; minute by Vansittart, 9 April 1939.
26. FRUS/1939/I Roosevelt to Hitler, 14 April 1939, pp. 130–3; for FDR's 'peace appeal' of 14 April 1939 see FRUS/1939/I, docs 120–166.
27. *Hansard*, House of Commons, Neville Chamberlain, 18 April 1939; Ickes, *Diary*, II, 23 April 1939, pp. 619–20.
28. For Hitler speech, 28 April 1939 (excluding references to FDR proposal) see Avalon Project, available at <https://avalon.law.yale.edu/wwii/blbk13.asp>; Ickes, *Diary*, II, 29 April 1939, p. 626; CAB/23, 26 (1939), item 1, 3 May 1939.
29. CAB/23, 24 (1939), item 1, 26 April 1939; see also CAB/23, 26 (1939), item 1, 3 May 1939; CAB 23, 27 (1939), item 1, 10 May 1939.
30. CAB/23, 22 (1939), item 3, 24 April 1939; CAB/23, 14 (1939), item 2, 22 March 1939; see also Reynolds, *Creation*, p. 61.
31. FO/371/22812, A151/98/45, Ogilvie-Forbes (Berlin) to Halifax, 5 January 1939; DGFP/D/V, doc 524, Thomsen to GFM, 12 January 1939; doc 526, Thomsen to GFM, 3 February 1939.

32. DGFP/D/VI, doc 34, Thomsen to GFM, 18 March 1939; DGFP/D/VI; doc 14, Thomsen to GFM, 17 March 1939; doc 24, Thomsen to GFM, 18 March 1939; doc 27, Director of the Economic Policy Dept (Wiehl) to Embassy, 18 March 1939; doc 33, Thomsen to GFM, 18 March 1939; doc 56, Thomsen to GFM, 21 March 1939; doc 130, memo by Director of Economic Policy Dept (Wiehl), 30 March 1939.
33. DGFP/D/VI, doc 107, Thomsen to GFM, 27 March 1939.
34. DGFP/D/VI, doc 283, Thomsen to GFM, 28 April 1939; doc 160, Circular of GFM, 5 April 1939; doc 179, Thomsen to GFM, 11 April 1939; doc 244, Thomsen to GFM, 22 April 1939; doc 201, Thomsen to GFM, 15 April 1939; doc 238, Thomsen to GFM, 20 April 1939; doc 244, Thomsen to GFM, 22 April 1939; doc 255, Thomsen to GFM, 24 April 1939.
35. See Watt, *How War Came*, Chapter 15, 'Muddled signals from Washington', pp. 255–70; DGFP/D/VI, doc 222, Wiedemann to Weizsächer, 17 April 1939; doc 264, note by Dieckhoff, Berlin, 25 April 1939.

11 'A Special Character', May–June 1939

Shortly after 4.00pm on 3 May 1939 Neville Chamberlain rose from the front bench in the Commons and requested that 'an humble Address' be presented to King George VI and Queen Elizabeth on the occasion of their upcoming visit to Canada and the United States. The visit, he said, not only would 'give immense pleasure and satisfaction to their subjects in Canada and further cement the ties of Empire', but it would also include a visit to the US, 'the first of the kind by a reigning Sovereign of this country'. He continued:

> The relations between ourselves and the people of the United States have long been of a special character on account of our common language, our common ideals and our common traditions, and we may be sure that the visit of Their Majesties to that country will be warmly welcomed in that great Republic across the Atlantic.

Thus, several years before Churchill referred to a 'special relationship' between Britain and the United States in his post-war Fulton speech, a British Prime Minister was speaking of the long-standing 'special character' of Anglo-American relations and alluding to the historical, cultural and ideological ties between the two countries.[1]

The perceived reluctance of the Chamberlain Government to move closer to the US had long been a staple in the Opposition's criticism of its foreign policy. Clement Attlee, who had replaced the pacifist George Lansbury as the Labour leader in October 1935, now hastened to support Chamberlain's motion on behalf of the Labour Party. 'We shall all hope that this voyage will be happy and successful, and that it will increase the close ties which bind this country to the people of Canada and to the people of the United States,' he said. 'In these days anything that can be done should be done to unite the great Democracy of the West to the sentiments of the people of this country and the other peoples of the British Commonwealth.' Similar views were expressed by Sir Archibald Sinclair, on behalf of the Liberals, and by the Archbishop of Canterbury, Cosmo Gordon Lang, in the House of Lords. Such speeches reflected an appeal to a common heritage and common ideals that contrasted markedly with those of the Fascist dictatorships in Germany and Italy.[2]

Royal Visit

This chapter argues that the Royal Visit to the USA in 1939 was an important element in FDR's strategy of forming what amounted to a 'tacit alliance' with Britain. The aim of this 'tacit alliance' was to 'keep Germany guessing' and thereby to deter Nazi Germany and her Axis partners from risking another major conflict that would sooner or later involve the United States, as had happened in the First World War. This strategy now accorded with the notion of a 'Peace Front' following the Anglo-French guarantees to Poland, Greece and Romania, and talks with the Soviet Union. FDR was also able to use the visit to present the royal couple not only as representatives of the mighty British Empire and its Navy, which acted as a buffer between Nazi Germany and the United States, but also as essentially democratic in their outlook, with many shared values with the United States. George VI was the perfect representation of this message as a naval officer who had served in the Great War and as someone who was personally modest and unassuming. The visit was additionally useful in consolidating Roosevelt's relationship with Canada and especially Mackenzie King – a key element in strengthening American coastal defences, including the use of the major naval base at Halifax.[3]

As regards British policy towards the Royal Visit, the worsening international situation meant that Britain's relations with both the United States and Canada were becoming all the more important as the likelihood of war increased. On top of Hitler's Reichstag speech on 28 April that threatened Danzig, the idea of a 'Peace Front' appeared to be making little headway in deterring Hitler, and Nazi propaganda was accusing Britain of orchestrating the encirclement of Germany. Chamberlain and Halifax were not keen on an alliance with Communist Russia but the fall of Litvinov, who had supported cooperation with the west, as Foreign Minister, and his replacement by Molotov, did not augur well for improved relations with the Soviet Union. The development of the Berlin–Rome Axis into a military alliance in the form of the 'Pact of Steel', signed by Hitler and Mussolini in Berlin on 22 May 1939, also suggested that the policy of driving a wedge between the Axis powers, by luring Italy away from Germany, was not succeeding.[4]

For Mackenzie King, the Royal Visit was an event of huge domestic and international significance and the fact that it was taking place at all was largely due to him, as he noted in his diary on more than one occasion. When he attended the coronation of George VI prior to the Imperial Conference in May 1937 he got on well with the new King and Queen, and it was agreed in principle that the new monarch would visit Canada, as the senior Dominion, at an early date. When progress proved to be slow, Mackenzie King asked Lord Tweedsmuir to raise the issue when he was in London during the summer of 1938 and it was subsequently agreed that the Royal Visit would take place in the early summer of 1939. When Roosevelt heard from Mackenzie King in August 1938 – during the President's trip to Queen's University – that George VI and Queen Elizabeth planned to visit Canada, he wrote to the monarch extending a personal invitation to Hyde Park – an invitation that was duly accepted.[5]

Royal Visit and the Imperial Question

At the same time, the Royal Visit potentially raised the difficult issue of American perceptions of the British Empire, and what might be termed 'the Imperial Question'. Should the United States render aid and thereby risk war for the sake of the British Empire? The isolationists argued strongly against. It was fortunate, therefore, that the visit took place within the context of a much longer trip to Canada and, indeed, the King and Queen were accompanied to the United States by the Canadian Prime Minister, Mackenzie King, rather than by the British Foreign Secretary, Lord Halifax – an arrangement that had been much discussed between London and Ottawa. This meant that it was the Canadian dimension of the British Empire that was uppermost in the minds of most Americans in the weeks prior to the brief Royal Visit to the US, especially as the progress of the royal couple through Canada was reported fully and enthusiastically by most American newspapers. Not only did Canada represent the senior Dominion within the Empire but it was also seen as a friendly neighbour. And, as recently as August 1938, FDR had said that the US would not stand idly by if Canada was threatened by a hostile state – that is, Germany or Japan.[6]

The positive image of Canada helped to counteract the negative image of the British Empire that was the common currency of many isolationists in relation to issues such as India, Ireland and Palestine. The Government of India Bill, which finally became law in July 1935, brought about a temporary reduction in the debate on Indian independence, although it did not satisfy either the Indian Congress Party, led by Mahatma Gandhi, or the so-called 'diehards' who opposed the legislation in the House of Commons. Chief among these was Winston Churchill, whose position on this issue and during the later abdication crisis, when he supported the cause of Edward VIII, helped to call his judgement into question when he argued for more rapid rearmament to counter the rise of Nazi Germany. He finally ended his opposition to the Bill in August 1935, declaring that 'dangers larger and nearer than Indian dangers gather upon our path' – that is, the rise of Nazi Germany. The existence of a vocal Indian independence movement led by the well-known figure of Gandhi, who was *Time* magazine's 'Man of the Year' in 1930, was a useful weapon for isolationists to use when arguing that the British Empire was fundamentally undemocratic.[7]

Many Irish Americans had little regard for Britain or her Empire but relations between Britain and Ireland were better in 1939 than earlier in the decade, which had witnessed a trade war between the two countries. This improvement in relations was brought about by the Anglo-Irish agreement of April 1938, which not only ended the tariff war and a long-running financial dispute but also transferred back to Ireland the three ports that remained under British control after the 1921 Treaty – Cobh (formerly Queenstown) and Berehaven (both on south coast of Ireland), and Lough Swilly (in northwest Ireland). The agreement had been criticised by Churchill for giving up important bases for British security for goodwill rather than any firm assurances from the Irish Government, but it was useful for relations with United States at least. So too was the decision to exclude Northern Ireland from the military conscription bill in April/May 1939. However, there were still security concerns about Irish dissidents, during the Royal Visit, especially when the King and Queen visited the New York World Fair.[8]

Perhaps the most pressing Imperial problem in May 1939 was the British mandate over Palestine, dating from the end of the Great War, which had proved to be a poisoned chalice. Following the Arab Revolt of 1936–39, a Government White Paper on Palestine, restricting Jewish immigration, had been prepared. Malcolm MacDonald, the Colonial Secretary, feared that the White Paper would meet with bitter opposition from Jews in America. 'It was true that this agitation might only last for two or three months', he told the Cabinet, 'but those might be vital months in which the full support of United States public opinion would be of immense value to us.' However, he later reported that Kennedy did not think publication would not have much effect on the Royal Visit. The White Paper was subsequently published on 17 May 1939 and the reception in the US was better than had been feared, partly because Hull and the State Department were very restrained in their comments about it.[9]

Pomp, ceremony and ideology

The bulk of the Royal Visit to North America took place in Canada, with a short detour into the United States in early June. The royal tour started on 17 May in Quebec, where George VI and Queen Elizabeth were met by Mackenzie King and the Governor General, Lord Tweedsmuir. After a few days in Ottawa they headed westwards to British Columbia and arrived in Victoria, on Vancouver Island, at the end of May. The royal party then headed back to the east, arriving at Niagara Falls on 7 June, before crossing the border to the US, where they were met by Lindsay, as British Ambassador, Cordell Hull and his wife, and other officials and dignitaries. There was no shortage of pomp and ceremony in Canada for this first tour of the Dominion by a reigning monarch and the short side-trip to the USA was also not without its symbolism, from highlighting the work of the New Deal to showing off Magna Carta and underlining the common heritage and ideals of Britain and the United States. Everything was done to accentuate the positive aspects of the Anglo-American relationship, and to avoid the negatives, including adjusting the timing of the semi-annual war debt note to Britain so that it was delivered in April 1939, rather than in June, when the King and Queen were in the US.[10]

After staying overnight on the royal train at Niagara Falls the King and Queen headed south and arrived at Washington, DC, on Thursday, 8 June, where they were met at Union Station by the President and First Lady. From Union Station there was a procession with pomp and ceremony much in evidence – the President in a top hat and the King wearing the uniform of the Admiral of the Fleet. The two heads of state rode together in an open-top car with a military escort along Delaware Avenue to the Capitol Building and then down Constitution and Pennsylvania Avenues on to the White House. The procession was followed by a formal diplomatic reception of chiefs of mission in the East Room and then a small informal lunch involving FDR, Eleanor Roosevelt, George VI and Queen Elizabeth, Mackenzie King and a few others. The King and Queen then had an hour of sightseeing in the capital, including the Lincoln Memorial, prior to a garden party at the British Embassy and then a state dinner at the White House, where they stayed overnight.[11]

At the White House dinner the President toasted his royal guests and said 'the entire United States is welcoming on its soil the King and Queen of Great Britain, of our neighbour Canada, and of all the far-flung British Commonwealth of Nations'. Then, referring to 'the bonds of friendship that link our two peoples', he said:

> It is because each nation is lacking in fear of the other that we have unfortified borders between us. It is because neither of us fears aggression on the part of the other that we have entered no race of armaments, the one against the other.

He then referred to 'a recent episode' when 'two small uninhabited Islands in the centre of the Pacific became of sudden interest to the British Empire and the United States as stepping-stones for commercial airplanes between America and Australasia'. Both nations had claimed sovereignty and both had good cases. To avoid 'a long drawn out argument' it was decided 'that the problem be solved by the joint use of both Islands, and, by a gentleman's agreement, to defer the question of sovereignty until the year 1989'. FDR hoped that with 'this kind of understanding' the two countries would grow 'ever closer' and 'their friendship would prosper'.[12]

On the morning of Friday, 9 June, the King and Queen went to the British Embassy, where they received members of the British community in Washington before travelling to the Capitol Building to meet members of Congress in the Rotunda. They then had lunch on the USS *Potomac* during a trip to Mount Vernon, where they laid a wreath at Washington's tomb before being driven back to the capital, stopping on the way at Fort Hunt to visit a Civilian Conservation Corps camp. Next came Arlington Cemetery, where the King laid a wreath at the Tomb at the Unknown Warrior before returning to the White House for an informal tea, and then on the British Embassy for a dinner in honour of the President and the First Lady. After this the King and Queen returned to the royal train, where they stayed overnight, ready for the short trip to New York City the next day.[13]

On Saturday, 10 June, the royal couple boarded a destroyer at Fort Hancock and proceeded with a naval escort along the Hudson to New York, to be met by the Mayor and Governor. They then headed to the New York World Fair, seeing Central Park on the way. At the Fair they visited the Canadian, Irish and British Pavilions, including the Australian, New Zealand and Colonial exhibits. The League of Nations pavilion was omitted from the royal itinerary because of lack of time. Pride of place during the visit was, of course, accorded to Magna Carta – a symbol of the common political heritage of the US and Britain. The World Fair was an integral part of the trip to New York in preference to other possibilities such as a visit to Harlem, which had been considered but rejected. It was the first time that Lincoln Cathedral's Magna Carta had been exhibited outside of Britain, and when the Fair closed in October 1939 the British Government extended its stay in the US because of the danger that it might be lost at sea if it was returned during the war. It was exhibited at the Library of Congress until April 1940, before being sent to Fort Knox for safe keeping, and was finally returned to Lincoln Cathedral in early 1946.[14]

Hyde Park talks

After the visit to the World Fair the royal party headed north – via a brief stop at Columbia University – to the Hyde Park home of FDR, where they spent the evening and all of Sunday, 11 June. In terms of political discussion, this was the most significant part of the visit. Lindsay and Hull had remained in Washington so Roosevelt, George VI and Mackenzie King were able to talk about the international situation quite freely, and this is what they did on

Saturday evening, after a very informal dinner at Hyde Park with the Queen, Eleanor Roosevelt and the Roosevelt family. In fact, the three men talked until 1.30 in the morning, with the President sitting in the middle, George VI to his right and Mackenzie King to his left. On Sunday morning the leaders attended church and then, after an informal lunch, the main feature of which was the hotdogs served up to the royal couple, the President and George VI went swimming while Mackenzie King had a nap. The Canadian later regretted excusing himself as the swim was followed by a private talk between Roosevelt and the King for about an hour in FDR's library. However, the President later gave the Prime Minister a report of his discussion with the King, which was largely an elaboration on what had been said the night before.[15]

During these conversations, the leaders covered a wide range of topics, all of which were recorded in detail by the Canadian Prime Minister and in a short memorandum by George VI. FDR appears to have done most of the talking and the conversation ranged far and wide. But it is possible to discern several main themes running throughout. Firstly, the President was very concerned at what he regarded as the German threat in South America and said that he had received a report that the British Government believed that there was a German submarine base off the coast of Brazil. He said that he intended to have a survey made of the area and that, in Mackenzie King's words 'he had a perfect right to keep European countries from sending warships off the coasts of America, whether it was north or south'. He also said that, if war came, he would like US ships to be able to use the Canadian port of Halifax for coal and equipment so that they could 'assist in keeping the waters of the Atlantic free of German ships'.[16]

Roosevelt also talked about the Neutrality laws, which he hoped would be repealed by Congress before the end of the session. In the meantime, pursuing the line he had taken in his annual message to Congress in January 1939 that there were 'methods short of war', the President said that he could allow the export of useful materials for aircraft production such as engines and wing parts, despite the embargo on 'arms, ammunition and the implements of war'. If Canada concentrated on developing assembly plants, then he would do his best to provide the necessary materials. 'His whole conversation with the King was to the effect that every possible assistance short of actual participation in war could be given,' recorded Mackenzie King. From George VI's notes of his conversation with FDR we see that the two men discussed war debts, amongst other things. The President had said that it was 'better not to reopen the question. Congress wants repayment in full, which is impossible, and a small bit is of no use, as they will want more later'. Financial credits were also discussed and the King recorded: 'USA will want nickel from Canada. They will buy our surplus rubber. In return they can send steel sheets which can be cut for aeroplanes wings. Rough castings with bored cylinders to be machined at home. Can be used for aeroplanes or motorboats. Roosevelt wishes to do.'[17]

A major theme of the talks was Atlantic defence and FDR discussed with George VI his ideas regarding North Atlantic bases. The King recorded these ideas in brief notes. 'Base for his fleet at Trinidad to fuel & replenish stores. From this base he can patrol the Atlantic with ships & aeroplanes on a radius of approximately 1000 miles on a sector of latitude of Haiti to latitude of Brazil. This patrol should locate any enemy fleet, which tried to get to S. Am. or the West Indies.' As well as this 'Trinidad Patrol', the King noted that FDR envisaged a Bermuda Patrol, the purpose of which was 'to patrol N. Atlantic from Cape Cod to Florida, with ships & aeroplanes to prevent submarines from attacking convoys'. FDR believed that Germany had an air base in Brazil at Natal Cape St Roques and a 'landing ground on the island of Fernando Noronha 200 miles from the coast'. The President also believed that 'Brazil is pretty sure to kick out the Germans. He would then use it himself. Haiti, Cuba, & West Indies are potential friendly bases. The idea is that USA should relieve us of these responsibilities, but can it be done without a declaration of war?'[18]

Clearly, the President was talking to the King as a friend and ally. When George VI and Mackenzie King were back in Canada, they discussed the significance of the American visit and the King asked Mackenzie King for his thoughts on their conversations with Roosevelt. 'I replied that it was clear to me that the President was anxious to do everything he possibly could to be of help, short of committing his country to war.' The King said, 'What a fine fellow he is!' and 'Obviously, he is the right man to continue on, if he cannot find anyone else with a similar purpose.' He then told Mackenzie King about his discussions with Roosevelt in the library the day before. He said that they had studied some maps of the Caribbean and discussed where 'the Germans were making their submarine base off Trinidad'. They had also discussed the likely military and naval situation in the event of war and the prime importance of air power and Canada's potential role in producing aeroplanes for the defence of Britain, with the help of parts supplied by the United States.[19]

George VI also reminded Mackenzie King of what the President had said on Saturday evening, when the three men discussed the international situation after dinner. Roosevelt had explained that he 'was trying to educate the American people to appreciate what it would mean to them if Germany were to win in a war and the French and British forces to be wiped off the seas. They would then lose entirely their export market, and if they were given a chance to import into those countries, it would be wholly on the terms of the Dictators themselves.' Pursuing this theme on Sunday, the King had asked Roosevelt 'what would move the Americans most in the event of a war between Britain and Germany'. The President had replied that 'if London were bombed, that would certainly stir the American nation'. The German 'blitz' in 1940–41 did indeed stir American public opinion, although not sufficiently to lead to a declaration of war, which occurred only after Germany declared war on the US after Pearl Harbor.[20]

The spectre of Churchill

George VI spoke quite openly to Roosevelt and Mackenzie King. He said that he was far from impressed by Eden, especially his guarded formality rather than the simple frankness that the King preferred. But he reserved his main criticism for Churchill, who, he said, during the Great War, had 'dismissed Prince Louis of Battenburg from the command of the navy on the score that he was a German but had later admitted he had done it in order to have the control of it himself'. The King also referred to Churchill's role in the ill-fated Dardanelles campaign and how he had ignored advice not to make the attack too soon. 'The King indicated that he would never wish to appoint Churchill to any office unless it was absolutely necessary in time of war,' noted Mackenzie King. 'I confess I was glad to hear him say that because I think Churchill is one of the most dangerous men I have ever known.' The King later mentioned that he had deliberately brought up Churchill's name to see what the President's reaction would be. He said he was anxious to see, as there was now talk of Churchill succeeding Chamberlain, how this might be regarded in America. 'He did not think the President viewed it too favourably,' recorded Mackenzie King. 'He told me quite frankly what he would rather do than have him at the head of a Government. I agreed that it would be inviting disaster, simply challenging Germany.'[21]

Significance of Royal Visit

When George VI asked Mackenzie King for his overall verdict on the visit, he said he thought 'it had surpassed all expectations' and was 'an unqualified success in every way'. The enthusiastic welcome that the King had received was 'a demonstration from the people themselves; was personal to himself, and the Queen, as well as expressive of sympathy with the British ideals of freedom and peace'. The King replied: 'This trip has meant a great deal to me, and a great deal to the Queen.' He had enjoyed the informal aspects of the trip and breaking away from the protocol that his father, George V, had regarded as essential to the monarchy. He also felt that the visit to America – and Canada – had helped to restore the image of the British monarchy after the recent abdication crisis that had ended the brief but troubled reign of his brother, Edward VIII. 'It is apparent that the American visit has made a tremendous impression on him,' concluded Mackenzie King. It had also made a great impression on Mackenzie King and he was especially gratified by FDR's very friendly attitude towards him, in contrast to the reticence of Lindsay and the British Embassy.[22]

This was also Lindsay's view. 'The royal visit which ended last night can only be characterised as a complete success,' he wrote.

> The whole visit has been a striking personal triumph of Their Majesties though at the cost of great personal fatigue to themselves due partly to the extreme heat of the weather. . . . I need hardly add that the President himself and his family were the embodiment of courtesy and friendliness.

He was sure that the visit had made 'a profound impression' on the US and enhanced the friendship between the two countries. 'Coming at a crucial moment it is of capital importance in the history of Anglo-American relations and its effects will not wear off.' As regards American Neutrality legislation, he was rather doubtful that the Royal Visit would have much influence on isolationist senators (such as Borah and Johnson). But the visit had certainly helped the British cause, so if war came prior to any change in the Neutrality laws, public opinion would certainly be in favour of revision. 'In other words, while we cannot at present feel certain of receiving an immediate dividend, we can be assured that our hidden reserves have been immensely strengthened.'[23]

This view was borne out in the US press coverage of the Royal Visit. As the *New York Times* noted: 'We like the British because we understand them better than most foreigners. And, after all, why shouldn't we? They gave us our speech, our manners and our customs, and after a little persuasion by the Continental army, our country itself.' The personal modesty of the King and Queen were often commented upon in the US press, as was their evident enjoyment during their hectic couple of days in the United States. Even the thorny issue of British imperialism took a back seat during the visit. Indeed, the triumph of the royal tour through Canada showed the most positive side of the British Empire and Commonwealth, and when George VI, in his occasional public statements during the US visit, referred to the Empire it underlined the belief that Britain, when it was committed to the defence of democracy, served as a major buffer to German expansion in Europe and Japanese expansion in the Far East.[24]

The very positive impact of the Royal Visit was also reflected in the British press. London's Sunday editions portrayed the welcome given to the King and Queen in New York as 'tumultuous'. It was also noted that the *Observer*, in an editorial headed 'Thanks America, a wonderful welcome', had used adjectives such as 'dramatic' and 'miraculous' to describe the reception given to the King and Queen. 'That the possibility of discord has been extinguished between two such nations is a fact of immeasurable import,' the *Observer* was reported as saying. The *Sunday Times*, in a three-column special article headed 'Old feuds forgotten in historic reunion', said:

> Americans are famous for hospitality, but the warmth of their welcome to the King and Queen surpasses anything that could have been expected. . . . The growing friendship between this country and the US makes the visit the principal bright patch in the surrounding gloom of international affairs.[25]

German press comment on the Royal Visit was as negative as the American and British coverage was positive and it included a significant article in a Munich newspaper, the *Neueste Nachrichten*, by the editor-in-chief. In line with German propaganda against Roosevelt, the article argued that the President regarded himself as 'the master of the democratic world bloc' and was 'trying to plunge the world into war in order to save America and capture a third term for himself'. The article characterised the Royal Visit as 'the most important link in the whole chain of measures whereby Britain has attempted during the last few years to tie America more firmly to British destinies'. The British were felt to have a network of organisations in the US that were trying to promote 'an Anglo-American alliance', including the Foreign Policy Association, the Carnegie Foundation and the *New York Times*. The royal tour was therefore seen as extremely effective in terms of British propaganda in the United States, especially if FDR was re-elected to a third term.[26]

Naval cooperation

At the end of June 1939 Roosevelt called Lindsay to the White House to follow up the ideas he had discussed with George VI. If war came, he said, he intended to establish a neutrality zone in the Western Atlantic that would stretch up to 500 miles from the coastline. A US naval patrol would then warn off any German or Italian warships that entered the zone. This would allow ships with goods from the Americas that were bound for Britain or France to collect safely at Halifax and be escorted in convoys from the neutrality zone to Europe. To facilitate this plan, FDR asked Lindsay to pass on to London a request for the use of the Canadian port of Halifax and for bases in the British West Indies – specifically Trinidad and Tobago, St Lucia and Bermuda – to be leased to the United States. His main aim was to defend the Americas, especially the Panama Canal and Latin America, but he also wanted to help the Allies, as he had told George VI in his Hyde Park talks, by supporting the British blockade in the neutrality zone and allowing Royal Navy ships to engage with the enemy elsewhere.[27]

Lindsay urged London to support the President's very unneutral proposal. The Foreign Office broadly welcomed the idea, despite its unorthodox nature, as did the Dominions Office and the Colonial Office. Formal permission from Ottawa to use Halifax as a base followed relatively easily in August but the Caribbean dimension proved more difficult as Foreign Office legal advisers raised various issues of concern. On 8 July 1939 Lindsay put these to the President, who was rather taken aback at the apparently negative

British response to his proposal, but he persevered and in August 1939 London agreed to lease coastal sites in Bermuda and Trinidad to Pan American Airways, so that they could be established as bases for the American Navy. The operation was suspended when war broke out in case it became known and provided ammunition for Borah, Johnson and the isolationists against the revision of the Neutrality Act. It was also delayed by the need to obtain sufficient naval personnel and planes to make effective use of the bases. But the plan came into its own in September 1940 as part of the destroyer-bases deal.[28]

Meanwhile, the increasingly threatening European situation meant that the British Government could no longer be certain that a fleet would be sent to the Far East in the event of a war with Japan. As a result, it was decided to renew the talks on naval strategy in the Pacific that had begun with the Ingersoll visit to London in January 1938. Commander T. C. Hampton was therefore sent to Washington for conversations with senior American officers. FDR had agreed to these talks only on condition that the utmost secrecy would be maintained as the Administration was somewhat paranoid about the possibility of press leaks and uncomfortable questions in Congress such as Admiral Leahy had encountered after the Ingersoll talks in January 1939. The Hampton talks therefore took place in Admiral Leahy's home and no joint record was made of them, although Hampton drew up a report. The talks went well, there was a spirit of cooperation and, in Hampton's words, both the President and the Admiral were 'extremely pro-British'.[29]

Hampton's report of the talks showed that American naval planning was moving along similar lines to British naval priorities. In particular, in the event of a European war, Washington's plan was to deter Japan by concentrating the American fleet at Pearl Harbor, while maintaining naval patrols in the Western Atlantic. Leahy went so far as to say that if an Anglo-American alliance were formed against the Axis powers, he personally would be prepared to move the American fleet to Singapore, provided that there was an adequate British force there as well. Thus the Hampton talks signalled the Anglo-American strategy that was adopted when war broke out in September 1939, with the British and French focusing on the Atlantic and Mediterranean, and the United States minding the Pacific. However, this tacit understanding depended on the goodwill of Franklin Roosevelt and it was by no means certain that his successor would be as accommodating to British interests if he decided not to run again for an unprecedented third term as President in 1940.[30]

The view from Berlin

The significance of the Royal Visit to America was not lost on the German Foreign Ministry. On 17 May 1939, the same day that the royal couple landed at Quebec after their transatlantic crossing, the German Embassy in Washington sent a significant despatch to Berlin entitled: 'The foreign policy of Roosevelt in the event of a European war, in particular a war between Germany and Britain'. Commenting on the impending trip to the United States, the Embassy remarked: 'The visit of the British King and Queen to America will serve to consolidate a relationship which for all practical purposes already amounts to an alliance, and which American patriots are opposing, apparently to no avail.' In the context of FDR's 'many speeches and hints, from which Britain and France have naturally been able to draw their own conclusions' – that is, that they had US support for their policy of a 'Peace Front' in Europe – the Embassy argued that 'one can only assume that the American people are to be systematically prepared for the fact that America's entry into a European war may possibly take place with lightning suddenness'. This was rather an exaggeration, but the Embassy was clearly under no illusions about the pro-British nature of FDR's foreign policy.[31]

The Royal Visit therefore strengthened the view of Thomsen and the German Embassy in Washington that there was a virtual alliance between the United States and Britain, and that, although US public opinion and Congress still supported the Neutrality laws, the Roosevelt Administration was working hard to undermine or bypass them in favour of Britain. 'The methods used to achieve this objective are as subtle as they are revealing,' argued Thomsen. FDR had never stated his opposition to the Neutrality Act 'openly and bluntly' – he had merely said that in certain circumstances it favoured the aggressor rather than the victim. Administration allies in Congress were aiming to do away with the arms embargo, while public opinion was also being 'systematically worked on'. FDR had played a leading part in this campaign through his speeches and pronouncements. 'From the quarantine speech in Chicago', Thomsen argued, 'there runs like a thread the effort to promote the idea that when the hour of decision strikes, America must be at the side of Britain and France as their natural ally.' Roosevelt's most recent speeches and actions showed this, Thomsen said, including the secret sales of aircraft to France, the imposition of countervailing duties, the reference to the frontier being in France that was made to the Senate Military Affairs Committee, and the announcement of 'measures short of war'.[32]

'The question therefore arises with all the force of logic', continued Thomsen, 'as to what America will do should a European war, especially a war between Britain and Germany, break out within the next year and a half.' The Embassy's reports had repeatedly stressed that 'America's entire economic and probably her financial might too will be available if Britain and France find themselves engaged in a life and death with the totalitarian Powers'. The isolationist leaders realised this and were trying to preserve the Neutrality Act. In the event of a major conflict breaking out between Britain and Germany, Thomsen said, the President was 'determined not to wait until America becomes a participant in the war as a result of her entanglement with the belligerents' but instead 'to espouse Britain's cause at a moment to be determined by himself'. Roosevelt feared that there was a possibility that Britain and France could be overwhelmed at the start of a European war, Thomsen reasoned, so he did not want to wait until the US joined the war before helping them.[33]

Encouragement was being given to Britain and France, Thomsen pointed out, despite the fact that American military aid was 'out of the question for the first year of a conflict'. This was because, after the outbreak of a war, 'Roosevelt personally will endeavour to come to the aid of our opponents as quickly as possible with the full moral weight of the US by creating the conditions for, and by skilfully timing, the entry into the war on their side.' Thomsen felt that Roosevelt probably expected that American support for the democracies would have 'a devastating effect on morale in the totalitarian States' and would encourage 'those Powers who, on the outbreak of a European war, might at first adopt an attitude of wait and see' to 'range themselves against the totalitarian States' instead. The President believed that 'by introducing the moral support of America in war as a decisive factor in world politics . . . he is contributing towards the active solidarity of all the "peace-loving" Powers and towards paving the way for their victory, and that he is vindicating his own claim to leadership'. In conclusion, Thomsen declared:

> We can expect no objectivity from this man. . . . Roosevelt rather seems resolved not only to join in Britain's policy of encirclement, but to exercise a decisive influence on it. The *leitmotiv* of Roosevelt's policy is America's participation in another war of annihilation against Germany.[34]

Notes

1. *Hansard*, Commons, Neville Chamberlain, 3 May 1939.
2. *Hansard*, Commons, Clement Attlee and Sir Archibald Sinclair, 3 May 1939; Ibid., Lords, Archbishop of Canterbury, 3 May 1939; for evolution of Labour Party foreign policy see Gordon, *Conflict and Consensus in Labour's Foreign Policy*.
3. For the Royal Visit see Langer and Gleason, *Challenge to Isolation*, p. 129; Reynolds, *Creation*, p. 43; Rhodes, 'British Royal Visit of 1939', pp. 197–211; Reynolds, 'British Royal Visit to the USA, 1939', pp. 461–72; Bell, 'The 1939 Royal Visit to America', pp. 599–616.
4. Bouverie, *Appeasing Hitler*, pp. 335–63; Shen, *Age of Appeasement*, pp. 226–58.
5. McCulloch, 'Mackenzie King and the North Atlantic Triangle', pp. 3–29; Roosevelt, *Roosevelt Letters*, 3, pp. 239–40, Roosevelt to George VI, 25 August 1939.
6. For Royal Visit to Canada see MacDonnell, *Daylight Upon Magic*.
7. See Clymer, *Quest for Freedom*; Gandhi, *Time* magazine, 5 January 1931.
8. See Cronin, *Washington's Irish Policy*.
9. CAB 23, 24 (1939), item 5, 26 April 1939; CAB 23, 27 (1939), item 5, 10 May 1939; CAB 23, 29 (1939), item 5, 23 May 1939; for US comment on White Paper see *NYT*, 30 May 1939; for background see Bethell, *The Palestine Triangle*.
10. See FO/371/22802-22803, file A385/45, for war debts in 1939. For a critical view of US attitude to war debts see Self, *Britain, America and the War Debt Controversy*.
11. Mackenzie King Diary, 8 and 9 June 1939.
12. President's toast for the King shared at White House State Dinner on 8 June 1939. Text in FDR Library, President's Secretary's File, 8 June 1939. For the long-running Pacific Islands episode see FRUS/1939/II, docs 271–285: the joint administration of Canton and Enderbury Islands was agreed in an exchange of notes, 6 April 1939.
13. FO/371/22800, A3880/27/45 for Royal Visit itinerary in United States.

14. For Magna Carta in the US see Library of Congress website, available at <https://www.loc.gov/exhibits/magna-carta-muse-and-mentor/magna-carta-comes-to america.html>.
15. Mackenzie King Diary, 11 June 1939.
16. Mackenzie King Diary, 10 June 1939.
17. Mackenzie King Diary, 10 June 1939. For the transcript of George VI's handwritten notes of his conversations with Roosevelt on 10 and 11 June 1939 see FDR Library, President's Secretary's File, Royal, King's notes transcript.
18. Ibid., George VI transcript.
19. Mackenzie King Diary, 12 June 1939.
20. Mackenzie King Diary, 12 June 1939.
21. Mackenzie King Diary, 10 and 12 June 1939. For Chamberlain's determination to keep Churchill out of the Cabinet see Phillips, *Fighting Churchill, Appeasing Hitler*, pp. xii–xiii.
22. Mackenzie King Diary, 12 June 1939.
23. FO/371/22800, A4139/27/45, Lindsay to Halifax, 12 June 1939.
24. *NYT*, 12 June 1939.
25. *NYT*, 13 June 1939.
26. FO/371/22801, A4467/27/45, German press comments, from British Library of Information.
27. FO/371/23901, W10051/9058/49, Lindsay to Halifax, 30 June 1939. See also Perras, *Origins*, pp. 81–5; Baptiste, 'The British Grant', pp. 5–37; Reynolds, *Creation*, p. 65; Watt, *How War Came*, pp. 269–70.
28. FO/371/23902, W10369/9805/75, Lindsay to Halifax, 8 July 1939; Perras, *Origins*, pp. 81–5; Baptiste, 'The British Grant', pp. 24–5; Reynolds, *Creation*, p. 65; Watt, *How War Came*, pp. 269–70.
29. FO/371/23561, report by Hampton, 27 June 1939; Johnsen, *Origins of the Grand Alliance*, pp. 50–5; Reynolds, *Creation*, pp. 61–2; Leutze, *Bargaining For Supremacy*, pp. 34–41.
30. Ibid.
31. DGFP/D/VI, doc 403, Thomsen to GFM, 17 May 1939.
32. Ibid.
33. Ibid.
34. Ibid.

12 Polish Crisis, July–September 1939

On 6 July 1939 William Borah declared in the Senate that the Munich agreement showed Britain and France to be no better than the dictator states when it came to abandoning the Czechs and looking after their own 'selfish and sinister' interests. In what the *New York Times* called a 'a bitter denunciation of the European democracies', Borah said that: 'When the time approaches for the dictators and the democracies to serve their own particular interests, they never differ unless their interests differ.' On 11 July Borah, Johnson and other isolationists and opponents of the President in the Senate Foreign Relations Committee voted by 12 to 11 to defer consideration of any revision of the Neutrality laws until the following session, scheduled to begin in January 1940. Borah also rejected the pleas of FDR and Hull at a last-minute White House conference on 18 July that urgent action was required to remove the arms embargo in wartime. Predicting a war by the end of the summer, Hull invited Borah to read the cables reaching his office. Apparently convinced that Britain and France would not go to war with Germany over Poland, Borah replied: 'So far as the reports of your Department are concerned, I wouldn't be bound by them. I have my own sources of information . . . and on several occasions I've found them more reliable than the State Department.'[1]

Roosevelt and Hull believed that the repeal of the arms embargo would demonstrate that the United States should not be discounted by Berlin, Rome and Tokyo in calculating their next moves. It not only would favour the European democracies in a future war, but it would also be a useful and timely contribution to the 'tacit alliance' with Britain and the burgeoning 'Peace Front' that was forming against Nazi Germany. Isolationists such as Borah and Johnson obviously realised that the repeal of the arms embargo would favour Britain and France and they therefore resisted the move. Roosevelt and Hull feared that the defeat of the arms embargo repeal would make another German move more likely as the democracies would not be able to buy arms and ammunition from the United States at the start of another war. Their temper was not improved by Borah's complacency regarding the European situation and they issued a joint statement on 14 July 1939 criticising the arms embargo decision as a blow to the Administration's efforts to maintain peace.[2]

'Missed opportunity'

The repeal of the arms embargo was eventually achieved in November 1939, but Hull later argued that the failure to repeal it in July 1939 was a missed opportunity. Repeal then, he wrote, 'would have been far more effective for the cause of the peace-loving nations if it could have been gained in the spring and summer of 1939 rather than in the autumn'. However, the main theme of this chapter is that while the failure to secure the repeal of the arms embargo in July 1939 was certainly a setback for FDR's foreign policy, it should not obscure other actions by the Administration to follow up the success of the Royal Visit, such as timely naval cooperation in the Atlantic and Pacific and the cotton–rubber exchange deal of June 1939. Other actions included the welcome accorded to the secret British mission headed by Lord Riverdale to prepare the ground for Allied purchases in the US in the event of war, diplomatic support for Britain during the Tientsin crisis with Japan in July 1939, and representations in Moscow urging Stalin to support the 'Peace Front' by joining Britain and France in a Triple Alliance against Nazi Germany.[3]

Lindsay explained to London that the Administration's defeat was due to domestic politics as well as the strength of isolationism in Congress. Republicans and conservative Democrats feared that the President was using the crisis in Europe to his own political advantage and that he might run for an unprecedented third term in 1940 if war ensued. Lindsay also pointed out that the majority against neutrality revision in the Senate Committee included Guy Gillette and Walter George, Democrats who Roosevelt had opposed in the previous year's mid-term elections. However, the failure of the Administration to secure the repeal of the arms embargo, while not a great surprise to Chamberlain, was a bitter blow to the Foreign Office and there was some criticism at what

Butler, Halifax's Parliamentary Under Secretary, termed another 'let-down' by the United States. In fact, it is unlikely that repeal in July 1939 would have made any difference in preventing the outbreak of war in September. There were other, more important, developments that undermined the notion of a 'Peace Front', not least the lingering suspicion – which Borah was not alone in harbouring – that the policy of appeasement would prevent Britain and France from going to war with Germany and the failure of the Anglo-French negotiations with the Soviet Union.[4]

One of the few world leaders who retained any optimism about the international situation was the Canadian Prime Minister, Mackenzie King. This was in large part due to the success of the Royal Visit. 'What this Royal Tour has done in the way of bringing the British and American peoples together no words will ever express & the world will never know,' he noted in his diary. 'The feeling has never been what it is today – In every direction it has surpassed expectations.' He also retained the belief that he had formed after his meeting with Hitler in May 1937 that the Führer did not want war if his ambition to unite the German people in one Reich could be achieved peacefully. The Canadian leader was certainly concerned about the strained relations between Nazi Germany and Poland but he hoped that Britain and France would not oppose the annexation of Danzig by Germany. Unlike FDR, he regretted the greater emphasis that the Chamberlain Government had placed on deterrence after the occupation of Prague as it allowed little room for manœuvre. But his most immediate fear was that Churchill and Eden might be brought into the Government, a move he believed would be regarded as a direct provocation by Hitler and one likely to lead to war.[5]

Danzig problem

Hitler's speech to the Reichstag on 28 April, as well as ridiculing FDR's 'peace appeal' and denouncing the Anglo-German naval agreement of 1935, also terminated the Polish–German non-aggression pact of 1934 that had guaranteed the status of Danzig for ten years. The Chamberlain Government was therefore anxious to make it clear that Britain's guarantee to Poland was not a bluff and that any further acts of aggression by the Nazi regime would be resisted. On 29 June Halifax delivered a speech at Chatham House that was intended to set out the Government's position and this was followed by Chamberlain's statement in the Commons on 10 July 1939 that Britain would support Poland if her national sovereignty was being threatened by another power. 'Recent occurrences in Danzig' had 'given rise to fears that it is intended to settle her future status by unilateral action', said Chamberlain. 'We have guaranteed to give our assistance to Poland in the case of a clear threat to her independence, which she considers it vital to resist with her national forces, and we are firmly resolved to carry out this undertaking.' But his statement did not rule out a solution to the Danzig issue if one could be found, and scepticism remained, both at home and abroad, as to whether Chamberlain had really abandoned appeasement.[6]

By July 1939 it was clear to Washington that the prospects for a peaceful solution of the Danzig crisis were looking bleak. Biddle reported from Poland that pro-Nazi Danzig officials were becoming more belligerent in their attitude towards Poland and Germany's apparent determination to settle the issues of Danzig, the Polish Corridor and Upper Silesia in favour of the Reich by the end of summer. Biddle reasoned that this might be part of 'Berlin's tactics of psychological terrorism' but if the current tone represented the true attitude of Berlin 'hopes for a reasonable and just settlement of the Danzig question seem remote'. Moffat, in a conversation with the French Ambassador in Washington, was told 'that the Germans had everything ready for the end of August and that they could, if they wished, strike almost without further preparation. No man's guess is worth anything as to how Hitler's mind would work. The Italians did not want war and would presumably argue against it, but that the decision would not be theirs.' From London, Herschel Johnson reported the Italian Ambassador in Berlin as saying: 'Great Britain must realize that Hitler is not to be intimidated by the Peace Front. He feels humiliated by having to watch its negotiations and would not wait indefinitely.'[7]

The position of the Polish Government appeared to be equally entrenched. Moffat reported a conversation with the Polish Ambassador, who, he said, 'had little to offer other than to reiterate the belief of his Government that German strength was overrated'. An alarmed Moffat further recorded: 'The whole conversation represented a point of view of unreasoning optimism and still more unreasoning underrating of one's opponent that, if typical of Polish mentality in general, causes me to feel considerable foreboding.' From Paris, Bullitt reported that Daladier 'considered it utter folly for the Poles to turn down a Russian proposal for genuine military assistance'. Meanwhile, Welles cabled the American Ambassador in Warsaw to say that Roosevelt, mindful of public opinion in the United States and elsewhere, believed that it was vital, in the event of a military crisis resulting from the Danzig issue, that the first offensive move should not be made by Poland. 'To use the Biblical phrase, a situation should not arise as a result of which it could truthfully be said that Poland "threw the first stone".'[8]

Cotton–rubber exchange agreement

The increasing likelihood of war was clearly signalled by the Anglo-American cotton–rubber agreement that was ratified by Congress in July 1939. The exchange agreement – often referred to as a 'barter deal' – originated as a move to help dispose of surplus US agricultural products and increase the US Government's stockpile of essential raw materials in the event of war. It first came to the notice of the Foreign Office when an article appeared in the London *Times* on 11 April 1939, regarding a plan announced by Senator James Byrnes for an exchange of raw materials that would have the double effect of aiding the democracies in the event of war and providing another outlet for surpluses of American farm products. The State Department contacted Kennedy on 18 April, saying that the US was in urgent need of strategic materials for emergencies and raising the topic of an exchange with Britain of cotton and wheat for rubber and tin supplies. It added that both Hull and FDR were interested in the exchange and Kennedy should remind the British Government of US efforts on its behalf, as help with this issue would command the attention of US public opinion.[9]

In London the exchange proposal was supported by the Foreign Office but it ran into opposition from the Board of Trade. Lindsay was therefore asked for his view of the likely impact of such a deal on neutrality revision. He replied that the Embassy felt that 'any serious achievement' in terms of acquiring surplus American cotton and wheat would have a useful political effect in Congress. However, 'we do not think it would seriously affect the attitude of Congress on Neutrality legislation and we suspect that Mr Kennedy has been exerting some high-pressure salesmanship'. Hull was 'avowedly lukewarm on the whole proposition' and thought a treaty was likely to be required. 'Nevertheless', Lindsay continued,

> on the principle that it is wise to cooperate with the US Government whenever invited to do so we think HMG would do well to do what they can to assist the US Government by making any counter proposals that may occur to them as regards the barter and by offering all possible help as regards purchase of commodities desired by the US Government. [10]

The Foreign Office was positive about the scheme as, according to Kennedy, FDR was 'personally interested'. It was not really concerned with the details of the proposal. 'Our sole interest in the matter is the effect on Anglo-American relations of the prosecution or abandonment of the attempt to reach agreement over some kind of barter deal,' minuted Balfour. 'The barter deal has aroused considerable public interest in the USA and if nothing materialises it would be a set-back to Anglo-American relations.' Similarly, at a meeting of the Cabinet on 14 June Halifax urged support for the deal. Chamberlain said that he did not think an exchange agreement would have much effect on modifying the American Neutrality legislation. But, he continued, 'it would be very unfortunate if there was a breakdown of negotiations, or negotiation in a grudging spirit, particularly at the present time'. With his support, an agreement was finally signed on 23 June. It was then ratified by Congress in July and came into force on 25 August – just in time for the outbreak of war.[11]

Wohltat talks

While Chamberlain was supportive of the cotton–rubber exchange agreement with Washington, he was also determined to maintain confidential channels to Berlin. On 18 July 1939, Sir Horace Wilson, Chamberlain's 'Chief Industrial Adviser' and one of his most trusted aides, had a secret meeting with Helmuth Wohltat, a trade official in the German Foreign Ministry and a confidant of Helmut Göring. The meeting took place in Wilson's office and, according to his own account, it was a general conversation about relations between Britain and Germany and how they might be improved, including the idea that a British figure should visit Hitler to discuss 'political, military and economic questions'. Wilson recorded that he had said to Wohltat that British policy was set out in Halifax's Chatham House speech and that British criticism of Germany had resulted from her 'troublesome behaviour'. Any initiative to improve matters needed to come from Berlin. In Wohltat's account of the meeting, Wilson suggested a non-aggression pact, an arms limitation agreement and an understanding that the two powers should not interfere in each other's sphere of interest. If relations could be improved along these lines, then Danzig would become a minor issue and the British guarantee to Poland would be unnecessary. Stressing the need for secrecy, Wilson apparently told the German official: 'You have Mr Chamberlain's political future in your hands. If this leaks out, there will be a great scandal and Mr Chamberlain will be forced to resign.'[12]

In fact, news of Wohltat's talks did leak out in London because on 20 July he also met with Robert Hudson, a Trade Minister in the Government, who suggested the idea of a huge loan to Germany in return for a more cooperative European policy. Hudson talked unofficially with journalists and the story became front page news in the *Daily Telegraph* and the *News Chronicle*. Chamberlain was then forced to deny the story in the House of Commons on 31 July when it was raised by Hugh Dalton on behalf of the Labour Opposition. Dalton said that Wohltat's talks with Wilson and Hudson risked endangering the 'Peace Front' as they suggested that the Government had not abandoned appeasement and that it was looking for a way to abandon Poland, just as it had done Czechoslovakia. Historians of the episode differ as to whether Hudson was a decoy used by the Government to distract attention from the more important Wilson talks or whether he was simply an ambitious young politician trying to make a name for himself.[13]

Berlin was fully aware of Chamberlain's great reluctance to abandon appeasement and knew that Wilson was speaking on behalf of the Prime Minister. According to Dirksen, the German Ambassador in London, Hudson's 'garrulity and incorrect presentation of the facts' had given the public 'a completely distorted picture' of the conversations. But the Ambassador thought that this was a good thing in many ways, as 'the really serious and significant part of the talks here – namely his two conversations with Sir Horace Wilson – has to some extent been kept dark; therefore the possibility of continuing them remains'. From Washington, the German Embassy reported that the Wohltat–Hudson conversation 'surprised and disappointed public opinion here'. The Embassy continued to regard the Roosevelt Administration as in a virtual alliance with Britain and, to that extent, a potential long-term threat to Germany in the event of war. But US policy would depend on the attitude of the British Government – if Britain was not involved in a war with Germany, then there was nothing to fear from the United States, even if Roosevelt was re-elected.[14]

Riverdale mission

As the European situation worsened, a secret visit by Arthur Balfour, Lord Riverdale, the British steel manufacturer and former President of the British Chamber of Commerce, was being planned that illustrates the military side of the increasingly close relationship between Britain and the US in 1939. The British Embassy in Washington had suggested early in the year that a purchasing agency should be established in America and this was taken up by a sub-committee of the Committee of Imperial Defence on 9 June 1939, chaired by Sir Arthur Robinson. The meeting recommended that a 'suitable person should proceed as soon as possible to the USA charged with the duty of studying the problem of purchasing our requirements (other than foodstuffs and oil products) in the USA in war, with particular reference to the question of setting up a purchasing agency, and of the type of organisation that would be suitable for such an agency.' This person was to consult with Government purchasing agents in Britain before proceeding to the USA and to make contact with Louis Johnson, the Assistant Secretary of State for War in Washington.[15]

Lindsay contacted the Foreign Office on 29 June 1939 to say that oral enquiries at the State Department showed that a purchasing agency would be welcome to both them and the War Department and that it could count on their 'discreet assistance'. Orders that were placed with manufacturers in peacetime would receive 'sympathetic treatment' by the US Government, which would also endeavour to permit the same proportion of orders placed by foreign governments to be maintained, compared with US Government orders, even in the event of war breaking out. Lindsay therefore urged London to send a 'scout' to the US in order to lay the foundations for setting up a purchasing agency as soon as possible, with its seat probably in New York and with a liaison officer in Washington. The Ambassador added: 'The State Department lay stress on the extreme desirability of avoiding all publicity until the neutrality legislation is passed and for this reason the scouting party should be as small and unobtrusive as possible, preferably only one man.'[16]

Leslie Burgin, the Minister of Supply designate, raised the issue at the Cabinet on 5 July 1939 and it was agreed to proceed along these lines. It was then decided that Lord Riverdale, a businessman who made frequent trips to America, would undertake the mission to explore the purchasing situation in the US. He left on the SS *Georgic* on 22 July and on the 31st he arrived in Washington, where he met with Louis Johnson. Riverdale had secret talks for several days with members of the State and War Departments, all of whom were very helpful, he said. Most of them, Riverdale reported, thought that the Neutrality Act and the Hiram Johnson Act would be repealed if war broke out in Europe. He was told by Louis Johnson that the President had expressed himself as '100 per cent in favour of what we are doing'. Riverdale had no doubt that a purchasing agency should be set up in the United States without delay so as to capitalise on American goodwill, even prior to the repeal of the arms embargo. This was agreed to by the British Cabinet on 28 August.[17]

Tientsin crisis

While the Riverdale mission was taking place, events in the Far East and Europe were coming to a head. As always, international relations in the two regions were very much entwined and this consideration continued to influence policymakers in both London and Washington and to affect the degree of 'close cooperation' between them. The key issue was whether Japan would join the Rome–Berlin Axis that had been agreed in October 1936 and formalised as a military alliance in May 1939 as the 'Pact of Steel'. The Japanese Government had joined the Anti-Comintern Pact between Italy and Germany – aimed at the Soviet Union – in November 1937 but was reluctant to join the Axis powers against the Western democracies until the balance of power in Europe was more clearly in their favour. The attitude of the Soviet Union was also a major factor as Japan was vulnerable to an attack from that direction. Berlin was pressing the Tokyo Government to join a full military alliance, so London and Washington wanted to avoid pushing Japan in this direction and risking coordinated action by the dictator states.[18]

This was the context of what became known as the Tientsin crisis during the summer of 1939. The crisis, which was closely observed in Washington, began in April 1939 when the manager of the Japanese-owned Federal Reserve Bank of North China was murdered in the Grand Theatre, located in the British concession within Tientsin. The local police, under British control, arrested four suspects but the Foreign Office was opposed to surrendering the men to the Japanese authorities. This led in June 1939 to a blockade of the Tientsin concession by forces of the Japanese North China Area Army that involved strip-searching everyone who entered or left the concession territory, including women and British Embassy staff, as well as regularly cutting off supplies of essential commodities such as milk. This provoked outrage in the British press and in the House of Commons, and accusations, discussed in the Cabinet, that the Government was not standing up to Japan on behalf of British citizens and interests.[19]

Eventually, talks between Sir Robert Craigie, the British Ambassador in Tokyo, and Hachiro Arita, from the Japanese Foreign Office, resulted in a formula that was to serve as the basis for a negotiated settlement. Under this formula, announced by Chamberlain in the Commons on 24 July 1939, the British Government recognised that the Japanese forces in China had 'special requirements for the purpose of safeguarding their own security and maintaining public order in the regions under their control' and said that British authorities and nationals in North China should not undermine these requirements. The statement was criticised in Britain by the Opposition and even by Tories, who regarded it as a humiliating retreat by the Government. Nor did it mark the end of the crisis as there were still the outstanding Japanese demands to be considered, including handing over the four Chinese nationalists and issues relating to Chinese currency and silver reserves – both of interest to the United States and France.[20]

Thus far, the US attitude to the British discomfiture over Japan's pressure on Tientsin had been sympathetic but non-committal. However, on 26 July the US Government denounced its commercial agreement with Japan dating from 1911. When Lindsay asked Hull about this he drew 'a complete blank'. As the Ambassador explained to London: 'Above all things', the Roosevelt Administration 'must be able to say with its hand on its heart that it was not impelled to act by any foreign pressure especially that of His Majesty's Government'. Congress was in 'full cry' so the State Department had to be careful not to be seen to be 'pulling the chestnuts out of the fire' for Britain. However, Lindsay felt that American abrogation of the 1911 treaty was doubtless intended to 'afford some relief to HMG in their present difficulties'. This was confirmed by the President himself when he saw Mallet at the White House and told him that he and Hull had wanted to take some action against Japan and did not have time to inform London beforehand. Mallet told Roosevelt that his action would be very helpful to Britain and the President replied that he hoped so, 'as something had to be done to warn the dictators'.[21]

The US move alarmed Craigie in Tokyo as he feared that it might be 'just another flash in the American pan' that would make it more difficult for Britain to reach an agreement with the Japanese 'moderates', which was the policy he advocated. However, it was generally welcomed in London as well as by the British Embassy in Washington. And it received overwhelming support during an adjournment debate on 4 August when MPs on all sides, especially Labour and Liberals, renewed their criticism of the British Government's perceived weakness towards Japan over Tientsin and the damage that they believed it was doing to the 'Peace Front' against the dictator states. By contrast, they heaped praise on the President for his leadership in standing up to Japan. Chamberlain's speech was much more circumspect and inevitably mirrored his policy of appeasement. Arguing that the crisis had come at a difficult time for the Government, he pointed out 'the fundamental difference between the United States, with its isolation from Europe, and this country'. However, he indicated that the Government was in touch with 'other countries' about the Far East – by implication, especially the United States.[22]

The constant references in the Commons debate to a 'Peace Front' and cooperation with the US, together with Chamberlain's statement on Tientsin, led to questions at a State Department press conference the next day. Sumner Welles replied that there was no understanding between the American and British governments for joint action in the Far East. While Washington might act in parallel with other nations when their interests were similar or the same, Welles said, no decision regarding collaboration in the Far

East had been taken, no conferences were being held and there was no specific understanding, although information was being exchanged with other governments on the Far East. As Halifax explained to Craigie, the Foreign Office view was that US policy was largely determined by a desire to 'maintain the appearance of acting only in US interests without collusion or even consultation with other Govts in order to be able to meet any possible criticism from isolationists'. Another factor was 'to put new heart into us by hints that we shall earn US sympathy and support in proportion as we show firmness'. It was felt that US policy would have 'a strong anti-Japanese and moderately pro-British bias', provided that the British government's own attitude 'showed some firmness in dealing with the present situation'.[23]

The Tientsin crisis was resolved – temporarily at least – on 11 August 1939, when the Foreign Office, acting on Craigie's advice, agreed to hand over the four Chinese nationalists to the local Chinese authorities, which, in effect, meant to the Japanese Army. They were eventually handed over after the outbreak of war – on 4 September – an action that led to accusations of a 'Far Eastern Munich', especially when the four men were publicly executed soon after. However, Japan subsequently broke off negotiations, which were not renewed until Tokyo resumed discussions with Craigie in October 1939. The British position in the Far East was aided by the announcement in Moscow on 23 August of the Nazi–Soviet non-aggression pact – an event that resulted in a new government in Tokyo and one determined to remain neutral in any European conflict – at least until it was clear which side was winning. Lothian reported that Roosevelt thought the pact would probably lead to complete a realignment of Japanese policy towards coming to terms with China with the assistance of Russia and the United States. 'He thought that our attitude should be friendly but that we should display no eagerness,' Lothian added, and if Japan became hostile again, he might move the American fleet to Hawaii.[24]

Invasion of Poland

As the crisis over Poland and Danzig gathered pace in August 1939, the Riverdale mission and FDR's meetings with Lindsay and Mallet showed the growing cooperation between London and

Washington 'behind the scenes'. More publicly, the visit to New York, from 13 to 18 August, made by the former Prime Minister, Stanley Baldwin, now Lord Baldwin of Bewdley, indicated the political and ideological dimension of the Anglo-American 'unspoken alliance'. Baldwin's visit grew out of a long-standing desire to visit America again after his previous visit regarding the war debt settlement in 1923. He was not able to meet the President, who was away at this time, but his speeches supported FDR's narrative regarding freedom and democracy. For example, he paid a visit to the New York World Fair and, after viewing the Magna Carta at the British Pavilion, he remarked to the press that he was 'enormously impressed before this foundation stone of our struggles for freedom for the individual, freedom of thought, religion and trade'. He continued by saying that 'this freedom has its inception in this document for which the common ancestors of the British and American peoples fought for 700 years and maybe will have to fight for another 700 years'.[25]

The ostensible reason for Baldwin's visit was to speak at the Congress on Education for Democracy about the need to defend democracy. Speaking at the Waldorf Astoria hotel on 16 August, Baldwin took as his theme the idea that democracy had to be ready to fight to save its ideals. The people of Britain and America shared a belief in freedom, he said, but it was easy to take it for granted. Freedom had been won at a great price and, especially since the Great War, it had been under constant threat. 'Ideas are on the wing,' he declared. Bolshevism, Nazism and Fascism might bring benefits such as low unemployment, but they came at a high price – an attack on freedom and Christianity. 'The world is not safe for democracy today,' he continued. 'We cannot make our own countries safe for democracy by letting things slide, nor can we educate our peoples by holding up our hands in horror at the actions of the totalitarian states.' How a country was governed was its own concern, but when totalitarian states imposed their system on other states, their actions became 'the concern of all free men'. As leading democracies, Britain and the United States bore a great responsibility to maintain freedom and democracy.[26]

Roosevelt did his best to urge the Soviet Union to join with Britain and France in the 'Peace Front' against Germany, but Stalin's replacement of Litvinov with Molotov in May 1939 was an ominous sign, as the former had been a leading advocate of an alliance with the Western democracies against Nazi Germany during the Spanish Civil War. The evidence shows that FDR took several steps to encourage the Soviet Union to join with Britain and France. For example, on 30 June he told Oumansky, the Soviet Ambassador in Washington, that if Russia did not conclude an alliance with Britain and France, then Hitler would be able to take on and defeat his enemies one by one. In July and August, Steinhardt, the US Ambassador in Moscow, was instructed to convey the same message to Molotov. However, German–Soviet negotiations had been moving forward rapidly, first with an economic agreement and then with the non-aggression pact on 22 August 1939.[27]

Just as FDR did his best – despite the failure to revise the Neutrality laws – to encourage the Soviets to enter into an alliance with Britain and France, so also he tried to delay the outbreak of war between Germany and Poland, or at least to place the blame squarely on Germany as the aggressor and to encourage Italian neutrality. On 24 August he appealed to the King of Italy to use his influence to avert a devasting war, while on 25 August he addressed appeals to Hitler and President Mościcki of Poland. He urged Germany and Poland 'to refrain from any positive act of hostility for a reasonable stipulated period' and to resolve their controversies by one of three methods: by direct negotiation, by arbitration or by conciliation with the aid of a neutral third party: for example, from one of the American republics. He sent a further message to Hitler along the same lines on 25 August, but to no avail. On 31 August the State Department was informed by Ribbentrop that the President's messages of 25 and 26 August were appreciated by Hitler but his attempts at an amicable settlement with Poland had been rejected by the Polish Government.[28]

The Polish reply to Roosevelt's message, accepting direct discussion with Germany or conciliation, arrived during his farewell interview with Lindsay on 26 August. FDR said that he would not summon Congress until war broke out. It might be difficult to persuade Congress to alter the Neutrality legislation, but he thought that he was in strong position to apply pressure. If war broke out, he would obviously have to proclaim an arms embargo but he would delay signing it for as long as he could – perhaps five days. The British government could then use this time to load up all available ships to carry arms and ammunition to Canada. 'There was every indication in his language that the US authorities would be anxious to cheat in favour of His Majesty's Government,' Lindsay said. Roosevelt also told Lindsay that in the event of war all foreign ships would be searched. In the case of German ships, a search might take up to two days but searches of British ships would be completed in half an hour. 'He spoke in a tone of almost impish glee', Lindsay added, 'and though I may be wrong the whole business gave me the impression of resembling a school-boy prank.'[29]

FDR's sympathy for Britain was much in evidence when Lothian presented his credentials as the new ambassador on 31 August. 'He could not have been more friendly,' he reported. 'There is certainly nothing neutral about the President's personal attitude towards the conflict between the dictatorships and the democracies.' Lothian told Roosevelt that British opinion was now entirely united in wanting to resist further German aggression in Europe. It was prepared to accept territorial change and the revision of frontiers by peaceful means but not by the threat or use of violence. 'With all this the President seemed fully to concur,' reported Lothian. 'He expressed the view that the most serious danger from the standpoint of American public opinion would be if it formed the conclusion that Herr Hitler was entangling the British Government in negotiations leading to pressure on Poland by England and France to abandon vital interests.' Roosevelt said that Hitler had no right to demand that a Polish representative should go to Berlin to be treated like the leaders of Austria and Czechoslovakia. He also reiterated his expectation that, in the event of war, Congress would revoke the Neutrality Act and he also repeated the details of his plan to declare a neutrality zone along the Atlantic coast that would be patrolled in the interests of Britain and France, thus relieving the strain on their navies.[30]

As can be seen from Roosevelt's conversation with Lothian, there was a lingering suspicion in the Administration, and in the United States more generally, that Chamberlain would be tempted to accept another Munich, and to push Poland into making unreasonable concessions to Germany, in order to avoid war. Indeed, at the end of August Horace Wilson, the Prime Minister's right-hand man, was still trying to reach out to Berlin to avoid a German attack on Poland in exchange for friendship with Britain. However, public opinion in Britain was in favour of a more resolute approach, and in the Cabinet discussions on 30 August even Chamberlain said that the German demand for a Polish emissary to go to Berlin was unacceptable. The Foreign Office kept Roosevelt and the State Department fully informed as to its discussions with Poland and

Germany throughout August, as well as its ultimatum to Berlin, following the German attack on Danzig and invasion of Poland, that Germany must withdraw its forces; otherwise, war would result. Receiving no satisfactory reply, Britain and France declared war on Germany on 3 September – although not without some delay on Chamberlain's part that, once again, raised doubts in the Commons about his determination to abandon appeasement.[31]

The view from Berlin

From the perspective of the German Foreign Ministry, it was of little consequence that the US Neutrality laws remained in place as it was assumed that they would be interpreted by the Roosevelt Administration as favourably as possible on behalf of Britain and France. However, German official propaganda, while mainly directed at Britain and the 'encirclement of Germany' in the guise of the 'so-called Peace Front', also targeted the American President. 'The ordinary German, to whom America is a strange and remote land, is given the impression that Mr Roosevelt now has his back to the wall and is fighting desperately to save what remains of his prestige after the worst reversal of his presidential career', reported the *Times* correspondent in Berlin. While care was being taken by Goebbels to avoid attacks upon the American people and American institutions, the President remained the butt of Nazi propaganda. 'He is presented to the German people as a dictator who, on the instigation of Jews, Communists, negroes and "the rabble" is bent upon dragging an unwilling America into war against Germany, while his own people groan under the burden of armament expenditure and the unemployed are starved.'[32]

A much greater blow to the 'Peace Front' than the US Neutrality law setback was the Nazi–Soviet pact, which, as the German Embassy in Washington reported, came as an 'unpleasant surprise' to US public opinion. 'It is considered that since the defection of Russia there exists a positive danger that Britain and France may suffer a defeat which would so alter the balance of power that the independence and existence of the United States would also be in acute danger,' reported Thomsen. Roosevelt, he continued, was therefore 'determined to support the democracies with the entire moral might and material power of this continent'. This would include the ending of the arms embargo, although, as Thomsen pointed out, the delivery of raw materials of military importance was unhindered since the expiry of the 'cash and carry' clause in May 1939. The *New York Times* had reported that 'an inventory of German assets in America has already been taken', while the press in general was doing 'everything in its power to establish Germany's war guilt unmistakably beforehand, and thereby to propagate the idea of intervention still more strongly among the people'.[33]

Thomsen continued in this vein as war approached. Arguing that US public opinion viewed Germany as 'a disturber of the peace and an aggressor who refuses to settle political problems otherwise than by force', he nevertheless believed that hostility towards Germany had not yet become strong enough to lead to active American participation in a European conflict, 'as memories of the world war are still too deep rooted'. But, he added, 'the pro-interventionist press' was arguing that the arms embargo 'amounted to support for the totalitarian powers, whereas support for the democracies would help to prevent an immediate threat to the United States'. Roosevelt himself considered neutrality to be 'despicable', said Thomsen, and he would do all he could 'to prevent the defeat of Britain and France and bring about the downfall of the totalitarian systems of government, especially that of Germany'. According to Thomsen, FDR did not think that Germany would succeed in defeating Britain and France early in a conflict – rather, the President expected a 'long war of attrition' with the outcome uncertain. Roosevelt also expected that the Allies' blockade would prove to be effective, and that Germany's position regarding supplies and food would quickly be strained, as in 1917.[34]

Thomsen also reiterated the Embassy's view that the US would 'resort to armed intervention if Britain and France were in danger of being defeated'. The despatch of large numbers of troops to Europe in under a year from the outbreak of war was 'technically impossible' but when Roosevelt judged that the time was right, 'the nation will be brought ruthlessly, by every possible means, to the required state of mind for intervention'. On the outbreak of war, the Neutrality Act would in theory come into force, but it would soon be abrogated, or circumvented, and the arms embargo would be repealed. 'Raw materials of military importance, as well as machines and equipment, will immediately be made available to Britain and France in unlimited quantities,' he continued. 'As this would help to overcome unemployment, no opposition to such supply is to be expected.' But because of the danger of war with Japan, 'the main fighting strength of the American fleet' would be 'tied down in the Pacific until further notice'. Thus the Embassy realised that direct US intervention in the first year of war was extremely unlikely, but that Roosevelt was committed to giving Britain and France 'all aid short of war'.[35]

Notes

1. *NYT*, 7 July and 19 July 1939; Dallek, *FDR*, p. 192 for White House conference and Borah quote.
2. *NYT*, 2 May 1939 for letter of 27 May from Hull to Pittman and Bloom, Committee Chairs, setting out State Department position; FO/371/22815, A4828/98/45, Lindsay to Halifax, 12 July 1939; ibid., A5051/98/45, Lindsay to Halifax, 14 July 1939. See also Hull, *Memoirs I*, pp. 641–53.
3. Hull, *Memoirs I*, p. 697.
4. FO/371/22814, A4583/98/45, minute by Butler, 3 July 1939; for British reaction to failure to repeal arms embargo see Reynolds, *Creation*, pp. 54–8; MacDonald, *US, Britain and Appeasement*, pp. 153–62, Watt, *How War Came*, p. 270.
5. Mackenzie King Diary, 24 June and 1 July 1939.
6. *Hansard*, Commons debate, 10 July 1939; for Hudson–Wohltat talks see Phillips, *Fighting Churchill, Appeasing Hitler*, pp. 291–9.
7. For US perspective on Polish situation see FRUS/1939/I, docs 167–234, April–August 1939; doc 198, Biddle to Hull, 12 July 1939; doc 204, memo of conversation by Moffat with French Ambassador, 2 August 1939; doc 231, Johnson to Hull, 19 August 1939.
8. FRUS/1939/I, doc 227, memo of conversation by Moffat, 18 August 1939; doc 228, Bullitt to Hull, 19 August 1939; doc 212, Welles to Biddle, 11 August 1939.
9. FO 371/22796, A2695/26/45, FO minute by J. G. S. Beith, 12 April 1939; *Times*, 11 April 1939; see FRUS/1939/II for negotiations between US and UK for exchange of cotton and rubber, docs 198–224; doc 198, Hull to Kennedy, 18 April 1939.
10. Ibid., A3446/26/45, Halifax to Lindsay, 15 May 1939; A3554/26/45, Lindsay to Halifax, 17 May 1939.
11. Ibid., A3664/26/45, FO minute by J. Balfour, 21 May; CAB 23, 32 (1939) item 12, 14 June 1939; CAB 23, 33 (1939) item 10, 21 June 1939; FO/371/22798, A5850/26/45, Kennedy to Halifax, 25 August 1939.

Polish Crisis 247

12. DBFP/3/VI, doc 354, Wilson memorandum, 18 July 1939; DGFP/D/VI, doc 716, memorandum by Wohltat, 24 July 1939.
13. See, for example, Phillips, *Fighting Churchill, Appeasing Hitler*, pp. 295–8; Mosley, *On Borrowed Time*, pp. 247–51.
14. DGFP/D/VI, doc 723, Dirksen to Weizsächer, 25 July 1939; doc 725, Thomsen to GFM, 26 July 1939.
15. FO/371/23989, W2487/326/50, Hoyer Millar to Nicholls (FO), 2 February 1939. FO/371/23989, W7822/326/50, Lindsay to Palairet (FO), 9 May 1939.
16. FO/371/23905, W12351/9808/49, report of Lord Riverdale's mission, August 1939.
17. Ibid., Riverdale report; CAB 23, 45(1939) item 3, 28 August 1939. See FO/371/22834-36, file A/6041/45, for establishment of British purchasing mission in US at the end of 1939; Hall, *North American Supply*, pp. 59–68.
18. FRUS/1939/IV, Far East, etc.; American interest in situation created by Japanese demands on the British concession at Tientsin, docs 197–295.
19. For Tientsin crisis see Langer and Gleason, *Challenge to Isolation*, pp. 157–9; Reynolds, *Creation*, p. 61; Kennedy, *Anglo-American Strategic Relations*, stresses US support for Britain over Tientsin, pp. 244–50; Watt, *How War Came*, Chapter 19, 'The Japanese Army Overplays its Hand', pp. 339–60; Dallek, *FDR*, pp. 192–6; CAB 23, 33 (1939) item 3, 21 June 1939; CAB 23, 35 (1939) item 8, 5 July 1939.
20. DBFP/3/IX, Tientsin crisis; doc 365, Craigie to Halifax, 23 July 1939; this statement – or formula – was made by Chamberlain in Commons on 24 July 1939; doc 379, Halifax to Craigie and Clark Kerr, Shanghai; doc 387, Halifax to Lindsay, 25 July 1939.
21. FRUS/1939/IV, docs 197–295 for the American attitude towards Japanese demands on the British concession at Tientsin; FRUS/1939/II, p. 189, US note to Japan, 26 July 1939; DBFP/3/IX, doc 443, Lindsay to Halifax, 2 August 939; doc 405, Lindsay to Halifax, 28 July 1939; doc 431, Lindsay to Halifax, 31 July 1939.
22. DBFP/3/IX, doc 463, pp. 381–2, Craigie to Halifax, 1 August 1939; *Hansard*, Commons, Chamberlain, 4 August 1939.
23. DBFP/3/IX, doc 468, Lindsay to Halifax, 5 August 1939; doc 488, Halifax to Craigie, 7 August 1939.
24. Shai, 'Was There a Far Eastern Munich?', pp. 161–9; DBFP/3/IX, doc 549, Halifax to Craigie, 18 August 1939; doc 590, Craigie to Halifax, 26 August 1939; doc 612, Craigie to Halifax, 3 September 1939; doc 603, minute by Butler, 29 August 1939; doc 569, Lothian to Halifax, 31 August 1939
25. *NYT*, 19 August 1939.

26. FO/371/22834, file 5870, Congress on Education for Democracy held at Columbia University, 15–17 August 1939.
27. FRUS/1939/I, pp. 293–4, Roosevelt to Steinhardt, 4 August 1939; see Steinhardt messages to Washington in FRUS/1939/I; FO/371/22967, C11723/15/18, Lindsay to Halifax, 17 August 1939. See also MacDonald, *The United States, Britain and Appeasement*, pp. 160–4.
28. DGFP/D/VII covers climax of Danzig dispute in August 1939; doc 328, memo by Weizsäcker, 26 August 1939 re further telegram from FDR to Hitler, 25 August 1939; doc 486, Ribbentrop to Washington Embassy, 31 August 1939.
29. DBFP/3/VII, docs 316, 317, 318, Lindsay to Halifax, 26 August 1939.
30. DBFP/3/VII, doc 568, Lothian to Halifax, 31 August 1939.
31. DBFP/3/VII, especially docs 360, 428, 431, 515, 541, 636, 671.
32. *The Times*, 14 July 1939.
33. DGFP/D/VII/doc 239, Thomsen to GFM, 24 August 1939.
34. DGFP/D/VII/doc 378, Thomsen to GFM, 28 August 1939.
35. Ibid., relaying views of Bötticher, Military Attaché.

Part 5

Tacit Alliance, 1939

13 'Winston Is Back', September–October 1939

On 3 September 1939, the Board of Admiralty signalled to all British ships 'Winston is back'. Churchill had just been appointed First Lord of the Admiralty, the post he had held at the start of the First World War. A week later FDR wrote to Churchill:

> It is because you and I occupied similar positions in the World War that I want you to know how glad I am that you are back again in the Admiralty. Your problems are, I realise, complicated by new factors but the essential is not very different.

He said he wanted Churchill – and Chamberlain – to know that he would like to be kept informed 'personally' about anything they wanted to tell him. Rather typically, he also flattered the British Minister by complimenting him on his recently completed biography of the Duke of Marlborough. In this fashion, Roosevelt initiated his now famous wartime correspondence with Churchill, who replied styling himself as 'Naval Person' and then, when he became Prime Minister, as 'Former Naval Person'. Eventually, over 1,700 messages were sent – about 1,000 from Churchill and 700 from FDR. The last message was written by Roosevelt on 11 April 1945 – the day before his sudden death at Warm Springs, Georgia.[1]

This highly unusual correspondence between the American President and a British Cabinet Minister has naturally been the subject of much discussion by historians of Anglo-American relations, some of whom have tended to downplay its significance. From the perspective of the current work, the Roosevelt–Churchill correspondence in many ways encapsulated the nature of the Anglo-American 'tacit alliance' denounced by William Borah in February 1938. Firstly, it was initiated by Roosevelt, in keeping with his well-developed penchant for personal diplomacy – as seen in his invitation to Runciman to visit him in January 1937. Secondly, the correspondence was highly secret and known only to a few trusted people in London and Washington, as FDR had suggested that Churchill could send him sealed letters via the system of diplomatic pouches that crossed the Atlantic on a regular basis. Thirdly, it drew upon the experience of the First World War when the intervention of the US on the side of the Allies in April 1917 had played a critical role in the eventual defeat of Germany. Above all, it reflected FDR's desire to establish a direct link with the man he had discussed with George VI and Mackenzie King during the Royal Visit to the US in June 1939 as potentially the next British Prime Minister.[2]

Roosevelt, Chamberlain and Churchill

The main aim of this chapter is to assess the state of Anglo-American relations at the outbreak of the war and the extent to which a 'tacit alliance' had come into being. Roosevelt's initiation of his secret correspondence with Churchill is one aspect of this assessment. But, as always, the President had to tread carefully – not only to avoid disturbing isolationists like Borah and Johnson, and US public opinion, but also to maintain cooperation with Chamberlain. On the same day that FDR wrote to Churchill he also wrote to the Prime Minister: 'I need not tell you that you have been very much in my thoughts during these difficult days and further that I hope you will at all times feel free to write me personally and outside of diplomatic procedure about any problems as they arise,' he said. 'I hope and believe that we shall repeal the embargo within the next month and this is definitely a part of the Administration policy.' The President's message to Chamberlain enabled him to contact Churchill at the same time, as it would have been unthinkable for him to write to Churchill without the knowledge of the Prime Minister. Roosevelt's message to Chamberlain gave him the diplomatic cover he required to establish his contact with Churchill – his first direct line to a member of the British Cabinet since his meeting with Walter Runciman in January 1937.[3]

Chamberlain's letters to Roosevelt were few and far between and the relationship between the two men was never close. However, shortly before the war had broken out Chamberlain had written to the President, requesting his help in acquiring for Britain the use of the secret Norden bomb sight which he had been informed was 'the most efficient instrument of its kind in existence'. This was obviously the kind of request that only a friendly – not to say allied – government could address to another government and the wording of Chamberlain's letter underlines this fact. Pointing out that war with Germany would challenge Britain's 'fundamental values and ideals', he continued: 'I believe they are values which our two countries share in common, and I am convinced that if there is a certainty, it is that our two countries will never go to war with one another.' FDR's response was couched in similarly warm terms that reflected not only US sympathy for the Allied cause but also his own strong support of the British war effort. 'I have been very glad indeed to receive your letter', he replied, 'and to hear from you directly with regard to the question set forth so clearly and so movingly therein,' adding that he would look at the issue again when circumstances allowed: in other words, after Neutrality revision.[4]

As regards Mackenzie King, he was naturally disappointed when war broke out despite his belief that peace would prevail. He had become very critical of British foreign policy since Munich, believing it had gone 'from bad to worse', especially since the guarantee to Poland. He personally felt that Danzig and the Polish Corridor should have been ceded to Germany, and Poland compensated 'farther East'. Despite these misgivings, he had no doubt that Canada should join Britain in war, provided that the Canadian Parliament voted to do so, as it did on 10 September. He was glad that Chamberlain and Halifax remained 'at the helm', and he blamed Churchill, and the Labour and Liberal parties, for pushing them towards confrontation with Germany after the occupation of Prague, and therefore driving the Empire to war. Nor was he pleased with the Prime Minister's response to Hitler's peace move after the defeat of Poland in October, believing that it should have been more conciliatory and was probably written by Churchill, who, he felt, saw himself as a great future wartime leader, like his ancestor, the Duke of Marlborough – a prospect that filled Mackenzie King with dread.[5]

Churchill and the War

Despite the failure of his peacetime policy, and doubts on the Opposition benches about his leadership, Chamberlain remained convinced that he was the best man to lead his country in wartime. He immediately formed a War Cabinet of nine members, which included Churchill at the Admiralty and Eden as Dominions Secretary but retained key allies such as Halifax, Simon and Hoare. The Prime Minister appeared confident that Britain's sound economy, vast Empire and powerful Navy meant that victory would be achieved through the traditional British policy of a naval blockade that would eventually undermine German resolve and lead to the removal of Hitler and the defeat of Nazi ideology. Nor was he alone in this view. Churchill had spoken warmly of the power of the blockade following the revision of the US Neutrality laws in May 1937 and the introduction of the 'cash and carry' principle, and Roosevelt had lectured his Cabinet during the Munich crisis about the blockade as the most effective weapon against Germany. However, once the war had begun, Churchill, like FDR, favoured a more active policy that increasingly contrasted with Chamberlain's approach.[6]

Back in government for the first time in more than ten years, Churchill had lost none of his flair for the big occasion and his short speech in the House of Commons made an immediate impact in the US as well as in Britain. He 'talked with the accents of a war leader', reported Ferdinand Kuhn, and 'electrified' the Commons as the Prime Minister had failed to do. Declaring that the trials ahead were 'not beyond the compass and the strength of the British Empire and the French Republic', Churchill acknowledged that it was a sad day. 'But at the present time there is another note which may be present, and that is a feeling of thankfulness that, if these great trials were to come upon our Island, there is a generation of Britons here now ready to prove itself not unworthy of the days of yore and not unworthy of those great men, the fathers of our land, who laid the foundations of our laws and shaped the greatness of our country.' Kuhn remarked that 'This was the kind of speech the House wanted to hear,' and 'its cheers re-echoed through the historic chamber'. Leopold Amery wrote: 'I think I see Winston emerging as PM out of it all by the end of the year.'[7]

As well as appealing to British martial pride, Churchill employed the kind of idealistic rhetoric that was closely aligned to FDR's appeals to international values and norms. 'This is not a question of fighting for Danzig or fighting for Poland,' he told the Commons. 'We are fighting to save the whole world from the pestilence of Nazi tyranny and in defence of all that is most sacred to man. This is no war for domination or imperial aggrandisement or material gain; no war to shut any country out of its sunlight and means of progress. It is a war, viewed in its inherent quality, to establish, on impregnable rocks, the rights of the individual, and it is a war to establish and revive the stature of man.'

Kuhn reported:

> Tonight, as the new Cabinet assembled for the first time, a crowd in Downing Street cheered Mr Churchill as Britons of a generation ago cheered Earl Kitchener. Mr Churchill's presence in the Cabinet is taken by the man in the street, as Lord Kitchener's was, as proof that this war will be carried through to victory.[8]

The sinking of the *Athenia*

Berlin certainly saw Churchill as an implacable enemy and as a 'warmonger', and he was the target of a great deal of German propaganda from the very outset of the war. When the British steamship *Athenia* was sunk by a U-boat off the coast of the Hebrides on the first day of the war, with the loss of fifty-four Canadian and twenty-eight American lives, the German Foreign Ministry was quick to deny that any of its submarines had been in the area. Primed by the Propaganda Ministry, German newspapers speculated that Churchill was behind the sinking in order to arouse US public opinion against Germany. This version of events was never seriously entertained in Washington as there was ample evidence from the British, supported by US officials, that the damage had been caused by a torpedo. But the State Department insisted on sworn testimony from the American survivors in order to counter speculation in the US amongst isolationists that the British might have been responsible. German documents captured after the war later proved beyond any doubt that the ship had been sunk by the German submarine U-30.[9]

Churchill was mindful of the US position from the outset of the war. When he reported to the War Cabinet on 4 September about the sinking of the *Athenia* with 300 Americans on board he pointed out that 'the occurrence should have a helpful effect as regards public opinion in the United States'. Two weeks later, on 19 September, he reported to the Cabinet on the sinking of the aircraft carrier HMS *Courageous*, which had been torpedoed 330 miles west of Land's End. Churchill 'said that this occurrence had drawn attention once more to the shortage of destroyers from which we were suffering'. As soon as the US Neutrality Act had been repealed, the Government should do everything in its power to purchase destroyers from the United States. 'They had a large number in their Navy', Churchill said, 'and even if we could only secure 20 of their old vessels, they would be of the greatest assistance to us.' The need to improve Britain's naval defences was also brought home by the sinking of the *Royal Oak* battleship by a U-boat that had penetrated the defences at Scapa Flow in the middle of October. When Churchill became Prime Minister in May 1940, he returned to the idea of acquiring US destroyers, which by then had become an even more urgent issue.[10]

James Reston reported from London that Churchill had emerged from the first few weeks of the war as 'the most inspiring figure in Great Britain' and as Chamberlain's likely successor. 'War is Mr Churchill's natural element,' he wrote.

> Like a happy old tugboat captain with a battered sailor's hat on his head and a dead cigar between his teeth he has looked and sounded like a war leader. And more than any other man he has spread a little confidence about the land.

His speeches were adding to his popularity, wrote Reston, but his reputation was built on the warnings he had given over the previous five years about the 'Nazi menace' and German rearmament. Attacks on him in the German press – for example, over the *Athenia* – merely added to his popularity. 'Even his old critics seem to agree now that he will make a great wartime leader', continued Reston, 'and many are beginning to believe that he and he alone has the drive and imagination to lead the British Empire through the greatest crisis in its history.'[11]

Neutrality and unneutrality

In Washington, the outbreak of war between Germany and Poland came as no surprise to the President or his Cabinet, especially after the announcement of the Nazi–Soviet pact, which, as Ickes put it, 'completely upset the diplomatic applecart'. What was less certain was whether British and French resistance to the mounting German pressure on Poland regarding the status of Danzig and the 'Polish Corridor' would continue in the light of the pact. 'Even Chamberlain's spinal cord gave evidence of becoming something more firm than wet spaghetti,' wrote Ickes. 'France seemed reconciled to the worst and England apparently was prepared, on this occasion at least, to carry out its agreement to go to the defence of Poland.' However, the pact stacked the odds against Poland. Roosevelt cut short a sailing cruise and returned to Washington to hold a Cabinet on 25 August and another one on 1 September. He told the meetings that he was watching the European situation 'from day to day' and would not call Congress into special session to revise the Neutrality laws until he was ready to act.[12]

Upon the outbreak of war on 3 September Roosevelt addressed the American people in a radio broadcast from Washington. 'For four long years a succession of actual wars and constant crises have shaken the entire world and have threatened in each case to bring on the gigantic conflict which is today unhappily a fact,' he said. He recalled the efforts he had made to avert war and reiterated his determination to keep the United States out of the war. 'As long as it remains within my power to prevent, there will be no blackout of peace in the United States,' he declared. But, unlike Woodrow Wilson in August 1914, he did not say that the US must be 'neutral in fact as well as in name', nor did he urge Americans to be 'impartial in thought as well as in action'. Instead, he said the US would remain 'a neutral nation' but added: 'I cannot ask that every American remain neutral in thought as well. Even a neutral has a right to take account of facts. Even a neutral cannot be asked to close his mind or close his conscience.' According to Norman Davis, Roosevelt totally empathised with Britain and France and felt 'very badly' about having to issue a neutrality proclamation, but he could not afford to provide ammunition for the isolationists in Congress at a time when he was aiming for the repeal of the arms embargo.[13]

FDR's Neutrality address set the tone for an American neutrality that was observed more in theory than in practice. Cordell Hull and members of the State Department, while relatively fastidious in observing the letter of the law, were also anxious to minimise the effect of the kind of issues that had greatly soured relations between Britain and the United States in the First World War, prior to American entry in 1917. Hull therefore suggested that a committee of experts from the State Department and the British Embassy should be established to draw up a suitable system to facilitate the Allied blockade of Germany. What he had in mind was an arrangement along the lines of the certificate system in operation during the latter part of the Great War that would reduce interference with American commerce. Specific problems requiring further attention could be dealt with as and when they arose. This arrangement appeared to work well in the first few months of the war, although problems arose in the new year. Overall, as a leading historian of this period has written, 'Britain's blockade against Germany after September 1939 did not evince the kind of emotive reaction it had in 1914–17.'[14]

By contrast, German interests received hostile treatment from various US government departments, rather as Harold Ickes as Secretary of the Interior had used his authority over the sale of helium to prevent its export to Germany before the war. Nor was the US government prepared to join with other neutrals in protesting against British blockade measures against Germany, under which 'all German goods of German origin or German ownership found on neutral ships would be seized in retaliation for illegal German use of mines'. Ribbentrop wanted the US government to take a stand with other neutrals against 'renewed breach of international law' by Britain. But when the German Embassy in Washington enquired about the British export blockade, it was informed that the US did not intend to protest in principle against this action or to participate in any collective protest by other neutrals. The State Department felt that the export blockade was admissible as retaliation against German mine warfare. Any cases of flagrant interference by the Britain blockade would be dealt with on an individual basis.[15]

Destroyers and bases

Following his neutrality address the President issued a series of proclamations invoking the Neutrality laws, as amended in May 1937. Proclamation 2348 identified the belligerents in the war and spelled out the details of the Neutrality Act regarding the neutrality of US territorial waters and the exclusion of belligerent vessels from them, while Proclamation 2349 covered the arms embargo prohibiting the export of arms and munitions to the belligerent powers. Proclamation 2352, on 8 September 1939, declared what Roosevelt called 'a limited national emergency'. At his press conference on 8 September, he explained this proclamation and stressed that 'there is no thought, in any shape, manner or form, of putting the nation, either in its defences or in its internal economy, on a war basis. That is one thing we want to avoid. We are going to keep the nation on a peace basis, in accordance with peacetime authorisations.' Despite this, the proclamation raised suspicions amongst his critics that he was preparing for war and he had to tread even more carefully while Congress debated the revision of the Neutrality laws.[16]

The proclamation of 8 September was followed by several executive orders intended 'to strengthen national defence relating to the Army, Navy, Marine Corps and the FBI and other investigating agencies that would be dealing with any foreign espionage'. The Army was brought closer to its authorised peacetime strength of 280,000 men by deploying more troops at key locations such as the Panama Canal and Puerto Rico. The size of the Navy was to be increased from about 115,000, closer to its authorised peace strength of 180,000 men. In addition, it was planned to use some of the most suitable out-of-commission destroyers. Roosevelt estimated that there were 116 of these decommissioned destroyers, of which about one-third would be put back into active commission 'to patrol US waters and enforce the Neutrality proclamations'. These were the destroyers referred to by Churchill in the War Cabinet on 19 September after the sinking of the aircraft carrier HMS *Courageous* as suitable for purchase for the British Navy and many of them were to figure in the Destroyer-Bases deal of September 1940, along with the Caribbean bases requested by Roosevelt before the outbreak of the war.[17]

Panama Declaration

As FDR had indicated to George VI during the Royal Visit, the US proclamations established a neutrality zone – an area along the Atlantic and Pacific coastlines of the United States, at least 300 miles wide, from which belligerent warships were excluded. The movements of any such warships entering the zone were to be reported by an American Neutrality Patrol. The principle of the neutrality zone was discussed and adopted by twenty Latin American republics at the Panama conference held at the end of September 1939, which had been proposed by the President and was attended by Sumner

Welles on behalf of the United States. As a result of the conference the Panama Declaration of 2 October was issued, banning belligerent submarines from entering South American ports, demanding the cessation of subversive activities within the republics, and announcing the formation of a 300-mile maritime security zone extending around the coast of South and Central America.[18]

Following the Panama Declaration, Churchill took advantage of his direct line to Roosevelt to send a message about the neutrality zone. Assuring the President that Britain wished to help the US in keeping the war out of the Americas, he said that the British Government liked the idea of a wide limit 'within which no submarines of any belligerent country should act'. However, surface ships presented more difficulties 'because if a raider operates from or takes refuge in the American zone, we should have to be protected or allowed to protect ourselves'. The British Navy did not mind how far south the prohibited zone went, provided it was effectively patrolled. 'We should have great difficulty in accepting a zone which was only policed by some weak neutral. But, of course, if the American Navy takes care of it, that is all right.' In fact, the US Navy was in a somewhat better position to 'take care of it' than it had been for many years. The increased expenditure on the Navy since the Naval Acts of 1934 and 1938 had led to a significant shipbuilding and modernisation programme that proved useful in September 1939 and aided the Destroyer-Bases deal of September 1940.[19]

Hitler's peace offer

A few days after the Panama Declaration, Polish resistance to the invasion by Germany, and on 17 September by Russia, finally collapsed. On 5 October Hitler viewed a victory parade in Warsaw and on the same day Russia pressured Latvia into signing a mutual assistance treaty that was similar to one already signed with Estonia and another one with Lithuania on 10 October. Soviet treaties with the Baltic states in September and October 1939, and war with Finland from the end of November, opened the way for a Russian invasion of the Baltic states in June 1940. Meanwhile, Hitler addressed the German Reichstag on 6 October, and after declaiming at length on the success of the invasion of Poland, he said that an international security agreement should be negotiated to prevent further destruction, which otherwise would not be confined to Europe. If the conflict was not halted now, he warned, 'it will reach far out over the sea'. Mackenzie King hoped that Roosevelt would offer to mediate 'on a basis which did not recognise the conquest of the war', although it was very unlikely that Hitler would have accepted any such proposal.[20]

Hitler's Reichstag speech was followed, according to the *New York Times*, by 'inspired Berlin despatches' suggesting that Hitler would call an immediate truce if Roosevelt offered to mediate. When the President was asked at a press conference on 10 October whether Washington had made any official overtures along these lines, he replied emphatically in the negative. However, the *New York Times* correspondent Felix Belair noted that Roosevelt did not say that he was against a peace initiative, only that he did not think much of the weekend despatches from Berlin. 'There are many officials here who believe he would certainly make such a move if assured publicly and in advance by Great Britain and France of their support of any mediation offer he might make. There is equal confidence that the President will not move without that assurance.' It was also pointed out that the President could not be expected to say anything about American participation in any kind of peace effort until Chamberlain had made his reply to Hitler's Reichstag speech.[21]

Chamberlain's reply came in a defiant speech in the House of Commons on 12 October. Declaring that Britain had embarked on war 'simply in defence of freedom', he said that Hitler had rejected all suggestions for peace until he had defeated Poland, having already overrun Czechoslovakia. Peace proposals were not acceptable if they involved the condoning of such aggression. 'The proposals in the German Chancellor's speech are vague and uncertain and contain no suggestion for righting the wrongs done to Czecho-Slovakia and to Poland. Even if Herr Hitler's proposals were more closely defined and contained suggestions to right these wrongs, it would still be necessary to ask by what practical means the German Government intend to convince the world that aggression will cease and that pledges will be kept.' Past experience had shown that the promises of Hitler's government could not be relied upon. 'Accordingly', Chamberlain declared, 'acts – not words alone – must be forthcoming before we, the British peoples, and France, our gallant and trusted Ally, would be justified in ceasing to wage war to the utmost of our strength.'[22]

It was a rousing speech, by Chamberlain's standards, and it was well received in the United States, although there was also foreboding about the future course of the war. Ickes lunched with Roosevelt on Friday, 13 October, and commented in his diary that the President 'was pessimistic about the international situation', especially Russia's designs on Finland and Scandinavia. At Finland's request, Ickes noted, Roosevelt had sent a personal message to Stalin urging restraint. As regards the war, 'the President believes that the French and English have more stamina than the Germans and that if the war goes in normal course, the Germans will crack'. At a US Cabinet meeting on 19 October, there was some discussion of Germany's next move. 'The fact is, however,' as Ickes pointed out, 'that no one knows when the blow will fall or in what manner.' The 'one bright spot' was that the Gallup polls were showing a big increase in Roosevelt's popularity and support for a third term. 'I have been insisting all along that the President is on top of the world politically,' wrote Ickes. 'From every quarter comes word that the people have confidence in the President in this international situation to a degree that they do not have it in anyone else.'[23]

The view from Berlin

Berlin was unaware of Roosevelt's correspondence with Churchill but knowledge of it would simply have confirmed the German Foreign Ministry's view that there was, indeed, a 'tacit alliance' between Washington and London. Churchill was seen as an implacable enemy and it was taken for granted that the President was determined to support Britain and France in every possible way, including the revision of the Neutrality Act. In the opinion of the Foreign Ministry, this situation made relations with the US even more important.

> We have a great interest in preventing the United States from throwing her weight into the scales on the side of our foes, and we must do everything to keep her in the group of the neutral powers, of which she, despite her hostile sentiments, has hitherto constituted one of the strongest and most important members,

wrote Weizsäcker, the Under Secretary. Ribbentrop, as Foreign Minister, went along with the policy of not antagonising the US, as did Hitler. But when Weizsäcker recommended that Ambassador Dieckhoff should be allowed to return to Washington to improve relations with the US, Ribbentrop vetoed the move, unless the US agreed to reciprocate.[24]

FDR's intention to ask Congress to repeal the arms embargo was fully recognised by the German Foreign Ministry. 'Anyone who knows the President and his attitude cannot doubt that he is working toward this goal with all his energy,' wrote Dieckhoff, now resident in Berlin. The American people were being 'continuously bombarded with anti-German propaganda by radio, press, lectures, and motion pictures' and were 'overwhelmingly anti-German' as a result. In the meantime, 'the American Government will do everything to circumvent the present neutrality regulations and facilitate, especially through Canada, the delivery of arms, etc. to our enemies'. Dieckhoff believed it was useless to send a protest or warning to the US regarding its Neutrality policy as Roosevelt would use any German objections for propaganda purposes against Borah, Nye and the isolationists by accusing them of making common cause with Germany.

> He has been pursuing his course consistently for years; through his attitude he bears the main responsibility for the stiffening of British policy in recent months, and in view of this man's determination and stubbornness, a change in his stand is not to be expected.[25]

FDR's support for Britain at the outset of the war was also stressed by the Ambassador's deputy, Thomsen, in Washington, who pointed out that the argument that the arms embargo constituted an unneutral act because it favoured Germany had made a strong impression on US opinion. 'For the time being', Thomsen said, 'Roosevelt believes himself able to keep the US out of war by strengthening the Allies' chances of winning the war through unlimited exportation of arms, military equipment, and essential raw materials.' But, if the Allies were threatened with defeat, 'Roosevelt is determined to go to war against Germany, even in the face of resistance in his own country.' In another despatch Thomsen reported: 'The American people as a whole are a good deal more hostile toward Germany and also more united than in 1917.' They therefore favoured 'helping the Allies to gain superiority by supplying armaments, especially aircraft, thereby shortening the war and forestalling active participation by America in the war through an early victory of the Allies.'[26]

Commenting on the course of the war at the end of October 1939, Thomsen reported that the expectation of US public opinion that 'total war would be waged' from the outset had been replaced by a more reflective outlook about the European war and its effects on the United States. One main school of thought saw the war as an ideological struggle against 'Hitlerism', he said, while the other main school viewed the war as primarily a European power struggle that did not concern the US. British policy was not always 'unreservedly approved', Thomsen noted; 'the abandonment of Poland, the lack of rational war aims, and the equivocal nature of British policy toward Russia are criticised'. But US support for the Allies remained steadfast. While the course of the war had so far strengthened the belief of most Americans that, despite warnings from the isolationists, the Allies could be aided without risking US involvement in the war, 'the belief that a defeat of the Allies is tantamount to a threat to America by Germany remains unshakable. Any threat to the Western Hemisphere would be interpreted by the people and Government as a cause of war.'[27]

Notes

1. Gilbert, *Churchill*, p. 624; FDR to Churchill, 11 September 1939, in Lowenheim et al., *Roosevelt and Churchill*, p. 89.
2. For varying estimates of the significance of the FDR–Churchill correspondence see McKercher, *Transition of Power*, pp. 279–81; Reynolds, *Creation*, pp. 85–8; Rock, *Chamberlain and Roosevelt*, pp. 210–11; and Leutze, 'Churchill–Roosevelt Correspondence', pp. 465–91.
3. FDR to Chamberlain, 3 September 1939 in Roosevelt, *Roosevelt Letters*, 3, p. 276.
4. Schewe, *FDRFA*, Chamberlain to FDR, 25 August 1939; FO/371/22799, A8357/26/45, Halifax to Lothian, 5 December 1939; CAB 23, 109 (1939) item 9, 9 December 1939; A8788/26/45, Lothian to Halifax, 16 December 1939.
5. Mackenzie King Diary, 1 July, 28 August, 15 September 1939. Chamberlain's speech was met with disappointment by Mackenzie King, Diary, 11 October 1939.
6. For Chamberlain's policy, September–December 1939, see Rock, *Chamberlain and Roosevelt*, pp. 209–46.
7. Gilbert, *Churchill*, pp. 623–4, including Amery quote, p. 623; *Hansard*, Commons, for Churchill speech, 3 September 1939; Ferdinand Kuhn, *NYT*, 4 September 1939.
8. Ibid.
9. DGFP/D/VIII, doc 4, memorandum by Weizsäcker, re *Athenia*, 4 September 1939; for US investigation into sinking see FRUS/1939/II, docs 245–264, 3 September–December 1939.

10. CAB 23, 65 (1939), 4 September 1939, item 6; CAB 23, 65 (1939), 19 September 1939, item 2.
11. *NYT*, 8 October 1939; see Gilbert, *Churchill*, p. 627 for similar views from critics of Churchill.
12. Ickes, *Diary*, II, 26 August 1939, p. 700 and 1 September 1939, p. 709.
13. FDR Neutrality address, 3 September 1939; Davis to Lothian quoted in Rock, *Chamberlain and Roosevelt*, p. 210.
14. McKercher, *Transition of Power*, pp. 284–5; see also Rock, *Chamberlain and Roosevelt*, pp. 214–29.
15. DGFP/D/VIII, doc 26, Thomsen to GFM, 8 September 1939; doc 393, Ribbentrop to Washington Embassy, 27 November 1939; doc 396, Thomsen to GFM, 28 November 1939.
16. FDR Proclamations of 5, 8 and 10 September 1939, available at: <https://www.presidency.ucsb.edu/node/210001>. FDR, excerpts from FDR Press Conference, 8 September 1939, available at: <https://www.presidency.ucsb.edu/documents/excerpts-from-the-press-conference-83>.
17. Ibid. FDR Press Conference, 8 September 1939.
18. Hull, *Memoirs I*, pp. 688–92.
19. Churchill to Roosevelt, 5 October 1939, in Lowenheim, *Roosevelt and Churchill*, doc 2, p. 90.
20. Hitler speech in Reichstag, 6 October 1939; Mackenzie King Diary, 6 October 1939.
21. *NYT*, 11 October 1939, Felix Belair Jr – headline – 'Roosevelt Denies Mediation Move'.
22. *Hansard*, Commons, Chamberlain speech, 12 October 1939.
23. Ickes, *Diary*, III, p. 37, 14 October 1939; 20 October 1939, pp. 44–45 and 50.
24. DGFP/D/VIII, doc 56, memorandum by Weizsäcker, 12 September 1939, re avoiding war with US and cover note dated 23 September 1939 with Ribbentrop's view.
25. DGFP/D/VIII, doc 22, memorandum by Dieckhoff, Berlin, 7 September 1939; doc 85, memorandum by Woermann quoting Dieckhoff, 17 September 1939.
26. DGFP/D/VIII, doc 54, Thomsen to GFM, 12 September 1939; doc 129, Thomsen to GFM, 24 September 1939.
27. DGFP/D/VIII, doc 315, Thomsen to GFM, 30 October 1939.

14 Allies' Arsenal, October–November 1939

On 3 November 1939, the day before Roosevelt signed the new Neutrality Act, Leslie Burgin, the British Minister of Supply, claimed that with the lifting of the US arms embargo the Allies would have access to 'an arsenal of tremendous resources'. Burgin was quoted as referring to the US as 'the Allies' Arsenal' and was criticised by the isolationist press as a result. The day after the repeal of the embargo Burgin made a broadcast to Germany, saying that with the aid of American supplies Britain and France would soon be able to produce twice as many aeroplanes as the Reich. 'We have seen a step taken by a great power which is going to have a far-reaching effect on the course of the war,' he said. The possibility of American production of planes was almost unlimited, and orders had already been placed for planes alone worth 'many millions of pounds'. Repeal of the arms embargo meant that the Allies could now 'draw upon the limitless resources of the United States' in addition to their own resources and those of the Empire. 'There is no end to the Allied supplies', he proclaimed, whereas 'there is an early end to German supplies.'[1]

Burgin's aim was clearly to undermine German morale by pointing out the disparity between the potential resources of Britain and France in comparison with those of Germany, even in terms of air power. Similarly, shortly after the revision of the Neutrality Act, Chamberlain wrote to Roosevelt:

> The repeal of the arms embargo, which has been so anxiously awaited in this country, is not only an assurance that we and our French allies may draw upon the great reservoir of American resources; it is also a profound moral encouragement to us in the struggle upon which we are engaged.

He continued, in an appreciative, if rather too optimistic, manner: 'I am convinced it will have a devastating effect on German morale.

We here have derived all the greater satisfaction from it because we realise to what an extent we owe it to your personal efforts and goodwill.' Indeed, Roosevelt had masterminded the repeal of the arms embargo and its replacement with the concept of 'cash and carry' – aided by Borah's incorrect assertion in July that there would be no war in 1939 and that further discussion of the Neutrality Act could therefore be safely postponed.[2]

Repeal of arms embargo

This chapter argues that the repeal of the US arms embargo was a central element in the 'tacit alliance' promoted by Roosevelt since the start of his second term in January 1937. One aspect of this 'unspoken alliance' was the President's determination to secure revisions to the Neutrality Act for the benefit of Britain, with her relatively strong finances and dominant Navy, despite the opposition of isolationists like Borah and Johnson. Although the strategy of deterring Nazi Germany from risking a general European war had failed, and 'doubts, hopes and fears' remained in government circles on both sides of the Atlantic, FDR hoped that the Allied blockade and benevolent American neutrality would strangle the German war effort. He was determined to keep the US out of the conflict, if at all possible, but he was also committed to supporting the democracies through the 'methods short of war' he had referred to in his 1939 State of the Union address. Hence – among other steps – not only his efforts to secure the repeal of the arms embargo but also his enthusiastic cooperation with the British Purchasing Commission that followed it.[3]

Historians of Anglo-American relations have tended to play down the importance of the repeal of the arms embargo as an indicator of amity between Washington and London, especially in comparison with the Destroyer-Bases deal some ten months later. For example, it has been pointed out that Cadogan, the Permanent Under Secretary at the Foreign Office, doubted that the American move would make any difference and suggested that it might 'only mean making money out of munitions'. Indeed, he 'continued to "feel sick" at the usual combination of inaction and lectures on the "high moral" plane' that he felt characterised US policy. In addition, although Chamberlain sent his message of thanks to Roosevelt, he did not mention the Neutrality repeal in his correspondence with his sister at this time. However, the *Sunday Times* summed up the general view when it said that the repeal of the arms embargo reflected 'the dual sentiments of the American people, which are a warm sympathy with the cause of the Allies and a great desire not to be directly involved in the war. . . . In law it is impartial; in fact, it is an assistance.'[4]

In support of the repeal of the arms embargo, and despite his misgivings about British policy towards Germany, Mackenzie King agreed to the Joint Air Training Scheme, whereby Canada, Australia and New Zealand would supply pilots and other personnel for the British Air Force, with financial support from the Treasury. An Air Training mission, led by Lord Riverdale, arrived in Ottawa on 15 October, and while Mackenzie King resented Riverdale's 'railroading manner' and British pressure on Canada regarding the funding of the scheme, the details were gradually thrashed out and he was able to announce an agreement on 17 December. But he was unhappy that the announcement was overshadowed by news of the scuttling of the *Graf Spee* on the same day and he was even more upset that, a day later, Churchill made a broadcast announcing the arrival of Canadian soldiers in Britain – news that he felt should have been delivered in Canada. Churchill's broadcast also irked him by seeming to emphasise the role of the British convoys rather than Canada's contribution to the war effort. And he thought that Churchill sounded as though he had been drinking. 'I shall be surprised if he carries through to the end of the war,' he wrote.[5]

Arms embargo debate

The outbreak of war – despite Borah's scepticism over whether Britain and France would support Poland – greatly improved the chances for the revision of the Neutrality law that had been thwarted in July. When Lothian met FDR on 18 September, he found him 'very confident' about having the embargo removed. On the 21st the President addressed Congress at the beginning of a special session to secure the revision of the Neutrality laws. After tracing the growing likelihood of war since January 1939, he referred to 'the so-called Neutrality Act of 1935' and said: 'I regret that the Congress passed that Act. I regret equally that I signed that Act.' Pursuing the line he had taken since January 1937 – that a pro-active foreign policy was more likely to keep the US out of war than a passive one – he said:

> I give you my deep and unalterable conviction, based on years of experience as a worker in the field of international peace, that by the repeal of the embargo the United States will more probably remain at peace than if the law remains as it stands today.

For good measure, he added: 'Our methods must be guided by one single, hard-headed thought – the keeping of America out of this war.'[6]

On 28 September, after a comparatively short hearing, the Senate Foreign Relations Committee, which had blocked repeal in July, reported in favour of Pittman's Bill to revise the Neutrality Act by 16 votes to 7. Lothian reported that the minority comprised 'a roll-call of the most committed isolationists in the Senate' – William Borah, Hiram Johnson, Champ Clark, Arthur Vandenberg, Arthur Capper, Robert La Follette Jr and Henrick Shipstead. The majority included Senators George and Gillette, whose adverse votes had turned the scale in July. The Bill then moved on to the Senate floor for a more general debate. The position of the President remained a factor, noted Lothian, because of the possibility of his running again in 1940, but the split in the Democratic Party that had opened up in 1937–38 was beginning to heal as the election loomed and Roosevelt allowed the New Deal to recede into the background.[7]

'Oratorical camouflage'

Arthur Krock once again pointed out the nature of the 'tacit alliance' that had formed between Washington and London when he argued that the Senate had wearied quickly of its 'great debate' over the repeal of the arms embargo, partly because of the lack of candour with which both sides – but particularly the Administration spokesmen – stated their case and engaged in 'oratorical camouflage'. Isolationists had also failed to convince Congress that the arms embargo was a step toward American involvement in the European war. Senators Norris and Connally had implied that the purpose of the repeal of the embargo was to remove its disadvantage for Britain and France, as it was in America's national interest that they should defeat Germany, wrote Krock. 'But this was furthest north in candour,' he remarked. 'The guns of Borah have roared, the guns of Vandenberg have thundered, and defenders of the Administration's wall have found, with a certain amount of surprise, that it stands firm.' However, he added, notwithstanding the repeal of the arms embargo, there was no doubt that American public opinion was solidly against involvement in the war.[8]

During the Senate debates in October 1939 the isolationists reiterated their well-known view that the sale of munitions by American arms manufacturers had been a major cause of the entry of the United States into the First World War. They also brought up the issue of unpaid war debts from Britain and France, the countries that would benefit most from repeal. And they argued that repeal would be the first major step towards taking sides with the Allies, thereby involving the United States in the war. 'We cannot become the arsenal for one belligerent without becoming the target for the other,' declared Vandenberg. Administration spokesmen deliberately played down the fact that repealing the arms embargo would aid Britain and France and, at the end of October, the Senate passed Pittman's resolution to repeal the arms embargo by 63 votes to 30. Attempts to reinsert the embargo in the House were defeated by comfortable majorities. The Bill was put in its final form by a conference of both houses and was signed by the President at midday on 4 November.[9]

British purchasing mission

Even before the repeal of the arms embargo, a British purchasing mission had arrived in Ottawa to place orders with Canadian firms, with the intention of establishing a purchasing organisation in New York. This had been recommended by the Riverdale mission in August 1939, and on 6 September the British War Cabinet approved the despatch of a mission to North America under John Greenly, who was the Chairman of the Prime Minister's Advisory Panel of Industrialists on Rearmament. As the Chairman of Babcock and Wilcox, he could go to the US and Canada ostensibly on private business. The plan was for a mission to be established which could be developed later into a full purchasing organisation, with Greenly as Comptroller General. Greenly and his team left Britain for Canada via New York on 23 September and arrived in Ottawa on 1 October, where they met Mackenzie King and Canadian officials. Canada was the original destination as it was still seen as the chief source of supplies in North America. In addition, Lothian reported that FDR was 'anxious on the eve of the impending Neutrality debate to avoid accusations of concerting with Britain and France so he wanted the mission to go to Canada before visiting the US'.[10]

Greenly then paid an unofficial visit to Washington between 10 and 13 October, during which time he met Morgenthau and other officials, including Pierrepont Moffat at the State Department. Morgenthau told Greenly that the President wanted to receive 'a weekly summary of the orders placed in the USA and the deliveries taken, including not only munitions but also raw materials, manufactured goods and foodstuffs'. He assured Greenly that this information would be treated as confidential. Similarly, he said that the British purchasing agency should keep its account at the Federal Reserve Board rather than a private bank, as he would be in a stronger position to avoid undue publicity for it there. Morgenthau also informed Greenly that he had become the primary channel of communication with the President regarding priorities for war supplies, rather than Johnson or Woodring in the War Department. 'We can fully confirm Riverdale's view that the United States administration are anxious and prepared to be entirely helpful so soon as the Neutrality Act is amended,' reported Greenly.[11]

On 8 November, shortly after the arms embargo was repealed, a press release was published in London, Washington and Ottawa, stating that the British Government was setting up a central organisation to be known as the British Supply Board in Canada and the United States, to coordinate purchases in the two countries. Greenly was to be the Comptroller-General and Chairman, and the Board would place orders in Canada through the Canadian War Supply Board under Wallace Campbell, while orders in the US would be placed through the British Purchasing Commission under Arthur Purvis, as Director-General of Purchases (US). Greenly had informed London that the US government was anticipating large orders of war supplies and he felt that it was important not to disappoint these expectations. However, Simon, as Chancellor of the Exchequer, had already made it clear to the British Cabinet that Britain's dollar supplies would have to be husbanded, so the

Anglo-American trade agreement was effectively shelved, and purchases of American foodstuffs were reduced to conserve dollars – a policy that was later to attract the ire of Cordell Hull. Detailed discussions about large-scale orders of US planes did not take place in Cabinet until 9 December and, even then, there were further delays, so that a major order was not placed until April 1940.[12]

Morgenthau–Purvis axis

Just as Morgenthau and FDR were instrumental in facilitating the 'cash and carry' arrangements on behalf of the British and French governments, so too they were keen to reduce the competition between them for US supplies. 'The President's aims', Morgenthau told Lothian, 'are the elimination of unnecessary profits, to keep prices steady and to avoid competition between the British, French and US governments.' This led to the setting up of the Anglo-French Purchasing Board under Purvis in Washington and the Anglo-French Co-ordinating Committee in London, with Monnet as Chairman. Purvis, as the Chair of the Anglo-French Purchasing Board in Washington, as well as head of the British Purchasing Commission (in New York) and the chief link with the Foreign Office, was naturally seen as the chief representative for the Allies regarding American war supplies. Morgenthau had regular meetings with Purvis and, in the words of the British Government's official historian, these frequent meetings 'set in motion a famous combination of two personalities which was the mainspring of British supply from America in the most critical period of the war'. Indeed, the 'Morgenthau–Purvis axis' was to play a vital role in Anglo-American relations in 1940–41, especially after the British evacuation from Dunkirk and the fall of France.[13]

On the US side, Morgenthau had the full confidence of FDR and represented him on the President's Liaison Committee, which Roosevelt had set up at his request 'to handle supply relations with the Allies'. This committee began to function informally in December, chaired by Captain Collins of the Treasury Procurement Division. FDR's sympathies towards Britain can be seen in the report by Collins of a meeting between the President, Morgenthau, Purvis and Pleven, the French representative, on 29 December. Purvis noted that the report was 'somewhat obscure in its phraseology' due to Collins's desire to 'avoid direct reference to certain items' that were discussed and approved by the President. As was obvious from his interviews with Morgenthau, reported Purvis, 'we have a fund of goodwill on which to draw, and the problem is how to capitalise on this to the best advantage within the political limitations involved for the US administration'. There was a 'very friendly atmosphere', said Purvis, and Roosevelt was very helpful. For example, he 'authorised Captain Collins to see that we are given access to prototypes of newly developed machines "off the record"'. Furthermore, at the end of the meeting, 'the President . . . made it clear the door would be open for further discussion as necessity arises'.[14]

Also in December 1939, Morgenthau informed Purvis that the President had under consideration various proposals to prevent essential alloys such as molybdenum and manganese, and other raw materials, from reaching Germany, Russia and possibly Japan. These proposals emanated from Ambassador Bullitt in Paris and Roosevelt saw in them 'grounds for the conception of a future policy for the maintenance of peace by depriving aggressor nations of essential raw materials'. Just before Christmas the Anglo-French Co-ordinating Committee in London authorised Purvis to inform Morgenthau that it 'warmly welcomed this approach and appreciated the helpful attitude of the US Government', but it pointed out that the Allies had a different policy towards Germany than to Russia and Japan. In essence, the US as a neutral country preferred a 'moral embargo' or a policy of withholding supplies because of other demands, whereas Britain as a belligerent nation would have to treat Germany differently from Russia and Japan.[15]

The Foreign Office had some qualms about these 'para-diplomatic exchanges' via Purvis but Roosevelt and Morgenthau were given credit 'for desiring to do all they can to help the Allied cause without exposing the United States Government to charges of dangerous partiality from isolationists, of breaches of neutrality from the Germans, or an unfriendly action from Russia and Japan'. In a good illustration of the nature of the 'tacit alliance' between Washington and London at this time, it was noted:

> Their idea is to explore to what lengths they can go *sub rosa* to make things as difficult as possible for our enemies, overt and covert, without appearing to have taken sides or to have increased the probability of the USA becoming involved in the war.

British policy must therefore be to help Roosevelt and his team 'not to know too much', so that if 'hailed before a Senate Committee' they could 'put their hands on their hearts and say that they have done nothing which they were not prompted to do by consideration for America's domestic and defence needs'. Any similarity between US actions and British policy 'must appear to be the result of accident rather than collusion and conformity and must be made to result from an exchange of ideas rather than from bargains'.[16]

'Missing the bus'

In the end, the moral embargo ran into too many obstacles to yield very much in terms of concrete results. But, in the words of the official historian of North American Supply, 'it helped in London and Washington to develop the habit of working together on matters of common concern'. Such cooperation may have been one reason for Chamberlain's growing confidence about the progress of the war. In December he wrote to his sister Hilda that Hitler had 'missed the bus' by not moving against Britain and France after the outbreak of the war, or at the time of the Munich crisis, when they were vulnerable to attack. He repeated the phrase at a Conservative conference in Central Hall on 4 April 1940 – shortly before the German invasion of Norway, which altered the tempo of the war and led to his replacement as Prime Minister by Churchill. This outcome might suggest that British policy was misconceived from the outset of the war. However, Chamberlain and his newly strengthened Cabinet appeared to be negotiating the initial stages of the war reasonably well. The War Cabinet was undoubtedly hard at work – meeting virtually every day and, on some occasions, twice a day. But while it was very efficient and businesslike, it was far from being dynamic or proactive, and proposals for action, especially by Churchill, were often delayed by the Cabinet, and delayed again if they required the agreement of the French, or the Dominions, or both.[17]

Chamberlain's own approach, in war as well as peace, tended towards caution and this was reinforced by his view that the resources of Britain and her Empire were much greater than those of Germany and that time was on the side of Britain as she would be able to outlast Germany, especially if the British Navy could blockade German goods. His quiet confidence was demonstrated in his speeches in the Commons and in a rare public broadcast on 26 November 1939. Pointing out that Germany was trying to squeeze British supplies through its use of U-boats and magnetic mines, he praised the merchant marine, which, he said, had provided for the nation since Elizabeth's days. Responding to the question, 'why are we not attacking the enemy?', he argued that Britain was not losing anything by delay. Every day the blockade was wearing down Germany – unlike the resources of the British Empire. The ultimate aim, he said, was to establish a new Europe, with a new spirit, marked by goodwill and the end of aggression.[18]

FDR largely agreed with this strategy at the start if the war. While determined to keep the US out of direct involvement in the war, including any idea of sending an expeditionary force to Europe, as had occurred in 1917, he was equally decided to support Britain and France against Nazi Germany. Having secured the repeal of the arms embargo in November 1939, he could do little more for the time being, apart from supporting the British economic blockade of Germany, which he had advocated to his Cabinet at the time of the Munich crisis. He was naturally concerned at the pessimistic reports being sent to Washington by Kennedy from London and Bullitt from Paris and the rumours of an imminent German invasion of Belgium and the Netherlands. He also had reservations about certain aspects of British policy, such as the pedantic nature of the naval blockade and, especially, the very tardy orders for aircraft and other military equipment after the repeal of the arms embargo. But for the first few months of the war, like the rest of Washington, there was little he could do, apart from watch the European situation closely and make sure that the United States was as well prepared as possible for any eventuality – for example, by sounding out Frank Knox, the Republican Vice Presidential candidate in 1936, about becoming Secretary of the Navy in the event of 'a real crisis' developing that would require a bipartisan Cabinet.[19]

Keeping in touch

Meanwhile, Roosevelt and Churchill were keeping in touch through their occasional naval correspondence and were beginning to develop something of a rapport. For example, FDR supported the actions of British warships that led to the scuttling of the *Graf*

Spee in Montevideo harbour on 19 December, despite the fact that they had ignored the rules of the Panama declaration's neutrality zone. Indeed, FDR had aided the British operation. In October he had asked the US Navy to step up its patrols in the neutrality zone and reports by various American destroyers and cruisers helped inform British warships about the location of several German raiders in the early days of the war. In the Battle of the River Plate on 13 December 1939, three cruisers, HMS *Ajax*, *Achilles* and *Exeter*, attacked the *Admiral Graf Spee* in the Plate River estuary off Montevideo and pursued the raider into the harbour, where it was scuttled on 19 December. Following the incident, the signatories of the Panama pact issued a joint statement protesting against the violations of the neutrality zone by Germany and Britain.[20]

Churchill wrote to FDR about the incident on Christmas Day and also sent him a seven-page report. While he apologised for the appearance of British submarines in the neutrality zone, he argued that 'as a result of action off Plate the whole of South America is now clear and may perhaps continue clear of warlike operations'. Churchill pointed out that a German victory would be a real threat to South America and to the USA, and he asked for the 'best construction' to be put upon the British action in the South Atlantic that was 'indispensable' to ending the war quickly and 'in the right way'. The President's reply was mollifying, to say the least. 'Ever so many thanks for that tremendously interesting account of the extraordinarily well-fought action of your three cruisers,' he wrote. On the issue of the Allied search and detention of American ships, he said: 'The general feeling is that the net benefit to your people and to France is hardly worth the definite annoyance caused to us. That is always found to be so in a nation which is 3,000 miles away from the fact of war.' And he ended: 'I wish much that I could talk things over with you in person – but I am grateful to you for keeping me in touch, as you do.'[21]

The view from Berlin

Meanwhile, in Berlin, the lifting of the arms embargo was taken as obvious proof that the United States, 'while posing as a neutral country, had in practice abandoned neutrality'. However, the

German Foreign Ministry decided not to make any official representations to the US Government. Keeping the United States out of the war remained the chief aim and nothing was to be done to provoke Washington. The Ministry also believed that any official protest would be counter-productive and that criticism in the press would make the attitude of Germany clear enough. Indeed, as the *New York Times* reported on its front page, the German press attacked the move to repeal the arms embargo as a blatantly unneutral act. While both the Foreign Ministry and the Propaganda Ministry said that the American action was 'no surprise and was to be expected', Nazi spokesmen were reported to have accused the United States of giving 'outright support' to Britain and France by repealing the arms embargo. Much of the hostility was directed towards Roosevelt himself, who was portrayed as following the same path as Woodrow Wilson – a path that had led the US into the First World War 'at the service of British imperialism'.[22]

Reporting from Washington, Thomsen was scornful of the debate over the repeal of the arms embargo. 'If the advocates of repeal were confronted with the clear-cut question whether the embargo would also be repealed if such a step were to benefit Germany, they would have to answer "no",' he wrote. The debates in Congress between isolationists and interventionists were evading the real issue, he continued, 'since the interventionists, out of regard for public opinion, are still reluctant to admit openly that they let themselves be guided less by a concern for American interests than by a desire to assist England'. The arguments previously deployed against the repeal of the arms embargo had been abandoned, he said, 'when it is a question of helping England'. The repeal of the embargo was 'an unfriendly and unneutral act, because it contradicts traditional American policy in all points'.[23]

But the reaction of the German Foreign Ministry was one of irritation rather than despondency – irritation similar to that felt at other examples of American unneutrality. It was realised that it would be difficult for the Allies to take immediate advantage of the repeal of the arms embargo. As Thomsen pointed out, 'after the creation of additional production facilities and provision for American armament requirements, it will in actual practice take considerable time for a repeal of the arms embargo for the benefit of the Allies to take *full* effect'. This was echoed by Bötticher.

'The armaments and aviation industries are continuing to increase their capacity,' he wrote. 'Nevertheless, it is to be noted that after the embargo was lifted the orders expected from the Allies did not come in to the extent anticipated in the aviation industry and only to a slight extent in other war industries, and therefore the expectation expressed by Roosevelt that the lifting of the embargo would lead to a rapid revival of the armaments industry and thus to greater war preparedness has for the time being not been fulfilled.'[24]

Indeed, apart from supplying the Allies, there was little sign that the United States would be able to enter the war before 'the late summer of 1940', even if public opinion was in favour of doing so. As Bötticher reported, after the first three months of the war 'adequate units of the Army and Air Forces as the basis for military intervention' were still not available. As a result, he said,

> doubt is beginning to be felt regarding the correctness of the American pre-war thesis that economic warfare would be the decisive factor in the struggle against Germany and that the present war would follow a course in accordance with the economic and military experiences of the World War.

Thus, Bötticher argued, the US authorities were 'moving towards a better realisation of the limits of their own power'. The US General Staff was 'working against war sentiment', he said, 'in contrast to the State Department's sterile policy of hatred and the impulsive policy of Roosevelt'. However, like Thomsen, he warned that, despite its limitations, 'the United States . . . will still enter the war if it considers that the Western Hemisphere is threatened'.[25]

Notes

1. *The Times*, 4 November 1939; FO/371/22836, A8254/6041/45, William de Krafft to Frank Ashton-Gwatkin, 8 November 1939; *NYT*, 6 November 1939.
2. PREM/1/367, Chamberlain to Roosevelt, 8 November 1939.
3. Reynolds, *Creation*, pp. 7–36.
4. Reynolds, *Creation*, p. 89 on Cadogan; see also his endnote 150 – Cadogan minute [between 19 and 27 November 1939], FO/800/317; endnote 151 – minutes of 25 November 1939, FO/371/22818. Rock, *Chamberlain and Roosevelt*, pp. 229–32 on Chamberlain correspondence. *Sunday Times*, 5 November 1939.

5. Mackenzie King Diary, 11 October, 17 October, 18 December 1939.
6. FO/371/22835, A6400/6041/45, Lothian to Halifax, 18 September 1939; Congressional Record, 21 September 1939, pp. 10–12; Hall, *North American Supply*, pp. 52–3.
7. FO/371/22817, A6879/98/45, Lothian to Halifax, 29 September 1939; FO/371/22817, A6895/98/45, Lothian to Halifax, 6 October 1939.
8. Arthur Krock, *NYT*, 8 October 1939.
9. Divine, *Illusion of Neutrality*, pp. 286–335.
10. FO/371/22835, A6041/6041/45, Robinson to Balfour, 6 September 1939; A6088/6041/45, Robinson to Ashton-Gwatkin, 7 September 1939; A6486/6041/45, Halifax to Lothian, 22 September 1939; A6115/6041/45, Lothian to Halifax, 8 September 1939; Hall, *North American Supply*, pp. 68–9.
11. FO/371/22835, A6847/6041/45, Lothian to Halifax, 4 October 1939; A6985/6041/45, Lothian to Halifax, 10 October 1939; ibid., A7204/6041/45, Report from Greenly to Robinson, 17 October 1939; Hall, *North American Supply*, p. 69 and pp. 96–7.
12. Hall, *North American Supply*, pp. 70–1 for press release; FO/371/22836, A8622/6041/45, memorandum for Halifax, 7 December 1939; CAB 23, 20 October 1939; CAB 23, 9 December 1939; Reynolds, *Creation*, pp. 88–92.
13. FO/371/22835, A7598/6041/45, Lothian to Halifax, 3 November 1939; Hall, *North American Supply*, pp. 70–1, 97–9.
14. FO/371/25136, W1609/79/49, Purvis to Monnet, 31 December 1939, enclosing memo by Collins on meeting with FDR, 29 December 1939; Hall, *North American Supply*, pp. 101–4.
15. FO/371/25136, file W/79/49 for alloys issue; see also WP(G)(1940) item 14, for War Cabinet memo, 19 January 1940 on 'Possibility of US Co-operation in Preventing Certain Vital Commodities From Reaching Germany, Russia and Japan' – good summary of issue.
16. FO/371/25136, W334/79/49, Foreign Office minute by Ronald, 8 January 1940.
17. Hall, *North American Supply*, pp. 80–94; Chamberlain to his sister Hilda, 30 December 1939, in Self, *Chamberlain*, p. 412. For Chamberlain speech, 4 April 1940, see *The Times*, 5 April 1940; Chamberlain to a Conservative Party rally, 4 April 1940, in Self, *Chamberlain*, p. 415.
18. Chamberlain broadcast, *The Times*, 26 November 1939.
19. Dallek, *FDR*, pp. 199–215; FDR to Knox, 19 December 1939, Knox papers, Library of Congress.
20. Dallek, *FDR*, pp. 205–6; Lowenheim, *Roosevelt and Churchill*, pp. 90–4.
21. Ibid., Churchill to FDR, 25 December 1939, doc 4, pp. 91–2; FDR to Churchill, 1 February 1940, doc 7, pp. 93–4.

22. DGFP/D/VIII, doc 323, footnote 1, GFM to Washington Embassy, 8 November 1939; *NYT*, 'Vote Angers Reich', 3 November 1939.
23. DGFP, doc 220, Thomsen to GFM, 9 October 1939.
24. DGFP, doc 220, Thomsen to GFM, 9 October 1939; doc 405, Bötticher and Thomsen to GFM, 1 December 1939.
25. DGFP/D/VIII, doc 405, Bötticher and Thomsen to GFM, 1 December 1939.

15 Conclusions: 'Tacit Alliance' Revisited

In his iconic 'Iron Curtain' address, delivered in Fulton, Missouri, on 5 March 1946, Winston Churchill argued that the Second World War could have been prevented if the democracies had formed a strong, secure and open alliance to deter Nazi Germany from threatening the peace of Europe. He also believed that a similar threat was confronting post-war Europe in the form of the Soviet Union. Hence his appeal for the revival of the 'fraternal association of the English-speaking peoples' or, as he also termed it, the 'special relationship between the British Commonwealth and Empire and the United States of America'. Otherwise, he warned, the mistakes of the interwar years would be repeated, the United Nations as the successor to the League of Nations would fail, and 'the dark ages' might return. But, he added, if such a fraternal association could be established, 'let us make sure that that great fact is known to the world, and that it plays its part in steadying and stabilizing the foundations of peace. There is the path of wisdom. Prevention is better than the cure.'[1]

In other words, Churchill was arguing that it was not enough to have a common front of the democracies against totalitarianism. An alliance or pact between the United States and the British Empire, if it could be achieved, had to be open and effective, like the Permanent Board of Defence between the US and Canada formed in August 1940, which he referred to in his speech. Otherwise, its existence would be doubted and its value as a deterrent undermined. This, he believed, was one of the main lessons of the 1930s – an open alliance between the United States and the British Empire would have acted as a deterrent to the expansionist aspirations of Nazi Germany, Fascist Italy and Imperial Japan. Indeed, Churchill was entitled to feel frustrated. While he had the benefit of hindsight in arriving at his post-war reflections, no one can read his pre-war newspaper articles and the texts of his speeches without being struck by the consistency and force of his warnings about the rapid pace of German rearmament after Hitler's coming to power in January 1933. Nor can there be any doubt that Churchill argued in the 1930s that a strong alliance between Hitler's opponents would have a deterrent effect in Berlin as well as in Rome and Tokyo.[2]

Key Questions

Churchill's argument that Hitler would have been deterred by a greater show of solidarity between the democracies, especially Britain and the United States, raises a number of points that take us back to the five main questions addressed by the current work. Firstly, what exactly was FDR's attitude towards the worsening international situation from 1937 to 1939 and how far was he prepared to go in forming an alliance of some kind with Britain against Nazi Germany, given the strength of US isolationism at this time, especially in Congress? Secondly, what was the attitude of the Chamberlain Government to Roosevelt's foreign policy in the context of British appeasement and how far did it welcome offers of cooperation by the United States? Thirdly, what role was played by Canada and especially Prime Minister Mackenzie King at this time in promoting Anglo-American understanding and cooperation. Fourthly, how was the growing evidence of closer Anglo-American relations in the late 1930s viewed in Berlin? Finally, to what extent can the degree of cooperation between Washington and London at the outset of the war be regarded as constituting a 'tacit alliance'?[3]

FDR and 'parallel action'

The current work argues, in contrast to the views of many historians of Anglo-American relations, that not only was Roosevelt anxious to support Britain in her diplomacy with Nazi Germany but that Washington had a strategy to do so – 'parallel action', a term that was used regularly by US policymakers in the late 1930s and that, as Arthur Krock, the *New York Times* columnist, pointed out, was designed to encourage the democracies and warn the dictator states while avoiding the ire of isolationist opinion in the United States. This clearly entailed a difficult balancing act, especially as, although London and Washington both favoured the containment of Nazi

Germany through a dual policy of deterrence and 'appeasement', Chamberlain was focused primarily on appeasement while Roosevelt, like Churchill, thought that deterrence was the most suitable approach, in the form of what became known as a 'Peace Front'. He believed that appeasement, in the sense of addressing the legitimate complaints of the 'have not' states, should be entertained only if they were abiding strictly by 'international norms'. 'Parallel action' with Britain was therefore selective and subject to US domestic as well as strategic considerations. It tried to signal to both the democracies and the dictator states, especially in the 'Quarantine' speech, that, notwithstanding the Neutrality laws, the United States Government was committed to 'active engagement' to tackle the deteriorating international situation and was ready to cooperate with like-minded powers to prevent another world war. Inevitably, that speech met with strong criticism from the isolationists and led Borah to speculate about a 'tacit alliance' between the US and Britain.[4]

Nevertheless, Roosevelt persevered. US foreign policy during 1937 had mainly involved 'parallel action' with Britain, especially in the Far East and Spain, but there were also discussions and meetings behind the scenes, which were continued in the form of the Ingersoll mission to London for naval talks in January 1938. FDR had been attracted, since his re-election, by the idea of calling a small international conference to include primarily the 'key players' in European affairs, but Chamberlain poured cold water on the 'Roosevelt initiative' put forward by Sumner Welles in January 1938 – a rebuff that contributed to Eden's resignation in February. Thereafter, the British Government pursued an enhanced policy of appeasement that was clearly in evidence following the muted British reaction to the German *Anschluss* with Austria and the decision to negotiate an Anglo-Italian agreement that recognised Italy's conquest of Ethiopia in return for reassurances regarding Italian policy in Spain and the Mediterranean more generally. Chamberlain's commitment to a policy of appeasement, culminating in the Munich agreement, meant that Roosevelt was confronted with a choice between isolationism and appeasement; feeling that he could not simply stand by, he supported the latter. But it was a temporary phase and thereafter he redoubled his efforts on behalf of the democracies taking a stronger stand against Hitler – hence his secret messages to Chamberlain via Arthur Murray in December 1938.[5]

The revival of Roosevelt's outspoken criticism of Germany, Italy and Japan as 'aggressor states', as highlighted by the Quarantine speech, was signalled by his State of the Union address in January 1939, which was a clarion call on behalf of democracy. This was welcomed, in public at least, by Chamberlain, especially after the German occupation of Prague, and the British and French guarantee to Poland, but he continued to hope for a modus vivendi with Hitler and to encourage his close associate, Sir Horace Wilson, to sound out Berlin. Meanwhile, Roosevelt actively encouraged the Peace Front that was taking shape against Nazi Germany, and the British Royal Visit to the US in June 1939 – aided by the Canadian Prime Minister, Mackenzie King – symbolised the arrival of a 'tacit alliance' between the US and Britain. But neither this, nor the Peace Front, minus Russia, were enough to deter Hitler from invading Poland, especially as he and Ribbentrop doubted the British Government's resolve. When war broke out, the neutrality proclaimed by FDR was followed more in theory than in practice and the repeal of the arms embargo showed the President's support of Britain and France, even though it was tacit in nature at this time.[6]

Chamberlain and British appeasement

As regards British policy, the main reason for Chamberlain's dogged pursuit of appeasement was his conviction that it would be possible to satisfy Germany's needs if only Hitler was prepared to negotiate and achieve his demands peacefully. At the same time, British resources were in danger of being overstretched if war with Germany broke out and the British Empire was also threatened by Italy and Japan. As regards the British attitude to FDR's policy, as Reynolds and other historians have pointed out, it was greatly influenced by 'doubts, hopes and fears' dating back to the First World War, especially the failure of the US to join the League, even though Woodrow Wilson had championed it and helped to shape its structure. Differences over issues such as war debts, naval limitation and policy towards Japan, especially during the Manchurian episode in 1931–32, also bedevilled relations. And, after an encouraging start to his presidency, Roosevelt's bombshell message to the London Economic Conference seemed to suggest that he was as unreliable as his predecessors.[7]

However, by the end of 1936, Eden and the Foreign Office were more optimistic that, after his re-election, Roosevelt II would prove to be an improvement on Roosevelt I – a change in opinion that was most noticeable in the outlook of Sir Robert Vansittart, the forceful Permanent Under Secretary. The Tripartite Currency Agreement of September 1936 and rumours of a possible US-led conference, together with reports that FDR and Hull intended to 'keep Germany lean' unless she mended her ways, all contributed to this view. So too did the Runciman visit in January 1937. However, 'doubts, hopes and fears' continued to influence Chamberlain and the British Government in its relations with Roosevelt and his New Deal Administration: for example, the well-known quotation from Chamberlain about expecting nothing from Americans except words. He was perfectly happy to seek FDR's endorsement of the Runciman mission to Czechoslovakia in 1938 but his basic attitude did not really change until after Munich and, even then, he was reluctant to give up on appeasement.[8]

There were also grave doubts in Washington about Chamberlain's commitment to opposing the dictators. Harold Ickes, for one, felt that the British Prime Minister lacked 'backbone', and he was not alone. Borah, Johnson and the isolationists took full advantage of British appeasement to argue that the British Government was unreliable and essentially no different from Germany itself. Thus, in July 1939, they opposed the repeal of the arms embargo desired by FDR and Hull, and Borah even argued that, because of British appeasement policy, there would be no war in 1939. In many ways, FDR's policy had more in common with that of Churchill and the Opposition than that of the Government. This was true of the Labour Party, especially when Ernest Bevin and the trade unions came out in favour of rearmament. It was also true of the Liberals, although both Labour and Liberals stressed the role of the League of Nations and the need for Britain and France to support the League – an institution that Chamberlain and many Conservatives felt was no longer 'fit for purpose'. Churchill believed that the League still had a role to play if it could encourage a coalition of powers, including Russia, as a 'Peace Front' against Germany, and Roosevelt and Hull were also sympathetic towards the League.[9]

Mackenzie King and the Canadian dimension

One reason for the British policy of appeasement was the attitude of the Dominions, not least the senior Dominion, Canada, led by Mackenzie King, whose visit to Berlin in 1937 to meet Hitler strengthened his support of British appeasement policy. Ironically, Chamberlain did not have a terribly high opinion of Mackenzie King and nor did the Foreign Office – partly because the Canadian was not keen on committing the Dominion to any sort of Imperial defence arrangement in peacetime. By contrast, FDR assiduously courted Mackenzie King from the outset, inviting him to visit Washington after his victory in the Canadian election of October 1935. Mackenzie King arrived in Washington on 7 November 1935 and had talks with FDR and Hull regarding a Canada–US trade agreement, which was concluded rapidly and signed just over a week later. The visit was also significant in establishing a rapport between the two leaders. According to Mackenzie King's own account, the President told him that he thought Canada could help him in his relations with Britain by acting as an 'interpreter' on some of the issues between the two countries. This also meant that FDR had to take into account Mackenzie King's strong support for Chamberlain's appeasement policy.[10]

FDR's view of Mackenzie King's role as an important link between Washington and London goes a long way to answering Stacey's question – raised in Chapter 1 – as to why the President paid so much attention to his northern neighbour during his presidency. Mackenzie King and Canada were to be of great significance for FDR during his second term in several ways. Firstly, the Canada–US trade agreements of November 1935 and November 1938 both aided the conclusion of the Anglo-American trade agreement by enabling concessions to the US in the politically vital agricultural sector. Mackenzie King also urged Chamberlain to attend the signing in Washington but, exhausted after Munich, he declined. Secondly, the regular meetings between Mackenzie King and Roosevelt enabled the Canadian to pass on the viewpoint of the British Government, and his own support for appeasement, which FDR had therefore had to accommodate, especially during the Munich crisis. Thirdly, the Canadian invitation to FDR to receive an honorary degree at Queen's University in August 1938 afforded the President the opportunity to pledge American defence of Canada in the event of war – effectively guaranteeing a key part of the British Empire.[11]

It was during the President's visit to Queen's University that he was informed by Mackenzie King that the Royal Visit to Canada was due to take place the following year. Roosevelt subsequently invited the King and Queen to undertake a side trip to the United

States and to stay with him at Hyde Park. The Royal Visit to America in June 1939 was of great significance, both symbolically and practically, in cementing relations between the United States and the British Empire on what proved to be the eve of war in Europe. The bond between Canada and Britain portrayed the positive and democratic side of the British Empire in contrast to other parts of the Empire such as India. Finally, by 1939, Canada was playing an increasingly important part both in Imperial defence and in North American defence. FDR was mindful of Canada's defence not only in his Queen's University speech but also in his willingness to defend the Canadian Pacific coastline and to include the naval base at Halifax in his North Atlantic strategy. These developments were followed up in the Ogdensburg agreement in August 1940, which resulted in the establishment of the Permanent Joint Board of Defence between US and Canada – referred to by Churchill in his Fulton speech as a model for the explicit and effective Anglo-American relationship he desired.[12]

The view from Berlin

Another key conclusion of the current work is that the German Foreign Ministry in Berlin was very aware of the existence of the close relationship between Washington and London, even though the US and British governments did not always see eye to eye. Especially from January 1937 onwards, numerous warnings from the German Embassy in Washington were sent to Berlin regarding the hostility of the Roosevelt Administration towards Nazi Germany and its determination to support Britain and France as the front-line democracies in Europe. The potential danger of an Anglo-American alliance in all but name was also pointed out on a regular basis by both of the German ambassadors in FDR's second term – Hans Luther (1933–37) and Hans-Heinrich Dieckhoff (1937–41) – and the Chargé d'Affaires, Hans Thomsen (who remained in post until December 1941). They had no doubt that there was some kind of 'tacit alliance' between the US and Britain. But they also acknowledged that Washington would ultimately take its lead from London in opposing Germany. In addition, as the German Military Attaché – Friedrich von Bötticher – pointed out, the US armed forces were very far from being ready to intervene in any conflict in Europe.[13]

While the German Embassy was certainly not above blaming 'Jewish influence' in New York for the Roosevelt Administration's criticism of Hitler and the Nazi regime, especially after *Kristallnacht* in November 1938, it maintained some semblance of proportion regarding the power of American Jewry, unlike figures such as Baron von Rechenberg, who sent a report back to Berlin portraying FDR as entirely under Jewish and Communist influence. Both the Embassy and the Foreign Ministry despaired of this report – and also of the German–American Bund – especially as Hitler appeared to be receptive to such propaganda. In addition, from February 1938, the staff of the German Foreign Ministry had to contend with von Ribbentrop as their Foreign Minister. Almost universally distrusted and despised by other diplomats and politicians, he was very far from being a 'safe pair of hands' in Berlin. As regards Hitler, Dallek stated that 'in general, he had little regard for the United States' or for the Neutrality laws, and this was certainly the view of earlier historians like Weinberg. But, more recently, Fischer has argued for a more nuanced viewed of Hitler's attitude to the United States. Indeed, Hitler's annoyance at Roosevelt's calls for the democracies to take a stronger line towards Germany can be seen in his speech of 30 January 1939 and his disdainful response to FDR's peace appeal in April 1939.[14]

It was taken for granted in Berlin that the Roosevelt Administration would not be 'more British than the British': that is, the US would take their lead from the British Government and FDR would not go further in moving away from strict neutrality if Chamberlain continued to prefer direct appeasement to deterrence. The German Foreign Ministry was also perfectly well aware that, even after the occupation of Prague, appeasement had not been entirely abandoned by the British Government and especially not by Chamberlain. In fact, it was considered more than likely that Chamberlain would put pressure on Poland to concede Danzig to the Reich, just he had done with Czechoslovakia. Attempts by the Prime Minister's Office, notably Sir Horace Wilson, to maintain a dialogue with figures considered close to the Nazi leaders, such as Helmuth Wohltat, supported this viewpoint. Ribbentrop and Hitler were not alone in assuming that Britain, and therefore France, would not go to war over Poland. Once war broke out, it became a major aim of German diplomacy to avoid direct US involvement as far as possible, even when provoked by Roosevelt's blatant lack of neutrality, as indicated by the repeal of the arms embargo in November 1939.[15]

A tacit alliance – five elements

Thus, despite the many 'doubts, hopes and fears' on both sides of the Atlantic, there was an increasing degree of cooperation and identity of interests between London and Washington from January 1937 that, by November 1939, definitely merited Borah's description of a 'tacit alliance'. This can be seen in five main areas: (1) ideology; (2) diplomacy; (3) economics, especially trade and war debts; (4) finance, including currency stability and the purchase of supplies from the US; and (5) national security and defence – including military and naval cooperation and the repeal of the arms embargo. The driving force behind this development was clearly the rise of Nazi Germany and the growing evidence from March 1935 that German rearmament on the ground and in the air was altering the balance of power in Europe, especially in the light of the Rome–Berlin Axis and the Anti-Comintern Pact with Japan. The Munich crisis, the annexation of the Sudetenland and the occupation of Prague raised the stakes still further and brought about the 'tacit alliance' feared by Borah and Johnson, as part of a Peace Front against Nazi Germany. This was not sufficient to deter Hitler from invading Poland and starting another European war, but the subsequent repeal of the American arms embargo meant that Anglo-American cooperation in November 1939 was a glass half full rather than half empty.[16]

Ideology

A major theme of the reports sent by the German Embassy in Washington to Berlin during FDR's second term was the growing ideological divide between the US Government and the Nazi regime. Indeed, at the centre of FDR's political philosophy as President there was a strong ideological conviction concerning the nature of democracy and the need to secure its future well-being. This can be seen very clearly in his State of the Union messages and his Inaugural Addresses, starting with his first Inaugural Address in March 1933 when he attacked the view that 'liberal democracy could not cope with a major crisis such as the economic depression'. In his 1936 State of the Union address he argued that the threat to world peace came from nations 'dominated by the twin spirits of autocracy and aggression'. He continued in this vein in many of his major speeches, including his Quarantine speech in October 1937, when he railed against the 'disease' of 'international lawlessness'. His State of the Union address in January 1939 included numerous references to the threat from abroad, which he now linked directly with American freedom, saying that where 'religion and democracy has vanished, good faith and reason in international affairs have given way to strident ambition and brute force'.[17]

The ideological dimension of foreign policy was much less evident in statements and speeches made by Chamberlain. This is not surprising, given the incompatibility of rhetoric about freedom and democracy with the ideologies prevailing in Nazi Germany and Fascist Italy. Baldwin was more inclined to bring notions of democracy and freedom into his public utterances, as can be seen during his visit to New York in August 1939 when he hailed the copy of Magna Carta that was on show at the New York World Fair and addressed the Congress on Education for Democracy. Chamberlain sometimes spoke of the common heritage and ideals of Britain and America, for example, at the time of the Royal Visit, but for the most part he adopted a very pragmatic approach towards the regimes that were in power in Berlin and Rome. He was often criticised for this by the Labour and Liberal Opposition – for example, after FDR's State of the Union message in January 1939 – but he began to echo the President rather more, during the course of that year, especially after the war began – although, even then, his speeches were invariably eclipsed by Churchill's oratory.[18]

Diplomacy

As well as setting the ideological agenda for US foreign policy during his term of office, FDR was keen to develop personal contacts with foreign, and especially British, policymakers. Hence the Runciman visit in January 1937 and the unsuccessful attempt via Norman Davis to invite Chamberlain to Washington later in the year. Cordell Hull, as Secretary of State, made regular speeches stressing what he called the 'pillars of peace' but his efforts lacked the impact of the President's addresses. Hull's main role was to supervise the details of American diplomacy along the lines favoured by the President and to advise him on any diplomatic initiatives. Hull's approach to almost any move by the President was one of extreme caution, especially in view of the likelihood that isolationists, in the press and in Congress, would seize upon any initiative that appeared to involve cooperation with a European power on political matters, and above all with Britain. It is significant that he did not forewarn Hull about his decision to employ the 'quarantine' metaphor in his Chicago speech in October 1937, which Hull believed unnecessarily aroused isolationist opinion in the US and set back his own programme to 'educate' the American public by several months.[19]

During his second term the President came to rely increasingly on Sumner Welles, the Under Secretary of State, who was appointed to succeed William Phillips in May 1937. For some time, the President had hankered after a conference to discuss the worsening international situation but, especially in view of the fate of the London Economic Conference, he favoured a much smaller meeting. The Foreign Office had got wind of this idea as early as September 1936 and Eden, although not wildly enthusiastic about it, saw it as a good sign insofar as the President clearly wanted to become more involved in international affairs. It was Welles who put Roosevelt's thoughts into practice in the form of the so-called 'Roosevelt initiative' but not before Hull had insisted that it should first be put to the British Government. Just as Chamberlain did not think very highly of Roosevelt's Quarantine speech, although he welcomed it in public, nor did he take to the conference idea in January 1938. He asked for it to be postponed, and although he reversed this request when Eden objected, the initiative never got off the ground and the disgruntled Foreign Secretary resigned soon after.[20]

Chamberlain feared that the conference initiative would cut across his bilateral diplomacy with Berlin and Rome but, as has been pointed out, he and the new Foreign Secretary, Lord Halifax, were perfectly happy to accept American involvement when it supported their appeasement policy. Hence the request for FDR to endorse the Anglo-Italian agreement in April 1938 and the quest to secure his support for the Runciman mission to Prague in July 1938 and the subsequent Munich agreement. It was not until 1939 that Chamberlain, under pressure from members of the Tory Party as well as the Opposition, began to adopt a stronger line against Germany, especially after the occupation of Prague. FDR's penchant for personal diplomacy extended to using friends like Arthur Murray to carry messengers to Chamberlain, as he did in December 1938. Arthur Willert, the former *Times* correspondent, was another frequent visitor to Washington, as was Lord Lothian – though Lothian was more of an acquaintance than a friend at this stage. Mackenzie King, the Canadian Prime Minister, and Lord

Tweedsmuir, were also important contacts. The Royal Visit to the US in June 1939 was a high point in Rooseveltian diplomacy prior to the war and was greatly aided by Mackenzie King.[21]

Economics

One reason why Chamberlain disliked the American initiative made in January 1938 was the rather convoluted arrangements that it involved, and its emphasis on broad economic issues – which Chamberlain did not believe would influence Hitler's outlook. For the same reason, he was rather dismissive of the Van Zeeland mission that eventually issued its report in January 1939 – a report that had little impact on the international situation. Chamberlain had more faith in bilateral financial and economic agreements – such as a major loan to Germany – hence the Wohltat talks in London in 1939. FDR also felt that the broad economic appeasement favoured by Van Zeeland was unlikely to have any effect on the dictators, but he favoured keeping Nazi Germany lean until such time as it accepted 'international norms'. The reason why the American initiative in January 1938 was couched in economic terms was to avoid accusations from isolationists such as Borah and Johnson that the US was dabbling in the political affairs of Europe and becoming entangled with European powers – especially Britain and France.[22]

While Chamberlain and Roosevelt both had their doubts about the efficacy of economic diplomacy, Hull remained a 'true believer' throughout his time as Secretary of State. Hull's commitment to – some might say obsession with – his trade agreements programme is well documented, not least in his own memoirs. For Hull, it constituted the basis of a 'world programme' of economic appeasement or, to use another phrase of which he was very fond, 'economic disarmament'. If the 'have not' countries like Germany, Italy and Japan that said they were denied access to raw materials and shut out of colonial markets took part in his trade agreements programme, they would share in the benefits of international trade and be able to reduce unemployment in their domestic industries by peaceful means rather than by investing in wasteful and dangerous rearmament programmes. The country with which Hull most desired economic cooperation and, above all, a trade agreement was Britain but 'Imperial Preference' was a major obstacle, although one mitigated by the efforts of Mackenzie King and Canadian officials. The Anglo-American trade agreement was not finally signed until November 1938, but it was an important milestone in Anglo-American cooperation during Roosevelt's second term.[23]

As Runciman observed during his visit to Washington, while FDR supported Hull's trade agreements policy in general terms he was by no means as interested in it as was the Secretary of State. FDR's main focus was on the deteriorating international situation, in both Europe and the Far East, and on amending the US Neutrality laws to give him more discretion to aid Britain and France against the dictator states. Economic diplomacy was a useful weapon in this respect, whether it was keeping Germany lean and imposing countervailing duties on German goods or abrogating the American trade treaty with Japan – both in 1939. As regards war debts, he informed Runciman that there was no prospect of any real progress in dealing with this issue as Congress was adamantly against a generous settlement. It was therefore better to let 'sleeping dogs lie'. Roosevelt made the same point to George VI during the Royal Visit. Indeed, although the isolationists raised the war debts issue during the debate on the Neutrality Act, it did not prevent the arms embargo from being repealed in November 1939.[24]

Finance

Financial diplomacy, as exercised by Henry Morgenthau Jr, FDR's Secretary of the Treasury, was a key element in the 'tacit alliance' with Britain. The 'Roosevelt bombshell' had ended hopes of a stabilisation of currencies in 1933 and soured relations between the US, Britain and France. Morgenthau had very little financial background and was not well regarded by the British Treasury when he was appointed but it was he who persuaded a sceptical FDR to put out feelers to London that resulted in the Tripartite Currency Agreement of September 1936. A strong critic of the policies of Nazi Germany, not least the treatment of his fellow Jews, Morgenthau regarded the agreement not only as a contribution to currency stabilisation but as a 'Tripartite Pact' between the three great democracies in defiance of German attempts to undermine French resistance to Nazi expansion. Morgenthau's view was that the Tripartite Pact was helping 'to save France from fascism'. With cooperation from Simon, as Chancellor of the Exchequer, he proceeded to defend the pact during successive financial crises in Paris that helped to maintain a degree of French financial stability until 1940.[25]

Morgenthau was anxious to build on his success in negotiating the Tripartite Currency Agreement by following up Runciman's visit to Washington with his own initiative to encourage cooperation between the Treasuries in London and Washington. To that end, he contacted Neville Chamberlain, as Chancellor of the Exchequer, via Bewley as a courier, to ascertain his views on what steps could be taken to prevent another war. Chamberlain's reply, largely drafted in the Foreign Office, was something of a disappointment as it largely focused on the problem of the US Neutrality legislation, and indirectly threw cold water on the idea of an international conference that might be summoned by the President. However, Morgenthau's initiative was useful in maintaining some momentum in financial diplomacy between London and Washington after the Tripartite Currency Agreement. The initiative also shows that it was the Roosevelt Administration that was making most of the running to cooperate with Britain in trying to avert another major conflict in Europe, rather than the other way round as might have been expected.[26]

Morgenthau was not shy of using his power as the Secretary of the Treasury or his influence as a close confident of the President to act against the dictator states. He supported loans to China in its struggle against Japan and was keen to put pressure on Nazi Germany through the device of 'countervailing duties' after the *Anschluss*. He finally had his way after the German occupation of Prague, when the ever-cautious Hull dropped his opposition to additional duties of 25 per cent on imports from Germany on the grounds that German exports to the US were heavily subsidised. The German Embassy in Washington was in no doubt that the real motive behind the duties was political. Morgenthau also played a major role in the financing of American defence production, especially of aircraft, both for the US and for France and Britain in the event of war, and when war broke out he liaised with the British Purchasing Mission in New York. The so-called Morgenthau–Purvis axis for purchasing American planes, weapons and so on greatly facilitated the large British orders placed from March 1940, and especially after the German *Blitzkrieg* in the spring of 1940 and the fall of France.[27]

National security

From the outset of his second term, it was a priority of Roosevelt and the State Department to secure the abolition, or at least the revision, of the Neutrality laws, especially the arms embargo. Whatever the merits of some aspects of the legislation, it limited the President's freedom of action at a dangerous time in international relations and was felt to give the advantage in terms of purchasing 'arms, ammunition and the implements of war' to states planning aggression. The issue had been discussed during the Runciman visit in January 1937 and was the main request put forward in Chamberlain's response – largely drawn up the Foreign Office – to the Morgenthau initiative in the following month. The Neutrality Act was revised in May 1937, with the introduction of the principle of 'cash and carry' for raw materials required for war, but Administration attempts to go further were thwarted by the isolationists in Congress, notably in July 1939. The arms embargo was finally lifted in November 1939 and was in many ways the culmination of FDR's efforts to support the democracies in their struggle against Nazi Germany.[28]

During his second term FDR also became increasingly concerned about US industrial mobilisation in the event of war. In 1937 he appointed Louis Johnson as Assistant Secretary of War – a significant post as the Secretary of War, Harry Woodring, had 'isolationist' tendencies. The two men frequently quarrelled but Johnson was praised in the Haldane report on US industrial mobilisation sent to London in February 1939. The British and French governments had both sent missions to the US to explore the possibility of importing American-made aircraft to make up for domestic shortages but found very few that were suitable for modern warfare. However, in the aftermath of the Munich crisis, FDR prioritised aircraft production and encouraged 'educational orders' from London and Paris that would develop American capacity for producing high-quality planes. As war loomed in 1939 the Riverdale mission was sent to Washington to explore the arrangements for establishing a British Purchasing Commission in the US that would be ready to take immediate advantage of the anticipated repeal of the arms embargo. When this duly occurred in November 1939, FDR and Morgenthau insisted on a joint approach by Britain and France, which led to the Anglo-French Purchasing Board in December 1939 and the Morgenthau–Purvis axis.[29]

Growing cooperation between the American and British navies was another important aspect of the Anglo-American 'tacit alliance' in 1939. Relations between the two navies had improved greatly since the dangerous rivalry of the 1920s, aided by the

London Naval Agreement of 1930 and the Second London Naval Agreement in 1936, which was primarily between the US and Britain as Japan had refused to take part. Following FDR's Quarantine speech and the *Panay* crisis, the secret talks regarding Pacific naval strategy conducted by Ingersoll in London in January 1938 were a considerable step forward towards Anglo-American cooperation and they were updated by the Hampton talks in Washington in June 1939. The Atlantic area of operations was discussed by FDR with George VI during the Royal Visit in June 1939 and resulted in the American neutrality zone established in September 1939, which generally favoured the British Navy. The issue of Caribbean bases was also discussed with George VI and followed up with Lindsay and the British Government thereafter, and this aided the negotiations that led to the Destroyer-Bases deal in September 1940.[30]

From tacit alliance to special relationship, 1939–41

The preceding chapters have shown that despite the difficulties attending the Anglo-American relationship in the 1930s – the 'doubts, hopes and fears' referred to by Reynolds and other historians – there was increasing cooperation between London and Washington over a wide range of issues during FDR's second term as President. It has also been shown that the initiative in bringing about closer Anglo-American relations in this period came very largely from the American side of the Atlantic in response to what the Roosevelt Administration perceived as the growing threat to the United States – and to the Americas as a whole – from Nazi Germany and the Axis Powers. This closer relationship was first signalled by the visit of Walter Runciman to Washington in January and gained momentum after FDR's Quarantine speech in October 1937. In February 1938 William Borah characterised the relationship as a 'tacit alliance', but it was not until after the Munich crisis, and Roosevelt's bold annual address in January 1939, followed by Chamberlain's rather reluctant adoption of similar rhetoric, especially after the occupation of Prague, that a 'tacit alliance' can be said to have come into existence – an 'unspoken alliance', as Robert Byron called it, that was symbolised by the Royal Visit in June 1939.[31]

However, the half-hearted 'Peace Front' instigated by the Chamberlain Government in the wake of the occupation of Prague, with

FDR's support, was a far cry from the 'strong and open' alliance that Churchill yearned for in the 1930s and returned to in his Fulton speech. Nevertheless, even after the demise of Poland, the 'tacit alliance' with the United States appeared sufficient at the outset of the Second World War, especially when the arms embargo was repealed in November 1939 and the Morgenthau–Purvis axis was established to smooth the system of purchasing of supplies between London and Paris and Washington. Although the Allies' defensive strategy and shortage of dollars at first curtailed large-scale purchases, the United States was recognised as potentially the 'Allies' arsenal' in a long war. The naval and military situation seemed to be reasonably satisfactory and Chamberlain gave a confident broadcast to the nation in November 1939, while writing to his sister that 'Mr Hitler has missed the bus'. In truth, Chamberlain had badly miscalculated and it was he who had missed the bus.[32]

Roosevelt had not envisaged the Allied collapse that occurred in May and June 1940, leading to an unprecedented third term as President, although he had certainly not ruled it out, as his conversation with Frank Knox in December 1939 shows. Even before the German invasion of Belgium and the Netherlands on 10 May 1940, Chamberlain had decided to resign following the much-criticised conduct of the Norway campaign, whereupon Churchill was appointed Prime Minister. Churchill was the preferred choice as Chamberlain's successor from FDR's perspective. His speeches and newspaper articles warning about the growing threat posed by Nazi Germany were much more akin to the President's own views than the one-sided appeasement policy towards Hitler pursued by Chamberlain and the British Cabinet, especially after the resignation of Eden in February 1938. Roosevelt had not joined in the strong criticism of Churchill by George VI and Mackenzie King during their discussion at Hyde Park in June 1939, during the Royal Visit, as to who might succeed Chamberlain. Indeed, the President had reached out to Churchill in September 1939, after the outbreak of war, when Chamberlain had finally brought the Tory rebel into his Cabinet and Roosevelt instigated their secret wartime correspondence.[33]

The Destroyer-Bases deal is often regarded as marking the beginning of the Anglo-American 'special relationship' and there is much to commend this view insofar as it marked the emergence of Churchill's concept of a 'special relationship' – that is, the one that he referred to in his Fulton speech in March 1946 and that he spelled out on many other occasions. This interpretation views the 'special relationship' as being, above all, an explicit display of cooperation between Britain and the US in the interests of the 'common good'. Only by being a 'strong and open' alliance could the Anglo-American partnership, supported by Canada and the rest of the Empire, act as an effective deterrent against potential aggressors such as Nazi Germany in the late 1930s and the Soviet Union after the Second World War. Notwithstanding their limitations, the Destroyer-Bases deal and the Lend Lease Act left no room for doubt that a 'special relationship' of the kind desired by Churchill had come into existence. An explicit understanding of this kind was politically impossible before the outbreak of the war but the 'tacit alliance' that developed between January 1937 and November 1939, largely thanks to Roosevelt and his Administration, laid the foundations that made it possible after the catastrophic events of May and June 1940.[34]

Notes

1. Churchill, 'The Sinews of Peace', Westminster College, Fulton, Missouri, 5 March 1946, available at <https://winstonchurchill.org/resources/speeches/1946-1963-elder-statesman/the-sinews-of-peace/>. See also Dimbleby and Reynolds, *Ocean Apart*, p. 116.
2. See his articles and speeches in Churchill, *While England Slept*, and Cannadine, *Blood, Toil, Tears and Sweat*.
3. See Chapter 1.
4. Reynolds, *Creation*, pp. 25–7, says that the US did not have a coherent foreign policy or 'policy towards Europe' in the mid-1930s or indeed until the summer of 1940. Adams, *America in Twentieth Century*, pp. 76–9, refers briefly to US 'parallel action' and see also his later but still brief account in 'The Concept of Parallel Action', pp. 113–30. But the significance of the concept for Anglo-American relations has been neglected by most recent historians. For the concept of 'parallel action' in 1937 see Chapter 4. For support for 'parallel action' with Britain by the *New York Times* see Chapter 5. For Krock's views see Chapter 6.
5. See Chapters 6, 7, 8 and 9.
6. See Chapters 10, 11, 12 and 13.
7. See Reynolds, *Creation*, Chapter 1, pp. 7–36 – 'Doubts, Hopes and Fears' (c. May 1937 to September 1938). See page 95 for summary of Part One of book, 1937–40. See also Rock, *Chamberlain and Roosevelt*.

8. Ibid.
9. Ickes, *Diary*, II, 26 August 1939, p. 700 and 1 September 1939, p. 709; Gilbert, *Churchill*. See also Stedman's chapter on alliances in *Alternatives to Appeasement*, pp. 119–60.
10. See also McCulloch, 'Mackenzie King and the North Atlantic Triangle', pp. 3–13.
11. Ibid., pp. 14–20; see also Stacey, *Canada in Age of Conflict, 2*, pp. 230–1.
12. McCulloch, 'Mackenzie King and the North Atlantic Triangle', pp. 23–9; Perras, *Origins*, pp. 65–92.
13. See, for example, DGFP/D/VIII, doc 220, Thomsen to GFM, 9 October 1939; doc 315, Thomsen to GFM, 30 October 1939.
14. See Dallek, *FDR*, p. 192; Weinberg, 'Hitler's Image of the United States', pp. 1010–13; Friedlander, *Prelude to Downfall*, pp. 15–26; Fischer, *Hitler and America*, pp. 9–45.
15. DGFP/D/VIII, doc 56, memorandum by Weizsäcker, 12 September 1939, re avoiding war with US; doc 323, footnote 1, GFM to Washington Embassy, 8 November 1939.
16. See Chapter 1.
17. McCulloch 'FDR and Democracy Promotion', pp. 69–85.
18. E.g. Chamberlain's speech of 28 January 1939, in *The Times*, 29 January 1939.
19. Hull, *Memoirs I*, p. 545.
20. See Chapter 6.
21. See especially Chapters 10 and 11.
22. See Chapter 6.
23. See Chapter 9.
24. See Chapters 3, 11 and 13.
25. See Chapters 2, 4 and 7.
26. See Chapters 3 and 4.
27. See Chapter 10.
28. See Chapters 3, 12 and 13.
29. See Chapters 10 and 13.
30. See Chapters 2, 11 and 13.
31. See Chapters 10, 11 and 12.
32. See Chapters 12 and 13.
33. See Chapter 13.
34. See Chapter 1.

Bibliography and Primary Sources

A note on sources

There is a veritable treasure trove of primary material relating to Anglo-American relations in the years 1937–39. On the American side, the most valuable primary sources are those of FDR himself and some of his key associates, such as Henry Morgenthau, the Treasury Secretary, housed at the Franklin Roosevelt library in Hyde Park, New York. Fortunately, much of the relevant material for the period 1937–40 has been included in the published volumes on FDR's foreign policy and in other key works such as the *Morgenthau Diaries*. The *Ickes Diary* is especially useful for Cabinet meetings and FDR's thinking in general. Another important resource is the *Foreign Relations of the United States* series, now on-line. It is very comprehensive but can be supplemented by the unpublished material housed at the US National Archives in Washington, DC, including the Treasury, War Department and Navy Department records. The private papers of key figures such as Cordell Hull, Norman Davis, Frank Knox and William Borah kept in the Library of Congress are also invaluable, as are those of Henry Stimson at Yale and Hiram Johnson at Berkeley, San Francisco.

On the British side, the papers of the Cabinet, the Prime Minister's Office, the Treasury and especially the Foreign Office are all extremely valuable and insightful. The Foreign Office papers are especially interesting as they include the detailed minutes by officials discussing the day-to day issues that arose in relations with the USA and other countries in the context of the deteriorating international situation between January 1937 and September 1939. These documents provide a very useful insight into British foreign policy and fully convey the 'doubts, hopes and fears' in London concerning US diplomacy. However, the disdain that the Foreign Office appeared to have for the alternative policies of friends and foes alike – not least those of the United States and France – needs to be taken into account. The *Documents on British Foreign Policy, 1919–1939* series is also very useful, although it prioritises relations with the European powers and Japan rather than the United States and it is not freely available on-line. Beyond these public records there are many private collections of papers relevant to Anglo-American relations in the late 1930s, especially the Chamberlain and Eden papers at Birmingham, the Halifax papers at York and the Runciman papers at Newcastle.

The main source used for the role of Mackenzie King, the Canadian Prime Minister during Roosevelt's second term, is the collection of his diaries and letters that are available on-line. From 1921 until 1948, Mackenzie King occupied the position of Prime Minister for all but three months (in 1926) and five years (1930–35). He was his own foreign minister and his dominance of the small department of External Affairs in Ottawa was virtually complete. The diaries are an excellent resource not only for Mackenzie King's outlook and motives but also for the detailed accounts they provide of his meetings with FDR, Hull and other US officials, especially during FDR's visit to Queen's University in August 1938, the signing of the Anglo-American and Canadian–American trade agreements in Washington in November 1938, and the Royal Visit to the US in June 1939. The Mackenzie King papers can be supplemented by the correspondence of John Buchan, Lord Tweedsmuir, the Governor General, who was a frequent discussant of the Canadian Prime Minister and on good terms with Roosevelt and Hull as well as Chamberlain and Halifax. Finally, the *Documents on Canadian External Relations* series is another useful source.

As regards the German perspective on Anglo-American relations, the main source for the present work is the excellent series *Documents on German Foreign Policy*, which includes a huge collection of documents relating to the diplomacy of the German Foreign Ministry between January 1933 and December 1941. This is a magnificent source, not just for German foreign policy during the Nazi era but for international relations in general, not least Anglo-American relations. It consists of almost twenty large volumes of correspondence, translated into English and selected from the documents captured in Berlin at the end of the war.

It is a source that is often mentioned in the bibliographies of works on Anglo-American relations in the 1930s but not so often used. In terms of English language sources, it can be supplemented by the archives of the London *Times* and especially the *New York Times*, which frequently provided reports on German press coverage of US and British foreign policy. The German ambassadors in Washington in the late 1930s, Luther and Dieckhoff, are quite well catered for in published works, in addition to key figures such as Ribbentrop, Göring and Hitler himself.

Primary sources – unpublished

Birmingham University Library, UK
Neville Chamberlain papers
Anthony Eden, Earl of Avon papers

Cambridge University Library, UK
Stanley Baldwin papers

Churchill College Archives, Cambridge, UK
Winston Churchill papers

Elshieshields Tower, near Lockerbie, UK
Walter Runciman private papers

FDR Library, Hyde Park New York, US
Adolf Berle papers
Walton Moore papers
Henry Morgenthau Jr papers
Franklin Roosevelt papers

Harvard University, Boston, US
Pierrepont Moffat papers
William Phillips papers

Library of Congress, Washington, DC, US
Robert Bingham papers
William Borah papers
Norman Davis papers
Herbert Feis papers

Cordell Hull papers
Frank Knox papers
Key Pittman papers

National Archives, Canada – Ottawa, Canada
Mackenzie King papers (diary available on-line)

National Archives of Scotland, Edinburgh, UK
John Buchan, 1st Baron Tweedsmuir
Philip Lothian, Lord Lothian papers
Arthur Murray, Lord Elibank papers

National Archives, UK – Kew, London, UK
Board of Trade papers (BT)
Cabinet papers (CAB/23, CAB/65)
Dominion Office papers (DO)
Anthony Eden papers (copies)
Foreign Office papers (FO/371, FO/800)
Prime Minister's Office (PREM/1)
Treasury (T)

National Archives, US – Washington, DC, USA
State Department paper (SD)
Treasury papers (T)
War Department files (WD)

Newcastle University, UK
Walter Runciman official papers

University of California, Berkeley, US
Hiram Johnson papers

University of Manchester Library, UK
Ramsay MacDonald papers

University of York, UK
Earl of Halifax papers

Yale University, New Haven, US
Robert Byron papers, especially Beinecke files, GEN MSS 605, Box 37, folder 593, 'Unspoken Alliance', pp. 1–36; 22 January 1939.
Henry Stimson papers

Primary sources – published

American Presidency Project (Gerhard Peters and John T. Woolley, eds)
https://www.presidency.ucsb.edu/people/president/franklin-d-roosevelt

Avalon Project, Yale Law School
<https://avalon.law.yale.edu/wwii/blbk13.asp>

Documents on British Foreign Policy, (DBFP), 1933–39
Available on-line via ProQuest as part of Documents on British Policy Overseas
<https://proquest.libguides.com/dbpo>

Documents on Canadian External Relations
Only volumes since 1946 are on-line
<https://www.international.gc.ca/gac-amc/history-histoire/external-relations_relations-exterieures.aspx?lang=eng>

Documents on German Foreign Policy (DGFP), 1933–39
Some volumes available on-line.

Foreign Relations of the United States (FRUS), 1933–39
<https://history.state.gov/historicaldocuments/roosevelt-fd>

International Churchill Society – Churchill speeches, etc.
<https://winstonchurchill.org/>

Mackenzie King Diary, 1933–39
Available on-line
<https://www.bac-lac.gc.ca/eng/discover/politics-government/prime-ministers/william-lyon-mackenzie-king/Pages/search.aspx>

New York Times, 1937–39
Available on-line

The Times (London), 1937–39
Available on-line

Washington Post, 1937–39
Available on-line

UK House of Commons debates (*Hansard*), 1937–39
Available on-line

UK House of Lords debates (*Hansard*), 1937–39
Available on-line

Secondary sources – books and book chapters

Abbazia, Patrick, *Mr Roosevelt's Navy: The Private War of the US Atlantic Fleet, 1939–1942* (Annapolis, MD: Naval Institute Press, 2016)

Adams, David, *America in the Twentieth Century* (Cambridge: Cambridge University Press, 1967)

Adams, David, *FDR, the New Deal and Europe* (Keele: Keele University Press, 1974)

Adams, David, 'The Concept of Parallel Action: FDR's Internationalism in a Decade of Isolationism', in Daniela Rossini (ed.), *From Theodore Roosevelt to FDR: Internationalism and Isolationism in American Foreign Policy* (Keele: Keele University Press, 1995), pp. 113–39.

Adams, David, *Before the Special Relationship: Colonel Wedgewood, MP, and Secretary Ickes, Fighters for Democracy* (London: Institute of United States Studies, 2002)

Adams, R. J. Q., *British Politics and Foreign Policy in the Age of Appeasement, 1935–39* (Redwood City, CA: Stanford University Press, 1993)

Adamthwaite, Anthony, *France and the Coming of the Second World War 1936–1939* (London: Frank Cass, 1977)

Adler, Selig, *The Isolationist Impulse: Its Twentieth Century Reaction* (New York: Praeger, 1974)

Allen, H. C., *Great Britain and the United States – A History of Anglo-American Relations, 1783–1952* (London: Odhams, 1954)

Avon, Earl of, *Facing the Dictators: The Memoirs of Anthony Eden, Vol. 1* (London: Cassell, 1962)

Bailey, Gavin, *The Arsenal of Democracy: Aircraft Supply and the Anglo-American Alliance, 1938–1942* (Edinburgh: Edinburgh University Press, 2013)

Bailey, Thomas, and Paul Ryan, *Hitler vs. Roosevelt: The Undeclared Naval War* (New York: Free Press, 1979)

Baylis, John (ed.), *Anglo-American Relations Since 1939: The Enduring Alliance* (Manchester: Manchester University Press, 1997)

Beard, Charles, *American Foreign Policy in the Making, 1932–1940* (New Haven, CT: Yale University Press, 1946)

Beard, Charles, *President Roosevelt and the Coming of the War 1941* (New Haven, CT: Yale University Press, 1948)

Beck, Alfred M., *Hitler's Ambivalent Attaché: Lt. Gen. Friedrich von Boetticher in America, 1933–1941* (Washington, DC: Potomac Books, 2005)

Bennett, Edward, *Separated by a Common Language: Franklin Delano Roosevelt and Anglo-American Relations, 1933–1939* (Lincoln, NE: Writers Club Press, 2002)

Berle, Beatrice, and Travis B. Jacobs (eds), *Navigating the Rapids, 1918–1971. From the Papers of Adolf A Berle* (New York: Houghton Mifflin Harcourt, 1973)
Bethell, Nicholas, *The Palestine Triangle: The Struggle Between the British, the Jews and the Arabs, 1935–48* (London: Futura, 1980)
Bloch, Michael, *Ribbentrop*, 2nd edn (London: Abacus, 2003)
Blum, John Morton, *From the Morgenthau Diaries, I: Years of Crisis, 1928–1938* (Boston: Houghton Mifflin, 1959)
Blum, John Morton, *From the Morgenthau Diaries, II: Years of Urgency, 1938–1941* (Boston: Houghton Mifflin, 1965)
Borg, Dorothy, *The United States and the Far Eastern Crisis of 1933–1938* (Cambridge, MA: Harvard University Press, 1964)
Bouverie, Tim, *Appeasing Hitler: Chamberlain, Churchill and the Road to War* (London: Bodley Head, 2019)
Bowman, Stephen, *The Pilgrims Society and Public Diplomacy, 1895–1945* (Edinburgh: Edinburgh University Press, 2018)
Brebner, John Bartlet, *North Atlantic Triangle: The Interplay of Canada, the United States and Great Britain* (New Haven, CT: Yale University Press, 1945)
Bruegel, W., *Czechoslovakia Before Munich: The German Minority Problem and British Appeasement Policy* (Cambridge: Cambridge University Press, 1973)
Breuer, William, *Hitler's Undercover War: The Nazi Espionage Invasion of the U.S.A.* (New York: St Martin's Press, 1989)
Bullitt, Orville (ed.), *For the President: Personal and Secret Correspondence Between Franklin D Roosevelt and William Bullitt* (Boston: Houghton Mifflin Harcourt, 1972)
Bullock, Alan (ed.), *The Ribbentrop Memoirs* (London: Weidenfeld and Nicolson, 1954)
Bullock, Alan, *Hitler: A Study in Tyranny* (New York: Harper and Row, 1962)
Burk, Kathleen, *Old World, New World: The Story of Britain and America* (London: Abacus, 2009)
Burk, Kathleen, 'Is There an Anglo-American Alliance? Or a Pact? Or an Agreement? Or Anything?', in Meliss Yaeger and Charles Carter (eds), *Pacts and Alliances in History* (London: I. B. Tauris, 2012), pp. 106–30
Burk, Kathleen, *Britain, America and the Sinews of War, 1914–1918* (Abingdon: Routledge, 2014)
Burk, Kathleen, *The Lion and the Eagle: The Interaction of the British and American Empires 1783–1972* (London: Bloomsbury, 2018)
Burns, James McGregor, *The Lion and the Fox, 1882–1940* (New York: Harvest, 1956)
Butler, Lucy (ed.), *Robert Byron, Letters Home* (London: John Murray, 1991)

Canedy, Susan, *America's Nazis: A Democratic Dilemma: A History of the German-American Bund* (Menlo Park, CA: Markgraf, 1990)
Cannadine, David (ed.), *Winston Churchill – Blood, Toil, Tears and Sweat: The Great Speeches* (London: Penguin, 1989)
Carew, Michael, *The Impact of the First World War on US Policymakers: American Strategic and Foreign Policy Formulation, 1938–1942* (Lanham, MD: Lexington Books, 2014)
Carr, William, *Arms, Autarky and Aggression* (London: Hodder Arnold, 1972)
Casey, Steven, *Cautious Crusade: Franklin D. Roosevelt, American Public Opinion, and the War Against Nazi Germany* (New York: Oxford University Press, 2001)
Cato, *Guilty Men* (London: Victor Gollancz, 1940)
Charmley, John, *Churchill: The End of Glory* (New York: Harcourt Brace Jovanovich, 1993)
Churchill, Winston, *The Gathering Storm* (London: Cassell, 1948)
Churchill, Winston, *A History of the English-Speaking Peoples*, 4 vols (London: Cassell, 1956–8)
Churchill, Winston, *While England Slept, Political Writings, 1936–1939* (London: Bloomsbury Press, 2015)
Clingan, C. Edmund, *The Lives of Hans Luther, 1879–1962: German Chancellor, Reichsbank President, and Hitler's Ambassador* (New York: Lexington Books, 2010)
Clymer, Kenton, *Quest for Freedom: The United States and India's Independence* (New York: Columbia University Press, 1995)
Cockett, Richard, *Twilight of Truth: Chamberlain, Appeasement and the Manipulation of the Press* (London: Palgrave Macmillan, 1989)
Cole, Wayne, *Senator Gerald P Nye and American Foreign Policy*, (Minneapolis: University of Minnesota Press, 1962)
Cole, Wayne, *Roosevelt and the Isolationists, 1932–1945* (Lincoln: University of Nebraska Press, 1983)
Compton, James, *The Swastika and the Eagle: Hitler, the United States, and the Origins of World War II* (Boston: Houghton Mifflin Harcourt, 1967)
Cowling, Maurice, *The Impact of Hitler: British Politics and British Policy, 1933–1940* (Cambridge: Cambridge University Press, 1975)
Cowman, Ian, *Dominion or Decline: Anglo-American Naval Relations in the Pacific, 1937–1941* (Oxford: Berg, 1996)
Craig, Gordon, and Felix Gilbert (eds), *The Diplomats, 1919–1939* (Princeton, NJ: Princeton University Press, 1953)
Cronin, Seán, *Washington's Irish Policy 1916–1986: Independence, Partition, Neutrality* (Dublin: Anvil Books, 1987)
Dallek, Robert, *Franklin Roosevelt and American Foreign Policy, 1932–1945* (New York: Oxford University Press, 1979 and 1995)

Danchev, Alex, *On Specialness: Essays in Anglo-American Relations* (Basingstoke: Macmillan, 1998)
Davis, Richard, *Anglo-French Relations Before the Second World War: Appeasement and Crisis* (London: Palgrave, 2001)
Dilks, David (ed.), *The Diaries of Sir Alexander Cadogan, 1938–1945* (London: Cassell, 1971)
Dimbleby, David and D. Reynolds, *An Ocean Apart: Britain and America in the 20th Century* (London: Hodder and Stoughton, 1988)
Divine, Robert, *The Illusion of Neutrality* (Chicago: University of Chicago Press, 1962)
Divine, Robert, *The Reluctant Belligerent: American Entry into World War II* (New York: John Wiley, 1965)
Dobson, Alan, *Anglo-American Relations in the Twentieth Century* (Abingdon: Routledge, 1995)
Dobson Alan, and Steve Marsh (eds), *Contemporary Anglo-American Relations: A 'Special Relationship'?* (Abingdon: Routledge, 2013)
Dobson, Alan, and Steve Marsh (eds), *Churchill and the Anglo-American Special Relationship* (Abingdon: Routledge, 2017)
Dockrill, Michael, *British Establishment Perspectives on France, 1936–40* (London: Palgrave Macmillan, 1999)
Doenecke, Justus, *Storm on the Horizon: The Challenge to American Intervention, 1939–1941* (Lanham, MD: Rowman and Littlefield, 2003)
Doenecke, Justus, and Mark Stoler, *Debating Franklin D Roosevelt's Foreign Policies, 1933–1945* (Lanham, MD: Rowman and Littlefield, 2005)
Doenecke, Justus, and John Wilz, *From Isolation to War, 1931–1941*, 4th edn (Chichester: Wiley, 2015)
Doerr, Paul, *British Foreign Policy 1919–1939* (Manchester: Manchester University Press, 1998)
Drummond, Ian, *British Economic Policy and the Empire 1919–39* (London: Routledge, 1972)
Drummond, Ian, and Norman Hillmer, *Negotiating Free Trade: The United Kingdom, The United States, Canada and the Trade Agreements of 1938* (Waterloo, ON: Wilfrid Laurier University Press, 1989)
Dumbrell, John, *A Special Relationship: Anglo-American Relations from the Cold War to Iraq*, 2nd edn (New York: Palgrave Macmillan, 2006)
Eayrs, James, *In Defence of Canada*, II: *Appeasement and Rearmament* (Toronto: University of Toronto Press, 1965)
Eldridge, Colin (ed.), *Kith and Kin: Canada, Britain and the United States from the Revolution to the Cold War* (Cardiff: University of Wales Press, 1997)
Faber, David, *Munich, 1938: Appeasement and World War II* (New York: Simon and Schuster, 2010)

Farnham, Barbara, *Roosevelt and the Munich Crisis: A Study of Political Decision-Making* (Princeton, NJ: Princeton University Press, 1997)
Feiling, Keith, *The Life of Neville Chamberlain* (London: Macmillan, 1946)
Fischer, Klaus, *Hitler and America* (Philadelphia: University of Pennsylvania Press, 2011)
Florence, Gregory, *Courting a Reluctant Ally: An Evaluation of US–UK Naval Intelligence Cooperation, 1935–1941* (Washington, DC: Joint Military Intelligence College, 2004)
Freidel, Frank, *Roosevelt: Launching the New Deal* (New York: Little, Brown, 1990).
Friedlander, Saul, *Prelude to Downfall: Hitler and the United States, 1939–1941* (London: Chatto and Windus, 1967)
Fuchser, L. W., *Neville Chamberlain and Appeasement: A Study in the Politics of History* (New York: Norton, 1982)
Fullilove, Michael, *Rendezvous with Destiny: How Franklin D. Roosevelt and Five Extraordinary Men Took America into the War and into the World* (London and New York: Penguin, 2013)
Gardner, Lloyd, *Economic Aspects of New Deal Diplomacy* (Madison: University of Wisconsin, 1964)
Gellman, Irwin, *Secret Affairs: Franklin Roosevelt, Cordell Hull, and Sumner Welles* (Baltimore: Johns Hopkins University Press, 1995)
Gilbert, Martin, *The Appeasers* (London: Weidenfeld and Nicolson, 1963)
Gilbert, Martin, *Churchill* (New York: Doubleday, 1980)
Gilbert, Martin, *Churchill and America* (London: Simon and Schuster, 2005)
Gordon, Michael, *Conflict and Consensus in Labour's Foreign Policy, 1914–1965* (Stanford, CA: Stanford University Press, 1969)
Gould, Harold, and Sumit Ganguly, *The Hope and the Reality: US–Indian Relations from Roosevelt to Reagan* (Abingdon: Routledge, 2019)
Graebner, Norman, *Roosevelt and the Search for a European Policy, 1937–1939* (Oxford: Oxford University Press, 1980)
Green, Jeremy, *The Political Economy of the Special Relationship* (Princeton, NJ: Princeton University Press, 2020)
Haglund, David, *Latin America and the Transformation of Strategic Thought, 1936–1940* (Albuquerque: University of New Mexico Press, 1984)
Haglund, David, *The North Atlantic Triangle Revisited: Canadian Grand Strategy at Century's End* (Toronto: Irwin, 2000)
Haglund, David, 'Is there a "Strategic Culture" of the Special Relationship? Contingency, Identity and the Transformation of Anglo-American Relations', in Alan Dobson and Steve Marsh (eds), *Anglo-American Relations: Contemporary Perspectives* (Abingdon: Routledge, 2013), pp. 26–51

Haglund, David, '"Strategic Culture" on the Road to (and from) Fulton: Institutionalism, Emotionalism, and the Anglo-American Special Relationship', in Alan Dobson and Steve Marsh (eds), *Churchill and the Anglo-American Special Relationship* (Abingdon: Routledge, 2017), pp. 19–42

Haight, John McVickar, *American Aid to France, 1938–1940* (New York: Atheneum, 1970)

Hall, H. Duncan, *History of the Second War: North American Supply* (London: HMSO, 1955)

Handby, Alonzo, *For the Survival of America: Franklin Roosevelt and the World Crisis of the 1930s* (New York: Free Press, 2004)

Harris, Brice, *The United States and the Italo-Ethiopian Crisis* (Stanford, CA: Stanford University Press, 1964)

Harris, Max, *Monetary War and Peace: London, Washington, Paris, and the Tripartite Agreement of 1936* (Cambridge: Cambridge University Press, 2021)

Harrison, Richard, 'The United States and Great Britain: Presidential Diplomacy and Alternatives to Appeasement in the 1930s', in David F. Schmitz and Richard D. Challener (eds), *Appeasement in Europe: A Reassessment of U.S. Policies* (New York: Greenwood Press, 1990)

Hart, Bradley, *Hitler's American Friends: The Third Reich's Supporters in the United States* (New York: Thomas Dunne, 2018)

Harvey, John (ed.), *The Diplomatic Diaries of Oliver Hardy, 1937–1940* (London: Harper Collins, 1970)

Hearden, Patrick, *Roosevelt Confronts Hitler* (Dekalb: Northern Illinois University Press, 1987)

Heinrichs, Waldo, *The Threshold of War: Franklin Roosevelt and American Entry into World War II* (New York: Oxford University Press, 1988)

Herman, John, *The Paris Embassy of Sir Eric Phipps* (Eastbourne: Sussex Academic Press, 1998)

Herwig, Holger H., *Politics of Frustration: The United States in German Naval Planning, 1889–1941* (New York: Little, Brown, 1976)

Herzstein, Robert, *Roosevelt and Hitler: Prelude to War* (New York: Paragon House, 1989)

Hildebrand, Klaus, *The Foreign Policy of the Third Reich* (Berkeley: University of California Press, 1970)

Hoenicke-Moore, Michaela, *'Know Your Enemy': The American Response to Nazism, 1933–1945* (New York: Cambridge University Press, 2010)

Holmes, Alison, and J. Simon Rofe, *The Embassy in Grosvenor Square: American Ambassadors to the United Kingdom* (New York: Palgrave Macmillan, 2012)

Hooker, Nancy (ed.), *The Moffat Papers: Selections from the Diplomatic Journals of Jay Pierrepont Moffat* (Cambridge, MA: Harvard University Press, 1956)

Howard, Michael, *The Continental Commitment: The Dilemma of British Defence Policy in the Era of the Two World Wars* (London: Penguin, 1974)
Hull, Cordell, *The Memoirs of Cordell Hull, I and II* (London: Hodder and Stoughton, 1948)
Ickes, Harold L., *The Secret Diary of Harold L Ickes*, II, *The Inside Struggle, 1936–1939* (New York: Simon and Schuster, 1954)
Ickes, Harold L., *The Secret Diary of Harold L Ickes*, III, *The Lowering Clouds, 1939–1941* (New York: Simon and Schuster, 1954)
Jeans, Roger, *American Isolationists: Pro-Japan Anti-Interventionists and the FBI on the Eve of the Pacific War* (London: Rowman and Littlefield, 2020)
Johnsen, William, *The Origins of the Grand Alliance: American Military Collaboration from the Panay Incident to Pearl Harbor* (Lexington: University of Kentucky Press, 2016)
Johnstone, Andrew, *Against Immediate Evil: American Internationalists and the Four Freedoms on the Eve of World War II* (Ithaca, NY: Cornell University Press, 2014)
Johnstone, Andrew, *Dilemmas of Internationalism: The American Association for the United Nations and US Foreign Policy, 1941–1948* (Abingdon: Routledge, 2016)
Jonas, Manfred, *Isolationism in America, 1935–1941* (Ithaca, NY: Cornell University Press, 1966)
Jonas, Manfred, *The United States and Germany: A Diplomatic History* (Ithaca, NY: Cornell University Press, 1985)
Jones, Thomas, *A Diary with Letters, 1931–1950* (Oxford: Oxford University Press, 1969)
Kennedy, David, *Freedom From Fear: The American People in Depression and War, 1929–45* (New York: Oxford University Press, 1999)
Kennedy, Greg, *Anglo-American Strategic Relations and the Far East, 1933–1939* (London: Frank Cass, 2002)
Kershaw, Ian, *Fateful Choices: Ten Decisions that Changed the World, 1940–41* (London: Penguin, 2008)
Kimball, Warren, *The Most Unsordid Act: Lend-Lease, 1939–1941* (Baltimore: Johns Hopkins University Press, 1969)
Kindleberger, Charles, *The World in Depression 1929–1939*, 2nd edn (London: California University Press, 1986)
Knox, James, *A Biography of Robert Byron* (London: John Murray, 2003)
Kottman, Richard, *Reciprocity and the North Atlantic Triangle, 1932–1938* (Ithaca, NY: Cornell University Press, 1968)
Kreider, Carl, *The Anglo-American Trade Agreement: A Study of British and American Commercial Policies, 1934–1939* (Princeton, NJ: Princeton University Press, 1943)

Krock, Arthur, *In the Nation 1932–1966* (New York: New York Times, 1966)

Krock, Arthur, *Memoirs: Sixty Years on the Firing Line* (New York: Popular Library, 1968)

Langer, William, and Everett Gleason, *The Challenge to Isolation, 1937–1940* (New York: Harper and Brothers, 1952)

Leigh, Michael, *Mobilising Consent: Public Opinion and American Foreign Policy, 1937–1947* (Westport, CT: Praeger, 1976)

Leuchtenburg, William, *Franklin D Roosevelt and the New Deal, 1932–1940* (New York: Harper Perennial, 1963)

Leutze, James, *Bargaining for Supremacy: Anglo-American Naval Collaboration, 1937–1941* (Chapel Hill: University of North Carolina Press, 1977)

Liebich, Andre, *Wickham Steed: Greatest Journalist of his Times* (Bern: Peter Lang, 2018)

Lowenheim, Francis, Harold Langley and Manfred Jonas, *Roosevelt and Churchill: Their Secret Wartime Correspondence* (New York: Dutton, 1974)

Lowenthal, Mark, *Leadership and Indecision: American War Planning and Policy Process, 1937–1942*, 2 vols (New York: Garland, 1988)

Lower, Richard, *A Bloc of One: Political Career of Hiram W Johnson* (Stanford, CA: Stanford University Press, 1993)

McCann, Frank, *The Brazilian–American Alliance, 1937–45* (Princeton, NJ: Princeton University Press, 1974)

McCulloch, Tony (ed.), *The Correspondence of Arthur Murray, 3rd Viscount Elibank, 1879–1962* (London: Microform, 2008)

McCulloch, Tony, 'Franklin Roosevelt and Democracy Promotion', in Michael Cox, Timothy Lynch and Nicolas Bouchet (eds), *US Foreign Policy and Democracy Promotion: From Theodore Roosevelt to Barack Obama* (London: Routledge, 2013), pp. 69–85

McCulloch, Tony, 'Churchill's Ambassadors – From Fulton to Suez', in Alan Dobson and Steve Marsh (eds), *Churchill and the Anglo-American Special Relationship* (London: Routledge, 2017), pp. 142–70

MacDonald, C. A., *The United States, Britain and Appeasement, 1936–1939* (London: Macmillan, 1981)

MacDonnell, Tom, *Daylight Upon Magic: The Royal Tour of Canada, 1939* (Toronto: Macmillan, 1989)

McFarlane, Keith, and David Roll, *Louis Johnson and the Arming of America: The Roosevelt and Truman Years* (Bloomington and Indianapolis: Indiana University Press, 2005)

McKenna, Marian, *Borah* (Ann Arbor: University of Michigan Press, 1961)

McKercher, B. J. C., *Transition of Power: Britain's Loss of Global Preeminence to the United States, 1930–1945* (Cambridge: Cambridge University Press, 1999; paperback, 2006)

McKercher, B. J. C., and Lawrence Aronson (eds), *The North Atlantic Triangle in a Changing World: Anglo-Canadian–American Relations 1902–1956* (Toronto: University of Toronto Press, 1996)

MacLaren, Roy, *Mackenzie King in the Age of the Dictators: Canada's Imperial and Foreign Policies* (Montreal and Kingston: McGill-Queen's University Press, 2019)

Maddox, Robert, *William E Borah and American Foreign Policy* (Baton Rouge: Louisiana State University Press, 1969)

Marks, Frederick, *Wind Over Sand: The Diplomacy of Franklin Roosevelt* (Athens: University of Georgia Press, 1990)

Medlicott, W. N., *The Economic Blockade, Vols I and II* (London: HMSO, 1952)

Medlicott, W. N., *Britain and Germany: The Search for Agreement 1930–1937* (London: Athlone Press, 1969)

Middlemas, Keith, *The Strategy of Appeasement: The British Government and Germany 1937–39* (Chicago: Quadrangle Books, 1972)

Morgan, Iwan, *Franklin Roosevelt: Transformational President in Depression and War* (London: Tauris, 2021)

Mosley, Leonard, *On Borrowed Time: How World War II Began* (London: Macmillan, 1971)

Mowat, Charles Loch, *Britain Between the Wars* (London: Methuen, 2012)

Murfett, Malcolm, *Fool-proof Relations: The Search for Anglo-American Naval Cooperation During the Chamberlain Years, 1937–1940* (Singapore: Singapore University Press, 1984)

Namier, Sir Lewis, *Diplomatic Prelude, 1938–1939* (London: Macmillan, 1948)

Neustadt, Richard, *Alliance Politics* (New York: Columbia University Press, 1970)

Newson, Scott, *Profits of Peace: The Political Economy of Anglo-German Appeasement* (Oxford: Clarendon Press, 1996)

Nicholas, Herbert, *Britain and the USA* (Baltimore: Johns Hopkins University Press, 1963)

Nicholas, Herbert, *United States and Britain* (Chicago: University of Chicago Press, 1975)

Nixon, Edgar D. (ed.), *Franklin D Roosevelt and Foreign Affairs*, 3 vols, 1933–7 (Cambridge: MA: Harvard University Press, 1969)

O'Brien, Phillips, *The Second Most Powerful Man in the World: The Life of Admiral William D. Leahy, Roosevelt's Chief of Staff* (New York: Penguin, 2019)

Offner, Arnold, *American Appeasement: United States Foreign Policy and Germany, 1933–1938* (New York: Norton, 1968)

Offner, Arnold, *The Origins of the Second World War: American Foreign Policy and World Politics, 1917–1941* (New York: Praeger, 1975)

Orr, Peter, *Peace at Daggers Drawn* (New York: Publish America, 2005)

Ovendale, Ritchie, *'Appeasement' and the English-Speaking World: Britain, the United States, the Dominions, and the Policy of 'Appeasement', 1937–1939* (Cardiff: University of Wales Press, 1975)
Ovendale, Ritchie, 'Canada, Britain, the United States and the Policy of "Appeasement"', in Colin Eldridge (ed.), *Kith and Kin: Canada, Britain and the United States from the Revolution to the Cold War* (Cardiff: University of Wales Press, 1997), pp. 177–203.
Ovendale, Ritchie, *Anglo-American Relations in the Twentieth Century* (London: Palgrave Macmillan, 1998)
Overy, Richard, *The Air War, 1939–1945* (Washington, DC: Potomac Books, 1980)
Overy, Richard, *1939: Countdown to War* (London: Penguin, 2009)
Overy, Richard, and Adrian Wheatcroft, *The Road to War: The Origins of the Second World War* (London: Vintage, 2009)
Parker, R. A. C., *Chamberlain and Appeasement: British Policy and the Coming of the Second World War* (London: Palgrave Macmillan, 1993)
Parker, R. A. C., *Churchill and Appeasement* (London: Macmillan, 2000)
Perras, Galen, *Franklin Roosevelt and the Origins of the Canadian–American Security Alliance, 1933–45: Necessary, But Not Necessary Enough* (Westport, CT: Praeger, 1998)
Phillips, Adrian, *Fighting Churchill, Appeasing Hitler: Neville Chamberlain, Sir Horace Wilson, and Britain's Plight of Appeasement, 1937–1939* (London: Biteback, 2019)
Pratt, Lawrence, *East of Malta, West of Suez: Britain's Mediterranean Crisis, 1936–1939* (Cambridge: Cambridge University Press, 1975)
Preston, Paul, *The Spanish Civil War: Reaction, Revolution and Revenge* (London: Collins, 2016)
Price, Christopher, *Britain, America and Rearmament in the 1930s: The Cost of Failure* (London: Palgrave Macmillan, 2001)
Rauch, Basil, *Roosevelt: From Munich to Pearl Harbor. A Study in the Reaction of a Foreign Policy* (New York: Creative Age Press, 1950).
Reardon, Terry, *Winston Churchill and Mackenzie King* (Toronto: Dundurn, 2012)
Reynolds, David, *The Creation of the Anglo-American Alliance, 1937–1941: A Study in Competitive Cooperation* (London: Europa, 1981)
Reynolds, David, *From Munich to Pearl Harbor: Roosevelt's America and the Origins of the Second World War* (Chicago: Ivan Dee, 2002)
Reynolds, David, *In Command of History: Churchill Fighting and Writing the Second World War*, 2nd edn (London: Penguin, 2005)
Rich, Norman, *Hitler's War Aims: The Establishment of the New Order*, 2 vols (New York: Norton, 1973–4)
Roberts, Andrew, *The Holy Fox: The Life of Lord Halifax* (London: Weidenfeld and Nicolson, 1991)
Rock, William, *Chamberlain and Roosevelt: British Foreign Policy and the United States, 1937–1940* (Columbus: Ohio State University Press, 1988)

Rofe, J. Simon, *Franklin Roosevelt's Foreign Policy and the Welles Mission* (New York: Palgrave Macmillan, 2007; paperback, 2015)
Rofe, J. Simon, 'Lord Lothian', in Priscilla Roberts (ed.), *Lord Lothian and Anglo-American Relations, 1900–1940* (Dordrecht: Republic of Letters, 2010), pp. 133–66.
Roosevelt, Elliott (ed.), *The Roosevelt Letters*, Vol. 3, 1928–1945 (London: Harrap, 1952)
Rosenman, Samuel, *The Public Papers and Addresses of Franklin D Roosevelt, 1933–1945* (New York: Harper, 1950)
Roskill, Stephen, *Hankey: Man of Secrets, 1931–1963* (London: Harper Collins, 1974)
Roskill, Stephen, *Naval Policy Between the Wars: The Period of Reluctant Rearmament, 1930–1939* (London: Harper Collins, 1976)
Rowland, Benjamin, *Commercial Conflict and Foreign Policy: A Study in Anglo-American Relations 1932–1938* (New York: Taylor and Francis, 1987)
Rowse, A. L., *All Souls and Appeasement* (London: Macmillan, 1961)
Schewe, Donald (ed.), *Franklin D Roosevelt and Foreign Affairs,* January 1937–August 1939, 10 vols (New York and London: Garland, 1979)
Schmitz, David, *The Triumph of Internationalism: Franklin D. Roosevelt and a World in Crisis, 1933–1941* (Washington, DC: Potomac Books, 2007)
Schmitz, David, *The Sailor: Franklin D. Roosevelt and the Transformation of American Foreign Policy* (Lexington: University Press of Kentucky, 2021)
Schorske, Carl, 'Two German Ambassadors: Dirksen and Schulenburg', in Gordon Craig and Felix Gilbert (eds), *The Diplomats 1919–1939* (Princeton, NJ: Princeton University Press, 1953), pp. 477–511
Self, Robert, *Neville Chamberlain: A Biography* (London: Routledge, 2016)
Self, Robert, *Britain, America and the War Debt Controversy: The Economic Diplomacy of an Unspecial Relationship, 1917–1941* (London: Routledge, 2006; paperback, 2012)
Shen, Peijian, *The Age of Appeasement: The Evolution of British Foreign Policy in the 1930s* (Stroud: Sutton, 1999)
Shepherd, John, *George Lansbury: At the Heart of Old Labour* (Oxford: Oxford University Press, 2002)
Sherwood, Robert, *Roosevelt and Hopkins: An Intimate History* (New York: Harper, 1948)
Shogun, Robert, *Hard Bargain* (New York: Scribner, 1995)
Soybel, Phyllis, *A Necessary Relationship: The Development of Anglo-American Cooperation in Naval Intelligence* (Westport, CT: Praeger, 2005)
Stacey, C. P., *Canada and the Age of Conflict, Volume 2: 1921–1948. The Mackenzie King Era* (Toronto: University of Toronto Press, 1981)
State Department, *Peace and War: United States Foreign Policy, 1931–1941* (Washington, DC: State Department, 1943)

Stedman, Andrew David, *Alternatives to Appeasement: Neville Chamberlain and Hitler's Germany* (London: I. B. Tauris, 2015)
Steiner, Zara, *The Triumph of the Dark: European International History, 1933–1939* (Oxford: Oxford University Press, 2011)
Tansill, Charles, *Back Door to War: The Roosevelt Foreign Policy, 1933–1941* (Chicago: Regnery, 1952)
Taylor, A. J. P., *The Origins of the Second World War* (London: Penguin, 1964)
Teigrob, Robert, *Four Days in Hitler's Germany: Mackenzie King's Mission to Avert a Second World War* (Toronto: University of Toronto Press, 2019)
Templewood, Viscount, *Nine Troubled Years* (London: Greenwood Press, 1976)
Thomas, Hugh, *The Spanish Civil War* (London, Penguin, 2003)
Thompson, Neville, *The Third Man: Churchill and Roosevelt as Revealed by Their Ally and Confidant, Mackenzie King* (Toronto: Sutherland House, 2020)
Thorne, Christopher, *The Approach of War, 1938–39* (London: Macmillan, 1967)
Thorne, Christopher, *Allies of a Kind: The United States, Britain and the War Against Japan, 1941–45* (Oxford: Oxford University Press, 1979)
Tierney, Dominic, *FDR and the Spanish Civil War* (Durham, NC: Duke University Press: 2007)
Tooze, Adam, *The Wages of Destruction: The Making and Breaking of the Nazi Economy* (New York: Penguin, 2007)
Toynbee, Arnold (ed.), *Survey of International Affairs, 1937*, Vol. One (London: Oxford University Press, 1938)
Traina, Richard, *American Diplomacy and the Spanish Civil War* (Westport, CT: Greenwood Press, 1968)
Trefousse, Hans Louis (ed.), *Germany and American Neutrality, 1939–1941* (New York: Octagon Books, 1969)
Trommler, Frank, and Elliott Shore (eds), *The German–American Encounter: Conflict and Cooperation Between Two Cultures, 1800–2000* (Berlin: Berghahn, 2001)
Turner, Barry, *Waiting For War: Britain 1939–1940* (London: Icon Books, 2019)
Vysny, Paul, *The Runciman Mission to Czechoslovakia, 1938: Prelude to Munich* (London: Palgrave Macmillan, 2003)
Wapshott, Nicholas, *The Sphinx: Franklin Roosevelt, the Isolationists, and the Road to World War II* (New York: Norton, 2015)
Watt, D. C., *Personalities and Policies* (Hoboken, NJ: Prentice Hall, 1965)
Watt, D. C., *Succeeding John Bull: America in Britain's Place, 1900–1975* (Cambridge: Cambridge University Press, 1984)
Watt, D. C., *How War Came: The Immediate Origins of the Second World War, 1938–39* (London: William Heinemann, 1989)

Weinberg, Gerhard, *The Foreign Policy of Hitler's Germany, I, Diplomatic Revolution in Europe, 1933–36* (Chicago: University of Chicago Press, 1970)
Weinberg, Gerhard, *The Foreign Policy of Hitler's Germany, II, Starting World War II, 1937–39* (Chicago: University of Chicago Press, 1981)
Weinberg, Gerhard, *Germany, Hitler, and World War II* (Cambridge: Cambridge University Press, 1995)
Wheeler-Bennett, John, *The Nemesis of Power: The German Army in Politics, 1918–1945* (London: Macmillan, 1964)
Wheeler-Bennett, John, *Munich: Prologue to Tragedy* (London: Macmillan, 1948)
Willert, Sir Arthur, *The Road to Safety: A Study in Anglo-American Relations* (London: Derek Verschoyle, 1952)
Williams, William Appleman, *The Tragedy of American Diplomacy*, 50th anniversary edn (New York: Norton, 2012)
Wiskemann, Elizabeth, *The Rome–Berlin Axis* (London: Collins, 1966)

Secondary sources – articles

Adamthwaite, A., 'The British Government and the Media, 1937–38', *Journal of Contemporary History*, 18 (1983), pp. 281–93
Allen, H. C., 'A Special Relationship', *Journal of American Studies*, 19 (December 1985), pp. 403–13 (a review essay of Watt, *Succeeding John Bull*)
Aster, Sidney, 'Appeasement: Before and After Revisionism', *Diplomacy and Statecraft*, 19:3 (2008), pp. 443–80
Baptiste, F. A., 'The British Grant of Air and Naval Facilities to the United States in Trinidad, St Lucia and Bermuda in 1939', *Caribbean Studies*, 16:2 (July 1976), pp. 5–43
Bell, Peter, 'The Foreign Office and the 1939 Royal Visit to America: Courting the USA in an Era of Isolationism', *Journal of Contemporary History*, 37:4 (2002), pp. 599–616
Bennett, Gillian, 'The Roosevelt Peace Plan of January 1938', *FCO Historical Branch, Occasional Papers, I*, FCO (November 1987), pp. 27–38
Borg, Dorothy, 'Notes on Roosevelt's "Quarantine Speech"', *Political Science Quarterly*, 72 (September 1957), pp. 405–33
Cantelon, Philip, 'Greetin's Cousin George', *American Heritage* (December 1967), pp. 6–11 and 108–11
Cole, Wayne, 'American Entry into World War II: A Historiographical Appraisal', *Mississippi Valley Historical Review*, XLVII (March 1957), pp. 595–617
Cole, Wayne, 'Senator Key Pittman and American Neutrality Policies, 1933–1940', *Mississippi Valley Historical Review*, XLVI (March 1960), pp. 644–62

Dobson, Alan, 'The Evolving Study of Anglo-American Relations: The Last 50 Years', *Journal of Transatlantic Studies*, 18:4 (December 2020), pp. 415–33

Doenecke, Justus, 'Non-Interventionism of the Left: The Keep America Out of the War Congress, 1938–41', *Journal of Contemporary History*, 12:2 (April 1977), pp. 221–36

Frank, Willard C., Jr, 'The Spanish Civil War and the Coming of the Second World War', *The International History Review*, 9:3 (August 1987), pp. 368–409

Haglund, David, 'Brebner's North Atlantic Triangle at Sixty: A Retrospective Look at a Retrospective Book', *London Journal of Canadian Studies*, 20 (2004–5), pp. 117–40

Haight, John, Jr, 'Roosevelt and the Aftermath of the Quarantine Speech', *Review of Politics*, 24 (April 1962), pp. 233–59

Harrison, Richard, 'A Presidential "Demarche": Franklin D Roosevelt's Personal Diplomacy and Great Britain, 1936–37', *Diplomatic History*, 5:3 (Summer 1981), pp. 245–72

Harrison, Richard, 'The Runciman Visit to Washington DC in January 1937', *The Canadian Journal of History*, 19 (August 1984), pp. 217–39

Harrison, Richard, 'A Neutralization Plan for the Pacific: Roosevelt and Anglo-American Cooperation, 1934–1937', *Pacific Historical Review*, 57:1 (February 1988), pp. 47–72

Hauner, Milan, 'Did Hitler Want a World Dominion?', *Journal of Contemporary History*, 13:1 (January 1978), pp. 15–32

Johnson, Gaynor, 'Sir Eric Phipps, the British Government, and the Appeasement of Germany, 1933–1937', *Diplomacy and Statecraft*, 16:4 (2005), pp. 651–69

Johnson, Paul, 'The Myth of American Isolationism – Reinterpreting the Past', *Foreign Affairs* (May/June 1995), pp. 159–64

Johnstone, Andrew, 'Isolationism and Internationalism in American Foreign Relations', *Journal of Transatlantic Relations*, 9:1 (March 2011), pp. 7–20

Kennedy, Greg, 'Neville Chamberlain and Strategic Relations with the US During his Chancellorship', *Diplomacy and Statecraft*, 13:1 (March 2002), pp. 95–120

Kimball, Warren F., 'Dieckhoff and America: A German's View of German–American Relations, 1937–1941', *Historian*, 27 (February 1965), pp. 230–2

Leutze, James, 'The Secret of the Churchill–Roosevelt Correspondence: September 1939–May 1940', *Journal of Contemporary History*, 10 (1975), pp. 465–91

Lowenthal, Mark, 'Roosevelt and the Coming of the War: The Search for United States Policy, 1937–1942', *Journal of Contemporary History*, 16 (1981), pp. 413–44

McCulloch, Tony, 'Franklin Roosevelt and the Runciman Mission to Czechoslovakia, 1938: A New Perspective on Anglo-American Relations in the Era of Appeasement', *Journal of Transatlantic Studies*, 1:2 (Autumn 2003), pp. 152–74

McCulloch, Tony, '"The Key Log in the Jam": Mackenzie King, the North Atlantic Triangle and the Anglo-American Rapprochement of 1935–39', *London Journal of Canadian Studies*, 20 (October 2005), pp. 45–68

McCulloch, Tony, 'Franklin Roosevelt and the Runciman Visit to Washington, 1937: Informal Diplomacy and Anglo-American Relations in the Era of Munich', *Journal of Transatlantic Studies*, 5:2 (Autumn 2006), pp. 211–40

McCulloch, Tony, 'American Isolationism in the 1930s', *Twentieth Century History Review*, 19:3 (January 2007), pp. 1–5

McCulloch, Tony, 'Roosevelt, Mackenzie King and the Royal Visit to the USA in 1939', *London Journal of Canadian Studies*, 23 (October 2008), pp. 81–104

McCulloch, Tony, 'Franklin Roosevelt as Founding Father of the Transatlantic Alliance: The Roosevelt Doctrine of January 1936', *Journal of Transatlantic Studies*, 8:3 (Autumn 2010), pp. 224–35

McCulloch, Tony, 'The North Atlantic Triangle: A Canadian Myth?', *International Journal*, 65:2 (Winter 2011), pp. 197–207

McCulloch, Tony, 'Mackenzie King and the North Atlantic Triangle in the Era of Munich, 1937–39', *London Journal of Canadian Studies*, 36 (Autumn 2021), pp. 3–29.

MacDonald, Callum, 'Britain, France and the April Crisis of 1939', *European Studies Review*, 2 (April 1972), pp. 151–69

MacDonald, Callum, 'Economic Appeasement and the German "Moderates": An Introductory Essay', *Past and Present*, 56 (August 1972), pp. 105–35

Mackenzie, Hector, 'Arsenal of the British Empire'? British Orders for Munitions Production in Canada, 1936–1939', *Journal of Imperial and Commonwealth History*, 31:3 (September 2003), pp. 46–73

Mackenzie, Hector, 'The North Atlantic Triangle and the North Atlantic Treaty: A Canadian Perspective on the ABC Security Conversations of March–April 1949', *London Journal of Canadian Studies*, 20 (2004–5), pp. 89–110

Marks, Frederick W., III, 'Six between Roosevelt and Hitler: America's Role in the Appeasement of Nazi Germany', *Historical Journal*, 28:4 (December 1985), pp. 969–82

Murray, Arthur, Lord Elibank, 'Franklin Roosevelt: Friend of Britain', *Contemporary Review*, (June 1955), pp. 362–8

Neilson, Keith, 'The Defence Requirements Sub-Committee, British Strategic Foreign Policy, Neville Chamberlain and the Path to Appeasement', *English Historical Review*, 118:477 (June 2003), pp. 651–84

Peden, G. C., 'Sir Horace Wilson and Appeasement', *Historical Journal*, 53:4 (December 2010), pp. 983–1014

Pratt, Lawrence, 'The Anglo-American Naval Conversations on the Far East of January 1938', *International Affairs*, 47:4 (1971), pp. 754–63

Remak, Joachim, 'Friends of the New Germany: The Bund and German–American Relations', *Journal of Modern History*, 29 (March 1957), pp. 38–41

Reynolds, David, 'FDR's Foreign Policy and the British Royal Visit to the USA, 1939', *The Historian*, 45 (1983), pp. 461–72

Reynolds, David, 'Lord Lothian and Anglo-American Relations, 1939–1940', *Transactions of the American Philosophical Society*, 73:Part 2 (1983), pp. 1–65

Reynolds, David, 'Rethinking Anglo-American Relations', *International Affairs*, 65:1 (Winter 1988/9), pp. 89–111

Reynolds, David, '1940: Fulcrum of the Twentieth Century?', *International Affairs*, 66:2 (April 1990), pp. 325–50

Rhodes, Benjamin, 'The British Royal Visit of 1939 and the "Psychological Approach" to the United States', *Diplomatic History*, 2 (1978), pp. 197–211

Rofe, J. Simon, 'Isolationism and Internationalism in Transatlantic Affairs', *Journal of Transatlantic Studies*, Vol 9:1 (March 2011), Introduction, pp. 1–6

Rofe, J. Simon, and John Thompson, '"Internationalists in Isolationist Times" – Theodore and Franklin Roosevelt and a Rooseveltian Maxim', *Journal of Transatlantic Studies*, 9:1 (March 2011), Introduction, pp. 46–62

Schatz, Arthur, 'The Anglo-American Trade Agreement and Cordell Hull's Search for Peace 1936–1938', *Journal of American History*, LVII (June 1970), pp. 85–103

Schwoerer, Lois, 'Lord Halifax's Visit to Germany: November 1937', *The Historian,* 32:3 (May 1970), pp. 353–75

Self, Robert, 'Perception and Posture in Anglo-American Relations: The War Debt Controversy in the "Official Mind", 1919–1940', *International History Review*, 29:2 (June 2007), pp. 282–312

Shai, Aron, 'Was There a Far Eastern Munich?', *Journal of Contemporary History*, 9:3 (July 1974), pp. 161–9

Smith, Kevin, 'Reassessing Roosevelt's View of Chamberlain after Munich: Ideological Affinity in the Geoffrey Thompson–Claude Bowers Correspondence', *Diplomatic History*, 33:5 (November 2009), pp. 839–64

Stewart, Gordon, 'What North Atlantic Triangle?', *London Journal of Canadian Studies,* 20 (2004–5), pp. 5–22

Trotter, Ann, 'The Dominions and Imperial Defence: Hankey's Tour in 1934', *Journal of Imperial and Commonwealth History*, 11 (May 1974), pp. 318–32

Watt, D. C., 'American "Isolationism" in the 1920s: Is It a Useful Concept?', *Bulletin (British Association for American Studies)*, New Series, 6 (June 1963), pp. 3–19

Watt, D. C., 'American Strategic Interests and Anxieties in the West Indies: An Historical Examination', *The Royal United Services Institute Journal*, 108 (August 1963), pp. 224–32

Watt, D. C., 'Appeasement: The Rise of a Revisionist School?,' *Political Quarterly*, XXXVI:2 (1965), pp. 191–213

Watt, D. C., 'Roosevelt and Neville Chamberlain: Two Appeasers', *International Journal*, 28:2 (Spring 1973), pp. 185–204

Watt, D. C., 'Hitler's Visit to Rome and the May Weekend Crisis: A Study in Hitler's Response to External Stimuli', *Journal of Contemporary History*, 9:1 (January 1974), pp. 23–32

Watt, D. C., 'Some Aspects of A. J. P. Taylor's Work as Diplomatic Historian', *The Journal of Modern History*, 49:1 (March 1977), pp. 19–33

Weinberg, Gerhard L., 'Hitler's Image of the United States', *American Historical Review*, 69 (July 1964), pp. 1006–21

Weinberg, Gerhard, William Rock and Anna Cienciala, 'Essay and Reflection: The Munich Crisis Revisited', *The International History Review*, 11:4 (November 1989), pp. 668–88

Witham, Charlie, 'Seeing the Wood for the Trees: The British Foreign Office and the Anglo-American Trade Agreement of 1938', *Twentieth Century British History*, 16:1 (March 2005), pp. 29–51

Index

Abyssinia *see* Ethiopia
admiralty, 53, 97, 111, 112, 113, 251, 254
African colonies, 44, 97, 114, 120, 130, 194, 204
Amau statement, 25
American Jewish Congress, 56
Anglo-American 'special relationship', 5, 17, 18, 21, 155, 172, 211, 281, 296–8
Anglo-American trade agreement, 40, 42–3, 49–50, 52, 63–4, 66, 85, 95–6, 101, 114, 153–4, 164, 170, 176, 178–81, 193, 233–4, 272, 286, 292–3, 301
Anglo-French guarantee to Poland, 204–5, 207, 212, 231–2, 235, 253
Anglo-French Purchasing Board, 295
Anglo-German naval agreement, 28, 204, 231
Anglo-Irish agreement, 214
Anglo-Italian agreement, 137–8, 149, 163, 202, 283, 291
Anschluss, 114, 129–31, 133–45
Anti-Comintern Pact, 34, 55, 95–6, 115, 123, 237, 289
appeasement, 5–6, 9, 11–12, 14–17, 23, 42, 52, 63, 65, 67–8, 70, 91, 94, 109, 115, 121–2, 129–32, 137–8, 143, 149–52, 154, 156, 163, 169, 170–1, 176, 193–5, 204, 231–2, 235, 239, 244, 282–6, 288, 291–2, 297
Arab Revolt, 215
Argentina, 184
arms embargo, 28, 44–6, 54, 75, 141–2, 174, 176, 200–1, 218, 225, 229–30, 237, 242, 244–5, 252, 257–8, 263, 266–71, 273–8, 284–5, 288–9, 293, 295, 297
Ashton-Gwatkin, Frank, 71
Asquith, Herbert Henry, 42
Athenia, 255–6
Attlee, Clement, 99, 204, 211
Australia, 217, 268
Austria, 121, 124, 129, 131, 133–6, 144, 150–1, 243, 283; *see also Anschluss*

Baldwin, Stanley, 11, 25, 28, 34, 41–2, 45–6, 65–6, 180–1, 241, 290
Balkans, 202
Baltic States, 260
Baruch, Bernard, 53–4, 172, 174–5
Battenburg, Prince Louis of, 220
Belgium, 63, 70–1, 107, 275, 297
Beneš, Edvard, 157–8, 161, 165
Bennett, Richard, 42
Berle, Adolf, 133, 151, 154
Bermuda, 219, 223–4
Bevin, Ernest, 6, 285

Index   323

Bewley, Kenneth, 47–8, 77, 294
Biddle, Anthony, 157, 232
Bingham, Robert, 34, 41, 48–9, 64–5, 67, 72, 75, 136
Blum, Leon, 33–4, 76, 139
Bonnet, Georges, 44, 56, 76, 151, 195
Borah, William, 3–7, 9, 28, 87, 90, 100, 116–17, 120, 130, 142, 201, 221, 224, 229–31, 251–2, 263, 267–70, 283, 285, 289, 292, 296, 300
Borchers, Hans Heinrich, 185
Bötticher, Friedrich von, 14, 277–8, 287
Brazil, 79, 103, 155, 184, 218–19
British armed forces, 42, 111, 161, 220
   Air Force, 27, 30, 42, 46, 132, 138–9, 160, 173–5, 177–80, 183, 196, 219, 220, 255, 259, 263, 266, 268, 272, 274, 275, 278, 294–5
   army, 30, 205
   navy, 3, 26, 30, 42, 53, 96, 97, 99, 111–13, 116, 143, 159, 169, 195, 212, 216, 219, 220, 223–4, 242, 251, 254, 255–6, 259–60, 267, 274–6, 295, 296
British Board of Trade, 40, 42, 66, 95, 148, 152, 233
British Cabinet, 26, 28, 41, 42, 89, 93, 95, 159, 204, 205, 237, 251, 252, 254, 255, 259, 270, 271, 274, 297
British Commonwealth & Empire, 4, 16, 18, 31, 45, 65, 93, 113, 131, 134, 144, 151, 155, 161, 200, 211–14, 216, 218, 222, 253–4, 256, 266, 274–5, 281, 284, 286–7, 298
British economic diplomacy, 4, 13–15, 25, 29, 33–4, 37, 41, 46, 48, 51–2, 63, 65, 66, 164, 178–9, 180, 234–5, 254, 275, 284, 289, 291–3
British economy & trade, 25, 33–4, 37, 40–52, 53–6, 63–4, 66–71, 76–9, 85, 89, 92, 94–6, 101, 108–9, 114–15, 139–41, 153–4, 164, 170, 176, 178–81, 184, 193, 198–9, 203, 207, 223–4, 226, 234–7, 259, 271–2, 274–5, 278, 285–6, 289, 292–5, 297, 301
British Embassy in Berlin, 22–3, 44, 121, 130, 145, 153, 165, 177, 200, 204
British Embassy in Washington, 22, 24, 42, 47, 49, 78, 88–9, 114, 141, 148, 159, 191, 216–17, 236, 239, 257
British Foreign Office, 22–4, 41, 47–8, 54, 70, 72, 85, 89, 91, 98–9, 108, 114, 115, 121, 141–2, 148, 152–3, 157, 159, 169–70, 182, 192, 193, 198, 199, 203–5, 223, 230, 233–4, 236, 238, 240, 243, 267, 272–3, 284, 286, 291, 294–5, 300–1
British Purchasing Commission, 267, 270–2, 294, 295
British rearmament, 6, 8, 12, 23, 27, 30, 35, 41, 55, 116, 119, 132, 138–9, 142–3, 145, 174, 191, 193–5, 196–7, 214, 270, 277–8, 285, 292
British Supply Board in Canada & US, 271
British Treasury, 25, 27, 54, 69, 70, 77, 268, 293, 300

Brussels conference, 92–6, 99, 117; *see also* Nine Power Treaty
Buenos Aires conference, 35–6, 37, 71
Bullitt, William, 34, 121, 174–5, 192, 233, 273, 275
Burgin, Leslie, 237, 266
Butler, R. A. B., 230–1
Byrnes, James, 33
Byron, Robert, 169, 171, 180, 192, 296

Cadogan, Alexander, 99, 109–12, 171, 203, 267
Campbell, Wallace, 271
Canada, 4–5, 9, 12–13, 16, 18, 22, 24, 31–2, 36, 42, 50–4, 65, 67, 69, 77, 85, 93, 109, 131, 139, 150, 154–5, 160, 176, 179–80, 183, 193, 202, 211–23, 225, 231, 242, 253, 263, 268, 270–1, 281–2, 284–7, 291–2, 298, 301
Canada–US trade agreements (1935 and 1938), 4, 24, 31, 42, 85, 176, 179, 286
Canadian election (1935), 24, 286
Canadian military and rearmament, 139, 174, 193–4, 218–20, 242, 255, 268, 270–1
Capper, Arthur, 269
Caribbean bases, 219, 223, 224, 259, 260, 267, 296–8
Chamberlain, Neville, 4, 6, 9, 11–12, 14, 16–17, 23, 26–7, 33, 41, 45–8, 51–2, 63–73, 77, 84, 89–90, 92, 94, 99–101, 107, 109–11, 114–15, 120–2, 129–32, 134, 137–8, 140, 148–53, 156, 159–63, 165–6, 169–71, 176, 179–83, 192–5, 197, 200, 201, 202, 204–6, 211–12, 220–1, 230–2, 234–5, 239, 243–4, 251–7, 261, 266–7, 274, 282–6, 288, 290–2, 294–7, 301
Chatfield, Lord, 109, 111, 113, 195
Chautemps, Camille, 76, 121
China, 23, 25–6, 64, 71–6, 85–9, 92, 95, 109–11, 134, 138–9, 142, 238, 240, 294
Churchill, Winston, 5, 11, 12, 18, 30, 54, 99–101, 115, 132, 150, 155, 171–3, 176, 194, 197, 205, 211, 214, 220–1, 231, 251–6, 259–60, 262, 268, 274–6, 281–3, 285, 287, 290, 297–8
Ciano, Galeazzo, 137, 195
Clark, Champ, 269
Collins, Captain Harry E., 272–3
commodities, 43, 44, 49, 53, 55, 69, 86, 90, 98, 101, 102, 107, 114, 176, 182, 203, 281, 233, 245, 263, 271, 273, 292, 295
communism & communists, 88, 91, 103, 116, 141, 183, 212, 241, 244, 288
Congress on Education for Democracy, 241, 290
Conservative party, 5, 89, 194, 274, 285
Cooper, Alfred Duff, 170, 173, 194, 197
cotton–rubber exchange agreement (1939), 230, 233–4
Craigie, Sir Robert, 47, 238–40

Cudahy, John, 122, 138, 196
Czechoslovakia, 11, 121, 129, 131–3, 148–52, 150–1, 154, 156–65, 170, 172–3, 175, 177, 200–1, 206, 229, 231, 235, 243, 253, 261, 284–5, 288–9, 291, 294, 296

Daladier, Édouard, 140–1, 161, 175, 195–6, 233
Dalton, Hugh, 235
Danzig, 204, 212, 231–3, 235, 240, 244, 253, 254, 256, 288
Davis, Norman, 7, 25, 41, 47, 52, 63, 92–3, 133, 143, 257, 290, 300
Defence Requirements Sub-Committee, 27
democracy, 31, 34–6, 56, 84, 103, 120, 122–3, 135, 150, 153, 170–1, 173, 184, 1 91–2, 194, 198, 201, 204, 211, 222, 241, 284, 289, 290
Democratic Party, 7, 34, 230
Destroyer–Bases deal, 224, 258–9, 260, 267, 296–8
Dieckhoff, Hans Heinrich, 78–9, 102–3, 122–4, 144–5, 165, 177, 183–4, 207, 262–3, 302
Dirksen, Herbert von, 153, 235
disarmament, 15, 26, 48, 55, 67–8, 70, 72, 107–8, 114, 116, 178, 292
Dodds, William, 44, 79
dominions, 11–12, 16, 22, 24, 29, 32, 42, 45, 50, 52, 63, 93, 113, 195, 223, 274, 285
Dunkirk evacuation, 11, 272

Eastern Europe, 89, 91, 97, 115, 298, 131, 151, 202
economic appeasement, 8, 52, 63, 65, 67–71, 94, 109, 154, 292
economic sanctions, 31, 80, 87, 89, 92, 96–7, 103, 108–9, 114–15, 164, 178, 180–1, 184, 191, 199, 207, 226, 259, 275, 278, 284, 289, 292–3
Eden, Anthony, 3, 4, 23–4, 28, 34, 42, 45–6, 48–50, 52, 63–5, 67, 71–3, 75–7, 84–5, 89–90, 92, 99–101, 109–15, 117–18, 120–2, 130, 137–8, 141, 150, 173, 181, 197, 220, 231, 254, 283–4, 291, 297, 301
Edward VIII, 32, 41, 214, 221
Elizabeth, Queen, 154, 164, 211, 213, 215–16
Ethiopia (Abyssinia), 28–9, 31, 114–15, 121, 134, 137–8, 149, 283, 310
Exchange Equalisation Account, 76

Far East, 4, 7, 11, 16, 17, 25–6, 37, 40, 46, 54–5, 66, 69, 71, 73–4, 79, 87, 89–90, 92–3, 96, 99–101, 111–13, 115–17, 130, 135, 193, 222, 224, 237, 239–40, 283, 293
fascism, 23, 31, 35, 54, 76, 88, 91, 102–3, 120, 141–2, 181, 194, 198–9, 212, 241, 290, 293
Federal Reserve Board, 271
Federal Union Club, 171
Finland, 260, 262
Fish, Hamilton, 53
Fisher, Sir Warren, 69
Foreign Policy Association, 223

France, 4, 6–7, 8, 11, 13–16, 23, 28–34, 37, 40, 43–4, 46–8, 54–6, 67, 72, 74–8, 84, 96, 101, 107, 113–14, 115–16, 119, 121, 129–33, 135, 139–41, 143, 150–1, 156, 158–62, 164–5, 170, 172–5, 177–8, 180, 192–3, 195–7, 199–205, 207–8, 212, 220, 223–6, 229–33, 238, 241–6, 254, 257, 261–2, 266, 268–72, 274–8, 284–5, 287–8, 292–5, 297, 301
Franco, General Francisco, 31, 75, 77, 121, 140–1

Gandhi, Mahatma, 214
Garner, John Nance, 97
George, Walter, 230, 269
George V, 32, 221
George VI, 41, 154, 164, 169, 211–13, 215–23, 252, 259, 293, 296–7
German–American Bund, 103, 123–4, 185, 288 13–14, 65
German–American trade relations, 30, 37, 44, 47, 55–7, 68, 86, 134, 184, 206, 285, 293
German Embassy in London, 65, 143, 170, 235
German Embassy in Washington, 13–14, 47, 103, 143, 163, 165, 177, 183, 185, 206, 225, 236, 244, 258, 287, 288, 289, 294
German Foreign Ministry (GFM), 9, 13 31, 79, 102, 103, 122, 124, 143–5, 153, 177, 183–4, 196, 197, 204, 207, 225, 234, 244, 255, 262–3, 277, 287–8, 301

German–Italian relations, 31, 143, 213, 223, 232, 237, 289
German rearmament, 23, 27–8, 44, 123, 139, 174, 256, 289
Germany, 4–6, 8–10, 12–15, 22–3, 26–31, 30–7, 40–2, 44, 46–8, 52–7, 63, 65, 67–8, 70, 74–5, 78–9, 84–6, 91, 94–5, 97, 102–3, 107, 109, 113–16, 120–4, 129–35, 137–41, 143–5, 148–66, 170–1, 173–8, 180, 183–5, 192–3, 196–208, 212–14, 218–23, 225–7, 229–38, 240–5, 252–6, 258, 260–4, 266–8, 270, 273–8, 281–5, 287–98, 301–2
Gillette, Guy, 230, 269
Goebbels, Joseph, 26, 56, 244
Göring, Helmut, 65, 121, 234, 302
Graf Spee incident, 268, 275–6
Greece, 202, 203, 205, 212
Greenly, John, 270–1
Grey, Sir Edward, 172

Hachiro, Arita, 238
Haile Selassie, Emperor, 31
Haldane, Graham, 197–9, 295
Halifax, Lord, Edward Wood, 11, 85, 121, 129, 131–2, 136–7, 139, 148–52, 156–8, 162–3, 170–1, 179, 182, 194–5, 201–2, 204–5, 212–13, 218, 223, 231–2, 234–5, 240, 253–4, 287, 291, 301
Hampton, Commander T. C., 224, 296
Harrison, Leyland, 74
Hawaii, 97, 98, 100, 110, 205, 240
helium, 258
Henderson, Sir Nevile, 121, 130, 145, 153, 165, 177, 200, 204

historians, 6–7, 9–18, 26, 27, 31, 41, 67, 84, 105, 115, 130, 139, 149, 169, 170, 173, 177, 193, 207, 212, 230, 235, 240, 251, 252, 258, 267, 272, 274, 282, 284, 288, 296, 297
Hitler, Adolf, 8, 11–15, 22–4, 26, 28, 31–3, 41–2, 46, 56, 65, 67, 91, 94, 103–4, 109, 120–2, 129–32, 136–7, 140, 143, 145, 149–51, 153–4, 156–9, 161, 165, 170–3, 177–8, 180, 182–3, 192, 196–7, 199–200, 203–8, 212–13, 231–2, 235, 242–3, 253–4, 260–2, 264, 274, 282–5, 288–9, 292, 297, 302
Hoare, Sir Samuel, later Viscount Templewood, 11, 28–9, 115, 149, 158, 162, 254
Hogg, Quintin, 202
Honolulu, 112–13, 205
Hoover, Herbert, 24–5, 87
Hopkins, Harry, 173
Hore-Belisha, Leslie, 132, 194
Hornbeck, Stanley, 72, 92
Ho-Umezu agreement, 26, 71
House, Colonel Edward, 8, 152
Hudson, Robert, 200, 235–6
Hull, Cordell, 7–8, 10, 24–5, 30, 32–6, 41–4, 46–9, 51–2, 56, 67–75, 77–9, 85–7, 91, 93–7, 99, 102, 109–11, 114, 117–20, 122–4, 133–8, 140–5, 149, 153–8, 163, 178–81, 201, 215, 217, 229–30, 233, 238–9, 257, 272, 285–6, 290–4, 300–301
Hungary, 107, 121, 159, 161

Ickes, Harold, 85–6, 97, 130, 159–61, 197, 203–4, 256–8, 261–2, 285, 300

Imperial Conference (1937), 42, 51–2, 65, 94, 139, 213
Imperial Preference, 18, 31, 42, 50, 52, 85, 93, 179–80, 292
Indian independence movement, 214, 287
Ingemar-Bernot, Alfred, 56
Ingersoll, Captain Royall, 111–14, 115–17, 224, 283, 296
Inskip, Sir Thomas, 30, 195
Internationalism, 6–8, 10, 14, 24–5, 34, 83, 87, 102, 108–9, 118, 134–5, 145
Interventionism, 3, 6, 8, 7–11, 25, 27, 31, 54, 74–5, 102, 113, 133, 145, 162, 199, 245–6, 252, 277–8
Ireland, 122, 196, 214, 217
isolationism, 3, 4, 5–7, 9–11, 15–16, 28, 32, 48, 50, 53, 65, 72, 73, 87–8, 90, 96, 100–2, 108–9, 116, 118–24, 130, 134–6, 142, 144, 153, 165, 172, 180–1, 191, 195–6, 198, 201, 213–14, 221, 224, 226, 229–30, 239–40, 252, 257, 263–4, 266–7, 269–70, 273, 277, 282–3, 285, 290–3, 295
Italy, 4–5, 10, 22–3, 27–9, 31, 34–5, 41, 55, 67–8, 70, 74, 75, 78, 84–6, 94–6, 97, 102–3, 107, 109, 113–16, 121, 123, 132, 134, 137–8, 140–1, 143, 149, 151, 155, 161–2, 163, 165, 193, 195–6, 199, 201–2, 204, 207, 212–13, 223, 229, 232, 237, 242, 281, 282–4, 289–92

Japan, 3–5, 10, 22–3, 25–6, 29, 33, 34–5, 41–2, 45, 55, 64, 66–8, 71–2, 74, 84, 86–9, 92–9, 101–2, 109, 111, 113, 116–17, 123, 129, 134, 137–8, 142–3, 171, 199, 205, 214, 222, 224, 230, 237–40, 246, 273, 281–4, 289, 292–4, 296, 301
Jews, 26, 36, 56, 103, 122, 134, 165, 171, 183–4, 197, 205, 215, 244, 288, 293
Johnson Act, 4, 33, 54, 66, 200, 237
Johnson, Herschel, 71, 76, 156, 232
Johnson, Hiram, 3–7, 25, 87, 117, 237, 269, 300
Johnson, Louis, 174, 198–9, 236–7, 295
Joint Air Training Scheme, 268

Kellogg–Briand Pact, 87, 154
Kennedy, Joseph, 136–7, 144–5, 156–8, 181, 201–2, 205, 215, 233–4, 275
Knatchbull-Hugesson, Sir Hughe, 74
Knox, Frank, 8, 10, 34, 275, 297, 300
Kristallnacht, 163, 166, 170–1, 176–8, 183–4, 288
Krock, Arthur, 23, 118–20, 136, 269–70, 282
Kuhn, Ferdinand, 194–5, 254–5

Labour Party, 5, 6, 28, 70, 99, 101, 150, 159, 172, 194, 211, 235, 239, 253, 285, 290
La Follette Jr, Robert, 269
La Guardia, Mayor Fiorello, 56
Lang, Archbishop Cosmo Gordon, 212
Lansbury, George, 6, 70, 211

Latin America, 35–7, 68, 79, 103, 107, 134, 176, 180, 184, 218, 223, 260, 276
Laurier, Sir Wilfrid, 193
League of Nations, 4, 7, 13, 16, 25–6, 28, 51–2, 74, 85, 87–8, 92, 94, 149, 172, 217, 281, 285
Leahy, Admiral William, 111–13, 116–17, 224
Leith-Ross, Sir Fredrick, 25, 71
Lend Lease Act, 298
Liberal Party, 5, 101, 150, 153, 159, 172, 194, 212, 239, 253, 285, 290
Lindenberg, Colonel Charles, 173
Lindsay, Sir Ronald, 24, 29, 43, 46, 48, 50–1, 53–4, 67–8, 95, 97–101, 107–12, 114–15, 121, 129–30, 142, 154–5, 158, 160, 163, 179, 215, 217, 221, 223, 230, 233–4, 236, 238–40, 242–3, 296
Lippmann, Walter, 101
Litvinov, Maxim, 212, 241
London Economic Conference, 33–4, 37, 284, 291
London Naval Agreement (1936), 26, 116, 143, 296
Lothian, Lord, Philip Henry Kerr, 152, 172, 199–200, 240, 243, 268–9, 270–2, 291
Ludlow, Louis, 118
Luther, Hans, 37, 47, 55–7, 122, 287, 302

MacDonald, James Ramsay, 11, 16, 22, 24–5, 27, 32, 42, 65, 93, 195, 215
MacDonald, Malcolm, 22, 24, 32, 65, 93, 195, 215

Index

Mackenzie King, William Lyon, 5, 9, 12–13, 24, 31–2, 42, 50–2, 65, 67, 85, 93–4, 109, 131, 150, 154–5, 171, 176, 193, 179–80, 193, 202, 205, 212–13, 215–21, 231, 252–3, 261, 268, 271, 282, 284–7, 291–2, 297, 301
McReynolds, Sam, 53
Maginot Line, 159
Mallet, Victor, 88, 90–1, 191–2, 196, 239
Manchurian Incident, 25–6, 71, 73, 134, 138
Marco Polo Bridge Incident, 26, 71, 87
Mediterranean, 77, 97, 113, 137, 141, 224, 283
Messersmith, George, 133–4
Mexico, 169
Middle East, 137, 203
Moffat, Jay Pierrepont, 129, 133, 138, 149, 158, 180, 232, 271
Monnet, Jean, 174–5, 192, 272
Monick, Emmanuel, 33
Morgenthau, Henry Jr, 30, 33, 41, 47–8, 66–8, 76–8, 97, 100, 111, 140, 175, 177–9, 192, 201, 271–3, 293–5, 297, 300
Morocco, 31
Morrison, Herbert, 138
Morrison, William, 95
Moscow, 30, 240, 242
Munich crisis & agreement, 5, 8, 10, 12, 15–16, 148–65, 169–73, 183, 192, 193–4, 200, 208, 229, 254, 274–5, 283, 286, 289, 291, 295–6
Murray, Arthur, Lord Elibank, 42, 66, 89, 153, 170, 172, 175–6, 182–3, 192, 195, 197, 283, 291

Mussolini, Benito, 8, 28, 31, 42, 46, 67, 91, 121–2, 137–8, 161, 195, 203–4, 213

National Association of American Manufacturers, 181
National Liberals, 42, 66
Nazi party, 26, 56, 151, 156
Nazism, 35, 54, 103, 173, 208, 241
Nazi–Soviet Pact, 160, 240, 242, 256
Netherlands, 101, 107, 275, 297
Neurath, Konstantin von, 65, 143
New Deal, 10, 15, 34, 191, 215, 269, 285
New York World Trade Fair, 214, 217, 241, 290
New Zealand, 217, 268
Nine Power Treaty, 87–9, 92
non-interventionism, 5, 7, 19, 31, 35, 74–9, 102, 117, 141
North Atlantic Triangle, 9, 12–13
Norway, 262, 274, 297
Nuremberg rally (1938), 156, 158, 171, 173
Nye, Gerald, 44–5, 53, 141–2, 196, 263
Nyon agreement, 77, 141

Ogdensburg agreement, 155, 287
Oliphant, Herman, 97
Ottawa agreements, 31, 36, 42, 45, 52, 179–80
Overton, Arnold, 179–80

Pacific, 46, 52, 97–8, 100, 110–13, 120, 205, 216, 224, 230, 240, 246, 259, 287, 296
Pacifism, 6, 28, 35, 88, 96, 102, 119, 124, 136, 142–3, 165, 211
'Pact of Steel', 213, 237

Palestine, 183, 195, 214–15
Panama Canal, 223, 259
Panama Declaration, 223, 259–60, 276
Panay crisis, 96–8, 110–11, 192, 296
'Parallel Action', 7, 14, 26, 61, 69, 72–4, 76, 97–101, 107–8, 110, 118–20, 130, 135, 138, 141, 143, 145, 164, 282–3
'Peace Front', 189, 205, 212, 225, 229, 230, 231, 232, 239, 241, 244, 283, 284, 285, 289, 296
'peace offer' by Hitler, 14, 260–2
Pearl Harbor, 6, 11, 174, 177, 205, 220, 224
Permanent Joint Board of Defence, 155, 281, 287
Philippines, 97, 113
Phillips, Captain Tom, 112
Phillips, Sir Frederick, 77–8
Phillips, William, 27, 67–8, 291
Phipps, Sir Eric, 22–3, 44, 133, 193
Pittman, Key, 53, 117–18, 201, 269–70
Pleven, René, 272
Poland, 11, 14, 57, 151, 157, 159, 161, 200–5, 207, 212, 229–46, 253–4, 256–7, 260–1, 264, 288–9, 297
President's Liaison Committee, 272
Purvis, Arthur, 271–3, 294–5, 297

'Quarantine' speech, 3–4, 67, 83–104, 114–19, 135, 122, 191–2, 205, 207, 225–6, 283, 289, 291

Reciprocal Trade Agreements Act, 178
Republican Party, 75, 230
Rhineland crisis, 30, 33, 196
Ribbentrop, Joachim von, 13–14, 65, 143, 147, 288, 302
Riverdale, Lord, Arthur Balfour, 230, 234, 236–7, 240, 268, 270–1, 295
Robinson, Sir Arthur, 236
Romania, 202–5, 212
Rome–Berlin Axis, 31, 213, 237, 289
Roosevelt 'Bombshell', 10, 24–6, 284, 293
Roosevelt, Eleanor, 175, 216–17, 218
Roosevelt, Franklin Delano, 3–6, 7–17, 22–37, 40–57, 63–71, 74–5, 78–9, 83–95, 97–103, 107–24, 130–9, 141–2, 144–5, 148–50, 152–65, 170–85, 191–208, 212–14, 216–27, 229–31, 233–4, 236–7, 239–46, 251–64, 266–78, 282–98, 300–2
Roosevelt 'peace plan', 22–4, 37, 50–2, 56, 90–2, 107–9, 114–15, 203–5, 207–8, 291–2
Royal Visit, 169, 211–22, 225–7, 230–1, 252, 259, 284, 286–7, 290, 292–3, 296–7, 301
Runciman, Walter, 4, 40–47, 51, 65–7, 84, 94, 139, 148–50, 152–9, 163–4, 172, 174, 252, 285, 291, 293–296, 301

Sayre, Francis, 179, 181
Scandinavia, 107, 262, 274, 297
Shipstead, Henrick, 269

Simon, Sir John, (later Viscount), 11, 25–6, 28, 66, 69, 73, 76–8, 97, 132, 139–40, 155–6, 181, 254, 271, 293
Sinclair, Sir Archibald, 99, 153, 212
Singapore, 98, 100, 110, 112–13, 224
Sino-Japanese War, 25–26, 64, 71–4, 85, 87–8
socialism, 6, 31, 141
Soviet Union, 18, 23, 31, 34, 75, 115, 141, 150–1, 160–1, 172, 199, 202, 212–13, 231, 233, 237, 240–2, 244, 260, 262, 264, 273, 281, 284–5, 298
Spain, 6, 31, 70, 74–7, 79, 86, 89, 121, 132, 137, 139–42, 144, 232, 283
Spanish Civil War 10–11, 31–3, 64, 74, 76, 78–9, 115, 132, 242
Stalin, Joseph, 230, 241, 262
Stanley, Oliver, 66
Steinhardt, Laurence, 242
Stimson, Henry, 8, 10, 25, 73, 87, 34, 38, 300
Streit, Clarence, 172
Sudetenland, 121, 129, 131, 148–51, 157–9, 161, 163, 165, 173, 289
Sweden, 107, 262
Switzerland, 24, 26, 32, 49, 51, 74, 107, 134

Tangku Truce, 25
Thomsen, Hans, 37, 164–5, 177, 184, 206–7, 225–8, 244–5, 263–4, 277–8, 287
Tientsin crisis, 230, 237–40
totalitarianism, 103, 108, 164, 206–7, 226, 241, 245, 281
Trading with the Enemy Act (1917), 97

Tripartite Currency Agreement, 4, 33–4, 37, 43, 47, 66, 70, 76–8, 139–40, 285, 293–4
Turkey, 25, 107
Tweedsmuir, Lord, John Buchan, 24, 32, 51–2, 67, 85, 93–5, 176, 193, 213, 215, 292, 301
Tyrrell, Walter, 197

US armed forces, 111, 113, 170, 174–5, 198–9, 224, 258–9, 272, 278, 287
  air force, 177–80, 192, 196, 201, 278, 294–5
  army, 6, 116, 177–8, 259, 278, 287
  navy, 3, 42, 97, 99–100, 110–13, 116–17, 142–3, 175, 177–8, 205, 207, 216, 218–19, 223, 224, 240, 246, 255, 256, 258–60, 275–6, 287, 295–6, 300
US Cabinet, 24, 85, 97, 130, 159–60, 161, 173, 179, 254, 256–7, 262, 272, 275, 300
US Congress, 7, 11, 25, 28–9, 37, 44, 51, 56, 63, 73, 88, 96, 100, 108, 116, 118–20, 123, 145, 156, 178–9, 191–2, 196, 201, 206, 214, 217–19, 224–5, 230, 233–4, 239, 241–2, 257, 259, 263, 268–9, 277, 282, 290, 293, 295, 300
US economic diplomacy, 7–10, 13–15, 25, 29–31, 33–4, 37, 48, 52, 55, 56, 259
US economy and trade, 25, 30, 33–4, 37, 43–7, 49–56, 63, 66–71, 72, 76–9, 86, 89, 92, 94, 108–9, 114–15, 139–41, 164, 178–81, 184, 198–9, 203, 206, 207, 226, 258, 259, 271–2, 278, 289, 285, 289, 292–4, 297

US Embassy in Berlin, 44, 79, 157, 177
US Embassy in London, 34, 41, 48–9, 64–5, 67, 71, 72, 75, 76, 136–7, 144–5, 156–8, 181, 201–2, 205, 215, 232, 233–4, 275
US House Naval Affairs Committee, 116
US industrial mobilisation, 16, 170, 176, 178, 182, 183, 197–9, 270, 295
US neutrality, 13, 28, 50, 53–5, 78, 83–4, 87–8, 98, 141–2, 176, 191, 221–2, 223, 234, 257, 258–9, 267, 296
US Neutrality Acts, 10, 15, 27– 30, 41, 53–4, 69, 71, 77, 75, 84, 88, 95–6, 119, 145, 174, 201, 224–6, 243, 245, 256, 258, 26 2, 266, 267–71, 293
US rearmament, 6, 8, 67, 118–19, 142–3, 145, 174, 178, 196, 198, 201, 218–20, 244, 263, 277–8, 292
US Senate, 3, 26, 53, 116–17, 142, 196, 197, 201, 226, 229, 230, 269–70, 274
US Senate Foreign Relations Committee, 117, 229, 269–70
US Senate Military Affairs Committee, 196, 226, 230
US State Department, 10, 30, 43, 47, 49, 52, 53, 55, 68, 74–5, 87, 95, 96–7, 102, 111, 115, 118, 120–1, 133–4, 138, 140, 141, 142, 149, 152, 159, 160, 177, 229, 233, 236–7, 239, 242, 255, 257, 258, 271, 278

US Treasury, 24, 30, 41, 47, 54, 66, 76, 140, 177, 178, 272–3, 293, 294, 300
US War Department, 177, 236, 237, 271

Vandenberg, Arthur, 269–70
Vansittart, Sir Robert, 22–4, 41–2, 51, 66, 203
Versailles Treaty, 8, 26–7, 30, 33
Vinson Naval Act, 143, 300–2

War Debts, 4, 17, 25, 33, 44, 47, 88, 95, 215, 219, 241, 270, 284, 289, 293
Washington, George, 7
Washington Naval Treaty, 26, 69, 112
Wedgwood, Colonel Josiah, 172
Weir, James George, 139
Weizächer, Ernst von, 102, 104, 144, 153, 164, 183–4, 262
Welczeck, Johannes Bernhard von, 164
Welles, Sumner, 68, 70, 79, 90–1, 102, 107, 110–11, 114–16, 121, 130, 133, 137–8, 142, 180, 201, 204, 206, 233, 239, 260, 283, 291
Wiedemann, Captain Fritz, 104, 145, 208
Wiley, John Cooper, 134
Willert, Sir Arthur, 30, 38, 199–200, 291
Wilson, Hugh, 157, 177
Wilson, Sir Horace, 94, 105, 170, 234–5, 243, 284, 288
Wilson Woodrow, 7–8, 16, 24–6, 32, 35, 48–9, 88, 162, 257, 277, 284
Woermann, Ernst, 183–4

Wohltat, Helmuth, 200, 234–5, 292
Wood, Sir Kingsley, 183
Woodin, William, 24–5
Woodring, Harry, 271, 294
World War One, 8, 13, 30, 42, 46, 49, 88, 91, 98, 112, 124, 131, 157, 175, 192, 193, 207, 212, 215, 251, 252, 257, 258, 270–1, 277, 284
World War Two, 5, 9, 11, 16, 18, 23, 41, 54, 79, 281, 297–8
WPA (Works Progress Administration), 173

Yugoslavia, 107

Zeeland, Paul van, 63, 70–1, 114, 292

EU representative:
Easy Access System Europe
Mustamäe tee 50, 10621 Tallinn, Estonia
Gpsr.requests@easproject.com

www.ingramcontent.com/pod-product-compliance
Lightning Source LLC
Chambersburg PA
CBHW070808300426
44111CB00014B/2452